The Great Films

Other books by Bosley Crowther

THE LION'S SHARE: The Story of an Entertainment Empire
HOLLYWOOD RAJAH: The Life and Times of Louis B. Mayer

THE GREAT FILMS

Fifty Golden Years of Motion Pictures

by BOSLEY CROWTHER

G. P. PUTNAM'S SONS · *New York*

For my sons
Bosley, John and Jefferson

Third Impression

Copyright © 1967 by Bosley Crowther

All rights reserved. This book, or parts thereof,
must not be reproduced in any form without permission.
Published simultaneously in the Dominion of Canada by
Longmans Canada Limited, Toronto.

Library of Congress Catalog Card Number 67–30265

PRINTED IN THE UNITED STATES OF AMERICA

Contents

Introduction

Practically everybody concedes the vast importance of motion pictures. We acknowledge that they are a major mass communication device of our age and a major new art form. We now know that much of our culture is encompassed and transmitted in them. Thus, for this and other obvious reasons, I feel that we should have a new critical sorting out and reexamination of the great works of the cinema, just as we have reexaminations of the great works of painting, music and literature. And so I venture and presume to make a full sweep of all the films that have been made to find the fifty that I feel merit re-viewing in perspective and in depth, revealing thereby, in their entirety, how the motion picture has grown and developed in the past half century as an art form.

To be sure, there are already several—a few excellent—historical and critical surveys that provide instructive and stimulating reflections upon the whole range of special areas of cinema. I am mindful of Lewis Jacobs' *The Rise of the American Film,* Paul Rotha's and Richard Griffith's *The Film Till Now,* Siegfried Kracauer's *From Caligari to Hitler,* Arthur Knight's *The Liveliest Art* and the various compendia of program notes assembled by the Museum of Modern Art Film Library and the British Film Institute. I have listed in my bibliography a generous selection of works which provide such reexamination and helpful orientation in films.

I feel and hope that this half-century presentation will afford a useful and graphic survey of the cinema's high points and give a concentrated comprehension of the expanding art of the medium and its historical growth. I also hope that these reexaminations will refresh many pleasant memories and stimulate the desire in many people to see the great films they have not yet seen.

You will note that I say the "great" films. I do not use that vulnerable word, the "best." Neither do I give myself a buffer by pretending that these are *my* "favorites." While most of the films in this selection are, indeed, ones I have supremely enjoyed and hold in fondest recollection, there are some that are not on this list which, as sheer motion-picture entertainment, I have enjoyed more than some that are. I have enjoyed them for reasons other than their artistic qualities and those distinctions they should have to justify them for inclusion on this list.

Naturally, my choices are arbitrary and a reflection of my experience, judgment and taste as a critic. I hope they are not a reflection of my personal sentiment.

What have been my criteria in making these selections of the great films? Let me explain this as clearly and explicitly as I can. My first rule has been to scrutinize those pictures that have been the breakthroughs, that have opened new ground, not just in techniques of expression but in the discoveries and revelations they have made. I have sought those films in which content has been of such originality and significance and has been so aptly combined with cinema technique—or style, if you wish—that it has resulted in those films being forceful and usually precedental works.

Thus the factor of content has been the crucial consideration. The technique of giving it expression has been a vital but secondary concern. That is to say, I have avoided picking the mere technical breakthroughs as such, unless they have been combined with strong content, as in the instances of *Potemkin* or *Citizen Kane.* Otherwise, I would have found myself picking the first story film or the first sound film or the first color film, and that would have led to loading this volume with examples of juvenilia that wouldn't interest even engineers.

Now, what have I considered strong content? It is that which in theme and substance makes for a fresh, stimulating, expanding and meaningful experience. It need not be serious or solemn or philosophically deep. It can be comedy or satire just as well as shattering tragedy. But it has to be content that has given us—and still may give us—new insights, new joys, new awareness of the human condition in exciting and absorbing ways.

Significantly, the great majority of films that have met this test have been ones that are strong on observation and criticism of society. The important and powerful motion pictures have been those that have contemplated the social scene, either seriously or with trenchant humor, and have said something acute about it. What they say may not be entirely accurate, it may not be altogether wise, but it is something that is strong and revealing and hasn't been said so well before in films. This is aptly illustrated by the first two films in the book (and you will note, incidentally, that all are treated in the chronological order of their release).

It is conspicuous from the dates of all these pictures that periods of great invention and artistic growth have been in times and in countries that have provided an environment of extraordinary tension and change. *The Cabinet of Dr. Caligari* was made in Germany right after the First World War and spearheaded a whole group of ultra-morbid and expressionistic torment films. *Potemkin* was made in Soviet Russia on the momentum of the Revolution, and set the pace and even the pattern for a famous culture of "social realism" films. *The Public Enemy* marked the onrush of the wave of angry, strident gangster films that boiled out of the period of the Depression and criminality in the United States. Most conspicuous is the surge of creativity in ferocious and radical styles that marked the great renaissance of cinema in Italy after the Second World War. One might ponder the melancholy question whether it does take misfortune and great tension, national agitation and even calamity, to arouse and inspire film-makers to dare radical leaps ahead and explode devastating expressions.

Noticeable, too, is the fact that so many of the great films include the occurrence of war and are moved to philosophical reflections by this most violent and tragic ritual of man. Look at the list—*The Birth of a Nation, Intolerance, Potemkin, All Quiet on the Western Front, La Grande Illusion, Gone with the Wind* and several others. War persists as a topic most apt to excite mass audience apprehension—or alas, intoxication.

What is termed "sheer entertainment," which is generally supposed to be the predominant and most appreciated commodity of the screen—that is to say, motion pictures that provide diversion and "escape"—has always been an area congenial to the efforts of artists with bents for expressing themselves and forceful ideas through humor and sly frivolity. The films of the great silent comedians—Charlie Chaplin, Buster Keaton, Harold Lloyd—and the later, more penetrating satires of the musical-minded René Clair, the Marx Brothers, Ernst Lubitsch (with *Ninotchka*), right down to Tony Richardson's *Tom Jones,* are evidence that a film doesn't have to be solemn in order to be eloquent.

In recent years, the marked trend of picture-making —in Europe, especially—toward introspective, psychological exploration and the development of philosophical ideas without the use of conventional narrative structure has resulted in some strong, exciting films (as well as some dismally obscure ones), and is the trend that many future films may take. The works of Ingmar Bergman (*The Seventh Seal, Wild Strawberries,* etc.) and Michelangelo Antonioni (*L'Avventura, Blow-Up,* etc.) indicate the intellectual nature and the cinematic character of this trend.

Placing such films in a relation to the great ones of the past, and likewise finding a basis for comparison of quality in early and later films, has been the most complicating challenge in making the selections for this book. Thus I have made evaluations on the calculation of what films have been, what they have represented, at the time of their release, and also how well they have held up as cinema expressions through the years.

It may be of some significance that my first exposure to every film in this book was at the time of its release, or close to it. My parents took me to see *The Birth of a Nation* in 1916, when I was a small (and quite impressionable!) child. But, of course, I have seen again and restudied every one of them in recent years, along with scores of others that I thought might qualify. A rule in my calculations has been that a great film must hold up; it must be forceful and engrossing when it is looked at today.

I have made a particular point of combining my critical comments with historical and anecdotal information about the making of these films and the context of the periods and the circumstances in which they were made. Thus I hope that this book will prove a sweeping and entertaining survey of the advance of all motion pictures, as well as an appreciative memorial of the most impressive or significant ones.

Most of all, I hope it will provide the reader with as much excitement and pleasure in reviewing these great films, or in "looking" at them for the first time as writing about them has provided me.

We speak glibly of the audio-visual image as the language and the art of today. But we also tend to be neglectful of the accumulation of this art, and we tolerate debasement of its classics and its lesser treasures in the most callous and indifferent ways.

The increasing abundant exposure of old movies, as they are termed, on television (which is, of course, but another mechanical means of transmitting motion picture) is rapidly gorging the great audience in this country and in other countries, too, with a massive smorgasbord of motion pictures, but without any order or manifest taste. These daily and nightly fillings of the popular craw with films picked at random from many countries, many periods and many types, without any points of cultural reference and without, at least, the chronological flow of techniques and topicality that prevailed at the time they were released, is causing a massive indigestion.

Even so, we might welcome this liberal and convenient dishing out of old films as a means of reminding or acquainting the worldwide public with a great cultural reservoir, if it were not that the showings on television are generally so damaging to the quality of the original works. What is extended with the right hand is shattered with the left. Not only are television showings so often interrupted and confused with frequent intrusions of flagrant commercials that mood and continuity are destroyed, but so many fine films are mutilated by senseless abbreviating cuts.

I have recently looked at television showings of two of the films discussed in this book—Satyajit Ray's *Pather Panchali* and Noel Coward's *In Which We Serve*—and was shocked to discover that the most eloquent and touching scenes in each were totally eliminated. (They are the scene in *Pather Panchali* where the children run through a flax field to see a distant train and the scene in *In Which We Serve* where the wife of the captain gives a toast to her husband's ship.) Such irreparable eliminations—and they are happening all the time—make me shudder at the dilution of motion pictures on television.

Yet there is no denying that millions of people, young ones, especially, are being brought to a new awareness and enjoyment of films through the Box. Four-Star showings (or whatever they call them) of outstanding pictures of past years are regularly pulling high ratings in prime time and causing ecstatic morning-after talk. And these, in turn, are encouraging more and more theatrical revivals of old films and opportunities for seeing them in the environment—the full screen, the spacious surrounding (the popcorn odors!)—for which they were designed.

There are many persons who have helped me greatly and whom I want to thank with assurance of my deep appreciation. For opportunities to research and look again at the films included in this volume (and many, many more), I am indebted to the staff at the Department of Film of the Museum of Modern Art, particularly Margareta Akermark and Joanne Koch; to Dan Talbot at the New Yorker Theater, Marshall Lewis at the Bleeker Street Cinema, Ursula Lewis at the Thalia Theater and the operators of the Hollis Theater in Queens. The archivists of the Theater Collection at Lincoln Center's Library of the Performing Arts and of the Academy of Motion Picture Arts and Sciences in Hollywood have been gracious and helpful. I also thank the authors of all the books listed in my bibliography.

For still photographs and generosity in obtaining them, I am much indebted to John Springer, James Card of Eastman House in Rochester, New York, John Ford, John Boulting, King Displays, Inc., Mark Ricci, Metro-Goldwyn-Mayer, Paramount, Warner Brothers, Janus Films, United Artists Corporation, United Artists TV, Columbia Pictures, Don Velde, Dan Talbot, Samuel Goldwyn, the Museum of Modern Art, Raymond Rohauer and the Gallery of Modern Art, David Mavity, Contemporary Films, Times Films, Edward Harrison, Fay Miske, Buena Vista Films, Astor Films, Arthur Canton and Brandon Films.

And finally, I am eternally grateful to my wife, Florence, who has put every bit as much physical and emotional effort into this book as I, not only doing the tough job of collecting and captioning the photographs, but that much more drudging one of typing the manuscript; and to my editor, William Targ, without whose counsel, enthusiasm and patience—the last beyond belief!—I can say without shame of redundance this book would never have been done.

The Birth of a Nation

"The Little Colonel," Ben Cameron (Henry B. Walthall), and his flower-decked horse typify the naïve gallantry of southern gentry as the Civil War first engulfs them.

The scope of Griffith's vision and the daring of Bitzer's camera work gave a powerful reality to the grim battle scenes. Here the Confederates are seen behind a bunker and the Union forces are mounting a charge.

1915

Adapted by David Wark Griffith and Frank Woods from the novel, *The Clansman*, by the Reverend Thomas Dixon, with additional material from *The Leopard's Spots* by the same author; directed and produced by David Wark Griffith for the Epoch Producing Corporation; assistant director: George Siegmann; cameraman: George W. (Billy) Bitzer; original musical score for orchestral accompaniment compiled by Joseph Carl Breil.

Ben Cameron, "The Little Colonel"	Henry B. Walthall
Flora	Mae Marsh
Flora (as a child)	Violet Wilkey
Margaret, the older sister	Miriam Cooper
Mrs. Cameron	Josephine Crowell
Dr. Cameron	Spottiswoode Aitken
Wade Cameron	André Beranger
Duke Cameron	Maxfield Stanley
Elsie Stoneman	Lillian Gish
The Hon. Austin Stoneman	Ralph Lewis
Phil Stoneman	Elmer Clifton
Ted Stoneman	Robert Harron
Lydia Brown, Stoneman's housekeeper	Mary Alden
Senator Sumner	Sam de Grasse
Silas Lynch	George Siegmann
Gus	Walter Long
White Arm Joe	Elmo Lincoln
Jeff the Blacksmith	Wallace Reid
Abraham Lincoln	Joseph Henaberry
General U. S. Grant	Donald Crisp
General Robert E. Lee	Howard Gaye
The Sentry	William Freeman
Laura Keene	Olga Grey
John Wilkes Booth	Raoul Walsh
Union Soldier	Eugene Pallette
Piedmont Girl	Bessie Love
Volunteer	Charles Stevens
Man Who Falls from Roof	Erich von Stroheim

It is nothing short of prodigious that the first of the world's great films, the first mature achievement with motion photography, should have had such intense dramatic volume and command of creative techniques as to render it still considerable as a crowning example of cinema art. Yet such is *The Birth of a Nation*, a massive drama of the American Civil War, which D. W. Griffith produced in the summer of 1914 and released the following year.

The sudden emergence of this picture, with all its chauvinistic fervor and power of intimate emotional persuasion, was as though a superb symphony had burst from the muck of primitive music within two decades after the invention of the horn. It was a phenomenal occurrence that grandly displayed and dramatized the vast potentialities of the new medium and the kind of influence it was to have.

Up to the time of its appearance, the moving pictures —or "flickers," as they were known—were mostly regarded as optical freak shows, not far removed from the penny arcades. Storytelling with this medium had barely gone beyond the basic stage of exposing simple dramatic actions, such as the holdup of a train and the attempted escape of the robbers, shown in *The Great Train Robbery* in 1903. Later pictures, though progressively longer and more involved as to plot, were still mechanical and impersonal in their portrayals of fictional happenings. Film-makers were still fumbling for a grammar, a system of pictorial harmonics, when *The Birth of a Nation* came along.

When it did, with its massive construction of visual rhythms and graphic displays of human feelings counterpointed to action, it fairly smashed through an age-old dike of natural confinement of the senses and inundated a new area of sensitivity. Suddenly the mind was penetrated by optical stimuli that excited imagination in a fresh and intoxicating way. People were simply bowled over by its vivid pictorial sweep, its arrangements of personal involvements, its plunging of the viewer into a sea of boiling historical associations and its consistently engrossing length. Where other films ran from forty to sixty minutes, this giant ran for nigh on three hours!

The Little Colonel accepts the grim facts of battle, no longer an equestrian gallant, but a leader of his troops, selfless and vulnerable.

Of course, Griffith did not come to it like a genius sprung from a tree. He was a former stage actor and playwright who had been directing pictures for the Biograph Company since 1908. In six years of tireless production of several-score one- and two-reel films, he had studiously found and developed many of the now-commonplace ways of making moving pictures more flexible, suggestive and articulate.

With his cameraman, Billy Bitzer, he had learned to move the camera around, to shoot a scene from more than one angle. He had worked out the use of the close-up to bring the audience magnetically near to expressive faces and objects and thus generate intimate emotional effects. Most important, he had developed unusual ways of assembling separate shots and scenes to construct a narrative continuity with cumulative force and clarity. His *Judith of Bethulia* (1913), the first American film to run four reels, presented an elaborate Biblical drama that clearly foretold his epic taste.

Now a zeal to do something bigger and more expressive than anything yet done (and this included the monumental costume dramas *Quo Vadis?* and *Cabiria* from Italy) possessed the aggressive director, and soon he found his story and his theme in a popular novel, *The Clansman*, which had to do with the American Civil War and its aftermath.

As the Kentucky-born son of a Confederate colonel, Griffith passionately and sincerely felt that the South had been wronged severely in the waging and the outcome of that war. He agreed with the Reverend Thomas Dixon, author of *The Clansman*, that the white people of the southern states had been stricken by northern carpetbaggers and by free Negroes incited by them after the war, and that they had bravely rid themselves of this affliction and reestablished justice by the organization of the Ku Klux Klan. This was to be the thesis, the epic exposition, of his film.

Griffith began photographing in July 1914, from a script which he and Frank Woods put together from *The Clansman* and another Dixon novel, *The Leopard's Spots*. His actors were mostly from a troupe he had trained at Biograph. Very soon it was evident to the company that he was embarked on a tremendous enterprise, with big battle scenes and outdoor actions more ambitious than anything they had done before. The $40,000 allotted to the production was soon used up, and the picture was nowhere near finished.

The story of how sufficient money was scraped together to finish the film is one of the great and characteristically garbled legends of the screen. A few lucky people invested; many others passed up the golden chance. Shooting was completed in October, and Griffith spent three months editing. Word got around that the

13

Once again the scene is opened dramatically to convey the bitterness of Sherman's march to the sea. A family, in the path of war, will soon see their small house in flames.

The thundering rise of the Ku Klux Klan was a natural outgrowth of Civil War turmoil. One evil, slavery, gave rise to another.

project ran to an impossible length, that it was "a dirty nigger picture," the brainstorm of a nut, and that it cost over $100,000, which was unheard of in those days.

Griffith and his associates decided they would have to exhibit the film, originally titled *The Clansman*, in a new way: on a two-a-day schedule of showings and at a $2 top admission scale. A special musical score, prepared by Joseph Carl Breil, was introduced to be played as an accompaniment by full symphonic orchestras set in the theater pits.

On February 8, 1915, the completed picture was first publicly shown in Clune's Auditorium in Los Angeles. Audience reaction was tremendous, unevenly divided between vociferous enthusiasm and ugly criticism of the film's contents and length. A print was brought east by Griffith. When Dixon saw it at a screening, he is said to have exclaimed, "It's great! It should be called *The Birth of a Nation!*" And that it was, when it was given its world premiere at the Liberty Theater in New York City on March 3. Openings in Boston and Chicago followed in a few days.

Reactions were swift and explosive. Negro leaders were shocked and dismayed at the gross and patronizing representations of their race. Mayor John Purroy

Mitchel of New York City demanded that several of the scenes be cut. The former president of Harvard, Dr. Charles W. Eliot, publicly denounced it as false. Critics and sober historians tagged it an inflammatory show.

It was, beyond any question. So powerfully did it excite romantic imagination and the sensitive vestigial remains of partisan feelings among the many Americans who were only one generation removed from the painful experience of the War Between the States that it sent audiences forth from theaters boiling with excitement and enmity.

Actually, the "documentary quality"—the "naturalness" with which Griffith made the viewer sense the vast eruption of a Civil War battle, the reek of carnage on a smoking battlefield, the dismal aspects of postwar desolation, the bold appearance of the charging Ku Klux Klan—was only one of the film's persuasive features, and not the most valid one at that. There was a good deal of lush romanticizing and exaggeration in Griffith's action scenes.

For all his meticulous staging and spotting of tableau "facsimiles" of key historical events, such as President Lincoln's putting his signature to the call for federal volunteers, the surrender at Appomatox and the assassination of Lincoln in Ford's Theater, and for all his deliberate imitating of Matthew Brady's Civil War photographs, it cannot be conceded that Griffith was a devoted realist. He was a remarkable reproducer of the dramatic look of things as the distended mind's eye would see them and as nostalgia would have them be.

In Dixon's original novel and in the fustian melodrama made from it for a generally unsuccessful stage production in 1906, the story was commonplace and hackneyed, typical of that day when the tragedy of the 1860's was a favorite topic in books and plays. But with the medium of motion pictures, Griffith was able to give a new charge to imaginations, a pictorial comprehension to the throb of dramatic events and a tingling illusion of personal reality.

Still impressive about *The Birth of A Nation* is the speed with which the issue is laid down, the characters assembled and the drama got under way. In the opening scenes, after the main titles, the theme of slavery is introduced with shots of Africans being brought to America and sold at auction in the South. Thus "were planted the first seeds of dissension," says the title, and slavery is naively proposed as the singular issue over which the Civil War was fought.

With this idea deftly planted, Griffith proceeds to set the stage with his major dramatis personae. To represent "the North," he has one family—the Stonemans of Pennsylvania—of which the imposing head is the Hon. Austin Stoneman, a United States Senator and abolitionist of fanatical fervor (he is Thaddeus Stevens in thin disguise). He has a lovely daughter, Elsie, and two light-hearted sons who are jolly friends of the Cameron family of South Carolina.

The Camerons represent "the South." They are plantation gentry—a father and mother who are plump parental types, two pretty daughters (the younger of whom, Flora, is full of perpetual joy) and three sons, the oldest of whom, Ben, becomes the hero—the Little Colonel—of the plot. They live in the town of Piedmont, but their cotton plantation is nearby. It is a place of idyllic beauty, with singing Negro slaves working in the fields.

The friendly association of the Stoneman and Cameron boys (with strong possibilities of romance developing with the sisters on either side) is quickly established as prelude to the shock of mortal conflict that comes as the southern states demand their right to maintain slavery and President Lincoln calls for troops to prevent them from seceding from the Union.

The drama now flows into the next phase, which includes the outbreak of war, the departures of the Stoneman and the Cameron boys to join the respective armies of the Union and the Confederacy, the bloody battles that follow, the difficulties on the southern home front, the slow defeat of the South, the surrender at Appomatox and the assassination of Lincoln.

The third phase has to do with the period of Reconstruction. Now Senator Stoneman comes to the fore as the impassioned champion of Negro equality in the South. But he is soon superseded as the villain by his mulatto lieutenant, Silas Lynch, a fierce and florid zealot for "black supremacy."

In this phase, the course of the drama, all of which takes place in the South, is from lurid and angry display of the arrogance of the Negroes, urged on by "scalawags" from the North, and the humiliation of the whites, to the founding of the Ku Klux Klan by the Little Colonel and its triumph in bringing "order" to the South.

Actually, the historical implications are vague and presumptive all the way. The tie-ups of the endless personal crises with political and social developments are loose at best. Griffith was not a historian, as his prejudices reveal, and he was not concerned with presenting a lesson in history. He was putting on the screen a strong romantic drama of personal hardship, humiliation and heroism. Historical truth and logic were only secondary and incidental.

Thus his summation of the issue is made in strictly personal terms. The ultimate debasement of the Negroes is demonstrated in two events. The first is an attempted rape of Flora by an emancipated house servant, Gus, to avoid which the Little Sister jumps off a cliff and is killed. Gus is captured, tried and executed by the newly formed Ku Klux Klan. The second event is an effort by Lynch to force Elsie Stoneman to marry him, with the promise that he will make her "queen" of a black empire.

The drama is brought to a thundering climax with the rising of the Klan, first to rescue Elsie, who is threatened with rape by Lynch, and then to rescue the entire Cameron family, along with one of the Stoneman boys, from a rabble of Negroes and carpetbaggers who have them besieged in a cabin on the edge of town. The arrival of the Klan—in both cases, just in the nick of time—and its tangible triumphs over the villains constitute the victories that symbolize the emergence of the South from its valley of defeat.

From the plateau of this emotional high point, Griffith grandly foresees, in quick tableaux, the union of the Little Colonel and Elsie, sitting poetically by the sea; the apotheosis of mankind in heaven; and the reign of peace and brotherhood throughout the world.

Obviously, *The Birth of a Nation* is not rational or intellectual. On the one hand, it is deeply sentimental; on the other, it is bitter and cruel, blazingly intolerant and shameful in its racist attitudes. But we refrain from condemning Griffith in the knowledge that prejudices were rampant in those days. And we forgive him because he gave us a tremendously illustrative film, the strength of which is evident in countless eloquent scenes.

One thinks of his simple clarification of the stabbing pain of war. In one scene the younger Cameron brother, charging across a battlefield, abruptly stops

Gus (Walter Long), accused of attempting to rape Flora, is captured by the Klan, tried and executed summarily, thus bringing a historical concept down to sharp personal terms.

beside the corpse of a Union soldier that he seems to recognize; he stoops, with evident apprehension, to scan the face of the fallen youth and sees with horror that it is his chum, the younger Stoneman boy. At that instant, a bullet strikes him and he falls dead across the body of his friend. The pathos in what might be a cliché is made to suffuse the simple scene as the camera holds for a thoughtful moment on the two still, immutably dead boys.

Griffith follows this with a second, broader comprehension of the horror of war. It is a sequence visualizing the siege and devastation of the South by General Sherman's forces, first with long shots of the firing of Atlanta and the flight of the populace, then a close corner shot of an anguished mother, sitting on the side of a hill and clutching a group of frightened children as she looks off down the hill. The scene opens out on a majestic expanse of fertile, forest-fringed valley through which a long line of Sherman's army marches off, while on the edge of the forest a small house forlornly burns.

So it goes. There is a stunning sequence depicting the

return home of the Little Colonel after the war. In a long shot, he is seen hobbling sadly and alone down the empty street (the street in which he has previously been seen leading his gallant company off to war). He comes to the gate of his own home and pauses briefly to note its disrepair. As he does, the Little Sister bounces joyously out the front door. But as she sees his tattered condition, the look of despair on his face, she stops in solemn amazement. Sadly the two embrace. Then, as the Little Sister guides the weary soldier to the door, the camera steps to one side to see tender hands reach out and slowly draw the Little Colonel inside.

There are notable touches of humor, many of them provided by the broad clowning of the family servants, referred to as Faithful Souls. The scene in which little Flora is chased through a sun-splattered woods by Gus is a classic example of dramatic contrasts achieved with light and shade. And all the mighty expositions of the gathering and the riding of the Klan have an eerie excitement about them that has seldom been surpassed on the screen.

It is easy to view the picture as a grotesque period piece, a changeless relic of a long-past style and taste—which it is, if one sees it only in contrast to a modern sound film. There is much that is florid about it. The subtitles flaunt such rhetoric as "The first flag of the Confederacy, bathed in glory at Bull Run" or "Bitter memories will not allow the poor bruised heart of the South to forget." The acting is broad and bold, full of extravagant gestures, which was the style of the day.

H. B. Walthall's heroic Little Colonel, Ralph Lewis' Stoneman, George Siegmann's Lynch, Lillian Gish's Elsie, Mae Marsh's Little Sister, Mary Alden's Lydia Brown, the mulatto mistress of Stoneman, and many more (including Joseph Henaberry's Abraham Lincoln) emote enthusiastically. But, to the understanding viewer, this sort of acting has historical authenticity, because it is a believable illusion of the natures of the people of those times.

There is no question that *The Birth of a Nation* was an explosive film, hot and demagogic. But it is precisely because it was that it detonated public interest, earned millions of dollars around the world (no one will ever know how much because of the looseness of film rentals then) and demolished forever the highbrow notion that moving pictures were merely a toy.

Intolerance

1916

Written, directed and produced by David Wark Griffith; cameraman, G. W. (Billy) Bitzer; assistant cameraman, Karl Brown; released by the Wark Producing Company.

THE MODERN STORY

The Dear One	Mae Marsh
The Boy	Robert Harron
The Girl's Father	Fred Turner
Jenkins	Sam de Grasse
Miss Jenkins	Vera Lewis
Musketeer of the Slums	Walter Long
The Governor	Ralph Lewis
Strike Leader	Monte Blue
A Crook	Tod Browning
A Prostitute	Miriam Cooper

THE BABYLONIAN STORY

Belshazzar	Alfred Paget
The Mountain Girl	Constance Talmadge
The Rhapsode	Elmer Clifton
The Princess Beloved	Seena Owen
Cyrus the Persian	George Siegmann
High Priest of Bel	Tully Marshall
King Nabonidus	Carl Stockdale
Mighty Man of Valor	Elmo Lincoln
Dancer	Ruth St. Denis

Slave Girls: Jewel Carmen, Carol Dempster, Mildred Harris, Colleen Moore, Alma Rubens, Pauline Starke, Eve Sothern, Natalie Talmadge, Anna Mae Walthall.

Soldiers, courtiers, etc.: Frank Campeau, Donald Crisp, Douglas Fairbanks, DeWolfe Hopper, Wilfred Lucas, Owen Moore, Sir Herbert Beerbohm Tree, Tammany Young and others.

THE FRENCH STORY

Brown Eyes	Margery Wilson
Prosper Latour	Eugene Pallette
Father	Spottiswoode Aitken
Mother	Ruth Handford
Catherine de Medici	Josephine Crowell
Charles IX	Frank Bennett
Duc d'Anjou	Maxfield Stanley
Marguerite de Valois	Constance Talmadge

THE JUDEAN STORY

The Nazarene	Howard Gaye
Mary	Lillian Langdon
Mary Magdalene	Olga Grey
First Pharisee	Gunther von Ritzau
Second Pharisee	Erich von Stroheim
Bride of Cana	Bessie Love
Bridegroom	George Walsh
A Wedding Guest	W. S. van Dyke
The Woman Who Rocks the Cradle	Lillian Gish

In the Modern Story, the Boy (Robert Harron) meets a prostitute (Miriam Cooper) through the evil influence of the Musketeer of the Slums (Walter Long), leading him eventually to jail and his young wife to near destitution.

Would success spoil D. W. Griffith?

That thought surely never occurred to anyone at the time *The Birth of a Nation* was vaunting the fame of the great director throughout the land. Such a triumph must certainly have seemed evidence of his infallibility. And, of course, people were not then as knowing about the evanescence of screen success as they have since become. But this question has been a speculation of students in later years: Did the great success of *The Birth of a Nation* generate in Griffith such a faith in the responsiveness of the public and in his own capabilities that he was moved to extend his virtuosity in a massive film that strangely proved his undoing?

This may seem a surprising speculation to anyone who has been told only that Griffith was *the* great creative genius of motion pictures in the early days, or to anyone not familiar with his sad decline in a matter of a few years. And it may seem off-key and infelicitous as a prefatory note to this review of what is generally regarded as his greatest (some even call it *the* greatest) of all films.

But felicitous or not, it is a question that inevitably occurs as we come to consider the next project that Griffith undertook. For the evidence is that the assurance *The Birth of a Nation* fired in him, and the parallel indignation caused him by the demonstrations against it in the North, charged him with such a confusion of vanity, vindictiveness and zeal that he was roused to make a film of such proportions that his critics would be overwhelmed. This was his great *Intolerance*, which ironically turned out to be the long-time peak of cinematic creation and the bane of Griffith's career.

Compared to *The Birth of a Nation,* this extraordinarily long and complex film is far and away more ambitious, involved and cinematically mature. Where *The Birth of a Nation* offers a fairly unified story line in which dramatic action is developed within a frame of history and time, *Intolerance* embraces four stories from four different periods of history, each separately evolved and carried forward to a dramatic climax of its own. Yet the unfolding of these four stories is done simultaneously, with cutting from one to another as they go along, so that they all reach their awesome climaxes in one great interweaving of action in the last tempestuous reel. The aim is to show the working of bigotry and injustice throughout time and to make a plea for tolerance, Christian charity and the brotherhood of man.

The construction of this elaborate picture looks comparatively awkward today, raw and elemental in conception and continuity. The stories are crudely motivated, and the development of the characters is weak. The film is mainly melodrama on an involved and spectacular scale. The strength of it lies in the sensations of the occurrence of exciting events and of the viewer's participation in them that Griffith stirs with his command of silent cinema.

Yet so tangled and complicated were the strands of its narrative to audiences uneducated to this kind of cross-cut cinema that it was hard for them to follow its dramatic intricacies for three hours or to grasp the philosophical intentions of Griffith's abstract theme.

As a consequence, though hailed by critics, it failed to be a popular success when it was offered in 1916. It was, in fact, the first big "turkey" that the expanding movie industry turned up. This callous rejection by the public caused Griffith to be even more confused than he was by the criticism that *The Birth of a Nation* drew. He became disillusioned and embittered. He was also financially strained, since he put most of his profits from *The Birth of a Nation* into this mammoth film. It cost more than \$2,500,000, a fabulous sum in those days.

The basis of this tremendous project was a modest scenario that Griffith wrote: a drama of social injustice called *The Mother and the Law,* about a working-class mother whose baby was taken from her and her young husband unjustly thrown in jail because of the heartless machinations of certain self-righteous meddlers of the upper class. It was the sort of plaintive story popular in those days, which insinuated social criticism with unblushing sentiment.

Griffith was set to shoot it when the triumph of his Civil War film brought upon him an expanding comprehension of his destiny. He wished now to do something mighty, in keeping with his new-found fame, and to humiliate the detractors who accused him of bigotry. He felt those who criticized his picture and wanted to have it suppressed were the actual bigots, blind and intolerant. In this frame of mind, he got an idea of what to do with *The Mother and the Law.* He would make this fervid story the central strand of a skein of four stories that would be woven together to show how hypocrisy, persecution and religious hatred have always afflicted and tended to destroy civilized men.

To go with this homely exposure of the contemporary oppression of the working class, he decided to have an account of the overthrow of Belshazzar and the destruction of ancient Babylon by the armies of Cyrus

A bibulous and self-indulgent Belshazzar (Alfred Paget) enjoys a Babylonian orgy with the sumptuous Princess Beloved (Seena Owen) and ignores the warning of the Mountain Girl.

In sixteenth-century France, a forceful and blindly superstitious Catherine de Medici (Josephine Crowell), supported by the Duc d'Anjou and other courtiers, urges Charles IX (Frank Bennett) to sign a proclamation against the Huguenots, the French Protestants.

A vast and expensive set, with a cast of thousands, was a paragon for filmic spectacles yet to come. Crowds of celebrants enjoy the fruits of Belshazzar's short-lived victory amid the shimmering temples and towers of the city of Babylon.

of Persia, with Cyrus instigated to this violence by the vindictiveness and treachery of a cabal of Babylonian priests; a drama of the religious persecution of the Huguenots by Catherine de Medici in sixteenth-century France; and, as a line of familiar spiritual reference, a tabloid account of the life of Jesus Christ.

Obviously, something would be needed to provide an introductory thought with which to arrest the audience and serve as a binder and reminder from time to time. For this Griffith hit upon the idea of Eternal Motherhood. Thus, he started his picture with a cameo shot of a mother rocking a cradle, over which is superimposed these lines from Walt Whitman: "Endlessly rocks the cradle, Uniter of Here and Hereafter—Chanter of Sorrows." This simple iconograph serves as a "chapter heading" for the separate dramas and as an occasional transition piece. Lillian Gish plays the Mother.

Today, this device seems stiff and pompous, literary and pretentious in the style of sentimental novels. But that was Griffith's taste. He was mawkish and moralistic, but he also had an exceptionally keen and accurate "camera eye" that accounted for some strikingly natural and trenchant passages.

For instance, he throws us off balance very early in his first episode—the drama of the daughter of a factory worker whose innocent, fun-loving proclivities are wickedly opposed by the blue-nosed sister of the boss

of the factory in which her father works—when he breaks away from a romantic and bouncy pictorial style to give a few sharply realistic scenes of a factory strike. This incident is weakly motivated (the workers go on strike because the boss has reduced their wages in order to support his sister's moral crusade), but it has a solid and authentic quality. It could be a recording of the seething labor troubles of the day.

In its substance, the whole romantic drama of the cruelly treated factory girl—the Dear One, as Griffith coyly calls her—is on the preposterous side. It is full of contrivance and coincidence as it recounts how this poor girl loses her father, moves to the nearby city, marries The Boy with whom she was in love back home and has to fend for herself and her baby against vice elements and the relentless do-gooders when her husband is unjustly put in jail.

Likewise, the fustian behavior of and relations among the characters in the Babylonian episode and in the grossly stilted drama of the tyranny of Catherine de Medici must be blinked at—or taken as amusing—in full-value payment for the still-overwhelming explosions of spectacle and action in these episodes.

The Babylonian section is undeniably the most ingenious and impressive in the film. For it, Griffith had constructed a mammoth outdoor set to represent the towers and temples of the city of Babylon. Huge portals

19

adorned with massive sculptures, walls 100 feet high and great vaulted Oriental chambers distinguished this unprecedented facility for spectacle. The conception and dynamism of it were on a scale that was to set the style, and the high mark, for future spectacle films. The elements of personal involvement that Griffith devised for this episode are neither profound nor convincing. It is the clashing, deadly action when the forces of Cyrus assault the walls of the city that is powerful—that and the eye-popping luxury and eroticism displayed at Belshazzar's feast.

Most unsubtle and amusing about the French Huguenot episode is the swaggering arrogance with which a busty Catherine steamrollers a simpering Charles IX into ordering the St. Bartholomew's Day massacre. But once the maneuver is launched and the French soldiers are pouring through the streets, battering down doors and finally nabbing the pretty heroine, the action is fierce and fine.

As for the story of Jesus, it is told, or represented, in solemn tableaux that are conventional illustrations of incidents in the last few years of the life of the Messiah.

The ultimate greatness of *Intolerance* is achieved in the momentum with which Griffith builds up the tension and excitement of all the separate dramas at the end—the Mountain Girl racing in her chariot to warn Belshazzar that he has been betrayed; the fiancé of the heroine struggling through the crowded Paris streets to try to rescue her before the Huguenot-killers reach her house; Christ groaning toward Calvary; and the Dear One speeding in an automobile to catch a train on which the governor is riding and get a pardon for her husband who is about to be hanged. These actions are flowed together as though they were all parts of one great conglomerate "chase."

It is this aspect of *Intolerance*, this demonstration of how to achieve illusion on several levels that is its genius. At the same time, it must be observed that its clearly conglomerate character is esthetically inharmonious and overwrought. In his great burst of power and ostentation, Griffith tried to do too many things with too little awareness of the necessity of cohesive form and style. He tried to equate a modern social drama and its implications of reality with the romantic and purely escapist exaggerations of pseudo-historical spectacle. He tried, in his surge of ambition, to blend two distinct types of films, apparently without an awareness of how distinctly different they are.

But throughout he is always the master of details that strike the eye and fire the imagination with concentrated emotional pull or shock. Scores of these have the distinction of being models for subsequent clichés—such things as the iron door banging behind The Boy as he is taken into jail and the little window in the door snapping shut with a shuddering finality; or the working of the trapdoor on the gallows being demonstrated by a close-up of the knife being drawn across cords, a simple detail which is repeated to develop great suspense when we are waiting breathlessly for The Boy to be hanged; or the close-up of the hand of the Dear One groping feebly across the floor for a discarded sock of her baby after the child has been taken from her; or the close shot of one of the Persian besiegers having his head completely lopped off by a swinging sword and a bulge of viscera spouting out through his gaping neck!

Inevitably, Griffith's disposition to moralize and preach comes out in an idealistic and grandiloquent epilogue. Having brought his separate illustrations of the evil of intolerance to an end (and having let only one, the modern story, conclude happily for the people involved), he envisions "the day when cannons and prison bars wrought in the fires of intolerance" will no longer prevail and "perfect love shall bring peace forever." A shot of battlefields, a shot of a prison, and then a dissolve to fields of flowers as a superimposed subtitle reads, "Instead of prison walls bloom flowery fields," and we see children playing happily on a grassy slope, clouds drifting serenely in the sky—and, as a final reminder, the mother rocking the cradle endlessly. . . .

Unfortunately for Griffith, unfortunately for the world, this elaborate sentiment for peace was disconcerting to those who saw the film. For even as *Intolerance* was bidding to attract middling audiences, the propaganda drums were beating to pull this country into the First World War. This was but one more reason for the public indifference to the film.

Griffith's disappointment and intransigence, his allegiance to an attitude and style that became "old-fashioned" and unpopular with youthful audiences after the war, arrested his growth beyond this picture. He did make others in which ideas and some scenes reflected his bold imagination and his command of the medium. The rescue of the drowning heroine from an ice-clogged river in *Way Down East* (1920); the stark, poetic beauty in *Broken Blossoms* (1919); the dignity of his last, *The Struggle* (1931), attest to the fact that Griffith was expressive to the end. But he was haunted by the failure of *Intolerance*. It broke his faith and his heart.

The Cabinet of Dr. Caligari

Dr. Caligari (Werner Krauss) urges Jane (Lil Dagover) to have a private audience with the somnambulist, Cesare (Conrad Veidt), who has fallen in love with her.

1919

Scenario by Carl Mayer and Hans Janowitz; directed by Robert Wiene; photography by Willy Hameister; design by Walter Reimann, Herman Warm and Walter Rohrig; produced by Erich Pommer for Decla Studio.

Dr. Caligari	Werner Krauss
Cesare, the somnambulist	Conrad Veidt
Jane	Lil Dagover
Francis	Friedrich Feher
Alan	Hans von Twardowski
Dr. Olsen	Rudolf Lettinger
A Criminal	Rudolf Klein-Rogge

It is interesting and ironic that the most original and exciting film to come from any country after the First World War came from defeated, devastated, disorganized Germany. It was *The Cabinet of Dr. Caligari,* a weird, macabre "monster" film, exceptional for its violent, stylized scenery and its generation of an air of insanity.

Much has been written about it, and many people have a vague idea that it is a slightly diseased and disreputable cinematic freak. That is because of the complexion Dr. Siegfried Kracauer has put on it in his book, *From Caligari to Hitler: A Psychological History of the German Film.* In framing his ingenious thesis that the postwar films of Germany anticipated and even assisted the national drift to the Nazi lunacy, Kracauer has found in this picture the first symptoms of the dark morbidity, sadism and self-delusion of the German people that he says infected their between-the-wars films. In his view, this extraordinarily weird, disturbing work was the first shot of cinematic poison to dope the Germans for the Hitler putsch.

To my way of thinking, Kracauer's theory that *The Cabinet of Dr. Caligari* was a piece of incipient propaganda finds more in it than it contains. But there is no doubt that this agonized picture does expose a disposition to "escape" into fantasies of maniacs and monsters that was common with the Germans after the war. Its grotesque melodrama of a madman obsessed with the thought that the head of the insane asylum in which he is lodged is a criminal maniac is morbid and disconcerting. It is an eerie excursion into a realm where reality dissolves into shadows and experience takes warped, unbalanced forms. But the striking thing about it is not that this strangeness implies political or social degeneration. It is that this strangeness is itself a brilliant way of giving expression to moods and ideas on the screen.

Prior to the emergence of this picture from Berlin's Decla Studio in the winter of 1919, the camera had been conventionally used as an instrument for recording the literal look of material things, no matter how erratic or fantastic the human performances might be. Except for the cinematic primitives of the Frenchman, Georges Méliès, which blithely departed from reality into such pictorially imaginary realms as the moon, hell and fairyland regions, there had been no films of any consequence in which the scenery had been purposely dreamed up and the actors expressly stylized to affect the mind of the viewer with a new concept of the look and order of things.

Then came this curious German picture. Naturalism as a logical aim of the pictorial stimulation was deliberately eschewed. Material surfaces were altered and twisted into abstract designs so that these became the prime apparatus of the creative element of the film. Oddly enough, this invention of a new form came by chance—or, at least, by a train of circumstances that was not calculated in advance.

In the fall of 1919, two disaffected young scenarists in Berlin, Hans Janowitz and Carl Mayer, submitted a story to Erich Pommer, producing director of the Decla Studio. It had to do with a series of mysterious murders which the audience would be brought to realize were being committed by a ghoulish sleepwalker under the hypnotic spell of a mad scientist. Pommer was taken with the idea, which he felt was in the old familiar vein of the macabre Grand Guignol melodramas that were always popular in Germany. Such previous German films as *The Golem* and the serial called *Homunculus,* which had to do with dangerous monsters fabricated by men, had been very successful during the war.

However, Pommer discovered that his authors felt the story should be photographed in a pictorial style approximating that of Alfred Kubin, a radical artist of Prague. Kubin was one of the disciples of expressionistic art, which was embraced with enthusiasm by restless and groping intellectuals in postwar Germany, not only as a style in painting but also for theatrical scenic use. Expressionism shifted the emphasis of art from the reproduction of the surface aspects of nature and phys-

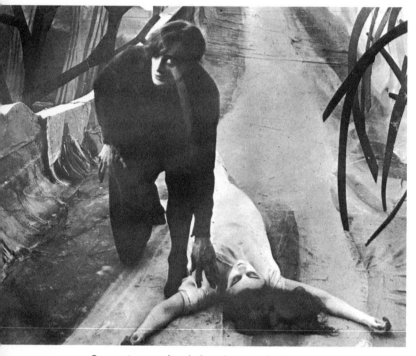

Cesare is apprehended in the act of kidnapping Jane.

ical objects to the development of sheer creative form. Its aim was to excite emotion not by descriptive and representational designs but by the construction and arrangement of formal patterns that "expressed" the artist's moods.

Pommer was dubious of this conception. As he has since recalled (in a program note prepared for a special showing of Carl Mayer's films in London in 1947), he knew he had to make an inexpensive, salable commercial film. He felt he could not afford a stylized experiment.

Some time passed before work started on the picture.

In that time, a young director, Fritz Lang, was selected to direct, but he was stopped by a prior commitment and Robert Wiene was given the task. And, since nothing was done about Kubin, four artists on Decla's designing staff—Herman Warm, Walter Reimann, Walter Rehrig and Robert Herlth—were put to designing the sets. They, too, were ardent disciples of the "new freedom" in art.

Pommer says they were also clever. Knowing the studio was limited on electric power and light, they came to him one day, he tells us, with a suggestion he thought absurd, even reactionary. "Why not paint lights and shadows on the sets for this *Caligari* film?" they asked. Pommer told them they were crazy, that it was impossible to put fanciful, "unreal" sets behind real people, that it would be a ridiculous return to primitive film-making. But the next day the artists brought in a series of designs, and persuaded him to let Wiene make a test scene against one of them. The test was so exciting that everyone was convinced.

During production, however, another issue arose which was handled not so favorably to the wishes of Mayer and Janowitz. Their story was meant to be presented as an account of actual horrors encountered by a young man who visits a traveling fair. But in the finished picture, these horrors are framed as nightmare fantasies of the young man's disordered mind.

The main story is that this young man, Francis, comes upon a shocking situation at the fair. He is led to suspect that a gnomish mountebank, billed as Dr. Caligari, who does what appears a harmless act with a cadaverous somnambulist that he keeps in a coffinlike box, is secretly a murderer, and that his sleepwalking confederate, Cesare, actually goes forth at night to do his bidding under the doctor's evil spell. This is proved beyond question one night when Francis' sweetheart, Jane, is attacked in her bedroom by this creature, who is supposedly shut up safely in his box. She isn't murdered, however; she is carried off by Cesare, who has conceived a passion for her, but she manages to escape and spread the alarm. In the ensuing search, the troubled Francis goes to an insane asylum seeking Cesare, and finds that the respected director of the asylum is none other than the interchangeable Dr. Caligari! The denouement is that the doctor, who indignantly denies the charge, reveals himself by going raving mad when the dead body of Cesare is brought to him.

At the suggestion of Fritz Lang, Wiene altered the story so that it comes out as the imagining of Francis, who is a patient in a mental institute. He tells his story to other patients in hopes of getting them to join him in a revolt against the director. When they refuse, *he* gets violent and is taken to the director, who remarks, "At

22

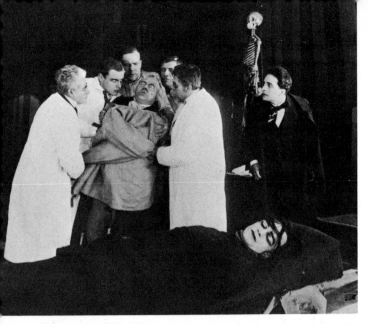

Francis (Friedrich Feher) discovers that the director of the asylum is none other than the frightful Dr. Caligari himself.

last I know his mania. He thinks I am the mythical Caligari. But now I know the cure." There isn't the slightest question that this alteration does dilute the orginal morbid proposition that a madman could actually be in control of other madmen or helpless victims in a social state. The harsh vicarious experience is disposed of as a maniac's fantasy.

Kracauer maintains that this treatment destroys not only the authors' intent, which he says (on the authority of an unpublished article by Janowitz) was to expose the tyranny of military authority—"unlimited authority that idolizes power"—but it also dissipates the logic of the radical artistic style.

This is a major criticism, *if* one is prepared to assume the specific political symbolism Kracauer says the authors meant. I am not, nor do I think it really matters in the basic evaluation of the film. To me, the picture's symbolism—if it is symbolism you want—is simply that of man as a mechanical creature susceptible to evil control, while others may be the helpless victims of whatever disorder this may cause. And I think this is just as impressive as a psychotic anxiety as it would be if it were presented as a horrid experience from life.

More cogent is the sometime criticism that the film is a triumph of stagecraft more than of creative cinema. The visual transmission of feelings of horror and disharmony is achieved in the design and manipulation of what is essentially painted scenery, rather than with the movement of the camera and dynamic editing.

This is true—to a point. The camera is generally static or set for every scene. Most of the weird articula-

tion of madness and the agony of a madman's mind is got in the scenery, the décor, erratic and askew, in effects achieved with lighting darted upon that décor, and in the grotesqueness of the actors in their makeups and attitudes.

For instance, in an early scene where Caligari goes to the office of the town clerk to get a license for his sideshow, the walls veer outward from the floor, broken by pyramidal openings instead of normal windows and doors, and are crossed by dark stripes that carry perspective into indefinite space. The clerk towers above the gnomish showman on a forbiddingly lofty stool. The scene conveys an air of utter coldness, brutishness and sterility. Or a scene in which a friend of Francis is murdered in his tiny room; this is deftly done without the victim or the murderer actually being seen, just silhouettes thrashing frantically on angular walls.

The most striking scene in the picture is that in which Jane is assaulted by the wild-eyed Cesare, played by Conrad Veidt. Here the hideous sleepwalker, a cadaver when first seen in his box, is now as ghostly and graceful as a shadow as he glides along a wall, en route to his mission in Jane's room, and as he comes upon her. There is a curious beauty about him, the terrible fascination of a snake. Cesare is never a person, never a fixed thing. He is a baleful, sometimes poignant chimera.

And the gnomelike, mephitic Caligari of the famed German actor, Werner Krauss—a stooped little trickster in a tall hat, striped gloves and with rheumy eyes that squint from behind thick-lensed glasses—seems a sadistic travesty of the kindly old men in sentimental German fairy tales. It is cruel to be shown this quaint magician at a place of such enjoyment as a fair turn out to be a foul deceiver and the fair turn into a noxious dream.

It is this that Wiene puts forth in this picture—a look behind the orderliness of things, a curious unsettling of dependence upon the substance of reality. Suddenly a motion picture becomes the opening into a psychic realm in which the unsuspecting, unprepared intruder finds himself in the toils of the insane.

To some extent, *The Cabinet of Dr. Caligari* is in the nature of a psychological film, a probe of a persecution complex in expressive pictorial terms. And while the clinical details of it may be open to professional doubt, it was the first real exploration in this later popular cinema genre. I wonder whether Franz Kafka ever saw this film and whether it might have had some influence on his writing of *The Trial*.

Nanook of the North

Nanook prepares to harpoon a walrus, his main source of sustenance.

1922

Scenario, direction and photography by Robert J. Flaherty; produced by Révillon Frères.

The first time a motion-picture camera was put to effective use and a photograph of motion was absorbed on film, it was a straight recording of an everyday, actual happening. The camera was conceived as a mechanism for picturing things as they are—for capturing the aspects of the real world and of movements as they occur—without any idea of creating illusions or fantasies.

And to this end, the camera continued to be used by countless photographers, even after the mechanism's utility for telling stories had been disclosed and the medium was being devoted mainly to the story film. Pictures of scenic wonders and beauties were early purveyed in specialized nickelodeon theaters got up to look like railway cars. These were the primitive precursors of the later familiar travelogues. A tremendously popular entertainment in the years before the First World War was a two-hour film made in 1913 by Paul J. Rainey, a Philadelphia sportsman and big-game hunter, called *Rainey's African Hunt*. Its pictures of African wildlife were uncontestably real. Martin John-

son's early *Orpheum Travel Weekly* was another favorite.

But the common characteristic of all these pictures was their purely objective point of view. They looked *at* their subjects, not *into* them. When they observed the African natives, the denizens of Zululand, the swarms of Indian swamis attending their durbar, they registered only the surface aspects, the outer appearances. When the picture was ended, the observer had a sense of having seen from afar. This is still the feeling one gets from many travelogues.

Such was the general situation with travel films until Pathé came up with a picture in 1922 which bore the exotic title of *Nanook of the North*. "Absolutely different from any picture you ever saw," the advertisements said on the opening of the picture at the Capitol Theater in New York, on June 11, 1922. And different it was, in a manner soon to be realized.

The film had been shot by Robert J. Flaherty, a mining engineer, in the area of Hudson Strait. In essence all it showed was scenes from life among the Eskimos who inhabited the regions of northern Ungava along the shores of Hopewell Sound at the upper tip of Quebec. But it did more than that. It brought the viewer close to the Eskimo.

Centered upon one family, of which Nanook was the

head and his jolly wife, Nyla, was the cohesive force, the film put one in the midst of the Eskimo's domesticity, made him feel a strong sense of participation with the sturdy people in their day-by-day affairs. It also caught a sense of the Eskimo's struggle to survive against the elements and showed the vast and awesome beauties of nature amidst which the Eskimo lived.

It was, in short, the first picture that clearly revealed "the film's power of imaginative natural observation," as Forsyth Hardy has said; the first in which the instinct of an artist and a poet had been applied to the photographic recording of actuality. And, as such, it possessed a reality and radiance so graphic and strong that it truly deserved to be touted as "different from any picture you ever saw."

What was indeed remarkable was the fact that it was Flaherty's first film, the first, that is, that he completed and brought to fruition on the screen. A trained and dedicated mining engineer, he had first gone into the Hudson Bay country on an exploring expedition in 1910. In the next six years, he made five more journeys into the frozen north.

Although the expeditions produced no discoveries of mineral wealth, Flaherty found himself greatly rewarded by his meetings with the interesting people of the Belcher Islands and Baffinland. He kept voluminous diaries of his months with them. Slowly he found himself becoming an anthropologist, ethnologist and poet.

On his journey in 1916, he took a movie camera and made a random photographic record of life with the Eskimos. When he returned to his home in Connecticut, he and his wife edited this footage into a sort of narrative film, but the negative was destroyed in an accident and the only print made from it was lost.

However, Flaherty now had an urge to show Eskimo life as it was, a vision of a cheerful, industrious people pitted against the hardships of a barren and difficult land. Then he met Captain Thierry-Mollet of the fur-trading company of Révillon Frères and imparted to him his ambition to do a film in the north.

Just at that time, the Révillon people were competing with the Hudson's Bay Company in the fur trade, and Captain Thierry-Mollet saw the publicity possibility of a film that would show one of the regions that produced this great resource. With John Révillon, he agreed to finance Flaherty in the making of a film. So in 1919, Flaherty went back to northern Ungava to shoot.

He chose as the base of his operations a trading post on Hopewell Sound and there discovered the family that would be the focus of his narrative. Nanook, on whom he would depend for most of his action, was a stalwart individual with a creased and weather-beaten face, bright little eyes in narrow sockets and an almost

Nyla, the Smiling One, was invariably cheerful, pursuing her wifely tasks in the starkness of native surroundings.

Childlike and unspoiled, Nanook takes a simple delight in the sounds of a phonograph seen at a trading post.

continual smile. His wife, Nyla, was a smooth-skinned woman with a sweet, benign expression and a natural grace that appeared in many of her movements, even within her layers of furs and skins. The other members of the family—two lively children, an infant which Nyla slung in a pouch inside the back of her sealskin parka, and several adults who are unidentified—completed the group of Eskimos with which the film-maker worked.

As became his custom, Flaherty did not start with a script. He allowed the occurrence of natural events to determine the pattern of his narrative as he went along. Thus his picture shows but a succession of everyday episodes in the patient, determined, monotonous life of the Eskimo. Yet it is just this feeling of casualness and informality that gives the film the air of reality in which the audience participates.

I would say that a good part of the attractiveness is

25

Nanook cuts bricks of ice for the walls of his igloo. To permit Flaherty's camera work, half the igloo was torn down, and the cast and crew uncomplainingly lost half their weather protection.

the humor which Flaherty gets from the beginning, the establishment of his people as perpetually cheerful and happy, despite successive problems and perils. In his first scenes, in which the family arrives at the trading post to sell the beautiful furs that Nanook has taken in the year (white fox and polar bear, which a title tells us has been taken barehanded with a harpoon), he shows us the recognized humor of the entire family piling out of a tiny sealskin kayak, like any country family coming to town in one wagon—with a puppy the last to pile out. This charming view of the ingenuousness and simplicity of these people is supported with shots of Nanook listening in amazement to a gramophone played by the trader at the post and one of the children enjoying a spoonful of castor oil.

Actually, the episodes of adventure are not so violent or prolonged as one might expect—certainly nothing to compare with some seen in later films. There is a fascinating bit of Nanook spearing fish along the edge of the ice—the little man alone on the great ice floe, looking for all the world like a woolly bear, in his polar-bear-skin pants, his sealskin boots and sealskin parka.

Similarly, there is a fascinating sequence of a group of Eskimo men creeping up to harpoon a walrus from a herd basking on the shore and then hand-hauling the line with the stricken creature at the end of it back to shore. The motif of family solidarity which runs through the film is here subtly counterpointed with shots of the walrus' mate coming in close to try to lock tusks and pull the harpooned animal away. Flaherty had a tender feeling for the natural instincts of man and beast.

But it is primarily the sense of relation to the people that is so keen: The speed and dexterity with which Nanook builds an igloo home for his family while off on an expedition, cutting out blocks of packed snow with a long walrus-bone knife and piling them up in a neat circle, cutting his way out from inside and then cutting a block of clear ice to fit into the small dome as a window. Then the family inside the igloo, naked to the waist under piles of robes, sleeping all packed together for companionship and warmth ("a few robes of deerskin, some pots and pans is all they have," a title says); Nyla chewing on Nanook's heavy sealskin boots in the morning to take the stiffness out of them so he can put them on his feet; Nyla licking and blowing upon her naked baby to warm it; Nanook watching his little son, Alee, playing with a puppy hitched to a tiny sled, or happily teaching the youngster to use a bow and arrow.

This is the composition of a truly pictorial poem of life—the original specimen of what John Grierson, the great documentary film-maker and critic, later called the "ancient dignities of man against the sky."

And at the end, when Nanook and his family lie down to sleep again in a deserted igloo in which they must seek shelter from a raging blizzard, Flaherty's cut from the face of the man to close-ups of the sled dogs lying in silent, ice-caked mounds outside in the snow, and then back to the face of the man for his fadeout is a metaphorical statement of nature's supreme encirclement.

This beautiful film of Flaherty's, which runs for only a few minutes over an hour, was, indeed, the beginning of what Grierson labeled "the documentary film," that is, the film in which the creative process is applied to real material, the film achieved with "a symphonic structure" and "dynamic editing."

And it was the initial expression of Robert Flaherty's lasting disposition to transcribe the poetic, the romantic aspects of man and nature into film. Henceforth he abandoned his profession as a mining engineer and persisted as a film-maker, usually with the financial sponsorship of such imaginative business organizations as Révillon Frères.

His next film, *Moana* (1926), is a study of the tattoo cult among natives in the South Seas. His *Man of Aran* (1934) is a rich appreciation of the rugged life of the Aran Islanders. And his last film, *The Louisiana Story* (1948), is a charming, romantic look at a nature boy living in the bayous who is struck with wonder when a floating rig of the Humble Oil Company is brought in to drill for oil.

Of course, the so-called "documentary movement" which he fathered went far beyond the impulse and spiritual urge of Flaherty. He remained a beautiful and pure creative soul. But the eloquent, poetic instrument he showed the camera could be with *Nanook of the North* was to be of tremendous service and satisfaction to mankind in years to come.

The Covered Wagon

1923

Scenario by Jack Cunningham from a novel by Emerson Hough; directed by James Cruze; cameraman, Karl Brown; produced by Famous Players-Lasky.

Will Bannion	J. Warren Kerrigan
Jesse Wingate	Charles Ogle
Molly Wingate	Lois Wilson
Sam Woodhull	Alan Hale
Jim Bridger	Tully Marshall
Mrs. Wingate	Ethel Wales
Jackson	Ernest Torrence
Jed Wingate	Johnny Fox
Kit Carson	Guy Oliver

Almost from the beginning of the making of films in the United States, a favorite source of inspiration and dramatic material was the American western frontier. The motion picture might have been invented with nothing but this union in view. The time was ripe for a medium that could readily and vividly translate the great national surge of excitement about the West into pictorial terms.

Ever more thrilling and engrossing to Americans after the Civil War were the stories, the legends and the fictions about the expanding frontier. This was a vast and fertile area of developing history and myth. The perilous westward migrations in the early part of the nineteenth century, the California Gold Rush in 1849, the building of the transcontinental railroads after the Civil War and the settlement of the western regions were sagas that grew and took on a glow.

Bret Harte and Mark Twain had written of the mining camps and the gambling saloons, the trips of the overland stagecoaches and the rugged life at the frontier forts. They and others had set the foundations for a stirring mythology that turned upon the facts and, more often, the fables of the West—the bad men, the gamblers, the cowboys, the sheriffs, the dance-hall ladies with hearts of gold. As the century drew toward its end, the romance had been taken up by the superheated writers of dime novels and the editors of the *Police Gazette*. The clashes of cavalry and Indians, the lore of holdups, lynchings, barroom brawls and the depredations of train robbers were luridly described in cheap print that was the literature of every schoolboy and many adults in the land.

Such were the originations of an American fantasy, a dream that engrossed every earthling hungry for "escape." What could have been more convenient and capable to make it materialize than the new device of the motion pictures, which happened to be invented at just the right time!

But, strangely enough, a quarter of a century was to pass before the film-makers achieved an effective representation of the western legend on a truly epic scale. That was *The Covered Wagon*, which a minor director, James Cruze, turned out for Famous Players-Lasky in 1922. Here was the first motion picture to use the full canvas of the screen as a medium for illustrating the magnitude of a western enterprise organized by a group of people as an assault against the vastness of the West. It tells of the perils and adventures of a covered-wagon trek from what is now Kansas City to Oregon in 1848, with the total success of the venture the most important aim.

Before this, the format of the western film had been tiresomely stuck on the interests and adventures of the individual. After *The Great Train Robbery,* a one-reel episode made in 1903, which has the reputation of being the first dramatic story film (it was made in the New York metropolitan area, with the shots of the holdup of a western train done on a stretch of the Delaware & Lackawanna Railroad, near Dover, New Jersey), there came a rush of little pictures about train robberies, Indian attacks, deeds of derring-do and self-sacrificial acts of charity by noble cowboys.

First of the popular cowboy actors was "Bronco Billy" Anderson, who played one of the bandits in *The Great Train Robbery*. He had never been west of Chicago and could barely ride a horse, but he made several

Will Bannion (J. Warren Kerrigan) comforts a small member of the wagon train with the idea that a doll casualty is replaceable.

A vast ranch holding, 200,000 acres in extent, in Sanke Valley, Nevada, was the location chosen by the Nevada-born director, James Cruze.

hundred one- and two-reel cowboy pictures between 1905 and 1912.

The roof blew off the western, however, with the arrival in 1914 of William S. Hart as an actor-director in *Two Gun Hicks* and *On the Night Stage*. Hart had spent his boyhood on the frontier and had a deep devotion to the West, which he manifested in his determination to put authenticity into his films. In the several-score westerns he made in the next ten years, he strove for a rugged realism in scene and character. As the central figure in all his pictures, he was the representation of the bold, self-sustaining, sometimes lawless but basically good and honorable man whose lot it was to wander lonesomely along the western frontier. His films were dramatizations of the power of the individual.

Hart was soon rivaled in popularity by another native westerner, Tom Mix, a former Oklahoma cowboy and town marshal who was spotted in the Miller's 101 Ranch Wild West Show by Col. William Selig, a pioneer producer of films, and started in little westerns of the two-reel type. William Fox later put him into five-reel features which quickly established his fame and his mammoth popularity. Where Hart was grim and realistic, Mix was flamboyant and wild. He was the romantic cowboy to satisfy fantasy. He wore fancy clothes, a white sombrero, and rode a beautiful fat horse, named Tony, which was almost as acrobatic, intelligent and popular as he. There was little likelihood or logic in the stories of the films in which he played, but Mix was one of the greatest personalities in silent films.

Even so, the inevitable monotony of the films of Hart and Mix and other less popular cowboy players (William Farnum, Douglas Fairbanks, Wallace Reid, William Desmond, etc.) resulted in a slow decline in the popularity of the western film. The formula of the single hero was definitely on the wane. To be sure, there had been developed, especially in the films of Hart, a sense of the natural beauty and poetry of the West. And, indeed, in a fairly spectacular five-reeler about a covered wagon trek, called *Wagon Tracks* (1919), Hart came close to realizing the epic potential of the screen.

Then the unexpected happened. A novel, *The Covered Wagon,* by Emerson Hough, had become a substantial best-seller in 1921 and was acquired by Famous Players-Lasky to be made into a conventional western film. Hough was a conservationist and his story of a wagon trek across the great plains and the mountains had good solid authenticity, even though it was heavily larded with elements of romance. George Melford, a hack director, was assigned to make it into a film, and a dainty young actress, Mary Miles Minter, was selected to be its star.

However, Jesse L. Lasky, one of the top executives of the company, happened to read the novel and became so captivated by it that he decided it should be placed in different hands. According to his story, told in his autobiography, *I Blow My Own Horn,* he persuaded Melford and Miss Minter to withdraw from what he warned would be only another western, then he turned the novel over to a young director named James Cruze. Cruze was rumored to be part Indian. At least, he was a native of Nevada. Lasky thought this good. Cruze was delighted with the novel and had some bold ideas for getting a maximum of excitement out of its many incidents, such as a buffalo hunt, a massive crossing of a river by the wagon train, an Indian attack upon the wagons and a prairie fire.

For the leading male role, that of Will Bannion, a stalwart fellow in charge of one section of the wagon train, Cruze suggested J. Warren Kerrigan. He had been popular in the years before the First World War, but he was beginning to slip. For the leading lady, he and

28

Ernest Torrence, on the right, was one of the old hands in this colorful recapitulation of America's move to the west.

Hundreds of horses, cattle, Conestoga wagons, reservation Indians and cowhand extras were used to flesh out for posterity a bravura episode in our history.

Lasky picked Lois Wilson, a wholesome young actress who was one of the lesser stars at the studio. Ernest Torrence, a redoubtable character actor, was selected to play a guide and fur trapper, Bannion's devoted pal; and Tully Marshall, another prominent character actor, was assigned to play Jim Bridger, the historic explorer, trader and scout.

On the approval of Lasky, a budget of $500,000 was set. When the word of this got back to New York, Adolph Zukor, the head of the company, knowing the status of westerns, assumed that in the transmission of the message an extra zero had been added by mistake. He was mollified, Lasky says, when told that the film would be an "epic."

Locations were scouted in nine states before Cruze finally hit upon a remote section in his home state of Nevada. Here, on the 200,000-acre Baker Ranch in Snake Valley, 85 miles from the nearest railway, a 500-tent encampment was set up and an army of actors, extras and crew was brought in. Several hundred Indians were gathered from reservations in Nevada and California, and prop men rounded up all the Conestoga wagons they could find in the West. Eight weeks were required to shoot the picture, a modest time today but a great deal in 1922. It was one of the most ambitious location ventures that a Hollywood company had ever done.

For the buffalo hunt and stampede, a site was selected on Antelope Island in Great Salt Lake. Cruze had the camera located in a stockade past which the beasts were driven in order to provide vivid close-ups. But the cameraman, Karl Brown, was almost killed when he stepped out of the stockade with a camera to try for proximity.

The production, as might well have been expected, went "over budget," coming in at $782,000. But it was worth it. The film, in ten reels, opened at the Criterion Theater in New York on March 16, 1923, and played there for fifty-nine weeks on a two-a-day schedule at $1.50 top admission price, breaking the long-run record of forty-four weeks held by *The Birth of a Nation*. From just the Criterion in New York and Grauman's Theater in Los Angeles, *The Covered Wagon* earned back its cost.

Undoubtedly the reason for the immense popularity of the film, and for its inevitable establishment as one of the all-time greats, was the vivid impression it conveys of the magnitude and peril of rolling across the vast, unsettled country in a wagon train. While the drama of individuals is very much to the fore, and, of course, gives opportunity for the vicarious association of oneself with one's favored individuals, the genius of the picture is that it places the viewer in the wagon train, makes him a participant in the adventure, an observer of the scene and an eventual sharer in the triumph of reaching Oregon.

The adventure begins at Westport Landing (now Kansas City), in 1848, as a great wagon train assembles. Conflicts are established at the start. Jesse Wingate, the wagon-train leader, is an austere, God-fearing farmer type, compelled to control the impatience of his people who want to start without waiting the arrival of the Liberty Boys, because he senses the wisdom of a large company on the westward trip. "I'm just as anxious to git my plow in Oregon soil as anybody," he says (in a subtitle, of course), as he grasps the handle of a homely farming implement, the symbolization of the purpose of the journey that runs all through.

His daughter, Molly, is affianced to Sam, his assistant, played by Alan Hale. But when the Liberty Boys and their section of wagons arrive—a great sweep of them against the sky—Will Bannion, the leader, and Molly begin making eyes. Wingate commands his

The part of Jackson, a member of Bannion's train, was one of many character roles played by Ernest Torrence in the early days of film.

daughter to keep away from Bannion, however, because he has learned that Bannion is "a renegade and a cattle thief to boot."

Thus, with the personal plot located, the long westward journey begins with the crack of a bullwhip, wielded by Jed, a staunch and valiant lad, and a blast on a trumpet. Then the great train lumbers forth, with a long shot of tiny wagons in a far-reaching single file, moving across the vast landscape under the great vault of the sky. It is an image of breathtaking beauty and inspiring pictorial eloquence, made more so by the surging music that rose to accompany it from the theater orchestras.

This is the touchstone of the picture, this image of men, women and children against space, against this great, awesome, beautiful, forbidding expanse of challenge and mystery. Space—the trackless, endless landscape; the open, windswept plains; the wide, formidable rivers; the elements-laden skies—this is the menace in the picture, the antagonist of man. It is the enemy he

has to conquer with his courage, ingenuity, strength and his meager mechanism, the wagon—this, and his own doubts and fears. The Indian out there in the vastness is no more a lurking peril than the broad, flat river imposing a crucial barrier, or the snow sweeping out of the heavens, or the dryness and choking dust.

Naturally, the personal story is romantic, full of egregious clichés, turning upon the rivalry of Bannion and Sam for Molly's hand. This inevitably leaves the company weakened when crises arise, such as an attack by Indians and the crossing of the Platte River.

The Indian attack and the firing of many wagons is most spectacular: the Indians creeping in, under cover of darkness, upon the circle of wagons in a box canyon, the arrows whizzing through the wagon covers, the savages racing around the wagons, the people fighting back.

And there is strong sentiment in many details, such as the burial on the open plains of old Mrs. Watters "that came all the way from Pennsylvania," with the folks gathered forlornly around as a young woman plays a battered violin. And then, as the order is given to put ashes and dust on the grave and drive the wagons over it so that the Indians may not find it, the shout comes from one of the wagons that a boy baby has been born. There is the incident of the woman who will not let them jettison her grandmother's walnut dresser and the rose cutting and flower seeds she has brought to start her new home when they are lightening the wagons to float them across the Platte.

But Cruze does not squander time stretching details for emotional effects. He whizzes through an incident such as Will saving Molly from a runaway horse, and he gives us but a few electrifying glimpses of an enterprise as crucial as the buffalo hunt. What he is actually doing is developing a saga of events. It is greater than the romantic drama, which is performed in the best expansive silent style.

What audiences of the day were left with—and what we can still appreciate, after hundreds of repetitions of the clichés have been seen on motion picture and television screens—is a deep admiration for the audacity of the western trek and a sense of the courageousness of simple people. But, most of all, we are left with the indelible image of those wagons, snaking across miles of open space, now looking tiny and vulnerable when seen from afar, now large and commanding in close-up. This is pictorial poetry. *The Covered Wagon* was the first motion picture to sing the song of the American frontier.

30

A country parson, Gösta Berling (Lars Hanson), given to excessive drinking and fiery sermons, excoriates his congregation for sin and hypocrisy.

Feeling degraded by Berling's accusation, the congregation set upon him, eventually defrock him, and send him away from his church.

The Story of Gösta Berling

1923

Adapted from the novel by Selma Lagerlöf. Scenario by Mauritz Stiller and Ragnar Hyltén-Cavallius. Directed by Mauritz Stiller; cameraman, Julius Jaenzon; produced by Svensk Filmindustri.

Gösta Berling	Lars Hanson
Majorskan Samzelius	Gerda Lundequist-Dahlstrom
Major Samzelius	Otto Elg-Lundberg
Melchior Sinclaire	Sixten Melmerfelt
Gustafva Sinclaire	Karin Swanstrom
Marianne Sinclaire	Jenny Hasselqvist
Countess Martha Dohna	Ellen Cederstrom
Countess Ebba Dohna	Mona Martenson
Count Hendrik Dohna	Torsten Hammeren
Countess Elizabeth Dohna	Greta Garbo

Here and there, on the vast and varied landscape of motion pictures as it spreads across the years, there loom certain films that have the stature of classics not only because of their strong cinematic distinctions but also because they present other aspects that render them imposing and inescapable in the culture of films. Such a one is *The Story of Gösta Berling*, made in Sweden in 1923.

This intensely romantic picture, which was written and directed by the now legendary Mauritz Stiller from a novel by Selma Lagerlöf, stands apart with a group of pictures that were the consequence of one of the most extraordinary phases of film-making. This was the phase we now refer to as "Sweden's golden age," the years between 1913 and 1924, when the making of films in that country developed so rapidly and achieved such artistic preeminence that Sweden emerged in this brief span as one of the most productive film producers in the world.

It was a period in which a mere handful of uncommonly talented men—Stiller and Victor Sjostrom and their producer, Charles Magnusson; the cameramen, Julius and Henrik Jaenzon; and possibly two or three more—managed to make this new medium an apt communicator of the spirit and quality of their environment, mainly inspired by the novels of Miss Lagerlöf. In a series of films that included such other outstanding works as Sjostrom's *The Phantom Chariot* (1920) and Stiller's *The Treasure of Arne* (1919), they captured the violent beauty of their country and the strong emotional nature of the Swedes in a manner that raised their motion pictures to the level of dramatic poetry. *The Story of Gösta Berling*, the last in this series of films, was the peak of the ambitions and achievements of the Swedish "golden age." It was also, for its social attitude, perhaps the strongest.

But more than its cinematic eminence and its historical importance combine to render *The Story of Gösta Berling* one of the classics of the screen. It was the first feature picture in which Greta Garbo appeared and

31

displayed the radiance and magnificence that were to make her perhaps the most romantic and exciting individual the screen has ever had.

Within this bulging drama of the adventures of a nineteenth-century country priest whose life is vastly troubled by a conflict of pride and shame, one may find all the interesting elements that characterized the early Swedish films, and, indeed, may be found in the more complex sound films of Ingmar Bergman of a later day. Here, in the story of Gösta—a handsome, defiant man who is defrocked because, in a drunken moment, he has berated his congregation for sin and hypocrisy—there flows the powerful, mystic spirit that is native to the Swedes and was expressed so vigorously in Miss Lagerlöf's writings.

If one were seeking the single circumstance that most strongly determined the characteristics of the "golden age" films, one would find it in the arrangement made by Magnusson in 1917 for film rights to all the novels and stories of Miss Lagerlöf. She was the bard of Sweden, its Nathaniel Hawthorne, its Sir Walter Scott. She wrote of the Swedish scene with a stark and stunning realism in the penetrating vein of the works of Strindberg and other iconoclasts of the day. And yet she transformed grim reality with a fervent idealism that gave to her subjects and her characters an unusual romantic glow.

The Story of Gösta Berling was her first novel, published in 1894 when she was a poor schoolteacher, and it very rapidly became extremely popular in her own country and then around the world. Its country-parson hero is essentially a weak and inadequate man, lazy, shiftless, alcoholic and full of whining pity for himself. But in Miss Lagerlöf's image he is a supreme Byronic type—handsome, generous, impulsive, a blend of bold strengths and human weaknesses.

Obviously, this heroic story was most appropriate for transfer to the screen, but it presented a mammoth challenge in the vast bulk and detail of its narrative. Stiller was given the assignment. Julius Jaenzon was his cameraman. The finest cast that could be assembled from the Swedish theater and films was drawn. Lars Hanson, the nation's leading matinee idol, was given the title role. Gerda Lundequist-Dahlstrom, a brilliant stage actress, was assigned the most difficult female part, that of an older woman who gives the hero wise counsel and encouragement and helps him eventually to accomplish the romantic union with a beautiful Italian countess that marks his return to a happy life.

To play the Countess, Stiller selected an unknown Swedish girl whom he had discovered at the Royal Dramatic Academy. Her name was Greta Gustafsson, and her only previous experience in films had been in two advertising trailers and as a bathing beauty in a com-

Berling comes to Ekeby Hall, a private residence for old soldiers, run by Major Samzelius (Otto Elg-Lundberg).

Countess Elizabeth Dohna (Greta Garbo), unsure of her future in the cold northern world, is comforted by Margaret (Gerda Lundequist-Dahlstrom).

edy short called *Peter the Tramp*. It was on the order of the Mack Sennett slapstick affairs.

How Stiller happened to pick her out of the many actresses that were available, and why he dared assign her to a secondary but romantically crucial role in this most important picture, are now more legend than history. Undoubtedly, he saw in her young body and in her strangely serene, unclouded face something of the wonderful quality that was to become her fascination in later years. Also, Stiller was looking for someone whom he could mold into a star. He saw that someone in young Greta, whom he renamed Garbo in place of Gustafsson.

It was realized that *The Story of Gösta Berling* would have to be a long film, but no one, not even Stiller, was prepared for the length it eventually ran— four hours, give or take a few minutes. And since that was considered well beyond the endurance of anybody, it was decided that the film should be cut in half, with the first half offered one night and the second half the next, the first time any such thing had been done.

It was soon realized, however, that this was annoying and impractical, and Stiller was induced to edit it down to a version that ran roughly two hours. As a consequence of such rigorous cutting many dramatic incidents were dropped, leaving gaps in the continuity and in the development of characters. It is this compacted

version that is available today, with sound effects added to give it a continuing commerciality.

Even so, and for all its disjunction, *The Story of Gösta Berling* remains an impressive motion picture, full of exciting events, crowded with energetic people in whom emotions run hot and large, breathing a passionate desperation and an air of poetry.

The time it covers is the period shortly after the Napoleonic Wars, in which Sweden had participated and from which it had acquired a class of superannuated soldiers who were a source of national pride and expense. The locale of most of its action is a country estate known as Ekeby Hall, a sort of private home for old soldiers, maintained by a wealthy ironmonger and his wife.

We are first introduced to Gösta carousing among the pensioners at Ekeby Hall, and are given to recognize him as a man of oppressive woe. For, in a flashback, Stiller shows us how he was removed from his pulpit by the bishops of his church for his forthright and fearless sermons—and for unrestrained drunkenness. Thus we see him at the outset as a noble creature, cruelly punished for an offense that might have been charitably forgiven by a society of less rigid and bigoted mold.

All the way through the picture runs this theme of the clash between enlightenment and reaction, candor and hypocrisy, compassion and moral condemnation, humanity and inhumanity. Each of Gösta's encounters with the women who fall in love with him is affected by conflict with forces opposing him for his past.

The first is a pretty girl named Ebba, whom he is employed to tutor after being evicted from Ekeby Hall. But she wastes away when she discovers the disgrace in Gösta's career. After this piteous experience, Gösta tries to commit suicide, but he is dissuaded by Margaret, the wife of the master of Ekeby Hall, who tells him in candid confidence of her own rather shameful past.

Next Gösta becomes friendly with a young lady named Marianne, but when her parents discover the liaison, they drive her forth into the snow. Gösta saves her from perishing and returns her to Ekeby Hall, from which he later rescues her during a calamitous fire.

Meanwhile, Margaret has been exposed to her husband as an adulteress, and he has banished *her*. In a scene that is really a digression, but one of the finest in the film, Stiller shows Margaret returning to the home of her peasant mother, from which she has been banished years before, and being silently accepted back by the old woman, humbly resigned to the way things are.

Earlier in this lengthy chronicle, Gösta has met at Ekeby Hall a very beautiful young Italian woman who

33

Countess Dohna and Berling are united romantically as Elizabeth is about to leave Sweden.

has recently wed a Swedish count. This stunning and sensible lady (whom Greta Garbo plays) has been fascinated by the young parson, by the sad story of his career and has tried to inspire and commend him, much to her husband's disgust. Now, after the burning of Ekeby, she encounters him driving through the late afternoon in his sleigh and tells him how much she admires his valorous deed. He takes her into the sleigh and seems to start toward her home, but suddenly he turns aside and drives furiously across a frozen lake. She thinks at first that he is determined to kidnap her, or worse, but then she discovers he is fleeing to escape a pack of pursuing wolves! This is a markedly vivid, suspenseful and exciting scene, achieved by some good photography and splendid editing.

After this wild adventure, the young countess tells Gösta of her faith and urges him to prove his atonement by rebuilding Ekeby Hall. The end of the picture is the uniting of Gösta and the countess at an inn just before she, having left her husband, is about to return to Italy.

The Story of Gösta Berling is one of the first significant films of social criticism and protest, in much the same spirit as the modern story in *Intolerance* (which see). Although it does not give a modern explanation for Gösta's addiction to drink, the reason is clearly implied in the conditions of repression and frustration under which he is forced to live. Thirty years later, a similar protest against the murkiness and bigotry of Swedish puritanism was evident again in the films of Ingmar Bergman, the one-man author of a new Swedish "golden age."

Within *The Story of Gösta Berling* are some beautifully constructed and acted scenes. That of Gösta's "trial" before the bishops and his congregation has a hard, literal, unrelenting, puritanical quality; and the sequence of the fire is well regarded as the most vivid and exciting in the film.

Notable, too, is the brilliance with which Stiller has portrayed the fashions and formal behavior of the upper classes in the nineteenth century and the absolute candor and severity with which he has exposed the social system and the moral code. Passions are quick and violent; vengeance is swift and strong. Yet, in the true romantic's fashion, the moralists are generally revealed as heartless and hypocritical; the sinners are the honest, generous ones.

As always in Stiller's pictures, the performances are rich in character. Lars Hanson's Gösta is romantic, persistently noble and strong, eloquent and graceful. Gerta Lundeqvist-Dahlstrom's Margaret, the mistress of Ekeby Hall, is a wonderfully disciplined woman in a stiff society. But, of course, the one performance by which we are most fascinated today is that of Greta Garbo, who plays the young countess with a strange sort of softness and aloofness that clearly foretells her later style. Her characterization is rather conventional, but her beauty and radiance are superb. There is a certain mysteriousness about her mouth and eyes; her skin has a glorious luminescence, which Jaenzon caught with his camera; and her piled-up hair and lusciously smooth bosom, revealed in her low-cut gowns, convey the warm and subtle feminine essence that were to be the magic of the later star.

The Story of Gösta Berling was the last great Swedish silent film because, even before its completion, the end of its era was in view. Sjostrom, Stiller's running-mate, had already departed for Hollywood, there to direct a succession of interesting, stylized films under the name of Victor Seastrom. (He returned to Sweden in 1929 to resume his career as an actor. By a fine poetic justice, his last role was that of the distinguished old professor in Ingmar Bergman's *Wild Strawberries*.)

Stiller, too, was ready—even restless—to move on. With his new female "find" and a print of his picture, he went to Germany. After a few misadventures, he and the actress were put under contract by Louis B. Mayer and, in 1925, made the fateful crossing to Hollywood.

There Stiller was never happy. He felt compromised and confined. After making a couple of undistinguished pictures (without Garbo), he returned to Sweden and soon died. But Garbo—well, that's another story! She was the phoenix that rose from the ashes—or, say, the glowing embers—of the Swedish "golden age."

The Thief
of Bagdad

1924

Screenplay by Elton Thomas (Douglas Fairbanks), based on the Arabian Nights Entertainment; directed by Raoul Walsh; photographed by Arthur Edeson; sets designed by William Cameron Menzies.

The Thief	Douglas Fairbanks
The Princess	Julanne Johnston
The Princess' Slave	Anna May Wong
The Thief's Companion	Snitz Edwards
The Mongol Prince	So-Jin
The Indian Prince	Noble Johnson
The Persian Prince	M. Comont
The Caliph	Brandon Hurst
The Holy Man	Charles Belcher

As long as the Thief of Bagdad (Douglas Fairbanks) and his companion (Snitz Edwards) have enough rope, their tricks can get them in anywhere.

In the lush chambers dreamed up by William Cameron Menzies (later a director) the Princess (Julanne Johnston) is ministered to by her hand maidens and, on the right, her slave (Anna May Wong).

It may not be chic to remember, in a day when anti-heroes are the style, that one of the most cinematic and popular screen actors who ever lived was the highly romantic Douglas Fairbanks, the first beau ideal of silent films. And it may not be wholly in accord with the modern sophisticates' taste to state that the best of his pictures was *The Thief of Bagdad,* presented in 1924.

Yet it cannot be disregarded that Fairbanks was, in his ingenuous way, a major and responsible contributor to the evolution of cinema. No one of his generation—not Tom Mix or William S. Hart or Rudolph Valentino or John Gilbert or even Charlie Chaplin—and no one since, was more of a picture *performer* or projected more personality than he. Neither did any, save Chaplin, do more to create a cinema style. And no one received more endorsement and affection from the fans.

As for *The Thief of Bagdad,* it gives us Fairbanks at the peak of his flamboyant style, which is frankly—and, in this case, outrightly—devoted to fabricating myth. And it still is a glowing example of magic-making in the silent spectacle film.

The interesting thing is that Fairbanks had a basic robust personality which he consciously evolved and adapted to several shifting entertainment purposes. When he first entered motion pictures in 1915, he came from the stage where he had a good reputation as a juvenile in light comedies. He was a bright, cheerful, cheeky fellow whose off-camera acrobatic tricks of vaulting over tables and flinging himself into chairs did not especially endear him to D.W. Griffith's Fine Arts-Triangle Company, with which he made a somewhat lurid melodrama entitled *The Lamb*. It is said that Griffith advised him he might better put his athletic skills to the slapstick comedies of Mack Sennett, who was also at Triangle.

Fairbanks was saved from that consignment, or from returning to the stage, by a happy crossing of paths with a young director at Triangle, John Emerson, and a young title-writer, Anita Loos. These two recognized in his manner a bold, uninhibited quality that might be put to good use in a sort of brassy, wisecracking comedy. They proved it with him in a waggish, action-packed semifarce, *His Picture in the Papers,* which was the real start of his screen career.

Between 1916 and 1919, Fairbanks played in some twenty-five films, comedies, melodramas, westerns, which bore such expressive titles as *The Half Breed, American Aristocracy, The Americano,* and *Reaching for the Moon.* Out of this body of pictures, there emerged the Fairbanks image: a vital, aggressive, optimistic, romantic young American businessman for whom no obstacle was too discouraging and who always came out happily in the end. All through his pictures ran a clear strain of vigorous self-confidence, a persistent endorsement of clean living and high morality. Fairbanks delighted in spoofing American manners and fads, but he was incontestably chauvinistic, 100 percent American.

In 1919, he joined with Mary Pickford, Chaplin and Griffith to form United Artists, an independent company designed solely to distribute their films.

The following year, Fairbanks and Miss Pickford, —who was, of course, the reigning female star, world-famed as America's Sweetheart, or Little Mary of the Golden Curls—were married, thus manifesting that Cupid also had a keen sense of good publicity.

Fairbanks, indeed, was quite as nimble and shrewd a businessman in real life as ever he managed to appear in any of his films. He was also a clever showman. He soon realized, after the First World War, that public taste was changing, that the kind of ingenuous comedy in which he had been so successful had just about run its course. So, in 1920, he made a tentative experiment with a new kind of costume picture, *The Mark of Zorro,* in which he used his style of acrobatic swash-buckling to play a charitable Spanish-American grandee, an aristocratic do-gooder, in the days of the Spanish occupation of California. It proved immensely successful and brought him to recognize there must be a waiting market for this sort of sprightly costumed farce. The following year he ventured an even more

ambitious go at derring-do. It was the role of D'Artagnan in a free-wheeling treatment of Dumas' *The Three Musketeers.*

Aware of the effectiveness of scenery in this new métier, he next chose a subject that would offer opportunity for noble display. He would do the outlaw hero from English ballads and legends, Robin Hood, and for this film he built a full-scale castle, surrounded by great Norman walls and moats. Within this huge scenic arena, he frolicked and leaped fantastically, fighting sword duels up long stone stairways and swinging on candelabra. His neatest stunt in this picture and probably his most memorable of all is a slide from a high balcony in the great hall to the floor in the fold of a huge tapestry. (The trick was very simple: the tapestry concealed a sliding board.) There are those who think that Fairbanks reached his peak in *Robin Hood* (1922).

But I say his paramount achievement in terms of self and cinema is his next film, *The Thief of Bagdad,* to which he devoted the better part of 1923. In this eclectic compounding of several of the Arabian Nights tales into a wildly romantic story of the adventures of a cynical rogue who falls in love with the Caliph's daughter and finally wins her by feats of derring-do, Fairbanks makes a full leap into the area of utter pictorial fantasy that had been opened by Georges Méliès in France but was almost totally neglected up to that time by the makers of American films.

To outdo the Norman castle he built for *Robin Hood,* he and his art director, William Cameron Menzies, now went to the extreme of constructing a fanciful city and palace, with shimmering domes and minarets, delicately sagging stairways and gracefully arching bridges that soar away into space. They made no pretense of simulating Oriental reality. Their dream city is a coalescence of illustrations from story books. The high silver walls were constructed and painted so that they would seem to float above polished pavements. The décor was created to suggest that it was insubstantial and weightless. And the designs for the Adventures of the Seven Moons, which comprise the latter part of the film, were unprecedented concoctions of animated scenery and trick photography.

Consistent with his moralistic concepts, Fairbanks meant this picture to convey a message of inspiration and hope. "Our hero," he reminded his scenarist, Elton Thomas (who happened to be himself), "must be every young man of this age and any age who believes that happiness is a quantity that can be stolen, who is selfish, at odds with the world and rebellious toward conventions on which comfortable human relations are based." This, he said, was a deception that must be

Typical Fairbanks derring-do clears the way for still more fantastic adventures and outwits the Princess' slave.

The Thief, endowed with magical powers, conjures up an army to rout the forces of the wicked Prince of the Mongols and save the people of Bagdad.

exposed. Fortunately, the primness of this precept does not noticeably intrude in the film, as it swings along gaily and spectacularly under the direction of Raoul Walsh.

It is the story of a handsome, charming, muscular and altogether adventurous rogue who runs about the crowded streets of Bagdad in billowy pantaloons, his torso bare and a piratical kerchief tied about his head. Then one evening he dares to enter the palace of the Caliph, gliding over the high, Maxfield Parrish walls by means of a magic rope.

Once inside, he is filching a string of pearls from a laden treasure chest when he comes upon the airy bed-chamber of the Caliph's daughter, sleeping in sweet repose with her Oriental handmaidens around her. From this moment, the thief is charmed by the beauty of the princess, and devises various deceptive ways to attain her attention and favor. The most successful is to disguise himself as one of the princely suitors who have

And off go the happy couple, on cloud-to-cloud carpeting, to a celluloid kingdom known for its piquant diversions.

come to Bagdad to seek her hand. He succeeds in being chosen (by the accident of being tossed from his horse into the very rosebush that, like a goal line, must be touched first by a suitor to win), but his disguise is penetrated, and the Caliph orders that he be flogged and flung to the ape. However, the Princess, now smitten by the gorgeousness and valor of the rogue, secretly fixes his release so that he may participate in the new contest the Caliph has arranged for the suitors: to bring back the rarest treasure from distant and magical lands.

It is in the series of adventures of the thief and his rivals as they strive to invade assorted fabulous regions, such as the Valley of the Monsters and the Citadel of the Moon, and there to obtain such treasures as the magic apple, the flying carpet and the winged horse, that Fairbanks and his designers project their most spectacular fantasies. The ingenuity and humor of their creations are delightful and prophetic indeed, for they prelude such later achievements in trick photography and miniature work as that in the fantasies of *The Lost World* (1925) and *King Kong* (which see).

Needless to say, it all ends with the thief winning the princess and the two of them riding away into the sky aboard the magic carpet, while stars twinkle and form into a sparkling title reading, "Happiness Must Be Earned."

Of course, there is a thoroughly insouciant incongruity about the whole thing, a blissful indifference to the logic of climate and character. The thief is an obvious Anglo-Saxon, a smiling American superman, and the princess, played by Julanne Johnson, is a beautiful Nordic blonde. Her father, as played by Brandon Hurst, might be a prosperous banker, and the mean Mongol prince is represented as a typical Occidental concept of Oriental villainy by an imported Siamese actor, So-Jin. This is pictorial thimblerigging for sheer entertainment's sake, a frank showing-off of Fairbanks' talent for prestidigious feats within a spectacular ambience of scenic and cinematic trickery.

And it is notably clean. It is not a cover for the sort of creeping pornography—the bathtub skin games and pagan orgies—that was evident in some concurrent costume films. Except for one scene in which the phallus of Fairbanks outcrops slightly within his pantaloons, there is not a trace of sexual agitation or suggestiveness in the whole film.

Strangely, *The Thief of Bagdad* was not as popular as *Robin Hood,* even though it was critically acknowledged as a more imperative work. It was probably too elaborately plotted, as *Intolerance* had been. And audiences were not then congenial to such unrestrained flights of fantasy.

After this, Fairbanks continued to make costume spectacle films, though not on a scale as ambitious or extravagant as this. In 1930, he and Mary Pickford made their first picture together and his first talking film. It was a rather bloodless adaptation of Shakespeare's *The Taming of the Shrew*. Professionally and domestically, it was the beginning of the end for both. Their images, cherished in silence, did not survive in sound. Fairbanks made four more pictures before he and Miss Pickford were divorced in 1935. That was the finish for him. He died in 1939, at the age fifty-six.

38

Greed

A wedding feast that is gross and ironic takes place in the house where McTeague has his office; this in an actual house in San Francisco, not in a studio.

1924

Screenplay by Erich von Stroheim, adapted from a novel by Frank Norris; directed by Erich von Stroheim; photography by Ben E. Reynolds, William H. Daniels and Ernest Schoedsack; abridged by June Mathis; produced by the Goldwyn Company.

Trina	Zasu Pitts
McTeague	Gibson Gowland
Marcus	Jean Hersholt
Maria	Dale Fuller
Mother McTeague	Tempe Pigott
Papa Sieppe	Chester Conklin
Mama Sieppe	Sylvia Ashton
Selina	Joan Standing
August Sieppe	Austin Jewell
The Sieppe Twins	Oscar and Otto Gottel

Next to D. W. Griffith, the most amazing and provocative director of American films in the turbulent silent era was a granite-faced, bullet-headed brute who had a congenital genius for making people furious. His name was Erich von Stroheim, and although he di-

rected only eight films—or, to be technical about it, one should say that was all on which he "worked"—he got such an evil reputation for being extravagant, quixotic and grotesque in his taste and in his demands for jurisdiction over his pictures that he was literally outlawed as a director in ten years. And yet, for all his perversity, for all his brazen and bitter temperament, which got him into so much hot water he inevitably became a hard-boiled egg, he turned out at least four pictures that may be counted among the best of their day. One was—and is—a classic: *Greed*.

This film, which became a legend because of the Spartan circumstances under which it was made and the fuss von Stroheim created by refusing to cut it to conventional length, deserves every bit of the deference it has been getting for the past three decades. It is a prime example of the use of the screen to impart, in a realistic manner, the meaner, uglier side of modern man. It delivers a brutal picture of the American lower-middle class in a style of naturalism that had previously been matched only in a few scenes in Griffith pictures and two or three other films. And because it departed so boldly from the romantic fashion of the day, because it followed so closely the radical literary trend of the "kitchen sink" school, it was a unique cinematic venture and a true trailblazer for a future style in films.

Greed was derivative, however. It was closely and studiedly made from a notorious naturalistic novel by Frank Norris, entitled *McTeague*. This corrosive and unrelenting novel was published in 1899 at the time the American debunkers and muckrakers were beginning to appear, and it tells a horrifying story of a quack dentist and his wife in turn-of-the-century San Francisco who are consumed and destroyed by a greed for gold. It is a studiously Zolaesque story which clearly reveals a frank disgust for the raw, urbanized, materialistic American bourgeoisie.

How such a man as von Stroheim came to pick such a book from which to make a film in the 1920's is a question that is hard to resolve. Born and brought up in Austria, where he was schooled for the cavalry, he came to America as a young man and knocked around in various pick-up jobs, including a hitch in the Mexican Army, before drifting to Hollywood. There he edged himself into the good graces of Griffith, who put him in a couple of bit roles in *The Birth of a Nation* and *Intolerance*. When the United States entered the First World War, he got into several pictures playing villainous German officers. The peak of his perfection at such villainy was in Griffith's famous war film, *Hearts of the World,* in which he played the hideous Heinie who betrayed and raped the American heroine. So nasty and noxious was he, so arrogant and cruel, with his monocle, his shaved head, his Iron Cross and his hideously saber-scarred face, that he became known as "the Hun you love to hate."

But that didn't satisfy von Stroheim. He wanted to write and direct. And it soon became apparent that he wanted to do so with no strings attached.

By camping on the doorstep of Carl Laemmle, the genial head of the Universal Company, he finally persuaded the little man, in 1919, to let him make what was promised as a modest film. The title of it was to be *The Pinnacle,* which sounded harmless enough. But the finished film was far from harmless. It cost three times as much as was intended, and it turned out to be an exegesis on the reasonableness of adultery. The title on release was *Blind Husbands,* which implied both a lecture and a leer.

Its success, and that of a second lesser film he was permitted to do (*The Devil's Passkey*), assured for von Stroheim a clearance to go to work on a third. This was to be a more ambitious story of a scoundrel, a bogus count, who preyed upon women at Monte Carlo, seducing and blackmailing them. Naturally von Stroheim played the scoundrel. The title was *Foolish Wives,* and Laemmle, or one of his lieutenants, approved a $75,000 budget for it. Imagine their surprise when they discovered von Stroheim was making a film that cost over $1,000,000. It was said that von Stroheim shot a total of 360 reels!

Even so, Laemmle allowed him to start another film, on the strength of the sheer sensation generated by *Foolish Wives.* This was to be another characteristic continental affair about a decadent Austrian prince and the crippled daughter of a carousel owner, to be called *Merry-Go-Round.* But this time von Stroheim was confronted by the first formidable producer he had ever known. This was young Irving Thalberg, who had just taken over as manager of the studio. Thalberg tolerated the extravagance and dawdling for just so long, then he yanked von Stroheim off the picture and put another director (Rupert Julian) on.

This might have scotched the arrogant Austrian as a director in Hollywood. Indeed, it did scotch him with Laemmle. But he was clearly an extremely talented man. While his films were inordinately expensive, they were also unusual and had style. He had brought a kind of sophistication and eyebrow-lifting skepticism to the American screen. In no time at all, he got Frank Godsol and Abe Lehr of the extravagant Goldwyn Company to let him make a film for them. The story he chose was, surprisingly, the Norris novel, *McTeague.*

Why? Again that question. Von Stroheim later told associates that he had read the novel in 1915 and always wanted to make it into a film. But the rights to it belonged to June Mathis of the Goldwyn Company. She arranged to transfer them to von Stroheim, and, with her endorsement, he proceeded to make the film.

He tipped his mitt as to the character he intended to give it by insisting on shooting all, interiors as well as exteriors, on location, mostly in the San Francisco area. He chose Gibson Gowland, a huge, blunt actor whom he had had in previous films, to play the principal role

For two solid hours McTeague (Gibson Howland) and Trina (Zasu Pitts) join in the wedding feasting.

of McTeague—or Mac, as he is called throughout the picture. (His first name is never revealed.) To play Trina, the timid immigrant girl who marries Mac, he got the delicate, sad-eyed and exceptionally talented Zasu Pitts. Jean Hersholt, a young Danish actor recently arrived in America, was cast as Marcus Schooler, Trina's cousin and former suitor, whose jealousy precipitates the act of vengeance that keys the downfall of the hapless McTeagues.

The company was almost nine months in San Francisco, during the fall, winter and spring of 1922–23, shooting in the area of Polk Street, the cheap commercial thoroughfare that figures so strongly in the novel and is the atmospheric radiant of the film. Von Stroheim sought out a house in which a man had actually murdered his wife to use as the home of Mac and Trina, and he even compelled his actors to live in it while shooting the scenes of their fatal estrangement.

Although, of course, the film is silent, von Stroheim wrote the precise dialogue his characters were supposedly speaking, then he made his actors learn it and speak it as accurately and expressively as though they were doing it in a play on the stage. Years later, Jean Hersholt told me that if they blew a line or didn't read it the way von Stroheim wanted it, he would do the shot again and again until they got it right.

When it came time to do the final phase of the story—the flight of McTeague to Death Valley after he has murdered his wife, his pursuit by Marcus, greedy for a reward for capturing him, and the conclusive struggle of the two men in the empty desert wastes—von Stroheim did a seemingly mad thing: he took his actors and camera crew right out to that brutal desert region and there, in the killing summer heat, he made poor Gowland and Hersholt enact their final nightmare scenes. It was as bold a move to get authenticity—and perhaps publicity—as any director has ever compelled.

Now came the big excitement. Von Stroheim's rough cut of the film ran forty-two reels, or close to nine hours (at an average of twelve minutes a reel.)

On the insistence of people in the Goldwyn Company, he cut this by half. That, he said, was as much as he could possibly cut, and he thereupon washed his hands of it. Miss Mathis, his sponsor, then undertook the final cut. She pulled it down to the ten reels (a bit over two hours) in which it was finally released. She also wrote the subtitles and changed the main title to *Greed.*

At just this time, the Goldwyn Company was sold to Loew's, Inc., to be merged with the latter's Metro Company, under the management of Louis B. Mayer. Mayer and his associate, Irving Thalberg (the same hard-headed young man who had thrown von Stroheim

Drunk and destitute, McTeague first pleads with Trina for financial help, then fights with her, finally killing her.

off *Merry-Go-Round*) looked at the still unreleased film, which now became their responsibility, and wondered what to do with it. They were not pleased with its theme, and there were certain contractual considerations that made it of no advantage to them to try to push von Stroheim's film. They sat on it for several months, had one of their cutters trim it a little more, and then finally sent it on for distribution. It opened in New York in December 1924.

It had a discouraging reception. Audiences laughed at some of its harsher scenes. Moviegoers were simply not accustomed to the sort of forthright realism it contained. The newspaper critics generally slammed it, calling it "the sour crème de la sour crème" and such. Only a few isolated commentators recognized it for the extraordinary work of art it is. Under the circumstances, it was not a box-office success.

Von Stroheim always protested that his masterpiece had been ruined by insensitive and mercenary people. He claimed he never saw it in the final cut. If that is true, it is too bad he didn't, for he might have been agreeably surprised.

To be sure, there are faults with the picture, faults that in large measure stem more from shortcomings in the novel than from the editing. *McTeague* is loosely constructed. It tends to grow by an accumulation of episodes rather than by a continuity of closely woven causes and effects. In recounting the fate of its hero, who is worn down and ruined by his wife's greed, it reaches its crucial situations more by coincidence than by logical consequences. Norris was, of course, pre-Freud. He was a storyteller who constructed his tale from dramatic assumptions and inventions, without psychologically reasoning why. Thus he does not explain Trina and the causes of her avarice. It is simply a foregone conclusion that she is a fanatically stingy woman. Nor does he explain why her cousin, Marcus, is jealous and vengeful or why he does the one crucial act of exposing poor McTeague as an unlicensed dentist, which destroys his means of livelihood. The novel is simply a harrowing exposure of people caught in the slow, sorrowful suction of a cheap, ugly, vicious and essentially materialistic environment. And so is the film.

Set in time some ten years later than the novel, it begins in a California gold-mining camp, where Mac is working as a miner and his mother as a cook. The latter, with simple ambition for the future of her son, persuades a transient quack dentist to take him as an apprentice to learn his trade. Time passes, and now we see Mac set up in his own office on Polk Street in San Francisco. One day, a tin-horn friend, Marcus Schooler, brings his cousin, Trina, to have her teeth fixed, and Mac falls in love with her.

The meeting of McTeague and Marcus (Jean Hersholt) in the desert climaxes with the death of both. Here again von Stroheim's passion for realism found his actors actually struggling in the gruesome heat of Death Valley.

With permission from Marcus, who is willing to surrender any interest he might have, Mac pays court to Trina. He is boorish and clumsy and she is shy, but after several visits to see her in the suburbs, he persuades her to become engaged. When she arrives at Mac's place for their engagement party, she is told by a charwoman from whom she had casually bought a lottery ticket that she is the winner of the $5,000 prize. This is the unexpected windfall that proves to be the burden in their lives.

The next phase of the picture, in a vein of good-humored irony, is a detailed description of the marriage of Trina and Mac in Mac's office. It is a tawdry, overshowy affair, with everything slightly exaggerated: the gaunt, solemn, plain-suited minister, the German immigrant family and friends, the comical German father (played elaborately by Chester Conklin) and a pair of mischievous, nuisance-making kids. Punctuating this low comedy, there are shots of a Roman Catholic funeral procession passing solemnly in the street outside. Then, at the wedding feast afterward, all the guests gorge themselves—a hideous but humorous exposure of human swinishness. This phase is sardonically concluded with Mac giving Trina a pair of lovebirds in a cage as a wedding present, and then the two going awkwardly to bed.

This is the peak of the rising action. From here on, it is all downhill for Mac and Trina. She hoards her pennies, allows Mac one night a week at the saloon. There, on one occasion, he is attacked by Marcus, who is jealous and resentful of his having got a woman who has $5,000. The fight is fast and vicious, and it brings their friendship to an end.

Boredom and a creeping estrangement between Mac and Trina now set in, as shown in a scene of them retiring, he talking to her about her money which she says is never, never going to be touched, clearly indicating her preference for her money over him. While he sleeps, she goes through his pockets and then wipes cold cream on her hands, which leads to a metaphorical insert of skinny, greasy hands twining over a pile of gold coins.

Marcus, acting nasty and supercilious, chewing gum vulgarly, comes to say goodbye. When he leaves, Trina says she is glad he is gone—and here von Stroheim dropped in another metaphor of a cat looking sinisterly at the two lovebirds in their cage. Then, a couple of months later, comes the disastrous blow: Mac is notified by an official letter that it has been learned he is practicing dentistry illegally and that he will have to give up his practice. Surprisingly, there comes one brief exposure of tenderness in the scene of Mac closing his office, preparing to wipe the slate on which he lists the appointments of his patients. Trina leans over, weeping, and says as her tears splatter on the chalk marks, "That's the way to rub it out, by me crying on it." In that moment, the two are revealed together and helpless in a bond of common calamity.

Then the plunge to destruction is continued. Mac loses his menial job, spends too much time in the saloon drinking, invariably comes home drunk. Trina will not let him have money, skimps and saves by buying stale meat. Finally, Mac leaves home and Trina takes a job as a charwoman (an ironic touch) in a school. One night, Mac comes back to see her, scratches drunkenly on the window and demands to be let in. Trina unwisely admits him, they fight, he murders her—and then on to the climax in Death Valley, with Mac and Marcus fighting and dying like animals.

Evidently von Stroheim was not capable of completing a film, of making the final decisions and performing the last creative chores of giving it cohesion and shape. He was brilliant and inventive, he overflowed with ideas, but he lacked the necessary pragmatism of an artist in this medium. His subsequent battles with Thalberg on his next film, a nonmusical version of Franz Lehár's *The Merry Widow*, with Mae Murray as the star, demonstrated this. Again he indulged in wild extravagance, took inordinate time and battled severely with Miss Murray. Again he threw up his hands and walked away from the picture after it was shot, leaving the job of cutting it to Thalberg and Metro-Goldwyn-Mayer.

After this, he did *The Wedding March* for Paramount, then *Queen Kelly*, with Gloria Swanson, which Joseph P. Kennedy, the father of John Fitzgerald Kennedy, produced. It was shot as a silent film and was completed just as sound was coming in. For reasons never clarified, it was not released. An abortive attempt to make a picture for Fox in 1932 (*Walking Down Broadway*) brought his career as a director to a close. Unable to get work in Hollywood, he went to Europe, where he resumed acting, achieving a great success in *La Grande Illusion* (which see), again playing a stiff-necked Hun. He returned to Hollywood to play General Rommel in *Five Graves to Cairo*, (1943) again a splendid job, and was, ironically, a major factor in the success of the film of a passé movie star and her old director, *Sunset Boulevard* (which see).

The Freshman

1925

Screenplay by Sam Taylor, John Grey, Ted Wilde and Tim Whelan; directed by Samuel Taylor and Fred Newmeyer; cameraman, Walter Lundin; produced by Pathé-Harold Lloyd Corporation.

Harold Lamb	Harold Lloyd
Peggy	Jobyna Ralston
College Cad	Brooks Benedict
College Hero	James Anderson
College Belle	Hazel Keener
Tailor	Joe Harrington
Coach	Pat Harmon

There is a prevailing disposition, enjoyed and encouraged, no doubt, by older folks with loving memories of their carefree moviegoing youth, to think of the years of silent pictures as the time "when comedy was king," when the merry purveyors of slapstick were the sultans of the screen. And there are, indeed, good reasons for this somewhat euphoric belief, over and above the compulsions of nostalgic memory.

For comedy in the silent movies was a wild and emancipating form that often departed entirely from the restraints of reality. It was largely fantastic fabrication of crazy and grotesque conceits that delightfully exaggerated and made fun of man's misfortunes, injustices and absurdities. This was true, especially, in the period of the Keystone comedies, which flowed from the studio of Mack Sennett, in the years before and during the First World War.

These ebullient little pictures, which ran for but one or two reels, were made up of violences exampled by the squash of a pie in someone's face or a whack across the seat of the pants with a slapstick that provoked a gross display of howling hurt. Their stories were inconsequential, the merest provocations to get the comedians launched into droll embarrassments, accidents, free-swinging conflicts and pell-mell chases on foot and in automobiles. Sennett's short films were usually climaxed by swarms of fat policemen giving chase to the key comedian in frantic demonstration of the ineffectualness of authority. These wonderfully nihilistic burlesques of the fearfulness of the hue and cry established an affectionate expression for menace of this sort: the Keystone cops.

The extravagances of these brief pictures betokened the opportunity the screen gave the traditional theatrical comedians to expand and elaborate their work. Where the old clowns of vaudeville and burlesque were limited by the confines of the stage and by the perils of physical damage that too much exuberance might wreak, the comics who played in the early movies—Ford Sterling, Fatty Arbuckle, Mack Swain, Ben Turpin, Snub Pollard, Mabel Normand, Max Linder (the great French comedian) and, later, Charlie Chaplin, Buster Keaton, Harold Lloyd, Harry Langdon and many more—were happily uninhibited by physical restraints. They could do anything they wanted through the flexibility of motion photography. They could drive an automobile through a city three times as fast as an automobile would go, smash one another with cudgels that would normally knock a person cold, run into walls and fall through windows without being noticeably hurt and do all sorts of impossible acrobatics that astonished the viewer with a literal mind.

The only limit on their exuberance and longevity was imposed by time. Time eventually made their repetitions and imitations disillusioning and dull. It also brought steady advances in the techniques and contents of films. The tendency to lengthen motion pictures after the First World War, to change their general characteristics, to put more narrative substance in them—all of which were but natural extensions aimed to serve more sophisticated taste—caused the little comedy pictures to seem skimpy and inadequate. The public wanted more, and the comedians were pressed to greater lengths. Thus was propelled the advancement of the great silent-film comedians.

What made them great was simple. They offered characters with distinctive traits and styles, not merely casual compendia of comical cutups by clowns. And they weren't just silly characters, either. They were basically characters in depth, each in his certain way reflecting fundamental human qualities and attributes. Of course, what they did was in a flippant, extravagant, farcical vein, carrying over into their feature-length pictures much of the "business" of the slapstick comedies —the sight gags, the wild exaggerations, the turmoils, the techniques of the chase. But the way each approached his problems conveyed the sort of person he was, and the sort was invariably reflective of deeply human and appreciable weaknesses and strengths.

The greatest of the silent comedians were Charlie Chaplin, Buster Keaton and Harold Lloyd. It is Lloyd's most significant film, *The Freshman*, that comes to attention first. He, like all the others, reached his eminence by years of hard work in one- and two-reel slapsticks. In several score of these films, which he made with Hal Roach and with Sennett, he appeared as a gawking clown known first as Willie Work and later, with certain variations, as Lonesome Luke.

Harold Lamb, the freshman (Harold Lloyd), comes to Tate College with high hopes, a flagrant wardrobe, and plenty of the "old college try."

Then one day he saw a movie—he has long since forgotten what it was—in which a peaceable, studious-looking parson who wore spectacles caught a thief after a chase. During the consequent tussle, which the preacher won, his glasses were knocked off. Afterward, he picked them up and replaced them on his nose, resuming immediately the appearance and attitude of peace. Lloyd thought the glasses so effective in creating a deceptive facade of bookishness and sissiness in a basically brave character that he adopted horn-rimmed eyeglasses as a permanent fixture of his costume. And thereafter he began to develop the famous Harold Lloyd personality, what he and his associates referred to as "the glass character."

This distinctively American individual—clean-cut, nice-looking, alert, athletic and acrobatic—acquired dimension in *Grandma's Boy* (1922), Lloyd's first feature film. In it, the young comedian played a timid small-town lad, a genial, gentle creature who was bullied and abused by other boys. But with the encouragement of his grandma and the exercise of his own will, he summoned the courage and resolution to fight back and triumph at the end. This ability to exercise will power was the core of "the glass character." He had a persistent and indomitable ambition to succeed.

A perfect example of this is in his memorable *Safety Last* (1923), which, next to *The Freshman*, is probably Lloyd's most fondly recollected film. In it, he is a minor store clerk who has been writing so boastfully to his girl about his success in the big city that, when she comes to visit him, he has to do something sensational to redeem himself in her eyes. His chance comes when he is forced by circumstances to substitute for one of the so-called "human flies" that thrilled people back in the 1920's by climbing up the outsides of tall buildings.

Here was a situation perfectly tailored for Harold (which was always the first name of the characters he played in his feature films). It was a challenge to skill and daring, fraught with imminent peril, but not beyond the range of possibility for an agile, courageous American lad. And it offered infinite opportunities to blend low comedy and thrills, as Harold edged his way up the building, missing toe holds and catching by his fingertips, dangling dangerously but drolly from the hands of a big building clock, and always wearing his horn-rimmed glasses and trying to keep a straw hat on his head. But, of course, the ironic humor came from the awareness that Harold had got himself into this predicament by trying to be something that he was not.

It was in *The Freshman*, however, that Harold's character and comic style were applied to the closest accomplishment of satire that he ever made. This

45

comedy was aimed to make fun of the rah-rah collegiate craze and the overemphasis of college football that were so prevalent then. Those were the days of college sheiks and shebas, the girls in their low-waisted dresses, decorated yellow slickers and flappy galoshes, and the fellows with their bell-bottomed trousers, their hair parted in the middle and slicked back. To go to college was the new ambition of the middle-class American boy and girl. But for what, was often the question. Was it to get an education? Perhaps. But the atmosphere of the Jazz Age made it seem for something else—to be a big man (or girl) on campus, to shine as an athletic star, to attain an uncertain social status that would be valuable to success in later life. It was this aspect of college that *The Freshman* satirized.

The tone is set in the first shot and subsequent sequence, with Harold in a close-up, clad in a monogrammed sweater and a college cap, leading a cheer. Then the camera pulls back, and we discover that he is standing before the mirror in his room at home practicing cheers from a manual, while his father, listening to the radio downstairs, starts at the weird and uncouth noises, thinking he is picking up some foreign station. Thus we meet a young man, full of enthusiastic hopes, prepared to embark upon something his father considers absurd.

Off to college goes Harold, and immediately sets out to make friends with the entire student body, admiringly eyes one of the girls and then, because he sees the way to fame and popularity is to be a football hero, goes out for the team. He is knocked about unmercifully, but he finally gets into the big game and, despite the opponents and his own follies, makes the winning touchdown.

There is more meaning to this character than there was to any one of the breezy chaps in Lloyd's previous pictures, and he and his associates sensed it only after they had started shooting. Lloyd, like most of the other silent comedians, did not work from a script. He would start with a basic idea, such as the freshman winning the football game or the store clerk forced to be a "human fly." Then he and his directors, Samuel Taylor and Fred Newmeyer, and their gag men would go into what they called "the idea room," where they would dream up the general narrative structure and the assortment of sight gags that would go into the film.

They had been shooting *The Freshman* for a week when they realized that to have "the glass character" involved in a brutal football game would be funny only if the cheekiness of the fellow was thoroughly set up. So they returned to "the idea room" for more material. It was in this expansion that the essence of the humor was derived. For the delight of the picture is in the consistent unfolding of Harold as a determined young fellow who won't be stopped by anything, not even by the devastating derision of his haughty collegiate peers.

The day he arrives at college, he steps off the train, green and unknown, yet he is ready to be the pal of everyone. He hails the dean of the college, who is there to meet someone else, with a big slap on the back, and piles himself and his baggage into the dean's auto. The students are laughing at him, but he isn't at all dismayed. He breezes into a circle of students and offers to treat them to ice-cream cones. They accept and start off with him to the ice-cream parlor in a medium shot. Then the camera pulls back and we see that practically the whole student body is tagging along to make a sucker of Harold.

When Harold first reports for football practice, he is still wearing his spectacles under his football helmet and atop a big rubber noseguard that almost covers his face. Again he is humiliated. The coach, after seeming to praise him for his exemplary qualities which all should emulate (but he is talking about another player who has walked away and whose place Harold has taken), assigns him to do service as a tackling dummy because the mechanical one is broken.

And then comes the day of the big game, with Harold animatedly warming the bench, shouting encouragement to his flagging teammates as they are getting their faces rubbed in the dirt. He is nothing daunted, though his team is being beaten brutally and players are being dragged off on stretchers. Then the last substitute is spent, and only Harold remains when another player is borne *hors de combat* from the field. The coach looks at him in dejection, but Harold begs then insists that he be sent in, so the coach waves him on.

The first time the ball is passed to him, he takes it and runs, hanging on to it for dear life, even after he is downed. The referee warns him severely to let go of the ball when he hears the whistle blow. Harold solemnly accepts the admonition. He is not one to resist authority. Sure enough, on the next play when he has the ball, he gets loose with it and runs toward the goal line. Just as he is about to score, a whistle on a factory outside the stadium lets go with a blast. (We are shown the whistle blowing in a close-up; the gag was augmented at the time by having the sound effect of whistles provided by theater orchestras.) When Harold hears the whistle, he obediently drops the ball and, of course, a rival pounces on it.

Thus it is through a delightful inventive and acrobatic series of plays. Harold runs in the wrong direction, he neatly avoids or leaps over tacklers, and in the final play, with only seconds to go, he races for the goal line and just barely gets the ball over for the winning

Harold, wearing a tuxedo held together by basting stitches, makes the artless mistake of plucking at a loose thread, to the vast amusement of the College Belle (Hazel Keener).

The first practice scrimmage is an awakening experience for Harold, one of many hilarious sight gags in the film.

score. The final scene shows Harold in the hospital, all bandaged and trussed, but reading a message from his girl and feeling proud of himself.

The camera work through the picture is fluid and imaginative, especially in the game sequence, which has great vitality. Lloyd shot some of it in the Rose Bowl at Pasadena during intermission in a Stanford–Southern California game, and shots of the crowds rising and cheering while the freshman performs on the field are well intercut to point the excitement and the spontaneity of the thrills in a football game.

"I always tried to make my gags possible," Lloyd told me recently. "They were not the cartoon gags of the slapsticks. They were things that *could* conceivably occur."

Lloyd saw to it that his heroines, the girls that Harold hopefully pursued, were sufficiently vibrant and unusual that their eventual interest in him could be believed. Jobyna Ralston is the girl in *The Freshman*, as she was in several other of Lloyd's films, and she has an amusingly arch and sympathetic air.

An indication of the basic social satire of *The Freshman* is the fact that it inspired a sound-film sequel, made by the distinguished later-day satirist, Preston Sturges, in 1947. Sturges, with Lloyd's permission, and with Lloyd himself playing the leading role, took the football-game sequence from *The Freshman* as the starting point for a farcical-satiric contemplation of what might happen to a college football hero in later life. This film, entitled *Mad Wednesday* (1947; it was originally called *The Sin of Harold Diddlebock*), was not commercially successful, nor was Lloyd especially winning in it. He was far from the slender, reckless youngster nostalgically recalled in the sequence of the game, far from the agile "glass character," who was distinctly a creature of silent films, even though Lloyd went on making sound pictures until 1938.

But the middle-aged man in *Mad Wednesday* is, indeed, what time has proved all too many of the college lads of the 1920's, with their built-in Babbitry, did become. He is the dismal dénouement of *The Freshman's* satiric spoof.

The College Cad (Brooks Benedict) pulls a fast one when he sticks Harold with the check for sodas for the whole class.

The Gold Rush

1925

Written, directed and produced by Charles Chaplin; associate director, Charles Reisner; assistant director, H. d'Abbadie d'Arrast; cameramen, R. H. Totheroh and Jack Wilson; released by United Artists.

The Lone Prospector	Charles Chaplin
Big Jim McKay	Mack Swain
Black Larsen	Tom Murray
The Girl	Georgia Hale
Chum of the Girl	Betty Morissey
Jack Cameron	Malcolm White
Hank Curtis	Henry Bergman

One generation passeth away and another generation cometh, and what has been fresh and full of charm for filmgoers of one generation may well be dull and boring for those of the next. But one joy that abideth forever in the magical medium of film, without losing any of its freshness, is Charlie Chaplin's Little Tramp.

Over the long years, since the genesis of this superlative comic character, in his small bowler hat, his tiny moustache, his baggy trousers and his reedy bamboo cane, attiring a cocky little figure of pliant grace and vitality, he has been a uniquely endearing source of delight to millions upon millions of people in countries all over the world. He is, beyond any question, the most famous and familiar character that has come into convincing existence in the folklore developed on the screen.

To grasp the essence of Chaplin, to understand why it was that his Little Tramp had such magnetism, such drollery, such pathos—and still does—I think it wise to consider his appearance before we turn to an analysis of *The Gold Rush,* the best of his silent films.

At first glance, the Little Tramp looks foolish, a callow and nondescript grotesque, too ludicrously put together to be anything more than a caricature. His large head set on narrow shoulders and topped by the antique bowler hat that requires frequent frantic clutching to prevent it spinning off into space; his diminutive, pencil-thin body packed into a too-tight coat, usually an old-fashioned jacket buttoned up to a bat-wing collar and tie; his oversized, baggy trousers; his obviously much too big shoes; his moustache; his bamboo cane—they shape up into an image that is outlandish and absurd.

When we see him moving along a sidewalk with his side-to-side waddling gait, stopping to look in store windows, peering out of those large exploring eyes that are the most striking and haunting feature of his curiously solemn face, he seems a haphazard scarecrow, a simulation of a human being made of assorted members and garments that just don't match.

But, then, as we grow accustomed to him, as we follow him gleefully in the erratic round of his adven-

Charlie Chaplin (a lone figure in the lower left corner) joins the mass trek to the gold fields in frozen Alaska.

Low on food, ammunition and human kindness, Black Larsen (Tom Murray) orders Charlie to head off into the blizzard, with the endorsement of another buddy, Big Jim (Mack Swain).

tures, like children tagging after a drunk, we begin to see how graceful and lovely he actually is. We sense a fineness in his features, the wonderful symmetry of his head. And especially we feel the beauty and expressiveness of his eyes, which appear in incongruous apposition to the foolish little tuft of moustache. Inevitably it comes upon us, no matter how impassive we may be, that this is no mere sawdust comic, no common flapfooted clown. This is an extraordinarily sentient and responsive human being, absorbed in his own complex feelings and his own mute but clearly fertile thoughts.

It must be this subtle recognition, whether consciously realized or not, that accounts for the sympathy and affection that millions have felt for the Little

Tramp. He is a profound articulation of our inner self, that hidden, gnawing gnome in our psyches which is never satisfied that all our beauty and goodness and generosity are coming through to the world. We look at him and unconsciously think how much of ourselves, how much that we know is *our* nature, is also veiled behind a misleading façade.

It is significant that Chaplin never clearly specified the ethnic background or origin of the Little Tramp. He never really tells us where he comes from or precisely who he is. He is just a lonely little fellow, a vagrant usually, who appears. He might be the slightly balmy castoff of an English lord. His exaggerated good manners and his awareness of the proprieties—his elegant use of tableware, for instance—could lead us to suspect that he is. In many of his one- and two-reel slapsticks he broadly parodied the English toff. In *The Gold Rush,* for example, his Lone Prospector could be one of those casual eccentrics who walked out of their London clubs—the kitchen, in this case, I would reckon—and went toddling off to the Klondike to pick up a bit of ruddy gold. Or he might just as easily be a "greenhorn," a new arrival from Middle Europe, as he was (without any country specified) in one of his best two-reelers, *The Immigrant.* He is, more or less, in the tradition of the duke in *Huckleberry Finn,* the prototype of all the Weary Willies with a pretense to class and elegance.

Here's another distinction, however. The Little Tramp is not a bum. He isn't lazy and sloppy, as most cliché Weary Willies are. He is signally energetic, ambitious, enterprising and neat. He aspires to improve his condition and will do anything to achieve that end, up to and including stealing. There is nothing pious about the Little Tramp. If he appears sanctimonious, it is usually to get what he wants. It is obvious that his experience has taught him that in this world, dog eats dog.

Actually, what he is seeking most truly and longingly are the respect and admiration of others and that ever-elusive thing called love. He wants to be recognized and flattered, because, like all of us, he tends to be vain. But he wants, most of all, to be noticed and appreciated by a beautiful girl. Just let a female smile at him— a young, attractive female, that is—and he will knock himself out to please her, to fan the spirit of friendliness behind that smile. The Little Tramp is ever gallant toward women, especially toward waifs, misfits or strays, like himself. He is seldom gallant, considerate or even friendly toward men. In *City Lights,* for instance, he does everything he can to please the pretty blind flower girl who suspects he is a dashing gentleman, but he barely endures the wealthy drunkard, who, in his cups, wants to shower largess on him. He trusts and adores the flower girl; he distrusts and shies away from the drunk. However, he accepts the latter's largess because that is a means to an end—the end being to survive.

It is, indeed, the struggle for survival that is the insistent theme of Chaplin's great silent film, *The Gold Rush,* which he wrote, directed and acted in 1925. In this indelibly brilliant picture, the longest he had made up to that time and thus the most severely demanding of the staying power of the Little Tramp, Chaplin chose a subject that gave him opportunity for full exposure of the character and his technique. It also provided the essentials of a subtle comment on acquisitiveness.

Here the Little Tramp is confronted with an adversary much more intense than any he had previously encountered, including the German army he roundly trounced in *Shoulder Arms.* Here he is up against the violence and fury of the arctic elements, against which he has the bland temerity to pit himself in his innocent quest for gold. It is the hideousness of winter, the howling blizzards in the empty, frozen wastes and the effects that these terrible conditions have upon the behavior of men that mostly confound his gentle nature and compel the exercise of all his ingenuity to survive.

Significantly, Chaplin starts the picture with an uncommonly realistic shot of a long line of men toiling slowly up a snow-covered mountain and disappearing through a gap between two formidable peaks which is identified as the treacherous "Chilkoot Pass." Thus, at the outset, he gives us a striking image of the bleakness, the cold, the physical hardship and the human competition involved in the historic Klondike gold rush, which this picture pretends to suggest.

But the next shot is in disarming contrast, for here, along a rocky mountain ledge which is so obviously artificial it could be no place but in a studio, comes the

A classic within a classic is Charlie's method of staving off starvation by delicately digesting stewed shoe as if it were a gourmet dish.

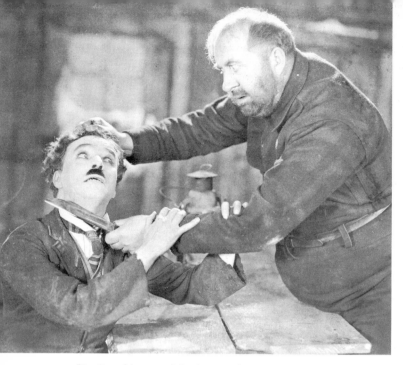

Big Jim, driven mad by hunger, has visions of Charlie as a four-footed animal and therefore a source of nourishment.

Little Tramp, here tagged the Lone Prospector. He is cheerful, unconcerned, debonair, wearing his usual outfit and swinging his incongruous bamboo cane. The only difference is that he is loaded with a conglomeration of prospector's gear, with a large frying pan hanging directly beneath his knapsack and spanking his bottom with each step of his waddling gait. He looks safe enough, but then the camera pulls back a bit and we see that he is unknowingly being followed at a couple of paces by a huge, inquisitive bear.

Thus we meet the little fellow, overburdened but plainly ill equipped for such a vicious country and venture as we have just seen described. He is an innocent in a cruel environment, cut loose among avaricious men, blithely pursuing his reckless fancy—and about to be eaten by a bear!

This is the comical beginning to the first, or "hunger" phase of the film, in which the Little Tramp must use all his ingenuity and all his portion of providential luck to find something to eat, and also keep from being eaten, first by the bear and then by two larger and hungrier prospectors with whom he is isolated in a tiny cabin in a storm.

It is here in this desperate situation that Chaplin spots what is probably the most magnificent and memorable piece of pantomime in all his films. It is the business of boiling and eating one of his hideous old shoes, carving it as though it were a turkey, portioning it out between himself and Big Jim, the less savage of his

In the barroom, amid the rough characters of the Klondike, Charlie's gentle ways seem to attract the sympathy of a hostess (Georgia Hale).

In the shambles of his cabin, Charlie scrapes together the semblance of a party for the dance-hall girls.

companions, with whom he is left when the other goes off in the storm; then briskly having at his sodden helping with the gustation of a gourmet, twirling the laces on his fork as though they were spaghetti and nibbling the nails of the sole as though they were succulent bones. He surrounds this frantic preclusion of starvation with the illusion of partaking of a gorgeous meal. It is a rich pantomimic performance and a charming display of the dauntlessness of the Little Tramp.

The second phase of the film is less macabre and more consistent with Chaplin's heart-tug style. It has the Little Tramp struggling bravely to survive the agonies of unrequited love. Having parted finally with Big Jim and come to a rough mining town, he has found himself thoroughly smitten with adoration of a beautiful dance-hall girl. He doggedly, delicately pursues her, and finally gets her and a few of her friends to promise to come to his small cabin for a party on New Year's Eve.

On the night of the anticipated party, he has a chicken roasting in the stove, party favors are set on the table, which is decorated with a scissor-trimmed newspaper as a tablecloth, candles are lit and there are paper streamers festooned about the room. Here again is a poignant token of the consideration and enterprise of the little man.

But the guests do not arrive on schedule. The host is waiting anxiously. Then there is a dissolve from a shot of him sitting at the table to the party going full blast. Everybody is happy. The little fellow, laughing and beaming, is urged by the girls to make a speech, but he

is embarrassed. He does a little act instead. He spikes two hard rolls with forks, and, holding them in front of him on the table as though they were tiny feet, he causes them to dance a joyous variety of capers, glides and Highland flings. The girl, Georgia, is delighted and ecstatically kisses him, which causes him to topple over backward—whereupon there is another dissolve, and we see that the little fellow has been dreaming. He is alone, the candles have burned down, and in the nearby dance hall he sees Georgia and the other girls with the big, rough men.

Such is Chaplin's depiction of the Little Tramp's adventure after gold. The pursuit turns into a prospecting for something more precious to him. And this is the consequence. But all is not over yet. Big Jim comes back and gets the little fellow to return with him to the distant cabin to seek his staked-out claim. After a hilarious experience with the cabin being blown about in a great storm, they find gold and become fabulously wealthy. On the ship going to San Francisco, the Little Tramp again runs into Georgia. Not knowing he is rich, she indicates that she loves him, and all ends happily.

It is useless to seek in *The Gold Rush* for anything more profound than this: this romantic suggestion that the getting of riches is generally quite fortuitous, and that much more gratifying than money is the achievement of the heart's desire. Chaplin was to be more accusative and cynical in later films. But he never gets any closer to the essence of the human quest than he does here.

53

Potemkin

1926

Prepared and directed by Sergei Eisenstein; assistant director, Grigori Alexandrov; cameraman, Edward Tisse; produced for First Studio of Goskino.

Vakulinchuk	Alexander Antonov
Captain Golikov	Vladimir Barsky
Ship's Officer	Levshin
Chief Officer Gilyarovsky	G. Alexandrov
Sailor	G. Gomorov

Sergei Eisenstein's *Potemkin* ranks as one of the great films of all time for perhaps a greater number of reasons than does any other film in this book. It is, first, a brilliant and exciting piece of recreated cinema reportage, based on an actual occurrence during the abortive Russian Revolution in 1905. That was the mutiny of the sailors aboard the Czarist cruiser *Potemkin* in the Black Sea and the subsequent rising of the people of Odessa in a great show of sympathy, when the ship was brought to port for the funeral of the leader of the sailors, who was killed in the mutiny.

Lean and economical in structure and vivid in its reportorial style—especially in a classic sequence showing the massacre of the Odessa demonstrators by Cos-sacks on a great outdoor flight of marble stairs—this extraordinary motion picture, made in 1925, moves with a subtle, savage rhythm and glows with a fierce, consuming fire. It is an intensely dramatic film.

That is because it is compounded of a number of skillful cinema techniques that were new and revolutionary when Eisenstein developed them and that still make their shock effects today. His use of carefully picked nonprofessionals to play the precisely imaged roles of sailors, ship's officers and civilians was radical and daring at the time. Now it is a common practice with the documentary-minded realists. Novel, too, was his manner of addressing the camera to the material at hand, his fanatic recourse to the close-up for detail and emphasis, his passion for reiterating an image or a point with repeated sequences and shots.

But the most bold and striking innovation was his radical use of montage, the name given to the kind of editing or cutting that is so notable in this film. Eisenstein was the master of a rigorous cutting style based on the logical assumption that rapid transitions of visual suggestion could generate shock. He found that in swift juxtapositions of contrasting images he could stir the emotions of the viewer to almost any pitch he desired. By carefully studying and equating the pictorial content and length of individual shots, then splicing them to-

Mutiny is, touched off when the sailors of the *Potemkin* are commanded to eat maggot-infested food.

gether in arrangements that were precisely calculated and timed, he developed a definite rhythm or periodicity in his sequences, which produces a subtle and unconscious psychological effect on the viewer. This is the marvel of *Potemkin*—its insinuating *rhythmic montage*. This impelled its esthetic reputation and secured its status as one of the world's great films.

Its unique distinction, however, is the fact that it was the spearhead for the wave of exceptional Soviet films which represented the first full mobilization of motion pictures in an explicit national cause. It was the primal achievement by the new and unproved group of youthful Soviet film-makers who had been charged by Lenin to put the motion picture medium to the promotion and glorification of the Soviet state. The fact that it accomplished this purpose with genuine artistry made it the eminent trailblazer for a cultural concept that was unprecedented at the time.

Eisenstein started in the theater after being trained as an engineer, and was a passionate exponent of realism. He carried his obsession to the point of staging one of his plays in a factory because he felt this would bring his audiences of workers closer to reality. From this disappointing venture, the director, at twenty-four, turned his hand to motion pictures, and, in his first feature-length film, *Strike,* a drama about an unsuccessful effort by a group of workers to form a union in the days of the Czar, he began laying down his basic technique of juxtaposing sharply contrasting images to develop shock. His photographer was Edward Tisse, an experienced news film cameraman, who became his indispensable collaborator on most of his subsequent films.

Although Eisenstein was not entirely satisfied with *Strike,* it made a tremendous impression on other Soviet film-makers, and it was sufficiently gratifying to its director to cause him to decide to stick with films. He was about to begin work on a picture recounting the achievements of the First Cavalry Army in the 1917 Civil War, when he was given a signal honor, on the basis of his direction of *Strike.* He was selected to direct a new film to be called *Year 1905*, which was to be one of the films celebrating the twentieth anniversary of the 1905 revolution. This film was to cover in eight episodes the entire range of the abortive revolt, from the disaster of the Russo-Japanese War to the armed uprisings in Moscow, with emphasis on the emergence of a new working class. One episode was to be devoted to the *Potemkin* mutiny and the subsequent strike and massacre of dockworkers in Odessa.

Eisenstein and Tisse started shooting in Leningrad in March 1925 and continued there for several months, doing the episode of the general strike. Then they went

In the midst of the mutiny, a priest vainly attempts to soothe the high feelings on board.

The ship's doctor, who has declared the sailors' food edible, is the first victim of the uprising.

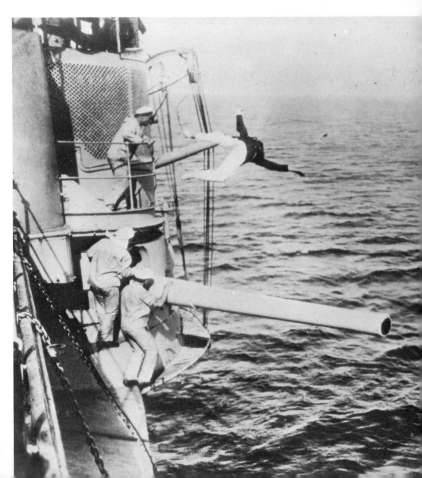

When the scene shifts to the waterfront at Odessa, the people who come to mourn the death of the mutiny's leader are themselves brutally massacred by the Cossack troops.

to Odessa to do the scenes of the strike and massacre there. This whole episode, including the *Potemkin* mutiny, was to be covered in forty-two shots, which were to convey a quick sense of the brutality of the Cossacks in chasing the people through the streets. But when Eisenstein got to Odessa and saw the great flight of stairs that go from the upper city down to the harbor, he knew that this must be the setting for the most terrifying and significant incident in the whole film. He threw away the scenario that had been prepared for him, and with Tisse, began the expansion of the famous scene of the massacre on the steps. As they proceeded, he realized that this episode of the mutiny and the massacre contained the essence of the nature and the meaning of the revolt of the masses in 1905. Later, in editing the

footage shot for *Year 1905*, he discarded all else but the *Potemkin* episode. This was offered as the anniversary film.

It is interesting to note the history of *Potemkin's* release—how it was previewed for a special Jubilee audience in the Bolshoi Opera Theater in Moscow on December 21, 1925, at which time it was evidently received warmly but with some guarded restraint; how it did not make much of an impression when it was first released to the public in Moscow on January 18, 1926; how it was later given a thundering reception by critics and the public when it was shown in Berlin; and how this (and its being banned in France and England) caused the Russian people to gain a new respect for it.

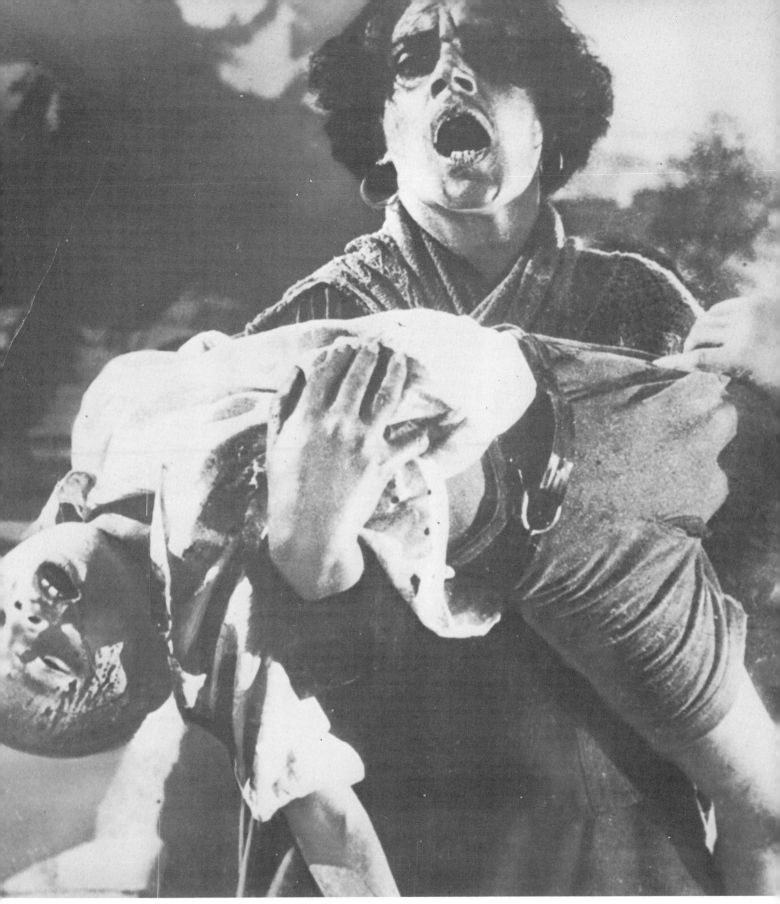

Unrelenting detail was used by Eisenstein to electrify the audience.

The film amply fulfilled the wish of its director that it should give a sense of the reality of the masses in a moment of history. In one hour, Eisenstein provides us with such a succession of experiences of an angry and harrowing nature that even a person who may have no political sympathy for the mutineers and the demonstrators must feel caught up and absorbed in their passion and agony and feel, for a moment or two, at least, the peril of death.

The structural form of *Potemkin* is that of classic tragedy; it is composed in five parts or phases, each filling roughly one reel. The first begins with ominous indications of smoldering unrest and discontent among the sailors aboard the battle cruiser at sea. They complain about the food they are being given. An allegedly offending side of beef is hung before them on the foredeck, and the ship's doctor, a perky little man with a ferocious beard and steel-rimmed spectacles, goes up to look at it. Through his spectacles, held close to it, we see maggots squirming in the meat. This sudden magnification through one of the lenses is the first shock effect in the film. This shot was considered so offensive that it was cut when *Potemkin* was first shown in New York. But the doctor proclaims the meat is all right, that it simply should be washed in brine, and the cook carries it to the galley. The hostile men go about their shipboard duties, as word spreads, "The rotten meat is in the soup!" At midday mealtime, the men refuse to go the the tables. They buy food at the ship's canteen, which causes the sounding of a bugle call for another muster on the deck.

Now we move into the second phase of the drama. At this point the captain comes on the scene, a great bearded man who emerges from a companionway with an air of immense authority. He orders the men who did not eat the soup to step out of ranks. Some of the sailors step forth. The captain orders them hung from the yardarm, with his finger pointing imperiously to the sky.

An armed guard is called to carry out the order, but, at a hastily arranged signal, the sailors break ranks and gather around a gun turret. For a few moments there is confusion on deck, a seething mass of white caps moving disorderedly, as seen from above. A few sailors try to dodge down the hatches, past the captain, but he drives them back and orders the guards to throw a huge tarpaulin over the mob of men.

As the guards bring up the tarpaulin and throw it over the men, an old priest, with wild hair and thick beard, appears on deck above the camera, holding aloft a crucifix. A subtitle reads that he calls on the Lord to remove the unruly spirit from the men, and a few pitiful forms are seen kneeling under the tarpaulin. But no time is wasted on religion. A firing squad is drawn up, and the forms under the tarpaulin shuffle and move about forlornly.

Then the stalwart leader of the sailors, Vakulinchuk, calls on the squad to throw down their arms. There is a moment of hesitation. The mutiny begins. There are many close-ups of angry faces, of officers and men, close-ups of men grabbing rifles and of feet running on the deck. Officers are chased into cabins. Some are caught and heaved overboard. In the confusion, the old priest is knocked down and his crucifix skates across the deck. Someone catches the ship's doctor. He is dragged, like the side of beef, to the edge of the deck

Massacre on the steps leading from the central city to the harbor of Odessa.

58

and, for all his terrified screaming and clutching at a coil of rope, is thrown into the sea. His spectacles are knocked off in the confusion, and the last comment on him is a close-up of these spectacles dangling ironically from a wire.

As the sailors are taking over, Vakulinchuk is shot by an officer and his body falls into the water. Several sailors dive in to rescue him and converge as in a vortex on the spot where he has gone down. But he is dead when they get him and, for the last shot in this phase, the camera irises in for a lingering and loving close-up of his battered and bloody face.

The sailors now place their leader's body on a small steam tender which moves ahead of the cruiser into Odessa harbor, amid the masts and spars of many boats. It is all very peaceful and poetic in the picturesque old port, where the body of Vakulinchuk is placed in a tent on a pier. There people come to view it and weep at a placard placed on the peak of the tent, reading "All for a spoonful of soup."

Dawn comes, and Eisenstein gives us a lovely shot of the great Odessa stairs, empty and quiet in the crystal morning, before dissolving to several long shots of hordes of people coming down the stairs and snaking along a curving seawall to view the body of the hero in the tent. In this phase, devoted to mourning and sympathy for the mutineers, the director develops a most affecting andante movement in the film. He shows us, in countless close-ups, the faces of the sorrowing populace. A little boy places a few coins in the dead man's cap. A clenched fist. A sign: "Down with the tyrants!" Well-groomed and haughty bourgeoises watch the mournful procession from the stairway and make contemptuous jokes.

Anger now swells among the mourners. "Shoulder to shoulder!" they chant. From the *Potemkin*, anchored in the harbor, the grateful sailors respond. "Together with the revolutionary workers of Russia!" they shout to the people on the quai, and the petty bourgeois snicker and mutter about "the Jews."

Then suddenly there comes an air of menace. A fast close-up to the top of the stairs shows a row of booted feet of soldiers starting to march down the stairs. The deadly barrels of their rifles, carried at the ready, come into view. A long shot shows people fleeing in terror down the stairs. Now the line of marching soldiers is seen by the camera from above, moving ruthlessly, metronomically upon the downward fleeing crowd. Thus begins the famous sequence of the massacre on the stairs.

Words cannot give a full description of the meticulous construction of this whole scene and the terrifying impact of it, the relentless redundancy with which Eisenstein shows the chaos of the victims and the march of the soldiers down the stairs. The steps are soon strewn with bodies. A mother, fleeing with her child, doesn't notice at first when her child falls. Then she stops and, with horror on her face, rushes back to snatch up the little body and lift it unbelievingly and accusingly in her arms. Frightened women try to plead with the soldiers, who push them aside and march on. The mother with the body of her youngster stumbles among the fallen, crying insanely, "My boy is ill!"

At the bottom of the stairs, a troop of Cossacks on horseback now comes into view and starts to ride up the stairs, with the chests of their horses a barricade against the down-rushing crowd. Panic grips the hemmed-in people. A baby is glimpsed in a baby carriage at the top of the stairs. The mother is shot and the carriage, untended, begins to roll down the stairs. The crescendo and climax of the sequence are paced by the accelerating plunge of that innocent carriage down the stairs, bouncing sickeningly over sprawled bodies, as onlookers watch in horror.

The final phase of the drama is almost anticlimactic after this, although it has some of Eisenstein's most urgent, proletarian picture-making in it. It has to do with the valor and efficiency of the sailors aboard the ship.

As night comes and the red flag is lowered, the men wait in silence and prepare for an anticipated engagement with an oncoming Russian fleet.

Then, as dawn breaks, the squadron is sighted. Men waken and rush to their posts. The order flies, "Prepare for action!" There is a jumble of men's faces, machinery, dials. Pistons plunge in cylinders. Water rushes past the hull. Guns are tilted in the turrets. Smoke pours from the stack. Then a signal is made to the oncoming squadron. "Join us!" the mutineers cry. The suspense is held for a few minutes as the ships converge. There is a close-up of the mouths of the big guns. Then the men on the other ships cheer. The men of the *Potemkin* answer. Thus the film ends trimphantly.

With *Potemkin*, a staggering succession of exciting Soviet silent films began. It included Pudovkin's *Mother, End of St. Petersburg* and his powerful *Storm over Asia;* Alexander Dovzhenko's *Arsenal* and *Earth,* Friedrich Ermler's *Fragment of an Empire* and Eisenstein's subsequent *Ten Days That Shook the World* and *Old and New.* It was a body of films that provided the people of the Soviet state an emotional identification with the revolution such as no other medium of communication or art could have achieved. And it certainly conveyed a moving concept of the fervor and vitality of the Russian people to people around the world.

Only Keaton would take out on foot to recapture his hijacked train.

The General

1927

Screenplay by Al Boasberg and Charles Smith; directed by Buster Keaton and Clyde Bruckman; photographed by Bert Haines and J. D. Jennings; produced by Joseph M. Schenck for United Artists.

Johnny Gray	Buster Keaton
Annabelle Lee	Marion Mack
Her Father	Charles Smith
Her Brother	Frank Barnes
Captain Anderson	Glen Cavender
General Thatcher	Jim Farley
Southern General	Frederick Vroom
Union Generals	Joe Keaton
	Mike Donlan
	Tom Nawm

As the last of the great silent comics to command a position in this book, Buster Keaton is perhaps the most elusive and therefore the least understood. Where Chaplin clearly expresses the poignancy of the "little man" valiantly seeking recognition and affection in a coldhearted world and Lloyd unmistakably mimics the go-getting all-American boy, Keaton presents us with a character just this side of a human question mark, a primly detached little stoic contending endlessly with nitwit people and anarchistic machines.

To the eye of the first-time beholder, he may appear an uninteresting sort, monotonous in his getup and stiff in his attitude. With grave eyes peering coolly out of a solemn, deadpan face which in its lean and high-cheeked structure fits with his underslung, starchly clothed frame he looks like a country undertaker or a small-time evangelist pondering the dismal possibilities of the next task he has to perform.

Yet this surface solemnity of Keaton is precisely the quality that makes his hidden nature so surprising and his reactions so droll. It soon becomes clear that his appearance is but a thin and foolish façade for a fiercely energetic individual with the pride of a potentate, the ingenuity of a wizard and the courage and persistence of a lion.

There has been a disposition among critics to put Keaton down as cold, an odd duck without emotions, a "deadpan automaton." He has been sometimes heedlessly figured as just a fast, frantic foil to machines, a mobile cigar-store Indian animated by quick impulses and instant springs. This is as false and unperceptive as

Finding a mortar on a flatcar, but knowing less about cannons than engines, Johnny Gray wonders how to go about firing it.

it would be to say that Lloyd is a supergymnastic cutup without a nerve in his body or a brain in his head.

It is quite true that Keaton's fellow politely eschews sentiment. He never makes a play for pity in the manner of Chaplin's Little Tramp. Neither does he beg for affection in the spaniel-eyed way of Lloyd, nor does he ooze wistfulness as does Harry Langdon, who also dwelled behind a fixed façade.

Keaton's is a dignified skeptic who is careful and cautious toward the world because he isn't quite sure how it will treat him with all its crazy, illogical people and its mischievous machines. Being supremely literal-minded, morally righteous and intense, he coolly distrusts all animate creatures and their wayward peculiarities. That's why he holds aloof from others, keeps his emotions in reserve, maintains a stoic appearance, never wears his heart on his sleeve. But to say that he is lacking in emotion or is without personal winsomeness and warmth is to miss entirely the distinction and subtlety of his character. For it is just because he does have spirit, ambition, self-confidence and pride, a will to exercise his independence, that he acts with such

swift precisiveness and reveals so much ire and impatience when things gang aft a-gley.

Keaton came by this character with the same co-operation of chance that assisted his peers in the development of the characters they portrayed. He picked up the idiosyncrasy of a deadpan countenance when he worked as a child with his parents in a vaudeville acrobatic act and was trained by his prescient father to keep a perpetually straight face. He is said to have been given the name of Buster by Harry Houdini, the famed contortionist, who was amazed by his ability to do hard stage falls without displaying so much as a wince. The habit acquired in childhood was propitiously maintained when he went into films in 1918 as an appropriately incongruous foil for the then full-blown Fatty Arbuckle and caught countless pies in that frozen face. With Fatty, he also perfected his essential acrobatic skill and learned the tricks of split-second timing that was so key to the comedians in silent films.

In the early 1920's, Keaton went on his own and began making feature-length pictures. *Our Hospitality* was a freakishly costumed chase film, turned out in

1923. The following year he made *Sherlock Jr.* and *The Navigator,* two memorable comedies which considerably extended his horizon and his popularity. The latter is sometimes considered his most sophisticated film, being an almost surrealistic study of Buster alone with a girl on a ship. But, to my way of thinking, *The General,* made in 1927, best combines the subtle character of Keaton with material that is perfect for his style.

The story, written by Al Boasberg and Charles Smith, with the customary aid of Keaton himself and all the wags he kept around him to dream up gags and play practical jokes, was based on an actual incident that occurred during the American Civil War: the hijacking of a Confederate supply train by Union saboteurs. Keaton and his people turned this incident into a perfect blueprint for a chase comedy, with Keaton as Johnny Gray, the outraged engineer of the stolen train who is inspired by his love for his engine—an old-time funnel-stack locomotive called the General—to go after it and return it home.

But passionate devotion to his engine, which is stated at the start of the film with shots of Johnny patting the locomotive lovingly, is not his only reason for going after the train and exposing himself to painful hardships and considerable military peril. He wants to be a hero and he wants to impress a girl. These are urges that burn fiercely in his seemingly saturnine soul. And

to fail to appreciate fully how dominant these urges are in motivating the little engineer to do the things he does—to penetrate the lines of the enemy, to resteal his intractable train, to drive it back against many dire obstructions and to be a hero in a military skirmish along the way—is to be misled by the notion that Keaton is just a spry automaton.

His Johnny is a valiant little fellow, an all too human being, and Keaton states it crisply and clearly in the first reel of the film. Rebuffed by his girl for being a slacker, for not joining the Confederate Army and going to war, Johnny tries to enlist and is turned down (he doesn't know it, but a leading citizen has told the recruiting officer he is more useful where he is). Thus denounced and humiliated, the little engineer is full of normal woe (and his solemn face piteously reveals it) when the train is suddenly stolen, with his girl accidentally aboard.

The galvanic reaction of Keaton when he sees his beloved engine and a couple of cars start off down the tracks is the first startling revelation of the electrically responsive mind and the split-second muscular reflexes of this deceptively solemn little man. He is off like a shot, racing swiftly on foot after the vanishing train, one arm waving magisterially forward, beckoning other men around the station to follow him, but not looking back for a second, so obsessed with pursuit is he. The

The train plunges from a burning trestle into a river. Buster is shown on the wreckage, peering from a funnel.

springiness of his running movement, contrasted with a glimpse of his stoic face, transmits at once the distinction of this human paradox.

The next significant revelation comes as Buster, seeing he is losing in the race, stops and swings about to rally with his followers. Lo, no one is there! The cohorts he thought were with him have blandly let him go it alone.

Now, what would an ordinary person do in a fix such as this? He would meekly return to the station, resigned to his discomfiture and loss. Not Buster. He is undaunted. He spots a handy handcar, wrestles it onto the tracks, leaps aboard and starts pumping wildly. He gets it going so fast it jumps the tracks and tosses him into the bushes, as it plunges down an embankment and burns. He is on his feet in a jiffy, looks about hopefully, spots an old-fashioned high-wheel bicycle at a nearby house and jumps on that. His belief in himself is so compelling and his spontaneity is so intense that it doesn't occur to him how incongruous it is to use a bicycle to try to catch a train.

In these initial happenings, the pattern of the picture is laid down, a succession of complications in which Buster attempts to mobilize whatever means or devices he can put his hands on to conquer a cantankerous machine. It is almost as though the General is being difficult on its own, conspiring with its larcenous human attachments to cause its master embarrassment.

Annabelle Lee (Marion Mack), rescued from the enemy and a runaway train by Johnny, makes Johnny a suitable mate—nerveless and brainless.

The contention of mechanisms, operated by frenetic human beings, is brought to a clear confrontation as Buster rides up to another settlement where a Confederate troop train is standing on a siding, with soldiers loafing about. Shouting and waving to the soldiers to get aboard the train, Buster leaps into the cab of the locomotive (the Texas is the name of this iron horse), pulls the throttle with professional precision and is off and chugging down the tracks. Only now does he turn around to look back and see—yes, it's happened again! The cars containing the soldiers are not connected. There is only the engine, the tender, one flatcar, and him. When Buster discovers this omission, not a trace of distraction clouds his face. There is just a flicker of amazement in his eyes. And this is a dandy demonstration of how these optical windows always give a delightfully droll delineation of what's going on in his mind.

Keaton was an absolute master of the double take, the trick of delaying a reaction for just a moment (or maybe two or three) to heighten the effect of the humor of a shock message hitting the brain. But he was able to do it entirely with his eyes. A prime example of this virtuosity, perhaps the best in all his films, comes later in the picture when he has got behind the enemy lines and has stumbled into army headquarters and into the officers' council room. He is trapped beneath the council table when the officers come in to make plans. Fortunately he is hidden by a low-hanging tablecloth. There is a small hole in the cloth, however, and through this he can see what's going on. Under the table with him, we watch him peeking out.

Then a shocking thing happens. Into the room, his girl is brought, a captive of the Union Army, presumably held as a spy. Buster's reaction to this (which is shown in an outside shot) is bound to be intense. It is the sort of surprise that should make him almost fall out into the room. And how are we shown this reaction? With a head-on close-up shot of Buster's one eye peering starkly through that hole in the tablecloth! Just one big eye, framed by the fabric, that stares incredulously for a beat or two, then blinks and stares again, this time with horror—that is all we see. Yet with this concise pictorial statement we are made to envision Buster's face and his whole startled, rigid perturbation. It is a brilliant stroke.

Another trait of Keaton's little stoic is his bland ingenuousness, which causes him to do sometimes clumsy and shockingly perilous things. For instance, after his discovery that he is alone on the pursuing train, the one he has picked up on the siding, he notes a stumpy howitzer sitting on the flatcar. Immediately this gives him an idea. He will load it and try to fire a broadside to hit the train ahead. But knowing nothing about ordnance, even less than the audience does, he first loads the howitzer with a pinch of gunpowder and a monster cannonball. Of course, the discharge is a fizzle. The howitzer gives a little puff and lobs the cannonball harmlessly into the engine cab.

Buster regards it coolly. He has evidently made a slight mistake. All right, he will rectify the error by going to the other extreme. He jams the whole keg of gunpowder down the muzzle and plunks in *two* cannonballs. This time he is seeing to it that this perverse little monster works! But as he lights the fuse, the vibration of the rattling flatcar causes the muzzle of the howitzer to lower. Now it points directly into the engine cab.

Naturally, the audience shudders. It knows the engine is going to be blown to smithereens and Buster, standing there so innocently, is going to be piled up in a terminal wreck. And then there comes a sudden shift of fortune of the sort that regularly occurs to save Buster from disaster. The engine starts around a curve and swings out of the line of fire just as the howitzer thunderously explodes. The two cannonballs burst from the muzzle, whoosh past the engine cab and zoom straight ahead to smash heroically close to the fleeing train a half mile up the track! Buster blinks with bland satisfaction and gives the howitzer an appreciative pat.

Buster's troubles are always compounded by the presence of the girl, who turns out to be more of a nuisance than a figure of sweet romance. After he has rescued her from the enemy, he tries to carry her, as a proper romantic hero should. But she is much too heavy. He soon has to put her down. While he is sitting on a log, limply resting, she comes up behind him and scares him half to death. Then she wanders away and gets caught in a bear trap. Trying to extricate her, *he* gets caught.

Some girl! She is constantly doing the wrong thing and getting in the way. Heading home in the restolen General, Buster finds they are short of wood. While he is breaking up things to feed the fire, he notes the silly girl is daintily tidying the cab by picking up small pieces of wood and tossing them out. In utter exasperation, he frankly throttles her. No wonder he is unmoved a few shots later when she is drenched by the overhanging pipe of a water tower.

But the final blow of the girl's stupidity comes when Buster, who has learned that the pursuing enemy is planning to focus a sneak attack upon the Confederates at the Rock River Bridge, runs his engine across the bridge and then gets down and goes back to pile up kindling and set it afire. What should happen but the girl lights the kindling with Buster on the wrong side! He has to dive off the bridge into the river and save himself as best he can.

However, in the succeeding battle, by dint of abundant zeal and despite some extravagant fumbles such as tripping over a sword and running up onto the back of a soldier which he thinks is a rock from which he can wave the flag, Buster manages to come out a hero. He is rewarded with the hand of the stupid girl and the uniform of a lieutenant, which is much too large for him. Thus, Keaton ends this exposition on a winsome and wistful note. Maybe romance and heroism aren't worth the effort, after all.

As usual, the cast in *The General* plays to Keaton with selfless loyalty. Marion Mack is magnificently un-intelligent and sexually vapid as the girl. And the rest, in small roles, strut and sputter, make trouble or get in the way, precisely as intended, like slightly nicked cogs in a machine.

This picture was vastly successful, as were all of Keaton's silent films, but he rapidly lost his magnetism, though not his recognition and fame, when sound came in. Teamed with Jimmy Durante, Wallace Beery and others in talkie comedies, he was denied opportunity to project his essence amid so much loquacity.

He virtually disappeared from pictures for many dreary years. Then in 1957 a screen biography, *The Buster Keaton Story*, was made. Donald O'Connor played the title role. Keaton was used as technical adviser. Not even his shadow appeared.

The Crowd

1928

Scenario by King Vidor, John V. A. Weaver and Harry Behn; directed by King Vidor; sets by Cedric Gibbons and Arnold Gillespie; photography by Henry Sharp; produced by Metro-Goldwyn-Mayer.

John	James Murray
Mary	Eleanor Boardman
Bert	Bert Roach
Estelle	Estelle Clark
Mary's Mother	Lucy Beaumont

There is an ingenuous simplicity about King Vidor's *The Crowd* that may cause it to seem somewhat naive to those who view it for the first time today. It elaborates the obvious in pursuing the poignant theme of the engulfment of a white-collar worker in the great gray marsh of society. It is frequently oversentimental. It abounds in what are now cornball clichés. And most of its dramatic forward movement is propelled by accidents.

Yet I find it the most revealing and honorable of the silent films that came in the late 1920's just as the medium was being converted to sound. It is humorously and touchingly expressive of the middle-class muddle of the day, whereas most of the films made in that period avoided reality like the plague. And the ending of the currently viewable version, the pick of several that were made, is a gem of thematic resolution done with true cinematic eloquence.

What is also interesting is that it portends the subjects and the techniques of the Italian neo-realists who were concerned about the state of the little people after the Second World War. Particularly, one may discover in the frustration and dismay of its middle-class hero an affinity to those of the worker-hero in Vittorio de Sica's *The Bicycle Thief* (which see).

Vidor has reflectively stated in his autobiography, *A Tree Is a Tree*, that he made *The Crowd* as a further exploration of the theme of his famous war film, *The Big Parade* (1925). In that film, he says, he described how his playboy protagonist, who was "neither an excessive patriot nor an active pacifist," was caught up in the First World War and carried along with it, simply doing what other people did and having his destiny determined entirely by the war environment. When Vidor came to make this other picture, he says he wanted to show how the peacetime life of the average fellow is also conditioned by his environment and by the flow of fortuitous circumstances over which he has no control.

That may be. Anyhow, as he tells it, he undertook the film virtually on the spur of the moment after a casual conversation with Irving Thalberg, his perceptive producer at Metro-Goldwyn-Mayer. Thalberg liked his suggestion for a picture about "an average fellow who walks through life and sees a lot of drama taking place around him," so Vidor went to work on a scenario with his collaborator, Harry Behn.

What they came up with was a story of a small-town American boy who finds that being an office clerk in the big city does *not* lead to a pot of gold, that the humdrum existence of a bookkeeper trying to raise a small family on a minimum salary is hardly the fulfillment of the great American dream. Further, they sketched the

John as a boy learns of the sudden death of his father.

66

A face in the crowd, a cipher in the office, John (James Murray) typifies the small city frog in the high white-collar pond.

hero as a genial, slightly boorish young man whose bland conceit is pathetically unwarranted by his evident mediocrity and whose stubborn anticipations of "the big break" are obviously not to be fulfilled.

It was the sort of story that Vidor and Thalberg could see should not be made in the customary format and with the customary casting of Hollywood. It needed to be developed for a strong illusion of reality, and that meant it had to be acted by people who could be thoroughly believed.

In reasonable line with this concept, Vidor gave the role of the wife to his own wife, Eleanor Boardman, who had been in several of his films. She had a quiet, natural beauty and was an excellent actress to boot. For the role of the husband, however, Vidor was determined to have a man who would be totally unfamiliar to moviegoers and would look and act exactly as though he had been plucked right off the street, a young fellow with a callow manner, a nice but commonplace face and an air of inborn indistinction. He should be one of the crowd.

One day, outside the casting office at Metro-Goldwyn-Mayer, a brash young fellow brushed past him. Vidor thought he recognized him. Then it came to him after the man had gone by that he fit the image of the character he had in mind. He hurried after him, caught him and asked his name. "Murray," the man snapped. Vidor asked what he did at the studio. The fellow warily acknowledged that he worked as an extra from time to time. Vidor then introduced himself as a director and told the man to come to see him the next day. Murray gave him a suspicious glance and went on.

He didn't show up the next day, or the next, and Vidor despaired. He figured the fellow imagined his leg was being pulled. Also he could not remember the name the man had given him. So he went to the casting office and patiently studied the list of extras. When he came to the name "James Murray," it rang a bell, and he asked that Murray be called to see him. Murray replied that he didn't have the time. Such a strange and cheeky reaction piqued Vidor's interest in the man. Finally, after much telephoning and an agreement by Vidor to pay him a day's wage, the extra came and made a screen test. Vidor signed him forthwith, confident, as was amply proven, that Murray was just right. He was of medium height, thin and narrow-shouldered, with a clean, open, average-looking face and a strong hint of Irish about him. In fact, he looked a lot like Vidor.

Others in the cast were small-part players whom

67

Vidor found at the studio, professionals of ordinary appearance who were not likely to be recognized. All turned out to be appropriate in their minor roles.

In accord with his aim to fill the picture with an illusion of authenticity, Vidor shot most of its exteriors in the streets and nearby areas of New York, often using a mobile "hidden" camera, which was quite unusual then. This maneuver may have been encouraged by the example von Stroheim set when he shot most of *Greed* (which see) in San Francisco in order to capture the urban atmosphere. For *The Crowd* gives ample evidence of having been planned and directed to achieve a kind of rawness and rightness of detail similar to that in *Greed*.

The opening shot of the birth of the hero, whose name is John Simms, at once conveys that this is an unconventional picture, done in what was then a startling way. It is a shot of the naked baby being lifted from its mother's bed by a family doctor who slaps it on the bottom and happily proclaims, as the baby begins to squall, "There's a little man the world is going to hear from!"

Likewise, the introduction of John Simms to New York, after his father has been killed in an accident and the run-of-the-mill young man is compelled to go forth to seek his living, is done with a striking sequence of realistic shots of him approaching lower Manhattan on a Hudson River ferryboat, bucking the crowds in the business district, being confused by the elevated trains (which are shown snaking weirdly among the buildings in a stunning shot from above). And Vidor completes this sharp conveyance of the hero's submergence in the

John and his blind date, Mary (Eleanor Boardman), are well matched, both groping for company.

crowd with a travel shot that is one of the finest impressionistic visuals in silent films. The camera, starting at street level, smoothly ascends the outside of a many-windowed skyscraper to a window on the top floor, then slides through and into a large room full of scores of identical desks set in monotonously straight rows, behind each of which sits a clerk. Slowly, incredulously, the camera dollies along one of these rows until it comes to Desk 137, and behind it we see the young man whom we saw just a few moments earlier debarking so hopefully from a ferryboat. Thus is the hero established as a cipher within this awesome enclosure of human adding machines.

In artful ways, Vidor continues to counterpoint the person and the crowd, to isolate and surround the individual within the hustle and bustle of the metropolis. At 5 P.M., John and his buddy, Bert, leap away from their desks, burst out of that mechanized pattern and join the stream of clerks that descends in a packed elevator to the crowded lobby, where they snatch two stenographers from the swarm and flee with them out into the city and to the top of a double-decker bus. Here, in lofty isolation, John can take a look at his girl, his pretty blind date, Mary, and feel triumphantly alone with her; or when the foursome jaunts to Coney Island and rattles joyously with other peas in the pods of the barrel roll, the roller coaster and the tunnel of love at the huge amusement park. Vidor concludes with John and Mary pressed close together on the homecoming subway train, oblivious of all around them, as he asks her to marry him.

It is a spinning impression of life in the city that we get in this first part of the film, and Vidor caps it with a beautifully constructed and topically witty montage: right from the subway sequence, the scene jumps to the two leaving Grand Central Station for Niagara Falls, confused and embarrassed in the Pullman on their wedding night, he stumbling into wrong berths, then sliding into the berth with her as the scene dissolves into a full shot of water roaring over the falls; then a pan to the couple embracing and promising undying love as they lie alone on a grass plot at the edge of the plunging falls.

Vidor has put together a precise and potent statement up to this point. It is the statement of a personal involvement within an ominous societal surround. John and Mary seem to be a happy couple embarked on a normal, happy life. But what of this megalopolitan milieu in which John has to get their livelihood? Will he, as they used to ask on the radio serials, be able to rise above it?

This is the contemplation in the remainder of the film. Unfortunately, it is not as cogent as is the early

part. Vidor and Behn did not stick squarely to the basic conflict in their scheme: the individual versus the crowd. They were more interested in presenting John's reactions to domesticity, and revealing his pathetically weak nature when hit by the blows of fate.

Even so, there is much that is genuine and poetic in *The Crowd*, much that is painfully human, despite its banalities. For instance, the tedious bickering of John and Mary after they have been married for a spell, the usual cataloging of irritations in their meager domestic ménage, is saved by a scene in which Miss Boardman simply and movingly conveys the fact that the wife is pregnant, done entirely through delicate pantomime.

Or the grotesque overstatement of John's grief which drives him to distraction when their little girl dies after an accident is erased by a brilliant comprehension of the pitifulness of it in a single long shot of a plain white hearse followed by two lonely automobiles winding mutely and forlornly through the drab city streets.

Even the maudlin business of John wavering on the brink of suicide after he has thrown up his job, gone to pieces and been threatened with abandonment by his wife, is redeemed by the luminous face of Murray looking lonely, frightened and ashamed when he finds he can't muster the courage or the abandon to jump in front of a train.

Actually, a lot of the clichés, or the seeming clichés, are Vidor's way of impressing the triteness and unoriginality of these middle-class people's lives. The scene of the visit from the in-laws on the newlyweds' first Christmas Eve is a calculated throwing together of all the hackneyed in-law jokes. John's constant twanging on the ukulele and playing the gramophone are tedious but effective indications of his essential boorishness. And the saccharine scene in whch the young son proclaims his idolization of his dad may be accepted as a means of exposing the superficiality and insincerity of that traditional wheeze.

Vidor has put so many realistic touches into the film —a frankly shown toilet, for instance; a little boy having to make a pee and letting everybody know it on a family picnic at the beach; a Negro sitting naturally among white men in a hospital waiting room—that the viewer is constantly astonished by his humor and honesty.

What pervasively and finally emerges is a realizaton that here, in this distinctively bourgeois environment and at the head of this average family, is a fellow who will never make it, who will never be much of anything in the way of a business leader or even a help to his son. He is a nice guy, and he has his one brief triumph when he wins a $500 prize in an advertisement-writing contest; but he is as doomed to frustration and anonymity as is the predestined loser in *The Bicycle Thief* (which see).

And Vidor completes this realization with an ending that says so much, yet says it so simply and softly that compassion wells out of it. John has come home to Mary after getting a modest job and buying her a conciliatory present, a gramophone record and a bunch of violets. She has told her unsympathetic brothers that she does not intend to leave John. "He has always depended so on me," she says. "I've got to make sure he has everything he needs."

Then John puts the record on the gramaphone; it's a popular old disc, "There's Everything Nice About You," sung by Johnny Marvin. The two dance uncertainly around the room, then laugh a bit, dance more ardently, stumble and fall laughing on the couch. Whereupon Vidor dissolves from a close-up of them laughing to a second close-up of them, still laughing, but now we see that they are sitting in a theater, their little boy with them, watching a clown in a vaudeville show. Proudly, John notices in the program an ad for Sleight-o-Hand, the Magic Cleaner. That is the brand name for which he won the prize. The three are caught for this moment in the spell of enjoyment and hope.

And that is how we leave them, as the camera trucks slowly back and more and more people sitting around them flow into the frame, until the camera has withdrawn to such a distance that we can no longer distinguish the three in a sea of laughing faces. They are lost forever in the crowd.

The irony and pity in this ending did not please Louis B. Mayer, associate of Thalberg and head of the studio. He sensed it was not a happy ending, so he insisted that Vidor shoot another one in which John got a good job, and, at the fadeout, was seen with Mary and the boy celebrating joyously around a Christmas tree. Exhibitors were given the choice of which ending they would show. The first-run theaters in larger cities generally took Vidor's; others generally took Mayer's.

This uncertainty about the picture was mirrored in the public response. Some viewers recognized and loved it for the rare slice-of-life film it is. Others, accustomed to the usual escapist make-believe of Hollywood, were puzzled and rendered uneasy by its candid view of the average man. Its romantic realism was almost as baffling as that of *Greed*. The concept was not in accord with the buoyancy of the American dream and the booming confidence of the 1920's. This was the year before the great Wall Street crash.

Six years later, toward the end of the Great Depression and after sound was firmly fixed on the screen, Vidor resolved to make what would amount to a sequel to *The Crowd*. It would be the story of John and Mary,

struggling to carry on during the years of depression by organizing and running a cooperative farm. (It was made independently by Vidor, and released in 1934 under the title *Our Daily Bread*.)

While casting it, Vidor thought of Murray and his haunting performance in *The Crowd*. He wished to find him, but it seemed that, in the interval, the actor had dropped out of sight. Then one day, as Vidor tells it, a bum came up to him in the street and asked for money. Vidor looked closely at him. Beneath puffy eyes and a stubble of beard, he recognized Jimmy Murray's wistful Irish face.

His child killed in an accident, John's despair is his only possession while still alone in the midst of the crowd.

70

The Blue Angel

1929

Screenplay by Karl Zuckmayer, Karl Vollmoller and Robert Liebmann from a novel by Heinrich Mann; directed by Josef von Sternberg; photography by Gunther Rittau and Hans Schneeberger; design by Otto Hunte and Emil Hasler; music by Friedrich Hollander; produced by Erich Pommer at Ufa.

Professor Immanuel Rath	Emil Jannings
Lola Frohlich	Marlene Dietrich
Kiepert, a magician	Kurt Gerron
Guste, his wife	Rosa Valetti
Mazeppa	Hans Albers
School Principal	Eduard von Winterstein
The Clown	Reinhold Bernt
Beadle	Hans Roth
Angst, a student	Rolf Muller
Lohman, a student	Rolant Varno
Ertzum, a student	Karl Balhaus
Goldstaub, a student	Robert Klein-Lork
Publican	Karl Huszar-Puffy
Captain	Wilhelm Diegelmann
Policeman	Gerhard Bienert
Rath's Housekeeper	Ilse Furstenberg

There is a rumble of premonition in the fact that the first talking film to make itself heard in this volume and therefore to lead to the sound parade is Josef von Sternberg's *The Blue Angel*, made in Germany in 1929. For above and beyond this picture's being a mordant work of cinema art and a surprisingly early example of effective wedding of picture and sound, it marks the first all-out screen appearance of a kind of woman and a quality of sex that have become progressively more insistent in the culture of talking films.

The woman that Marlene Dietrich exudes in this dark, degenerate tale of the destruction of a German schoolmaster by a faithless cabaret girl is so far advanced beyond the limits of the sleek, husband-stealing vamps, the poignant, self-sacrificing mistresses and the shimmying bowlfuls of "it" that so inadequately stated the attraction of women for men in silent films, it's no wonder she caused a world sensation, launched Miss Dietrich on a fabulous career and became, as it were, the grandmother of a whole slew of notable screen sluts.

Some critics say *The Blue Angel* is important primarily because it so presciently shows the immaturity and sadism of the German middle class. It does this, beyond any question. In its singular contemplation of

The cabaret singer, Lola, flaunts her attractions in the cheap nightclub where students gather and where the hapless professor goes to spy on them.

"Falling in Love Again" is the song with which Lola thrills the customers, but not the other female entertainers.

the sudden disintegration of a pillar of bourgeois society under the quick, corrosive influence of a strong application of gutter sex, it starkly reveals the imperfection and fraudulence of the façade of middle-class decency and discipline that its ponderous hero represents. It sourly suggests the soggy culture out of which Nazism oozed. And in the sadistic frenzy of the schoolboys to torment and destroy their hated teacher after they have witnessed his weakness for the cabaret girl, we may spot the incipient viciousness of later Hitler Youth.

But I find *The Blue Angel* most engrossing because of the opening it makes upon the whole darksome, subter-ranean area of psychoneurotic sex. Where the custom in silent pictures was simply to treat the primal urge as a powerful but usually unholy and sinful appetite that overwhelms men *and* women by its sheer physical rush and urgency, the revelation in this picture is a sickly image of sex as a passion mixed up with deep obsessions to dominate and get revenge. And where the evil of it in the silents was mainly its immorality, the evil of it in *The Blue Angel* is its corruption into a social disease that infects the aggressions of people and causes them to act in debased and vicious ways.

The great Professor Rath, its stern protagonist, is no

The scorn with which Lola (Marlene Dietrich) views her suitor, Professor Rath (Emil Jannings), is manifest from the first, but never turns him away.

more than a petty brute whose badgering and bullying of his teenage pupils is apparently his only means of releasing his inhibitions and rewarding his stuffy bachelorhood. Thus it would seem a mere extension of his desire to rule the boys that causes him to trail some of them to The Blue Angel, a low-class cabaret, when he discovers they are going there to ogle a female entertainer whose photograph he has snatched from one of them. And likewise it would seem but a fervor to show his boastful authority that first sends him to the dressing room of Lola, the sultry singing star.

But, of course, it is the pull of voyeurism and a resentment of her attractiveness that hauls him into her presence, and it is desire to vaunt his masculine command, as much as it is lust for fornication, that makes

him fall for her lures to go to bed. Likewise, it is his ignominy, rather than any vestige of physical desire, that keeps him attached to the woman after she has deceived and degraded him.

Similarly, the basic urge in Lola, this insolent cabaret girl with the long legs, the bare thighs, the garters, the provocatively ornamented crotch, the smoldering eyes, the moistening armpits and the husky voice that sings "Falling in Love Again," is not to enjoy coition. It is to vanquish and debase this stupid man who has dared to intrude himself upon her with his air of superiority. It is the urge to take vengeance upon him, which is the usual latent urge of prostitutes, and, in this particular case, to show contempt for the smug middle class he represents.

These strange and ugly intimations which creep out like worms in the film were a new kind of Freudian dissection of human behavior when they were first shown on the screen. They still stand as startling revelation in the overworked sex-drama genre.

The Blue Angel was made by Sternberg at the personal and urgent request of Emil Jannings, the distinguished German actor, whom he had directed in Hollywood in *The Last Command* (1928). Sternberg was a young American director who, in four years and nine silent films, had advanced himself from the obscurity of a cutter to the gaudy distinction of being the most aggressive *enfant terrible* (outside of Erich von Stroheim) in American films. Although there had been some friction between him and Jannings while they were making *The Last Command,* the famous actor apparently trusted the director enough to seek his help when he went back to Berlin and got ready to make his first plunge into the uncertain realm of the talking film.

For this initial venture, which was to be done in German, of course (with, as it turned out in production, an English version shot simultaneously), Jannings chose a novel, *Professor Unrat*, by Heinrich Mann. It was a story of an eminent school teacher who lost his position and caste when he married a demimonde singer and thereafter disgraced himself in gambling and cheap politics. It was a bitter arraignment of society at the time it was published, 1905.

Evidently Jannings chose it because it followed the general line of the kind of stories in which he had been popular since his brilliant appearance in F. W. Murnau's *The Last Laugh* (1924). These were stories of fallen idols—men of substance and authority who, for one reason or another (usually women), were reduced to ruin and shame. In *The Last Laugh,* he was a hotel doorman who got drunk and lost his job. In E. A. Dupont's superb *Variety* (1925), he was a stellar trapeze performer who succumbed to jealousy. And he likewise was several sorts of failures in the silent films he did in Hollywood—*The Way of All Flesh* (1927), *The Patriot* (1928), *Sins of the Fathers* (1929) and *The Last Command*.

With Mann's complete endorsement and the nominal collaborative help of three German writers, who Sternberg maintains in his amusing autobiography, *Fun in a Chinese Laundry,* had virtually no hand in it, the protean director prepared a screenplay which departed considerably from Mann's original story. His changes were mainly in the cutting of the latter part, updating it and reshaping the role of the girl.

Of major importance, as a consequence, was the choice of an actress to play this role, a subtly corrosive creature who is the *dea ex machina.* Sternberg describes with zest and humor the circumstances under which he found an undistinguished actress who was then in a play in Berlin and perceived her exquisite possibilities, despite their complete obscurity to Jannings and everyone else. This may be. Erich Pommer, the producer of *The Blue Angel,* once told me that Sternberg tried at first to get a prominent German actress, Greta Massine, to play the crucial role. When he couldn't get her, he fretfully settled for this odd and unpromising girl, whose name was Marlene Dietrich and who *had* sung in cabarets. There is no point in quibbling about it. The important thing is that Sternberg did pick Miss Dietrich to play Lola and got a famous performance from her. It is not to take one whit from his credit or from Jannings' to say that it is the aura exuded by Miss Dietrich that gives this film its unique cachet.

Jannings is fine, beyond question, and his powerful projection of Rath provides the dramatic provocation for the subtle reactions of the girl. His deft establishment of the teacher in the opening scenes—with his loftiness toward his landlady when she brings his breakfast to his rooms, his arrogance toward his pupils, the way he domineers them (especially the more timid and toadying), the way he wipes his glasses, blows his nose, struts his command of English by speaking Hamlet's "To be or not to be" soliloquy—provides an immediate and repugnant indication of a bloated egotist.

And it is he who propels the drama forward with the obtuseness of a charging bull, as he lunges for the raw temptations that Lola so deliberately waves, rushes for her sly seductions, puts himself in the way of being speared. His brutish reaction to the business of her tossing her panties in his face the time he first goes to berate her in her smoky dressing room is like the first arrogant, contemptuous tangle of a bull with a fluttering cape. He snorts at the miserable insult, but he returns the next night for more. (Incidentally, Sternberg's staging of this scene in the dressing room is so cumulative of detail, so suggestive of closeness and heat, one

practically experiences with the teacher the tousled garment's odor and warmth.)

Going on, Jannings' truculent performance of Rath's bullheaded conceit when he is got drunk and falsely adulated by the manager of the cabaret is vividly illustrative of his bovine plunging toward doom. So is his dudgeon toward the school's headmaster when he is censured for the scandalous thing he has done and pugnaciously accepts his dismissal, or his fatuous responses to the flattery of Lola's associates when they get him to crow like a cock at the wedding night. In every respect, Jannings gives us an excruciating understanding of vanity, lust and brute aggression that drives this man to his ruin. And he finally presents a haunting picture of the last stage of Rath's decay in a fit of maniacal cock-crowing on the cabaret's smoky stage before an audience of his former pupils who have come to hoot at him.

But the air of evil and corruption that wafts so heavily through this film comes from the sultriness of

Irresistibly drawn to Lola, the professor seals his doom when he persuades her to marry him.

Sternberg, too, used unrelenting realism to tell his sordid story of puritanism debauched, exemplified by the professor and the cabaret singer, with Guste (Rosa Valetti) as an interfering virago.

Lola, from the intensity with which she is played. How much of this is Sternberg, his sense of the mechanics of a slut and his skillfulness in surrounding such a creature with a noxiously steamy atmosphere, and how much of it is Miss Dietrich is hard to analyze. Sternberg suggests she was the puppet, that he manipulated the strings.

Certainly he was the master who had her do such impertinently obscene things as the business of tossing the panties, grossly spitting into her mascara box, dropping cigarettes under her dressing table and making Rath get down and pick them up so that he will be within inches of her bare legs and her contiguous erogenous zone. It was Sternberg who gave her the

cruel line, "You've come back; they always do," when the ponderously proud schoolmaster returns to her dressing room. And it was he who directed Lola's sudden and viciously autocratic switch from seductress to commanding virago on their fatal wedding night.

But it is Miss Dietrich's own magnetism, her weird way of sinking her eyes behind an enigmatic curtain, her ability to blend just the right tones of come-hither and go-to-hell in that "Falling in Love Again" song that put individuality into the character the director shaped for her.

It is notable that Sternberg does not give us any scenes of Rath and Lola making love, none of the sort of erotic acrobatics that have shown up in later sex-

75

charged films. This is tremendously important, for it is all too suggestively implied in the few shots he shows of the teacher fumbling clumsily and grossly with the slut that any sex act between them would be disgustingly callow and crude, totally without pleasure for either of them. This leads us back to the premise that it is sex in its more neurotic form that is the essence of this picture. It is the lust-bloated arrogance of a man who thinks he can impose his domination and his whole stuffy, sterile way of life simply by having a woman go to bed with him.

The clue to this fatuous self-deception is the early attitude of Rath that he can have relations with Lola in the conventions of the hide-bound middle class. When he wakes up in the morning after his first night with her in her room, he has the indolent air of a burgher after a stodgy rut with his *frau*. Likewise, he is deluded when the manager of the Blue Angel boasts that his own special skill as a magician puts him in the professorial class. Rath actually thinks his stuffy status as a "herr professor" is looked up to in this place. And he falls for the mocking deception of Lola wearing a proper bridal gown for their obscenely vulgar wedding. He still thinks he has conquered her.

Thus the crux of the drama is the explosion of this ridiculous conceit with the denouement of Lola's cruel perversion of the purpose of sex. Suddenly and shockingly she shows Rath on their wedding night that her seeming interest in him was but means to delude and dominate. By making him pick up the bundle of lewd photographs of her that he has spilled on the floor in indignation, she drives home the devastating point that her sex is but an article in commerce and she uses it as she will. From his smug and smiling contentment, shown in the way he smokes a fat cigar, he is suddenly dumped into a strange state of shock and bewilderment. The flimsy props of his illusions are knocked out from under him, and he finds himself stricken and helpless in an alien and hostile milieu.

From here on, the morbid demonstration is the sucking of this brutally deflated man into the maw of the vulgar environment that Lola and the Blue Angel exploit—the environment of common, sex-starved people gorging sausages, swilling beer and ogling the fat, concupiscent women who rouse their animal appetites. It is an environment from which the broken bourgeois ironically crawls at the end to die at his desk in the schoolroom from which he detached himself so arrogantly.

This being an early talking picture, it is interesting to see how economical Sternberg is with talk. He packs some essential information and personality into the dialogue, which is as it should be, and he develops a great deal of stimulation with Lola's naturally included song. But most of his best communication of character and atmosphere come in the pictorial presentation that is done with silent techniques. So able is Sternberg with details, so graphically does he describe the setting of the Blue Angel, its personnel and its clientele, that one can almost sense the body odors, the stink of stale beer and cheap perfume. It is as though he has commanded in this picture not only the dimension of sound but that of smell. This is one of the things about *The Blue Angel* that makes it an extraordinary film.

Significant and premonitory is the fact that Lola, for all her perversity, is still a provocative creature when we last see her in the company of a handsome new actor. She is unloving and self-serving, but she has that kind of arrogant allure that makes her the secret envy of women and a vicarious challenge to men.

It was this quality that Sternberg tried to carry on in the series of films that he made with a glamourized Miss Dietrich in Hollywood during the next several years. The first of the lot, *Morocco,* which has Gary Cooper as co-star, was released in America in 1930, ahead of *The Blue Angel* in fact. It is the best of the Hollywood series, but neither Sternberg nor Miss Dietrich ever again reached, together or separately, the level of this ground-breaking classic German film.

Paul Baumer (Lew Ayres) is a young student in Germany when the fiery slogans of the First World War make the Army irresistible to him and his classmates.

All Quiet on the Western Front

1930

Screenplay by Dell Andrews, Maxwell Anderson and George Abbott, from the novel by Erich Maria Remarque; directed by Lewis Milestone; cameraman, Arthur Edeson; musical score by David Broekman; produced by Carl Laemmle, Jr., for Universal.

Katczinsky	Louis Wolheim
Paul Baumer	Lew Ayres
Himmelstoss	John Wray
Tiaden	George (Slim) Summerville
Muller	Russell Gleason
Gerard Duval	Raymond Griffith
Kemmerich	Ben Alexander
Peter	Owen Davis, Jr.
Mrs. Baumer	Beryl Mercer
Poster Girl	Joan Marsh
Suzanne	Yola d'Avril

War being man's most murderous, monstrous and melodramatic means of joining in mortal conflict, it is natural that it should have been a perpetually fascinating subject for the makers of films. No action could be more graphic than the clash of men at arms, no spectacle more horrendous than that of masses of people charging to their deaths. And in the dramatization of warfare, which could be done on the screen with a

77

The boredom, the homesickness that war imposes on young men was brilliantly caught by director Lewis Milestone.

magnitude and realism possible in no other medium, a maximum host of emotions might be aroused in an audience. Fear, pride, hatred, chauvinism, agony and grief—these and many more could be excited by the reenactment of the aspects of war. And war in any age, in the present or in the story-book ranges of the past. It is amazing how many motion pictures have been about, or have included, the occurrence of war.

It is also amazing how varied have been the dramatists' points of view on this most vast and inhuman method for resolving the animosities of men. In *The Birth of a Nation* and *Intolerance* (which see), Griffith presented war as brutal but bold and romantic. In the heat of battle, the Little Colonel displays the bravery, zeal and compassion that are so nobly compacted in him. In the assault of the army of Cyrus on the walls of Babylon, the massive murderousness of warfare is magnified into a morbid, majestic symphony. Likewise, in his 1918 epic, *Hearts of the World*, Griffith represented war as a sort of Herculean conflict in which the defenders of a right and noble cause oppose a dark and despicable enemy, despoiler of women, the hated Hun. This was the general sentiment and attitude in all the American films, even the slapstick comedies, that were made at the time about the First World War.

During the 1920's, a trend toward "debunking" war

and emphasizing its anguish in close-up, personal terms was developed by novelists and playwrights. John Dos Passos' novel, *Three Soldiers*; Maxwell Anderson's and Laurence Stallings' play, *What Price Glory?*; and R. C. Sherriff's sensitive English drama, *Journey's End*, were pacesetters in an onrush of cries against the cruelty of war. As usual, this trend was evident, in a few years, on the screen.

The first truly overwhelming American film about the First World War was *The Big Parade,* directed by King Vidor, which came out in 1925—the same year, incidentally, as Sergei Eisenstein's *Potemkin* (which see). It gives a stupendous comprehension of the accumulation of military power in famous scenes of the American forces moving up to the front, an awesome concept of the rifleman's viewpoint on a battle (Belleau Wood), and the shock and horror of killing and seeing one's comrades killed. But it is, in the end, a familiar acquiescence to the romantic myths of war: the hero, engulfed in patriotism and looking for thrills beyond those of his usual rounds as a playboy, enlists in the American Expeditionary Force, goes to France as an infantry soldier, joins in the camaraderie of the lusty doughboys, has a romance with a French peasant girl, is moved into battle, fights grimly, sees his buddy killed, loses his leg from shrapnel and comes out a seasoned,

78

Realistic battle scenes gave dimension to the great anti-war story.

serious man who returns to France when the war is over to find his peasant sweetheart again. It is, in short, a war film that concludes triumphantly.

Up to this time, the changeless thesis of the Hollywood war movies was that courage, perseverance and power, the kind of power that "our side" could muster, would prevail over all adversities. And, of course, beyond any question, our side was always right. Then, in 1929, a German novel, *All Quiet On the Western Front,* was written by Erich Maria Remarque, a journalist who had been drafted into the German Army at eighteen and had been wounded five times in the First World War. It was immediately published in English in the United States. Although it was not a story of "our side" but of the German foot soldier in the war, and was passionately pacifistic, it became a roaring bestseller overnight and was bought right away by Universal, which assigned Lewis Milestone to make it into a film.

Mindful, no doubt, of the sensational success of *The Big Parade,* and advantaged now by the opportunity to communicate more with dialogue, Milestone attacked the task of putting this novel on the screen with emphasis on realism and total, despotic tragedy. Huge sets were built on the back lot: a French town, an entire battlefield; and extraordinary time and care were taken in making the picture "right." The world premiere was in April 1930, at the Cathay Theater in Los Angeles, and critical and public admiration was as great as it had been for *The Big Parade.*

All Quiet tells the story of a German boy who is aroused by the fervent talk of his schoolmaster to believe that in war the human spirit has its greatest opportunity to express its nobility, and, at the same time, the individual can best serve the fatherland. With such myths in his head, the youngster goes into the Army with a group of his friends, expecting the experience of warfare to be something like an athletic game.

He has his first taste of brutality and sadism from a roaring drill sergeant, a former friend, who compels the trainees to crawl in mud, endure hardships and suffer personal indignities. When sent to the front, however, our lad discovers that this training only began to foretell the harsh humiliation of the battlefield. The unit goes into the trenches, has its first horrible brush with death and faces the ultimate awareness that war is without humanity or hope.

More strongly than by any previous war film, save perhaps *The Big Parade,* the viewer was pulled into this experience, made to identify almost totally with the German lad and his comrades. Such complete self-association with soldiers in German uniforms was, indeed, a new sensation for American audiences. The fact that the actors spoke English without a trace of accent did allay the shock of feeling sympathy for what was then still regarded as "the enemy."

The point of dramatic explosion, the initial flash of horror in the film, is the first encounter of the fresh troops with actual death. This is the point of collision of the myth and reality, the smash of the mind filled with ideals and totally unprotected against the sudden, stabbing comprehension of the ghastliness of this awful thing. Milestone made this scene unmercifully vivid. The company has gone into no-man's-land at night to stretch barbed wire. Though the mission is regarded as routine, and the men even joke about it nervously at the start ("I'll give you all clean underwear when we get back," the wise old sergeant promises), the group is fired upon out of the darkness and one of the men is hit. He screams in agony out there someplace. We hear his terrified cries, along with the young and startled soldiers. One, pierced by his comrade's agony, rushes away to rescue him. When he eventually returns, he is lugging the youth's dead body. And, in front of the others, the sergeant roundly upbraids him for exposing

Not even a cemetery is sacred ground when the attack is launched.

himself to bring in a dead man. "It's just a corpse," he says, "no matter whose it is."

This is the moment at which all slogans, all the cant about the glory of war, are blown away. From here on—and from the scene which follows, wherein the shaken hero, the next day, has a sudden attack of the screaming meemies (or shell shock, as it was later called) and runs berserk through the trenches—the picture piles horror upon horror, fatality upon fatality, until the ironic end. It says that the life of the soldier is exposed to a murderous anarchy. He is just a warm body in the tumult of a senseless fate. The individual is of no importance whatsoever; he has to protect himself from the great, nebulous and inefficient military organization in which he is caught up as much as he does from the gunfire and the sudden onrush of the so-called enemy. This is evidenced by the instinctive way the

soldiers band together in small groups to scrounge for food, which is not provided in adequate quantity by the military machine, and to seek comfort and survival in their own small, cooperative comradeship.

The pattern of existence is circumscribed by the fight for food and the fight for survival, which is most harshly represented in vivid scenes of bloody hand-to-hand trench warfare, in which faceless waves of grimy French poilus charge the German trenches with their deadly fixed bayonets, overwhelm befuddled comrades, are frenziedly beaten off and forced to withdraw, and then face a ferocious counterattack by the remaining Germans. Within this endless pattern, which includes visits to rest camps behind the lines, the slow and inexorable erosion of the human body and spirit goes on.

Paul, the smooth-faced, sensitive hero, played by the

80

young Lew Ayres, goes with a couple of other fellows to visit one of their comrades in a field hospital. The lad's leg has been amputated and he is dying from shock and loss of blood, which provides the morbid material for his discovery of the loss of his leg and then for Paul's horror at discovering that the medics will pay no attention to the dying soldier. While his comrades are with him, the wounded boy dies, and his friends go away from the hospital carrying his cherished watch—and his shoes.

Next, Paul is stunned by the experience of killing a Frenchman himself. In a sudden, lone encounter in a shellhole, he drives his bayonet into the Frenchman's gut, then is forced to stay with him through the night while the fellow slowly dies, muttering his pain. In the dawn, Paul addresses his dead body, "Forgive me, comrade," and then cries, "Oh, God, why do they do this to us? We only wanted to live, you and I!"

This is followed by an interlude of pleasure with a trio of French peasant girls—a declaration that there is no animosity between individuals—and an idyllic bit in which Paul and one of the girls make love, off screen, while we hear their voices speaking softly in an old farmhouse. The scene is too idealistic, but it serves as a valid contrast to the hideousness of war.

But the menace reappears the next morning when the fellows are marched off to the front past piles of coffins that have been stacked in preparation for the next big assault. On this trip to the front, Paul is wounded, sent back to the hospital and beholds the terror of a man who thinks he is being taken into what the men called the "dying room." Here again is a grisly indication of the feeling of distrust and helplessness the men have toward their own organization, which supports the major theme of the horrible insignificance of the individual in the deadly mechanism of war.

Now Paul is sent home. He is triumphant. He has not been killed. But he finds home no comfort, no answer. His mother treats him as though he were a boy—in a scene that is much too maudlin, incidentally, for present-day taste, but was hailed at the time because of the performance of Beryl Mercer, a favorite actress of mother roles in silent films. And Paul is disgusted and driven to an angry outburst when he visits his old school and finds his teacher still rousing the schoolboys with chauvinistic cant.

Paul is returned to his company, finds it almost completely changed, with new boys in the places of old comrades who have been killed or lost. But he is happy to find his top sergeant, Katczinsky, the father image, still there. Maybe, with "Katz" to protect and guide him, Paul will be miraculously safe. In the next scene, however, the two are in an open field when an enemy airplane swoops out of the sky and ruthlessly machine-guns the defenseless men. The sergeant is hit. Paul lugs him to a dressing station, the burden of responsibility now reversed, and he stays beside him while Katczinsky dies.

The last episode in the picture is a classic scene in films. Paul is back in the trenches, looking through a watch-hole into no-man's-land. Someone offscreen is playing wistfully on a harmonica. Paul sees a butterfly clinging to a weed in front of the sandbag parapet. Momentarily heedless of danger—or fatalistically indifferent, perhaps—he stretches his arm gently toward the butterfly. He wants to touch this singular symbol of beauty and innocence in a nightmare world. As Paul exposes himself, Milestone cuts to a close-up of a French sniper drawing a bead on him, then has a slow, ominous montage of close-ups of Paul and the sniper, back and forth. Just as the hand is about to close on the butterfly, we hear the sniper's shot. The hand goes slack, the fingers dangle. The harmonica continues playing for a few beats. And that is the end of the picture, except for a tear-wiping epilogue in which we see a ghostly file of soldiers marching obliquely away from the camera, into a misty void, looking back silently at the audience with sad, accusing eyes.

Inevitably, this picture—the haunting title of which implied the irony in the familiar phrase so often used in daily press dispatches, "All quiet on the Western front" —staggered observers accustomed to some sentimental reprieve, some hope, in films of war. It stunned and

Happily reunited with his old top sergeant, Katczinsky (Louis Wolheim), Paul regards the tough veteran as his personal amulet.

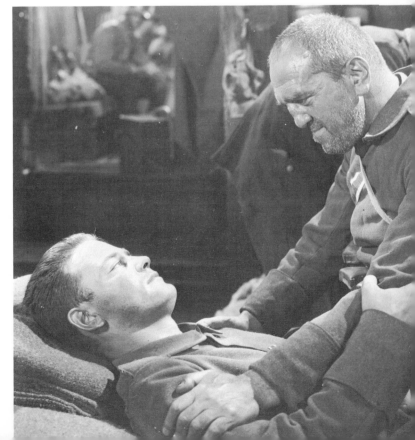

overwhelmed them with its illusion of reality, which was considerably enhanced by its blunt (but often mawkish) dialogue. The latter, incidentally, was dubbed into the language of each country in which the film was shown.

Louis Wolheim, a rock-faced stage actor, was praised for his playing of the role of Katczinsky, a performance that injected a vital measure of manly sentiment. George "Slim" Summerville is dry and pungent as a spavined corporal, and Raymond Griffith, a popular comedian of the "silents," is good in the cameo role of the Frenchman who dies in the shellhole. But Lew Ayres is superior as Paul. His performance in this picture launched him on an interesting career which included his origination of the role of the humanitarian physician in the series of *Dr. Kildare* films and his public avowal as a conscientious objector (he served in the Army Medical Corps) in the Second World War.

When *All Quiet* was first shown in Germany in 1930, it was very well received, but Nazi agitators, flooding the country, endeavored to sabotage it by releasing snakes and rats in theaters where it was shown. It was totally banned by Hitler when he came to power in 1933, and was not allowed again in Germany until 1952, when it was shown in some 4,000 theaters in West Germany, to large success. Several times through the 1930's, it was re-released in the United States, and a heavily cut version of it was circulated in 1950 at the time of America's involvement in Korea. But for all its pacifistic message, it could not discourage recurrences of war. It was—and is—a haunting guidepost that rises starkly and unheeded on the screen.

In the trenches and dugouts of the front line, the irony of war is underscored when Paul is killed while reaching out to touch an errant butterfly.

1931

The Public Enemy

Screenplay by Harvey Thew, from a story by Kubec Glasmon and John Bright; directed by William A. Wellman; photographed by Dev Jennings; produced by Warner Brothers.

Tom	James Cagney
Matt	Edward Woods
Mike	Donald Cook
Mamie	Joan Blondell
Mother	Beryl Mercer
Gwen	Jean Harlow
Bugs Moran	Ben Kendricks, Jr.
Paddy Ryan	Robert Emmett O'Connor
Nails Nathan	Leslie Fenton
Bess	Louise Brooks
Putty Nose	Murray Kinnell
Kitty	Mae Clark

The deadly chatter of machine guns and the piercing screech of automobile tires on vehicles wildly careening around the corners of city streets were among the most iterative noises that blared from the screen in the years immediately following the introduction of sound. These were the characteristic noises that accompanied the wave of gangster films that came, like a swarm of hornets, with this new element.

Historically, there is a question whether the big rush

Tom (James Cagney) and Matt (Edward Woods) grow up together in the slums, go from petty thievery to hijacking and finally to bootlegging as their way of making it.

of films about crime and the folkways of racketeers and gangsters, which was a major manifestation in the culture of American films, would have come—at least, in the volume and with the overwhelming impact that it did in the early 1930's—without the dimension of sound. It is obvious that the physical propulsion and shock effect of these films, good or bad, were due in large measure to the newness and amazement of having one's ears filled with noises of crime and the unaccustomed lingo of the tough guys, their lurid jargon and their punctuating snarls.

But of equal historical reason for this outbreak of gangster films was the simultaneous conjunction of two major social trends. The surge of organized crime that came in this country in the 1920's as a consequence of the Prohibition law and the inducement it gave to the expansion of illegal traffic in beer and liquor reached an explosive climax in 1929 with the St. Valentine's Day massacre in Chicago. This horrifying incident, in which a whole platoon of gangsters was lined up against a wall and shot by a firing squad of rivals, finally brought home to a torpid nation the immensity and ferocity of organized crime.

In that same year, the flimsy figment of financial prosperity and the illusions of endless luxury that went with it came tumbling down in the great Wall Street crash which prefaced the terrible Depression of the next few years. This shocking and soon too-painful notice that our vaunted security had been based on faulty economics and deceptive salesmanship disillusioned the public and left large segments of it prone to the cynicism and rebellion that whined and snarled in the gangster films.

Significantly, the movie-makers—and the novelists and playwrights, too—had been slow in discovering and deciphering the surge of organized crime. The first

A historic scene of social alienation—Tom pushes a grapefruit in the face of his mistress Kitty (Mae Clark) to assert his rise in the world.

novels on this subject did not come until the mid-1920's. The first stage play to treat it realistically was *Broadway* in 1926. The first film to identify the Prohibition gangster was Josef von Sternberg's *Underworld,* turned out in 1927 from a scenario by a Chicago newspaperman, Ben Hecht. It was followed the next year by such items as *The Drag-Net, The Racket* and *Dressed to Kill,* all silent and unsensational as statements of a sweeping social plague.

But with the coming of sound and the prompting of mounting crime waves and massacres, the gangster film suddenly broke the barrier and became a dominant genre. Ten or twelve of them were turned out in 1929. Scores came along in 1930 and 1931. The coupling of them with the headlines and with the awareness of such new kings of crime as Al Capone, John Dillinger and Owney Madden caused them to seem real exposés, vivid and true-to-life reflections of what was happening in the blazing underworld. The fact that they were mostly overstatements, blatant compendia of clichés picked from the journalists of gangland, was not sensed by the public at first. They satisfied a morbid curiosity. Also, they moved excitingly; the action scenes were usually shot with mobile silent cameras, and sound effects, were added later on.

The most important thing they did, however—the three or four great ones, that is—was give a fearful intimation of the nature of the gangster mind. This notorious criminal individual, what sort of creature was he, with his brazen proclivity to private warfare, his willing exposure to mortal peril and his readiness to betray his partners, all in his passionate quest for power? He was an awesome enigma, the modern-day badman of the West, but with a difference. He was a consequence of societal conditions. The public wanted to know about him.

The first classic revelation is that given by Edward G. Robinson in *Little Caesar,* made by Mervin LeRoy for First National (Warner Brothers) in 1930. It is a brilliant and chilling picture of a sardonic and sentimental Italian-American, modeled more or less on Capone, who goes after power with a vengeance and is betrayed and destroyed in the end. Robinson's Ricco (Little Caesar) may be a fictional character, skillfully realized by the actor from a script by W. R. Burnett, but he is consistently concentrated and he is believable.

However, Ricco comes at us fully fledged and professionally skilled. He is a postgraduate criminal when the picture begins. Therefore, I find a better drama and, indeed, the most compelling gangster film to be *The Public Enemy,* made by William Wellman with James Cagney in the leading role and released by Warner

Brothers six months later, in April 1931. This is the first one to offer speculation on how the gangster evolved, his social origination and his seduction into a life of crime and then into gangland complications by the opportunities that society itself held out, all with incisive graphic detail and illustration of corrosive character.

It follows the standard format of all the early gangster films—the initial insignificance of the hero, his strategic thrust for power, his brief enjoyment of underworld preeminence and then his sudden, ignominious rubbing out. The devices for these steps may have varied, but the consequence was always the same. In *The Public Enemy,* however, the inspection of the hero's life begins much earlier than usual. It begins with his boyhood in a Chicago slum, child of a widowed Irish mother and pal of a swayable scamp with whom he fetches pails of beer for neighbors and shoplifts in big department stores. In a 1909 urban environment, which Wellman pictorially describes as a welter of crowded streets, stockyards, beer wagons, corner saloons and Salvation Army Bible-thumpers, the youngster is already launched as a vandalistic mischief-maker and a committer of petty crime.

Now it is six years later, in the chronological phasing of the film, and our hero, Tom, and his pal are poolhall roughnecks, ready to move along under the tutelage of a small-time Fagin, a sleazy character named Putty Nose (whose pastime is playing "I'm Forever Blowing Bubbles" on the tinny piano in the back

Tom and Matt, gaudy racketeers now, pick up a wealthy society girl, Gwen (Jean Harlow), who is on the prowl for excitement.

room), to the intermediate step of a fur robbery and an initial ugly tangle with the police. Now the role is taken by Cagney, a small, wiry, impudent youth (or apparent youth, at this stage), and the character begins to take form. Tom is a hard, brazen, cheeky little ruffian, schooled for a criminal career and contemptuous of the patriotism of his older brother, who is prepared to go off to the First World War.

Wellman indicates clearly that his delinquent gets caught in the pull of big-time crime because he and his pal are available to do jobs for the barons of booze who are bootlegging illegal liquor to the good citizens crying for it. A shot of crowds of bottle-smuggling homegoers on 1920 New Year's Eve makes the point that Prohibition made lawbreakers of the citizens and stimulated the traffic the professional criminals battled to control. Tom's introduction to it is through a caper whereby he and his pal, Matt, are assigned to steal booze from a warehouse by syphoning it out of vats into a gasoline truck and making off with their haul in a hail of gunfire. After this, Tom is on the move. He abandons the cheap cap of his boyhood. He gets outfitted in tailor-made clothes, with snap-brim hat and camel's-hair coat. He is a slick, sporty, on-the-way-up punk.

Thus our underprivileged slum boy, who might have gone on to a bleak career of common crime if it hadn't been for Prohibition, is now involved in this new nefarious trade, which is practiced openly and boldly, with the paid-off connivance of the police, and is given such social encouragement that Tom can boast of his connections to his family. The fact that his brother scorns him when he returns wounded from the war is only further indication that his brother is a sap.

The requirement of this new brand of criminal is that he conform to the mores of the mob, that he take orders—kill, if he is told to, or put himself in the way of being killed. The enemy is the rival outfit, which is more assertive and formidable than the police. The maintenance of equilibrium is according to tacit rituals and codes. But such is the nature of the "business" and such are its possible rewards that it aggravates ambition, stimulates a hunger for power. The meanest qualities of the individual are brought out by the competitive atmosphere. Moves to upset the equilibrium result from changing attitudes. It is change in the individual that is the foremost fascination in the gangster film. And it is this manifestation of evolution that Cagney does so well.

His tough little guy, who stands so boldly with his feet spread, his head drawn back, his arms by his sides and extended outward with the fingers half clenched in fists, is an image of fierce determination and tightly controlled energy, and his quick, gravelly way of speaking conveys impertinence, impatience and brusque command. You see in him from the beginning a piece of human machinery that seems geared for no other action than that of propelling itself, rapidly, smoothly, quietly and satisfactorily to itself alone. He has the grace of a prizefighter or a dancer. This isn't surprising; Cagney was both before he came into motion pictures in 1929.

But what he slips into the role so slyly and with such

Tom and Matt come to the inevitable parting of the ways when the way is led by Gwen.

chilling effectiveness is a sense of the change of the gangster into a species of fiend. This is best illustrated in the film's most original scene, which is now one of the most famous and most often cited in gangster films. It is that in which Tom and his first mistress, acquired as a status symbol of his rise, are having breakfast in their cluttered apartment. He looks cheap and dimestore tacky in his rumpled silk pajamas; she looks dull in her dressing gown. The atmosphere reeks of Tom's boredom and restlessness. In an attempt at refined conversation, the mistress, played by Mae Clark, asks him what he would wish. He looks at her coldly, and, with a mean smirk, he snarls, "I wish you was a wishing well; then I could tie a bucket to you and sink you!" She whimpers foolishly, "Maybe you've found somebody you like better." For a moment, he doesn't move. Then he calmly picks up the half of grapefruit from his plate and, with a sudden, vicious forward thrust, as though throwing a punch, shoves it squarely and forcibly into her face.

This was and remains one of the cruelest, most startling acts ever committed in a film—not because it is especially painful (except to the woman's smidge of pride), but because it shows such a hideous debasement of regard for another human being. This simple act swiftly changes the audience's feeling for Tom, erases the expectation that he may by some miracle be redeemed. From here on, we know he is committed to power and violence, to his own private route of self-advancement and self-indulgence, which does not even have room for his pal, Matt. He is a vicious little monster, still fascinating to watch, but as erratic, unreliable and dangerous as a fer-de-lance.

We watch him go out now and make contact with a dazzling, slippery blonde, played voluptuously by young Jean Harlow, and we are engrossed and amused by the fulfilled prospect of fireworks and treachery here. We watch him move in on the layout of his fallible confederates in crime and ruthlessly, icily bump off his old boyhood preceptor, Putty Nose. This is a fine scene, incidentally, with the camera cutting away from the victim and panning around the room as Tom shoots Putty Nose at the piano; there is a jangled termination of the old "Blowing Bubbles" song; we hear the thump of the body as it hits the floor, and then the camera comes full on Tom's face as he says casually to Matt, who is with him, "Guess I'll call up Gwen. She may be home now."

We laugh at the utter bizarreness of Tom, in a riding costume, going to the stable in the suburbs where the horse that threw and killed his big-shot friend, Nails Nathan, is kept, at the outraged swagger with which he breezes into the barn, and then at a shot from the in-

side, which tells us that this ruthless little brute has actually taken gangland vengeance on a horse! There is grotesque humor in this action, but there is a sobering irony, too, for it tersely says that this hardened gangster knows no difference between people and animals. Furthermore, he has no compunction about shooting whatever he doesn't like.

Such is the concept of this strange breed that Wellman and Cagney present. The gangster, in his soaring egotism, becomes a frenzied anarchist. This creature, whom the public has fostered, is inevitably the public's enemy.

His elimination is standard. First his sidekick, Matt, is mowed down in a running gun battle with rivals. Tom abandons Matt to his fate. Then he himself is riddled in a fated fusillade. As he staggers away from this encounter, bloody and soaked by rain, he mumbles his first acknowledgment of vincibility: "I ain't so tough."

But Wellman and the authors have concocted a final retributive twist. They have planned it so that Tom is only wounded in that penultimate clash. He is taken to the hospital, where he and his brother are mawkishly reconciled, and arrangements are made for him to come home to mother to recuperate. To welcome him home, the family gathers; and, when there comes the knock at the door, the brother throws it open. There, standing in the hall, is the stiff form of Tom, swathed in bandages like a mummy out of a tomb. For a moment, it appears the living person. Then, as it starts to fall face forward into the camera, we sickeningly see it is a corpse and realize that Tom's gangland enemies have taken grisly vengeance on him.

This coldly conclusive image of the fate of the gangster was enough—or should have been enough—to carry the message that that sort of life did not pay. But it was questionable whether all the people who saw this film in the bleak years after its release—the out-of-work men sitting forlornly in the theaters that were their havens in Depression times, the youngsters who were fearful of the future—were revolted by it. Did they not feel with the gangster their own resentments against society? Did they not envy him his affluence and vicariously enjoy his burst of power?

Many people worried about this, and, in 1931, there came a wave of public outcry against the showing of gangster films. Pressure reached such intensity that the motion-picture industry was compelled to take steps to restrict the output. This contributed to the adoption of a Production Code. At the same time, an excess of crime pictures created audience apathy. The public soon shoved a grapefruit into the faces of the public enemies.

A Nous la Liberté

1932

Screenplay and direction by René Clair; music by Georges Auric; sets by Lazar Meerson; photography by Georges Périnal.

Emile	Henri Marchand
Louis	Raymond Cordy
Jeanne	Rolda France
Uncle	Paul Olivier
Paul	Jacques Shelly
Foreman	André Michaud
Maud	Germaine Oussey
Old Gentleman	Leon Lorin
One-time Prisoner	William Burke
Orator	Vincent Hyspa

How to put music to movies in order to achieve something more in the way of entertainment than a picture of someone singing or dancing or (what was simplest) just a picture with background music to set a mood was a much tougher challenge to film-makers than how to intrude dialogue. That, after all, was but a matter of controlling the mechanics of talk—keeping the action going and the actors from saying too much. But the trick of combining audible elements to reach a new cinematic form—a pattern of eye and ear enchantments to generate a sense of delight—was an esthetic problem much more difficult to solve.

It was appropriately, a young Frenchman, the dance-minded René Clair, who, along with Ernst Lubitsch in America, did most to discover and lay down the sightlines for using music to construct a new screen form, to liberate the musical motion picture from what he called "filmed theater." He found ways to, harmonize the rhythms of visual and aural images and make them rouse vibrant thoughts and feelings through a kind of choreographed cinema. His paramount achievement was a stunning conjunction of his style with a devilishly sharp, satiric story in *A Nous la Liberté*.

Clair had begun in the early 1920's as a maker of trick and abstract films with grandly exaggerated ideas —virtual fantasies they were, as farfetched and visually eccentric as Mack Sennett's wild comedies. His *The Crazy Ray* (1923), *Entr'acte* (1924) and *The Italian Straw Hat* (1927) are tokens of his understanding of the graphic aspects and energies of the medium.

With the coming of sound, he was doubtful that this mechanical fixture could be used to improve what he and many considered an exclusively visual device. Although hampered by commercial restrictions and governmental restraints imposed on French film-makers, he began to experiment. His first sound film, turned out in 1930, was *Sous les Toits de Paris* (*Under the Roofs of Paris*). It is a delightfully fanciful lark about an assortment of lyrical Parisians which begins with a street singer hawking the sheet music of the title song, thus starting a progressive pickup of the tune by singers and dancers all around. The following year came *Le Million*, which again is a fanciful tale of people in Paris spinning wildly around a bedeviled love affair, with action ranging from scenes at the Paris Opéra to a ludicrous football game. And in 1932, he presented *A Nous la Liberté*, an extraordinary social statement in the flexible form of a song film.

The secret of Clair's invention is that he never pretends or indicates that he wants the viewer to be literal or logical. He leaps at once into a process of pictorial and aural forgery in which the intimations of reality are frankly and clearly counterfeit. His settings, though reasonably natural, are just enough out of this world to let you know you are not expected to take them as the real thing. And his characters, though they look like real people and have recognizable traits, do not behave like real people. They jump out of the customary grooves of normal and even romantic behavior and go bouncing off on their own. And, of course, they frequently sing and get involved in patterns of movement that have the spontaneous rhythms of ballet. Yet they make very true and touching statements about life— especially in *A Nous la Liberté*.

Substantially, this joyous entertainment (the title of which loosely means *Freedom for All*) is an irreverent blast of objection to what it philosophically perceives as the enslavement of man's energies and spirit in a mechanized industrialized world. It mocks at the ambiguous system whereby men, tethered to machines, monotonously toil to manufacture the claptrap means of their own enjoyment. And it ends in a wonderfully spirited and hilariously satiric thrust at the indignity and absurdity of men wasting their lives chasing after wealth.

For it, Clair and his designer, Lazar Meerson, created sets that have the cheeky exaggeration of their free imagining. There is the industrialized prison in which we initially meet the two heroes. It bears a remarkable resemblance to a modern factory. There is the phonograph shop which Louis, the hero who first breaks out of jail, acquires by nefarious double-dealing. It looks like a noisy phonograph. And there's the big, shiny phonograph factory which Louis builds in his next step up and in which he so sternly regiments his workers that it has the air of a penitentiary. There are also subsidiary settings—Louis' office, his apartment, a workers' park—that convey, in their overelaboration, a subtle and mischievous wit.

The gist of the ironic thesis is put in the opening scene as the camera brings us in on a close-up of toy horses moving along on a conveyor belt in what we naturally assume from the evidence to be a toy factory. Then the camera dollies back and we discover that the men who are doing the work on these innocent, pleasure-giving items are prisoners in a penitentiary. As they perform their routine functions, they sing the title song in a slow mechanical tempo which sets the rhythm for their humdrum work. Thus the Liberty song is established as the ironic threnody of the enslaved.

This thought is carried on in the next sequence when Louis breaks out of jail, with the sacrificial help of his cellmate, the benign and cheerful little Emile, and makes his escape from the region by knocking a fellow off a bicycle and taking it, only to find himself involved in a bicycle race. While the cyclists are grinding along grimly, presumably *pour le sport,* they are accompanied by an auto filled with people—idlers, obviously—who tacitly taunt the athletes by happily singing the Liberty song.

It is the Liberty song, too, that the workers in Louis' phonograph factory sing as they punch the time clock, march to their places on the assembly line and go through the mechanical motions of putting together phonographs. The analogy to the prisoners and the implication that the working class is caught in a similar imprisonment—at least, in this factory—is clear.

The antithesis to this concept is represented by little Emile, who has no intention of working when he gets out of jail. He lies in a field of waving grasses and listens to a lyrical little song that is sung by the reedy voices of a chorus of invisible girls. But Emile, too, is susceptible to a kind of imprisonment. He is unwittingly captured by the illusion of romance.

Hauled back to prison for not working ("To work is freedom!" a pinch-nosed schoolmaster drones to his pupils in a comical insert), little Emile, at the window of his cell, hears a dulcet voice singing. Then he sees, in a vine-framed window across the way, a pretty girl who he thinks is doing the singing. He instantly falls in love with her, and, with only the barest effort, pulls the bars from his window and escapes. Outside in the street, beneath her window, he sees she is no longer there. However, the singing continues. Then he sees the girl come out the door. At the same time, the singing runs

Escaped from prison with a pal, Louis (Raymond Cordy) gets a job in a record shop, but is struck with a vision of big business.

down slowly. The charming voice has been coming from a phonograph! Yes, it has been coming from one of those boxes manufactured to delude man. Little Emile, so romantic and trusting, has been bewitched by a piece of merchandise!

Even so, his heart has been captured, and he follows the girl to the factory, where she and her uncle are clerical workers. And there he becomes a slave himself. Only he is not enslaved by the system. He is enslaved by love, which he thinks is as natural and attainable as it is played up to be in the popular songs. So he makes an unsatisfactory worker. He is so bewitched by the girl that he won't pay attention to business and fouls up the assembly line. He has workers stumbling over one another trying to catch up with the work they have missed. For this he is chased from the factory and lands in the office of the boss, who is Louis, of course, his old cellmate, now a well-tailored capitalist.

Here Clair injects a characteristic bit of symbolism and sentiment. At first, Louis is haughty toward Emile. He refuses to recognize him. Then later, alone with him in his big office, he pulls a gun on him. Emile laughs at this melodramatic gesture. Then Louis, fearing he will be betrayed, offers Emile money, a wad of banknotes, to go away. This cuts little Emile deeply. He looks into Louis' ice-cold eyes and shakes his head slowly and sadly. Louis clasps and squeezes his wrist, until his ring cuts into the flesh and drops of blood splatter on the banknotes on the desk. Both men observe this indication. Louis slowly takes his handkerchief and binds the wrist. There is a long pause. Emile winks at his old cell-

Louis' pal, Emile (Henri Marchand), is enraptured by the sight of a flower when he leaves prison behind—a Chaplinesque touch.

mate, and, as the strains of their Liberty song hum plaintively in the background, Louis solemnly winks back. They embrace now. The subterfuge is ended. And, as the music swells, they swing, arms locked, around the office and sing the last bars of the Liberty song.

From here on, the heroes are united in concealing the secret of their past and in recognizing the absurdity of their environment. That evening they get drunk at a big party (wherein Clair gloriously travesties the pomposities of expensive living), and finish by throwing spitballs at a portrait of Louis on the wall.

The next day, in Louis' office, he resolves to play cupid for Emile, and seeks the girl from among the employes by putting the information into a computing machine. The machine sends up her uncle, who is a greedy and venal old cuss, but he is willing to allow Emile to court her, in view of his friendship with the boss. Thus is romance reduced to the level of a mercenary deal.

The climax comes when Louis' identity is discovered by a gang of crooks who try to blackmail him, and he decides to take it on the lam. Before he goes, he has one function he is determined to perform. This is the dedication of a new automated factory, at which speeches are made by pompous statesmen and Louis is praised by the President of France.

But right in the midst of the ceremonies, while the suspicious police are closing in and a pompous speaker is following Louis' impromptu announcement that he is giving the factory to the employes, a mighty wind arises. It starts to blow the pages of the speaker's speech, then the high hats of the dignitaries. Then a satchel full of 1,000-franc notes, which Louis had in-

tended taking with him, slips from a hiding place on the factory roof and falls open, releasing the banknotes, which are blown into the yard below. As they sprinkle down over the assemblage, the astonished dignitaries clutch cautiously for them, then abandon their hats and grab greedily when a rain of money descends.

In a moment, the wind is whistling, the pages of the President's speech about liberty, equality and fraternity are being blown away, banknotes and high hats are swirling and the assemblage has broken up in a mad melee of undignified dignitaries chasing money while the cops chase Louis and Emile. It is an unspeakable shambles which, in a fluid montage, becomes resolved into a pattern of groups of people—dignitaries, workers, cops—racing rhythmically like dancers in a ballet, all to music, of course.

The end of the film is a completely sentimental conceit. In the lately cluttered yard of the new factory, the liberated workers are playing bowls. Others are fishing in the river. Others are dancing to the title song at an outdoor park. And Louis and Emile, in old clothing, are walking off down a country road, avoiding the dust of a passing limousine and happily singing "A Nous la Liberté." The terminal implication is that a spirit of freedom still resides in the soul of the average Frenchman—although, of course, this happy conceit is as

Louis' vision comes true when he makes himself the head of a huge company which manufactures records and the portable machines to accompany them.

much a sentimental fiction as are the characters and their environment.

Actually, the amount of music that Georges Auric composed for this pioneering picture was ridiculously limited, as compared with the amount that is generally written for a musical today. The title song does protean service. Otherwise there is the romantic tune, played on phonographs and barrel organs. There is a neat satiric hymn of praise sung by an offscreen male chorus as the phonographs roll off the new automated assembly line in the climactic scene. As a consequence, there is a certain monotony of the major melody. But that can be forgiven. The picture's infectious quality is in its wit, its rollicking tempo, its nutty performances by Henri Marchand and Raymond Cordy and its perpetual musicality. It is never sober or solemn. Work is for the birds, and commerce, social ritual and governmental dignity are overrated and absurd.

It is not surprising, however, that the film baffled the critics and audiences when it opened in Paris in January 1932. They were troubled by Clair's comprehension of industrial efficiency. They thought it too intellectual, not sufficiently farcical and gay. And, of course, they were still a bit wary about the musical form. However, its sharp sophistication was increasingly appreciated as years went by, and many film-makers drew inspiration from *A Nous la Liberté*.

One may note a strong strain of Charlie Chaplin's social philosophy and his idealization of the free spirit in the early musical films of Clair. Four years after the release of this picture, Chaplin's *Modern Times* came along, with a sequence that repeated almost exactly the comic business of the fouled-up assembly line. Someone asked Clair if he wasn't angry at Chaplin for cribbing from his film. "Of course not," Clair cheerfully answered. "After all, I've taken plenty from him."

And Emile winds up on the assembly line of Louis' factory, a condition not unlike the one he suffered in prison.

King Kong

Ann (Fay Wray), kidnapped by Kong, is protected by him against a giant lizard that threatens her.

1933

Screenplay by James Creelman and Ruth Rose, from an original story by Merian C. Cooper and Edgar Wallace; directed by Ernest B. Schoedsack and Mr. Cooper; technical director, Willis O'Brien; chief photographer, Edward Linden; musical director, Max Steiner; executive producer, David O. Selznick; produced by Radio-Keith-Orpheum.

Ann	Fay Wray
Denham	Robert Armstrong
Driscoll	Bruce Cabot
Captain Englehorn	Frank Reicher
Weston	Sam Hardy
Native Chief	Noble Johnson
Witch King	Steve Clemento
Second Mate	James Flavin
Lumpy	Victor Wong

The chief distinctions of this famed monster picture are conceded in the area of techniques—in the skill of manipulation of its miniatures and trick photography—and on the level of popular entertainment achieved with these mechanical effects; but they are seldom considered sufficiently adult to assign it to the ranks of the elite. *King Kong* is usually classed by highbrow critics among the lower order of cinema freaks, or among the higher order of what they lightly term *kitsch* or "camp."

Yet I find this fantastic fable of the capture of a giant primeval ape in an anachronistic, prehistoric jungle and its removal to the alien environment of New York City, where it breaks loose in a surge of love for a human female and is finally destroyed atop the Empire State Building, to be a pictorial allegory with implications more spacious and profound than had ever before been generated in a mere monster or science-fiction film. It is a pure photographic phantasm in which the range of the evolution of man from primate to urban cliff-dweller is spanned in one imaginative conceit, and several ironies of social imbalance are remarkably and morbidly symbolized.

I am sure that most of the millions who have seen and thrilled to this film in its perennially popular circulations have not calculated what it is about it that stirs their apprehensions and leaves them troubled and even distressed. Most viewers simply see it as an uncommonly awesome and amusing monster film. And I suspect that if they were confronted by the suggestion that it seeds their minds with a series of subconsciously connnective and disturbing images—images of the brutality and cruelty of civilized man, of the enslavement of the strong but ignorant masses, especially those of the Negro race; of the frustration of sex in a society dominated by machines—they would laugh at such an idea, as they laugh at much in the film—until they thought about it. Then they might see why I have picked this film.

King Kong is a prime example of a composite. It was compositely fabricated entirely in a studio, with miniature animated models of prehistoric beasts, including that of the monster hero, Kong, which was only eighteen inches high. These models were animated and photographed on strips of film with blank backgrounds,

On a ledge to which he has taken Ann, Kong is attacked once again, by a pterodactyl, another prehistoric masterpiece of the film's technicians.

and these were superimposed on matching photographs of live human action, fanciful paintings of jungle settings and such, to achieve the completed picture. And it was a composite in concept, being a conscious combination of the classic monster-picture plot with the currently expanding conventions of the popular true-life travel-adventure films.

It follows closely the pattern of *The Golem,* first made in Germany in 1915, which tells of a medieval statue into which a rabbi imparts life and which then falls in love with a young woman, only to be repulsed by her. Driven mad by this frustration, the creature goes berserk and plunges to death from a high tower. This is the basic pattern of most of the German monster films, which were made during the 1920's, and the series of films about deformed humans and frustrated freaks made by the ingenious Lon Chaney—*The Hunchback of Notre Dame* (1923), *The Phantom of the Opera* (1925), *London After Midnight* (1927). Such films of fanciful occurrence were extremely popular.

But in *King Kong,* this formula was combined with the character and atmosphere of the then increasingly more popular travel and wild-life films. Indeed, Ernest Schoedsack and Merian C. Cooper, who made *King Kong,* had distinguished themselves originally with this type of stranger-than-fiction film. Their *Grass* (1925) is a magnificent documentary of migratory herdsmen in Persia, and their *Chang* (1927) is an excellent documentary-fiction film that tells of a primitive family living in the jungle of Siam. These films, along with such others as Robert Flaherty's *Moana* (1926), W. S. van Dyke's *Trader Horn* (1931) and Frank Buck's *Bring 'Em Back Alive* (1932), had served to acquaint the public with wild and exotic areas and condition its abundant credulity for geographical and zoological caprice. Thus the illusory power of the motion picture gave a certain plausibility to the totally unscientific anthropological fantasy of *King Kong.*

An appeal to this power of illusion is made at the beginning of the film, with a realistic simulation of a travel-film enterprise. An expedition is departing New

93

A daring rescue by Jack Driscoll (Bruce Cabot) brings Ann back to the expedition ship and leads to the capture of the huge monster.

York City for an uncharted island in the Indian Ocean off Sumatra, where the expedition's director has learned there is a fantastic collection of strange beasts. It is his intention to make a motion picture of this mysterious place.

It is notable that Robert Armstrong, who plays Denham, the director, bears a certain resemblance to Frank Buck and has much the same quality of a carnival showman that Buck had. Also the fact that Denham picks up a beautiful, starving girl off the streets of New York on the night before departure to go along and play the heroine in his film had a similarity to the much-publicized episode of W. S. van Dyke selecting an unknown, inexperienced female extra to take to Africa to play the White Goddess in his location-made *Trader Horn.*

Schoedsack and Cooper have also continued to emphasize the real-life nature of the expedition, with the motion-picture camera conspicuous on the deck of the ship to make test shots and do rehearsals with the inexperienced girl, played by Fay Wray. It is only as they approach the mystery island, known as Skull Island because it has a mountain on it that looks like a skull, that they begin to intrude the air of menace that was conventional in jungle films. Mists hang around the island, great black birds hover over it and Max Steiner's monitory music rumbles ominously.

The arriving expedition discovers one end of the island to be separated from the vast interior by a great wall. It is on the other side of this wall, says Denham, that the strange animals live. As the people from the ship approach the near end, where the human inhabitants dwell, they hear the thumping of drums and a weird chant rising from a thousand human throats, "Kong! Kong! Kong!" Then they see through the trees the eerie glow of a strange, wild ceremonial taking place. The natives, some dressed as gorillas, are dancing in a circle around an altar to which a terrified native girl is lashed. When they spy the people from the ship, and especially the white girl, Ann, they become greatly excited. They want the "golden girl" to give as a sacrifice to Kong. Here is the first suggestion of the appeasement of this mysterious beast, this creature that calls up an image of the legendary minotaur, with the flesh of a human female. And the further suggestion that the beast would be gratified with *white* flesh enhances the erotic hint.

Of course, Denham and the ship's captain refuse the witch doctor and the native chief when they demand that Ann be turned over to them. But that night the natives kidnap her and take her back to the island, where they prepare her for sacrifice. They tie her to a large stake and place this in the ground on the far side

A pathetically subdued and shackled Kong is exploited in New York by Denham (Robert Armstrong), with the contrasting assistance of Ann and Jack.

of the wall; then they strike a huge gong to summon Kong from the interior and line the top of the wall to watch.

Now, out of the twisted trees and giant vines rises the huge black shape of the dreaded gorilla, with his great hideous face and shining eyes. Ann twists and writhes in terror, but of course there is no hope, as the menace music thumps like a heavy heartbeat and smoke from a hundred torches rises into the night. With his eyes flashing anticipation, Kong deftly lifts Ann from the stake and, clasping her to his vast chest, lumbers off into the jungle beyond the wall.

No sooner has this happened than a group of men from the ship arrive, led by Jack, the mate, who has by now become enamoured of Ann. When they learn what has happened to her, they boldly plunge into the jungle beyond the wall, hopefully going to her rescue—and

thus do we plunge from the initial period of comparative reality into the first phase of pure fantasy. For here, in the depths of this strange jungle, the men encounter giant beasts. "Something from the dinosaur family" is brought down with a gas bomb. While crossing a lake on a makeshift raft, they are attacked by a giant water monster.

On ahead, Kong, with Ann in his giant paw, comes upon one of the men on a log bridge. Very gently, Kong sets the girl on the ground, heroically thumps his chest a few times, then grandly destroys bridge and man. Ann escapes, but Kong rushes to her when he hears her screams and rescues her from a huge lizard in a marvelous prehistoric wrestling match. Kong wins, of course. He ends the battle by ripping the lizard's jaws apart, then tries, in his mute way, to show Ann that he is very fond of her—with the mood music slyly helping him.

Later on, there's another thrashing battle between Kong and a huge water snake, and yet another with a giant pterodactyl on a mountain ledge. But while this struggle is raging, Jack arrives and makes off with Ann, a perilous maneuver which Kong tries in vain to prevent.

Meanwhile, back at the wall, the scattered crewmen have reassembled and are wondering what to do, when Ann and Jack emerge from the jungle, with Kong crashing through not far behind. The giant ape, fired with passion, pushes down the gate, scatters the terror-stricken natives and goes after the whites, who are trying to escape in a boat. As a last delaying maneuver, they fling a gas bomb at the ape and, sure enough, it stops him. He falls anesthetized in his tracks! Now Denham realizes what a treasure they can have by lashing Kong in chains and taking him back to America. "We're millionaires, boys!" he exults. "I'll share it with all of you! We'll have his name up in lights on Broadway: Kong, the Eighth Wonder of the World."

Dissolve now to the inside of a theater. Denham comes out on the stage to introduce the show. "We have brought back the living proof of our adventure," he says. The curtains open and there on a platform is the heavily shackled Kong, and on the stage beside the platform stands Ann in an evening gown. "Look at Kong," shouts Denham. "He was a god in his world!" The great ape wrenches at his shackles. "There the beast and here the beauty!"

Then Jack is brought on in dinner jacket to pose with Ann for photographers and to announce the romantic culmination of the expedition. But Kong, seeing him, is infuriated with jealousy and hate. Further, the surprise of the photographers' flashes causes him to leap with fear. With a great crash and rending, Kong pulls free from his chains. The audience flees in panic. Kong breaks through the wall of the theater and terrifies pedestrians and motorists as he bursts into the street. Making straight for the building into which Jack has fled with Ann, he scales the outside of it, shoves his huge

King Kong on the loose in New York is a high point of the film, especially when he fights off a plane attack from the top of the Empire State Building. Illusion, animation, and composite photography also reached a high point in this final scene.

arm through the window of the room in which the two are fearfully cringing, grabs Ann in his giant paw and departs with her over the rooftop and then down the outside of the building to the street below. Still clasping his precious handful, he rips up the elevated tracks and looms in front of an oncoming train which crashes calamitously through the gap he has made.

The city is in an uproar. Police are calling for help. Now a flash goes out over the radio: "Kong is climbing the Empire State Building!" And, in a splendid distance shot we see the creature—superimposed, of course—climbing up the outside of the familiar pylon-topped skyscraper.

Perched on the top of the pylon, with Ann clasped in his hairy paw, Kong is the symbolization of the gross power of primitive, emerging man. Then modern man —civilization—calls forth the ultimate weapon to bring him down—airplanes—and in a moment, a swarm of them converges on the tower. As they near Kong and start firing at him with machine guns, he gently places Ann on a narrow ledge, and, with his arm thus free, lashes wrathfully at the planes which seem like tiny gadflies as they swoop past. He catches one plane that ventures too close and flings it, crumpled, to the street far below. But it is in vain. He is hit again and again by screaming bullets. He picks up Ann for a last loving, tender-eyed caress—all he has ever been able to show her—while she cringes in horror, then places her back on the ledge.

Now the great brute wobbles. His hideous face shows crinkled agony. Then he lets go of the pylon and plunges at last to the ground. On the street below, policemen and reporters are gathered around Denham. "Well," says one, "the airplanes got him." And Denham sadly and solemnly replies with what is clearly a howling understatement, "Oh, no, it was beauty killed the beast."

No matter how used to the illusions of motion pictures one may be, there is an irresistible excitement to be got from this fanciful film, outside of the wildly imaginative tale it spins. Perhaps the freakish power of its suggestion pricks some depth of atavistic fear, touches some subconscious stratum of primitive animal dread. Kong is more physically substantial and therefore less difficult to believe than the monsters evolved out of statues or the gruesome specimens of human deformity. And since he is a manifest of nature, he becomes an affecting metaphor just as do all folk-tale animals when they are presented as symbolizations of humankind.

Remember, *King Kong* was initially released in March 1933, at the depth of the Great Depression, when millions were out of work and a sense of inhuman betrayal by the social system was surging through the land. Though critics and audiences did not hail it as an allegory of the times, nor did Kong leap forth as a symbol of the helpless working man, there was obviously some strange empathy felt toward this cruelly badgered beast by millions of unemployed who saw the picture in 1933.

Likewise there is inducement for subconsciously sensing Kong as a massive symbolization of the segregated Negro race. Kong is black. He is taken from the jungle and transported to America in chains. Here he is used to serve a white master who exploits him unmercifully.

But most suggestive and pervasive in the picture is the theme of frustrated sex, which is superficially funny but essentially sad and ominous. An irony (undoubtedly unintended) is that poor old Kong finally retreats to the top of the Empire State Building, which is—or was, until its peak was adorned with spiky television antennae—the most elaborate phallic symbol in the world.

King Kong was immensely popular. It is the only film that ever played the Radio City Music Hall and the Roxy Theater in New York simultaneously. The figure of Kong became synonymous with the concept of superhuman strength and quickly merged into the folklore of our mechanical age.

It Happened One Night

Zeke's Wife	Blanche Frederici
Gas Station Man	Irving Bacon
Gordon	Charles C. Wilson

A New York-to-Miami bus figures with Clark Gable and Claudette Colbert in the romantic comedy that sold almost as many bus tickets as it did theater tickets. Ward Bond is the driver.

1934

Screenplay by Robert Riskin, from a story by Samuel Hopkins Adams; produced and directed by Frank Capra; photographed by Joe Walker; a Columbia picture.

Peter	Clark Gable
Ellie	Claudette Colbert
Alexander Andrews	Walter Connolly
Shapeley	Roscoe Karns
King Westley	Jameson Thomas
Danker	Alan Hale
Bus Driver	Ward Bond
Lovington	Wallis Clark
Henderson	Harry Bradley
Reporter	Charlie Brown
Auto Camp Owner	Harry Holman
His Wife	Maidel Turner
Zeke	Arthur Hoyt

A new category of screen humor as unique and significant as that of the great pantomimic comedians in American silent films was comparatively slow in evolving after the arrival of sound. It took a few years of experimenting before a true American comedy genre emerged.

At first, there were the Marx Brothers and their turbulent slapstick-with-words which we will get to in the chapter on *A Night at the Opera* (which see). Then there were other word comedians of assorted characteristics and costumes—W. C. Fields, Will Rogers, Jimmy Durante, Eddie Cantor, Ed Wynn and blowzy old Marie Dressler and Wallace Beery, who briefly made a popular low-comedy team. There was a deluge of classy but static stage-derived high comedies, such as *Holiday* (1930) and *The Guardsman* (1932). And there was Mae West with her travesties of a sex queen, which she began with *She Done Him Wrong* (1933). But the industry's moral guardians soon got Mae with their new Production Code and purged all the lustiness and humor out of her modifications of old-time burlesque jokes. Obviously something different remained to be devised.

The something different, something modern and appropriate to the contemporary American mood and taste, finally emerged with the evolvement of a group of mischievous, topical films which we call screwball comedies. These blended sight and verbal humor, freakish mix-ups and witty dialogue, screwy twists that were possible but unlikely and take-outs based on surprise, to tell stories that seemed to be legitimate in the nature of the current social scene but were really quite fanciful, romantic, idealistic and hard to believe. Their cheerfully simple solutions of the problems of economics and sex were hopelessly unrealistic, when one stopped to give them some thought. But they were beautifully optimistic, so who wanted to stop and think? This was the 1930's, when the wounds of the Great Depression were still raw. People went to the movies expecting to be entertained. And that was the fundamental purpose of the screwball comedies, the first, and, for me, the most delightful, of which was Frank Capra's *It Happened One Night*.

The gist of this frisky recounting of a romance that burgeons between a millionaire's runaway daughter and a roguish newspaperman who are brought into unlikely contact on a bus trip from Miami to New York is that one doesn't need money to have a good time. Indeed, money and high social station are supreme disadvantages. And the blissful and buoyant realization the girl finally gets through her head is that these things can be well abandoned for the greater satisfactions of true love. Obviously such an outpouring of unrealistic romance would be and would *have been* bromidic, even to the audiences of its day, who were hardly empathetic to social snootiness and wealth, if it weren't done with enough versatility, ingenuity and quick colloquial wit to disguise its essential nonsense and its incongruities. But these were precisely the virtues that Capra brought forth in his film and that became the recognizable elements of screwball comedy.

Capra had started as a gag man in the studio of Hal Roach and had advanced to become the director of the wistful, improbable comic, Harry Langdon. He went on to talking films and gained distinction with *Lady for a Day* (1933), a colloquial, sentimental fiction about an aging Broadway apple vendor who is set up briefly to play an elegant lady by a bigtime Broadway gambler in order to impress her daughter who hasn't seen her in years. It was done in a Damon Runyon idiom that weds romanticism and toughness in a way that deluded the audience into feeling it was observing a marriage that would last.

This is what he does to perfection in *It Happened One Night*. The idea for it was taken from a short story titled "Night Bus," written by Samuel Hopkins Adams, that appeared in *The Saturday Evening Post*. It was turned into a sparkling screenplay by Robert Riskin, Capra's good write hand. The story itself is simple: this out-of-work newspaperman, trying to beat his way homeward from Miami to New York, encounters the runaway daughter of a millionaire on a bus, soon discovers her incognito and smells a great exclusive story for himself. While she is fleeing her father to join a society parasite she has wed, our fellow will stick close to her and gather data for a firsthand feature on "Society Girl's Mad Flight to Happiness." She is outraged by his purpose, but there's nothing she can do.

En route, it becomes apparent she is unable to take care of herself, that she, in her rich girl's incompetence, is compelled to rely upon him. She must let him find lodgings for her on a night they are stopped by a washed-out bridge, protect her from mashers, and especially handle the very small amount of cash she has. And he, in turn, must bear the burden of putting up with this foolish, snobbish dame in order to get the story that will reestablish him with his managing editor.

There is no need to notify what happens. She is grudgingly enchanted, of course, by the adequacy, sex magnetism and repartee of what is beyond any question the first real man she has known. And he is unsuspectingly smitten by the winsomeness of this girl, who is

The offensive familiarity of another passenger, Shapeley (Roscoe Karns), brings Ellie (Claudette Colbert) a chivalrous assist from Peter (Clark Gable).

obviously much more human than she has ever been encouraged to be. In the face of the evident obstruction of her wealth and position, they fall in love, and, after a flood of complications, are demurringly encouraged to elope.

What is delightful about it is the illusion it easily conveys of being modern and realistic because of its rich contemporary *mise en scène*—bus stations, buses, lunch counters, highways and autocamps—its aura of sex sophistication and its flow of colloquial wit, and yet how aggressively romantic and idealistic it is. This is entirely consistent with the American mood and taste. Capra's films in the 1930's—this one, then *Mr. Deeds Goes to Town* (1936) and *Mr. Smith Goes to Washington* (1939) are loaded with optimism and high integrity. The measure of their accord with common feeling was their immense popularity.

To be sure, *It Happened One Night* had going for it the perfect chemistry of Clark Gable and Claudette Colbert in the principal roles. And both were in the picture by sheer chance and good luck. Capra originally wanted Robert Montgomery and Myrna Loy to play the leads. But Montgomery was not available from his home studio, Metro-Goldwyn-Mayer; and Gable, who was somewhat in the doghouse at the moment, was loaned instead as a disciplinary measure for what was expected to be just an ordinary film. Neither was Miss Loy available, so Miss Colbert was borrowed from Paramount, where she was momentarily stagnating in stereotyped roles, seeking a change.

Gable was antagonistic and sullen at the start, but as soon as he sensed the rare abundance of the character, he was all for the film. What he liked especially were the scenes in the autocamp, which are, indeed, the crucial conveyors of the basic idea. For it is in these scenes that the essential sex confrontations occur and the bar-riers of social inequality are undercut with a sly, seductive tease.

The first such scene is presented the night they are stuck in the bus by a washed-out bridge and the reporter decides they should seek shelter in a nearby autocamp. The girl is antagonistic and apprehensive, but she goes with him to a cabin he has got for them to share together, registered as husband and wife.

Stringing a line from wall to wall between the two beds and hanging a blanket over it, he tells her, "Behold the walls of Jericho! Maybe not as thick as the ones Joshua blew down with his trumpet, but a lot safer." And then he adds, "You see, I have no trumpet." That remains to be seen!

The Walls of Jericho—a blanket hung on a clothesline—satisfied the morals mentors of the movies and, incidentally, Ellie.

In the face of her rueful hesitation, he proceeds to get undressed, with a mischievous running commentary on the ways a man may take off his clothes. This ingenious business is in the nature of a masculine striptease, beginning the teasing quality of all that happens in the rooms of the autocamps.

The girl goes behind the curtain on her side, proceeds to get undressed and don the pajama top he has generously handed over to her. But when she heedlessly drapes her slip and silk stockings over the line supporting the "walls of Jericho," he politely requests her to remove them. "It's tough enough as it is," he says—and the audience is given full assurance he is not so innocent of an urge.

When they are both bedded down and lying separately in the dark, she somewhat indifferently asks him, "By the way, what's your name?"

With a sly smile, he artfully teases, "Why, I'm the whippoorwill that cries in the night. I'm the soft morning breeze that caresses your face."

Unamused, she interrupts, "You've got a name, haven't you?"

He answers, "Yeah, I got a name. Peter Warne."

"Peter Warne," she repeats. "I don't like it." She sniffs and turns her face to the wall.

But the sexual electricity is turned on. The situation of an attractive girl and a strange, very obviously virile man in the same bedroom, snug against the rain in the darkness, with only a blanket suspended by a cord separating them was very daring in 1934, and is still sufficiently seductive to agitate audiences.

Their playful conversation the next morning, when he chases her out in his bathrobe to take a shower while he scurries up some breakfast, his teaching her how to dunk a doughnut in a cup of coffee, and then their spontaneous falling into an act of a snarling husband and wife to fool detectives who come around in a dragnet search for the missing heiress, all done with lively dialogue, brings them closer together. When they reboard the bus, they are feeling entirely folksy, and join the rest of the passengers in happily singing "The Daring Young Man on the Flying Trapeze."

That is the first autocamp scene. And the second, more disturbing, comes after they have had some droll adventures together. They have had to leave the bus because a masher who tried to flirt with Ellie—the girl —has soon discovered her identity and Peter has chased him off by pretending to be a gangster surreptitiously kidnapping her. They have spent a night in a haystack, eating raw carrots for their only meal and they have snitched an old jalopy from a thieving farmer who has responded to their cute attempts to thumb a ride. In this latter scene, incidentally, Ellie has her only

Hopefully thumbing for rides, Peter and Ellie make it back home in time for her to call off an unsuitable social marriage and for him to write a happy ending to his story.

chance of asserting feminine superiority. She gets a lift for them by showing her leg.

Now they have come to another autocamp for their last night before reaching New York, and the blanket—the "walls of Jericho"—is put up for the last time. Sadly and with misgiving, they retire to their separate beds. You know she doesn't want to join her husband and Peter doesn't want to expose the story of this "flight."

In the dark, they begin a conversation, and he reveals his romantic dream of going to an island in the Pacific. Ellie listens. Her eyes glaze. Then she is around the "walls of Jericho," at his bedside, looking luscious in his pajama top.

"Take me with you, Peter!" she beseeches. "Take me with you to your island!"

This is it. This is the moment when they would logically fall into each other's arms. But that would be too sudden, too obvious and too at variance with the essence of romance. It would also be too easy a surmounting of social barriers. So Capra and Riskin archly work out their cheerful comedy with a cascade of incidents to display Peter's rugged independence in refusing a reward from Ellie's father, and then Ellie's own stubborn-

ness, before finally bringing the two again to an auto-camp, married, and ending the film by showing a blanket hitting the floor.

Capra's formula for this happy demonstration that the rewards of goodness go to the just, that the poor, honest, smart, ingenious fellow confounds the rich scalawags in the end, is tart and amusing dialogue, combined with fast action and genuinely comic incidents. He uses his camera casually, as a stand-off observer most of the time, only now and then letting it creep in to scan Ellie's radiant face as she feels love's mysterious stirrings or shudders in moments of dismay.

In addition to Gable and Miss Colbert, who are charmingly unpreposterous, Walter Connolly is nicely demanding as the permissive millionaire and Roscoe Karns is a perfect vaudevillian as the tinhorn masher who is frightened off.

It Happened One Night was the beginning of a wave of romantic comedies, such as *The Thin Man* (1934), *My Man Godfrey* (1936), *Nothing Sacred* and *The Awful Truth* (1937). Its uniqueness is attested to by the fact that it is the only film ever to receive all five of the major Academy Awards—best film, best screenplay, best director, best actor and best actress.

Since Peter is a newspaper man and Ellie is a runaway debutante, what else should he teach her but how to get full flavor by dunking the morning doughnut.

Out in the boondocks and out of money, Peter and Ellie stave off starvation by pinching carrots from a convenient farm.

Gypo Nolan (Victor McLaglen), a weak and destitute member of the Irish rebellion, tears down a poster asking for the capture of his best friend, Frankie McPhillip (Wallace Ford), but cannot erase the reward from his memory.

The Informer

1935

Screenplay by Dudley Nichols, from the novel of Liam O'Flaherty; directed by John Ford; cameraman, Joseph H. August; musical director, Max Steiner; produced by Cliff Reid for R-K-O.

Gypo Nolan	Victor McLaglen
Katie Madden	Margot Grahame
Dan Gallagher	Preston Foster
Mary McPhillip	Heather Angel
Frankie McPhillip	Wallace Ford
Mrs. McPhillip	Una O'Connor
Terry	J. M. Kerrigan
Mulholland	Joseph Sauers
Rat Mulligan	Donald Meek
Tommy Connor	Neil Fitzgerald
Blind Man	D'Arcy Corrigan
Donahue	Leo McCabe
Flynn	Francis Ford
Madame Betty	May Boley
The Lady	Grizelda Harvey
Daly	Gaylord Pendleton

I would venture to guess that few motion pictures have stuck so tenaciously in the minds of those who saw them when they were first released as John Ford's *The Informer* or few characters have lingered so hauntingly in the memories of older film fans as the great lout whom Victor McLaglen plays in this drama of treachery and retribution in strife-torn Dublin in 1921. It was almost as though the sombrous story of Gypo Nolan, the outcast who betrays his best friend, a fugitive rebel, to the Black and Tans for a £20 reward and then

Gypo betrays his best friend to the Black and Tans for the £20 reward that will buy passage to the States for him and his girl.

cracks beneath the press of the avengers and the mounting comprehension of his guilt, were a distant recollection of an experience the viewer himself had been through back in those dark days when the Irish were fighting the British to be free.

So expressively does this picture suggest the brooding atmosphere of Dublin during "the trouble" and so compellingly does it obtrude a sense of the confusion and anguish of a fellow who commits an odious deed, that it deeply affected the feelings of those who saw it in 1935, when we were not too long removed from the history it so bitterly recalled. And, except for a mawkish ending and a few disturbing flaws along the way, it remains a tremendously absorbing psychological melodrama to this day.

Also, one of the reasons *The Informer* caused such a stir among critics and smart moviegoers when it was released was the fact that it came as a startling and reassuring surprise. It offered a solid anti-hero in contrast to the brash romantic types that were blooming in the middle 1930's. And it was quite unexpected from Ford.

He was a bread-and-meat director who had come to prominence in 1924 as the youthful, energetic creator of the railroad-building epic, *The Iron Horse*. The many and varied pictures that he made in succeeding years included the talking adaptation of Sinclair Lewis' medical novel, *Arrowsmith* (1931), and an interesting desert-warfare picture, *The Lost Patrol* (1934). After the success of the latter, he determinedly importuned the heads of the R-K-O studio to allow him to do an adaptation of Liam O'Flaherty's novel, *The Informer*, with which he, as a stalwart Irishman (born with the Christian name of Feeney), had fallen in love.

The studio heads had every reason (by their lights)

to say no. The story was murky and melancholy; the hero was a brute, a gross, jugheaded Judas, who was destroyed at the end. There were strong strains of Communist involvements in the O'Flaherty book, which had been published to a mixed reception in 1925. Furthermore, the story had already been used by Arthur Robison for a silent film in England in 1928, and that film had been a washout. The prospects were not good. However, Ford was insistent, and he was finally given permission to proceed, with the explicit understanding that it would have to be a modest and cheaply made film. Ford agreed (he once told me the reason his Dublin streets are so shrouded with fog, an effect that adds considerably to the atmosphere, was to hide the fact that they could not afford background sets).

Dudley Nichols, a skillful scenarist who had previously worked with him, did the adaptation and finished the screenplay in a remarkably short time (Ford has told me six days, but that is hard to believe). It is a tight and compact screenplay that considerably departs from the book. (For an interesting analysis of the changes, see George Bluestone's *Novels into Films*.)

The film was made in a studio annex and was completed in seventeen shooting days, an achievement that eloquently attests to the concentration and assurance of Ford. When it was first shown for studio executives, they were restless and obviously displeased. Ford was sick with apprehension until he went outside the screening room and found his good friend, Dudley Digges, the Irish actor, who had just come from seeing the film, sitting in an automobile weeping. That sufficiently reassured him.

When the picture opened in New York at the Radio City Music Hall, it was glowingly reviewed, but attendance in the one week it played there was poor. Not until it was continued in a smaller theater did the audiences arrive and public interest and enthusiasm begin to build. Its selection by the New York Film Critics as the best picture of 1935, and the selection of Ford as best director, gave it a critical cachet that has not been tarnished by the weathering of the years.

The basic force of *The Informer* is in the spartan simplicity with which it graphs a psychological disaster in clear cinematic terms and pulls the viewer into a vortex of intrigue and anguish with an economy of images and sounds. It has the straight line of classic drama in moving from cause to consequence: from the horrible temptation of Gypo to betray his patriot friend, Frankie McPhillip, on to the primary crisis of his doing so; and then from the apex of this action through the night-long closing in of the relentless avengers and of Gypo's own conscience until he is drawn, like a great bull is hectored in the bullring, to his inevitable doom.

Gypo on the binge, through the seamy bars and brothels of the Dublin slums, has accused Rat Mulligan of turning in Frankie.

It all happens in a period of one night, from dusk to dawn, within an area of a few blocks in Dublin, and interest is centered entirely upon one man.

It is actually a drama of dishonor, which is an unusual theme for a Hollywood picture, a revelation of one man's weaknesses driving him to betray not only his best friend but, more importantly, himself. Gypo, the great stupid rebel who would like so much to belong, but has been dropped from the organization (we are told) because of his ineptitude and cowardice, is essentially an informer upon his own inadequacy, upon his hopeless lack of those qualities that might put him among the hero breed. And the fact that he finally faces his cravenness and shame is the agony that brings to a climax our accumulating pity for him.

It is surprising how few critics have noted how similar *The Informer* is to a 1930's gangster picture, with its atmosphere of secrecy and stealth and its spewing of violence and vengeance in a shadowy underworld. Gypo is the conventional squealer, the stoolie, who tips off the cops and against whom the gang takes gangland measures. But the great and important difference is that here the organization operating outside the law is that of the Irish Rebellion, a romantic and patriotic cause, endowed with an aura of valor and heroic self-sacrifice. Treachery against this organization is a shocking and sacrilegious thing, meriting excommunication—which *The Informer* comes close to meting out.

It begins in the murky streets of Dublin, with the large, hulking shadow of a man moving along a wall for a moment. Then the man himself comes into view. He is Gypo, a massive fellow with a rough, granitic face. He wears a cloth cap, a scarf and shabby jacket. He stops in front of a poster on a wall which blazons the photograph of Frankie McPhillip, wanted for murder, and offers a £20 reward. Gypo pauses briefly before the poster, looks at it in disgust, then rips it from the wall, crumples it angrily, casts it away from him and hastens on along the sidewalk, where lonely street lamps pierce the gloom and a sweet-faced Irish tenor sings the plaintive "Rose of Tralee." The angry man stops to listen, as a small patrol of Black and Tans, menacingly armed with rifles, passes, frisks the singer and goes on, counterpointing the thump of their rough boots against the sadness of the song. Thus, in the shorthand of a few shots, the tension and enmity of the occupation of Dublin are effectively imposed.

As swiftly and atmospherically, the torment of Gypo is introduced. He is attached to a shabby streetwalker, and wants enough money to escape with her to America. Then, when he comes upon McPhillip, back in Dublin by stealth for one night to visit his mother and sister, Gypo, haunted by the image of that poster, is rashly inspired to turn him in for the reward.

The account of the betrayal is vulpine. A furtive Gypo enters the headquarters of the Black and Tans, cap in hand, nervously wiping his sweaty face with it and haltingly dropping the fatal words to the officer at the desk, "I've come to gain the twenty pounds you offered for Frankie McPhillip." Sharply, there is a cut to lorries, crowded with Black and Tans, roaring away from headquarters, then back to Gypo sitting in a chair, waiting for something to happen, while a clock on the wall ticks ominously, the graphic and aural suggestion of time closing in on him.

The capture of Frankie comes swiftly, with the Black and Tans crashing into his home, fighting a gun duel on the stairway and ferociously shooting him down as he tries to escape through the back yard. It has the hideousness of a killing in a gangster film, and leaves an inerasable image of violence and calamity in the viewer's mind.

This is very important, as is indicated by the next scene. Back in the Black and Tan headquarters, the

Mortally wounded and disgraced, Gypo staggers into a church to ask forgiveness of Frankie's mother (Una O'Connor) before he dies.

telephone rings. An officer answers. "McPhillip was killed trying to escape," he repeats. Gypo hears it and stiffens. Then the officer pushes the folded pound notes, the fateful blood money, across the table to Gypo, with the point of his swagger stick, remarking coldly, "You'd better count it." Thus the treachery is done.

Now the falling action of Gypo's undoing begins—his spontaneous throttling of a blind man as he leaves headquarters by a back door, his imagining he sees the poster of Frankie still glaring at him from the empty wall, his thinking he hears the voice of Frankie taunting him as he drinks in a saloon, his flaring up at his girl-friend, Katie, when she joins him and innocently asks where he got the money to buy booze.

Everything he does is a betrayal of his accumulating sense of guilt. He visits the home of Frankie, where the wake is already begun, uneasily joins the mourners and drops four telltale coins onto the floor. With all eyes riveted upon him, he shouts, "I swear by all that's holy, I warned him to stay away from this house!"

Taken before the captain of the organization, Gypo is nakedly confused. He guzzles whisky impulsively and is much too quick to invent a patently phony accusation that it was the tailor, Rat Mulligan, who informed. Gypo is obviously suspected, and is told to report to a secret court at 1 A.M. He goes now and gets wildly drunk with a rabble of gutter types, including the little tout, Terry, who, in his sychophancy and deceit, plays a wickedly minor obligato to Gypo's major treachery.

In most of the analyses of *The Informer,* little mention has been made of the development of a gallows humor in this phase of the film. When Gypo gets drunk with the cackling rabble and treats everyone to fish and chips, the comical behavior is boisterous. Terry is a weaselly mountebank. He takes Gypo to Aunt Bessie's, which is represented as a sort of social hall (in order to avoid the censure of the Production Code), but is actually a swank bordello. Here Gypo has a comical brush with an officious little rooster who threatens to throw him out of the place.

But all through this morbid buffoonery, we are mindful that the riddled body of Frankie is lying back there in that mournful house and that a great and cruel betrayal of friendship and honor has been done. And when Gypo boozily demands that eveyone sing "Those Endearing Young Charms," the incongruity of his sentimentality points up the grisly farce.

Even at the court of inquiry, a strain of comedy is laced through the deadly proceedings by the rambling testimony of Rat Mulligan, a finicky little fellow who sets up an easy alibi. Thus the force is that much more compelling when the spotlight is suddenly swung upon Gypo, sitting there uneasily in the crowded court, and

the barrage of accusatory questions is relentlessly leveled at him, until finally, stunned and staggered, he shouts in frantic defense, "I didn't know what I was doing!" Thus Gypo informs upon himself.

Actually, the drama is over at this explosive point. The psychological third degree has been successful; Gypo has been exposed. From here on, the flow is melodrama of a progressively more obvious and mawkish sort. It concludes with a maudlin business of Gypo, mortally wounded in an ambuscade, staggering into the dawn-lit church where Frankie's mother is praying, begging forgiveness of her and then falling dead before the image of Christ, with the dying words, "Frankie, your mother forgives me!"

Such is the cathartic ending of this ironic tale. And since the sentiment of it seemed less bromidic than it does today, it brought to an effective climax the surge of audience sympathy. People went out of theaters moist-eyed, weeping for the loneliness of man. And Gypo, the great betrayer, became an immortal of the screen.

Much credit for his compelling image must go to McLaglen, who portrays the denseness, the animal cunning, the childlike naïveté, the sinister brute power, the groping terror that are compounded in this man. It is a performance that won McLaglen an Academy Award and gave rise to a shameful rumor that Ford, to get him to play as well as he did, kept him full of whisky through the shooting of most of the film. This is a legend that Ford has discredited with a contemptuous word: "Absurd!"

Other performances vary. J. M. Kerrigan's Terry is true, an evil and noxious little weasel that ruthlessly sucks the blood of man. Preston Foster is conventionally noble as the rebel commandant. Heather Angel is bland as Frankie's sister, Wallace Ford is tough as Frankie himself, Una O'Connor is apt as the weeping mother, Donald Meek is limply droll as Mulligan and Margot Grahame is conventionally saccharine as Katie, the whore with a heart of gold.

The musical score of Max Steiner seems a bit hackneyed today, with its obvious significations, such as snatches of "Wearin' o' the Green" as the sullen Irish rebels glower at the passing Black and Tans or faint strains of "Yankee Doodle Dandy" to signify Gypo's and Katie's longing to get away. But the score, on the whole, marked a considerable advancement in the use of music for that day, and it still rates high marks for its subtle interweaving of the poignant "Rose of Tralee" theme.

With *The Informer,* Ford leaped to the forefront of American directors. We will see him reach the peak of his achievement with *The Grapes of Wrath.*

A Night at the Opera

1935

Screenplay by George S. Kaufman and Morrie Ryskind, from a story by James Kevin McGuinness; directed by Sam Wood; music by Nacio Herb Brown and Arthur Freed; cameraman, Merritt P. Gerstad; produced by Irving Thalberg for Metro-Goldwyn-Mayer.

Otis B. Driftwood	Groucho Marx
Fiorello	Chico Marx
Tomasso	Harpo Marx
Rosa	Kitty Carlisle
Ricardo	Allan Jones
Mrs. Claypool	Margaret Dumont
Gottlieb	Sig Rumann
Lassparri	Walter King
Captain	Edward Keane
Henderson	Robert Emmet O'Connor

Considering that the Marx Brothers first appeared on the screen at the time of the big switchover to sound in 1929, this may seem a somewhat tardy moment at which to be catching up with them and their creative capacities for combining slapstick and talk. The explanation is simple: I am one who thinks *A Night at the Opera* is the grandest, the most inventive and satiric of all their japes, the one in which their unique combination of commentary and craftsmanship reached its peak. But because I am putting my selections in the chronological order in which they came, and they did not make this picture until 1935, we are just now coming upon them. This implies no lack of regard.

Indeed, it makes little difference to the permanent estimation of their work at what point one chooses to grapple with the Marx Brothers and their style, for they and their brand of humor are as changeless as Chaplin's Little Tramp. True, they provided a departure of fresh

and explosive surprise when they first crashed the screen from the theater with *The Cocoanuts* in 1929. And their way of bombarding the viewer with sight and word gags in a barrage that added din to the familiar demolition of the visual did, indeed, help break the way into sound. But they, their character conceptions and their illusory construction of the world in which all the conventions of normal behavior are permittedly flouted and ridiculed, are the same in *A Night at the Opera* as they were in the succession of films the boys flung at an idolizing public after *The Cocoanuts.*

Groucho, the spearhead of the combine, is always a confidence man—a fast talker and a swindler who is forever trying to take somebody in. His monstrous eyebrows, his grease-paint moustache, his perpetually mobile cigar, his shoddy frock coat, his rasping chatter and his way of gliding in a headlong, foxy slouch betray beyond any question the egregious conniver he is. He may be anything—a snake-oil peddler, a quack professor, a fake psychiatrist—anything, just as long as it is shady and gives him plenty of room to move around. In a *A Night at the Opera,* he is posing as an international impresario who promises to get a rich and socially ambitious woman involved in a New York opera—naturally, for a price. Of course, he has no connections, no knowledge of music, no prestige, nothing but unlimited ingenuity, impudence and nerve.

His invariable sidekick is Chico, a casual scapegrace with the innocent façade of an Italian organ-grinder—a peaked cloth hat, a round and open face, a short, tight-fitting jacket, baggy pantaloons and an oily Sicilian accent that suggests the docile immigrant. But Chico is far from docile. He will swindle without shame or restraint, and often, in his bland and stolid fashion, he will beat the crafty Groucho at his game.

Chico's companion is Harpo, an apparently lunatic mute whose broad, beaming face is sweetly haloed by a

Getting there is more than half the fun in Groucho's stateroom, and this is only half the crowd that piles in for one of the film's more hilarious scenes.

mop of wild, curly hair (it was pink on the stage and in color pictures). He wears an out-sized raincoat and a squashed plug hat. Harpo is the pixie, the totally free spirit of the team. He responds without guile or inhibition to all sorts of spontaneous whims. He will pick up a powder puff and eat it with the nonchalance and relish of a goat. He will jump aboard the banister of a circular staircase and slide down it at a dizzying speed. He will fish into the baggy, catch-all pockets of his raincoat and snatch forth an antique bulb-blown auto horn which he will honk with smiling satisfaction and as a message of his ebullience to his friends. And often, when he spies a pretty female, he will take out after her in frantic chase, eyes glistening, coattails flying and arms stretching for a rapacious embrace.

The relations of these three rascals are usually nebu-lous and vague, except that they seem to work together whenever there's a swindle to be pulled. (In their films before this, a fourth Marx brother, Zeppo, is an obvious fifth wheel. He's just a good-looking schnook who is usually as much a butt of their jokes as any of the other befuddled characters who happen to get involved, and his excision from the combine was an intelligent move.)

Obviously Groucho and Chico are established confederates, for all their tries to hornswoggle one another in the course of their nefarious deals. And obviously Chico and Harpo are inseparable friends, with Chico always gentle and protective toward the loveable mute, clearly understanding his weird sign language and translating it astonishingly whenever Harpo signals him with a shrill whistle and semaphores wildly with his hands.

109

This friendship between these two eccentrics is one of the subtle felicities of the team, pointed up by the usual annoyance and impatience of Groucho toward the mute. And it is always brought to a touching climax, at least once in every film, when the two do a musical number, Chico playing the piano (which he does with comic flourishes) and Harpo playing the harp. This bond of melody between the zanies intrudes a touch of poignancy into their pranks.

It is futile and thoroughly nonessential to seek a plot in a Marx Brothers' film. The logic of a narrative arrangement is one of the conventions they deliberately defy. Once they have set a point of departure and indicated whom they are out to take, the occurrence of events thereafter is as vagrant as a tornado. Anything can happen. A random character coming on the scene can draw their abusive attention to a totally extraneous

dead end. Then they can pop back to their swindle as though they had never been away, and, indeed, as though the pulling of the swindle were a matter of casual concern. Or they can find themselves involved in a verbal bladdering of one another with horrible puns that eventually ends up as nothing but a comical *non sequitur*.

So it is in *A Night at the Opera*. It begins with Groucho making a pitch as one Otis B. Driftwood to interest a Mrs. Claypool (Margaret Dumont) in investing in a nebulous opera which he promises to produce. He says this will greatly elevate her in New York society.

But all this is secondary to Groucho's establishing himself by blazing away with the shotgun banter that is his particular forte. Indeed, he makes his entrance in a possibly Parisian restaurant by barking imperiously at a

Harpo, Chico and Ricardo (Allan Jones), having stowed away, hijack the uniforms of some foreign generals in order to disembark legitimately.

Harpo has promised a Met debut to Rosa (Kitty Carlisle), but he's far from having solved the problem of bringing it off.

waiter who has been paging him, "Waiter, won't you please stop calling my name around here! How would you like to have me go around calling your name?" It is a characteristically blatant and egotistical crack which immediately calls the attention of Mrs. Claypool and the audience to himself. And he goes right on in this manner. Interspersed with his pitch are random verbal asides, such as asking the waiter, "Do you have any milk-fed chicken? . . . Well, squeeze the milk out of one and let me have it," or loudly complimenting Mrs. Claypool on being an excellent businesswoman, then topping it with the glib remark, "There's something about me that brings out the business in every woman." That's Groucho, always pushing himself.

Harpo is brought into the picture as the brutally ban-

ished valet of a pompous opera tenor who has caught him gleefully ransacking the dressing room; and Chico, who is the manager of a struggling young tenor (Allan Jones), arrives at this moment to help Harpo get out of the jam he's in. Thus is the standard bond of friendship between these two scamps laid down.

Typical of their verbal hassles is a conversation between Groucho and Chico. They have sat down in a bar to discuss the drawing of a contract—it doesn't matter for what—but before they begin, Groucho calls, "Two beers, bartender," and Chico, without batting an eye, calls out, "I'll have two beers, too." Then they attack the contract, each with a copy in his hands, swiftly running over its clauses and tearing off those they think nonessential or they don't understand. A few minutes

111

of this and Groucho holds his copy away from him. "If my arms were a little longer I could read it," he says. Then he nonchalantly asks, "You haven't got a baboon in your pocket, have you?"

They continue with the tearing-off business. "Now what have you got?" Chico asks.

"I've got about a foot and a half," says Groucho. "How much have you got?"

Chico is miffed. "How come your contract is longer than mine?" he wants to know.

Groucho has the logical answer: "You must have been out on a tear last night."

When they come to the last item, Groucho says, "That's what they call a sanity clause."

Chico looks at him and chuckles wisely, "You can't fool me. There ain't no Sanity Claus."

Soon everybody is embarking by ship for New York: Mrs. Claypool; the Paris opera company, which includes an ingenue (Kitty Carlisle), with whom Chico's aspiring tenor is in love; Groucho, breezing along busily as custodian of Mrs. Claypool's trunks; and, for some reason, Chico and Harpo, who are evidently taking a free ride.

Now comes a classic scene of bedlam. Groucho and a huge steamer trunk are moved into a tiny stateroom, he beefing indignantly but climbing in nonetheless, with Chico climbing in after him. Groucho, with much agitation, opens a drawer of the trunk to get a shirt, finds the innocent Harpo curled up and sleeping inside. "That can't be my shirt," snarls Groucho. "My shirt doesn't snore."

The steward comes to take a food order, and some

Sig Rumann as the impresario, Gottlieb, is a sturdy foil for the mad antics of the Brothers Marx.

fast dialogue follows. "Have you got any stewed prunes?" asks Groucho.

"Sure," the waiter replies.

"Well, give them some hot coffee," says Groucho. "That'll sober 'em up."

Two maids crowd in with the three fellows, presumably to make up the berth. Then Allan Jones arrives; then a manicurist, whom Groucho tells to cut his nails—short. Down the corridor waddles a fat man, and we anticipate the gag. He shoves into the room, and Groucho hollers from where he is squashed against the wall, "Hey, is it my imagination, or is it getting crowded in here?"

Along comes a big charwoman, announcing, "I came to mop up." Groucho greets her warmly, "You're just the woman I'm looking for!" Then the waiters approach with trays of dishes, the door flies open and all fall out, knocking trays over teacups. That's the blackout, of course.

There is a cascade of chaos hereafter. The boys cut off the beards of three uniformed foreign generals and debark wearing the beards and uniforms themselves. They are greeted as visiting dignitaries and speeded to a reception at City Hall, where they are soon exposed as impostors and have to flee, with Groucho shouting back, "This means war!"

Eventually, they get to the opera and turn the place into a shambles by slipping the sheet music of "Take Me Out to the Ball Game" into the orchestra score, and then hawking peanuts and popcorn in the aisles when the tune pops up in *Il Trovatore*. Chico and Harpo, dressed as peasants, get on stage and start a riot, kidnap the villainous tenor and put Allan Jones in his place. He is a sensation, Mrs. Claypool is happy, and the boys are hauled off to jail.

One can see the essence of the Marx Brothers' brand of comedy: it is a complete ridiculing of reason and reality. There is no regard for the disciplines by which so-called normal people behave (or pretend to behave) in the chaos of their outrageous actions and words.

They mock and exploit the modes and manners of bourgeois society, making fun of anything that smacks remotely of prudence or pomposity. Mrs. Claypool's social ambition, the esthetics of opera, the formality of municipal receptions, all the clichés of classy etiquette and genteel conversation that considerate people observe are turned upside down by the Marxes in this apogee of their films. They are, in their way, as disdainful of the sober and self-restricting rules of the capitalist establishment as their unlikely namesake, Karl.

Here in *A Night at the Opera*, we see them using the cinema medium with a sharpness of staging and tempo and a mechanical refinement of wit that were absent or generally uneven in their early films. It is interesting that they pretested many of the separate episodes, such as the mix-up in the stateroom, on a West Coast vaudeville tour so that they could find the laughs and pace the action before putting them in the film.

While they worked with several directors (Sam Wood directed this one) and had many writers of their scripts, the compulsion of writers and directors was to adapt material to them. The creative pattern was as standard as Miss Dumont, always in the role of foil to Groucho's lurid swindles and mugging displays of lechery, or Harpo's equally preposterous sallies after girls. They also invariably included a strain of musical-comedy romance, which is carried in *A Night at the Opera* by Miss Carlisle and Jones. The best to be said for the latter is that it affords a break from the bedlam of the boys.

Needless to say, the Marx Brothers eventually became monotonous when they and their congenital swindling began to degenerate. The last film they made together was *Love Happy* in 1949. But in the span of one decade, they managed to put a kind of neo-slapstick on the screen that is much more presentable and potent today than that of Mack Sennett's famous cops. It is significant that many new comics, including that British foursome the Beatles, have been discovering this.

Camille

1936

Script by Zoë Akins, Frances Marion and James Hilton, after Alexander Dumas' novel and play *La Dame aux Camélias*; directed by George Cukor; cameraman, William Daniels; produced by Irving Thalberg for Metro-Goldwyn-Mayer.

Marguerite	Greta Garbo
Armand	Robert Taylor
Monsieur Duval	Lionel Barrymore
Nichette	Elizabeth Allan
Nanine	Jessie Ralph
Baron de Varville	Henry Daniell
Olympe	Lenore Ulric
Prudence	Laura Hope Crews
Gaston	Rex O'Malley
Gustave	Russell Hardie
Saint Gaudens	E. E. Clive
Henri	Douglas Walton
Corinne	Marion Ballou
Marie Jeanette	Joan Brodel
Louise	June Wilkins
Valentin	Fritz Lieber, Jr.
Mademoiselle Duval	Elsie Esmonds

Now comes the time to encounter that exquisite phenomenon of films that we first brushed against in this volume in *The Story of Gösta Berling* (which see).

This is, of course, Greta Garbo, the most entrancing of all the female stars that have contributed their kinds of personal magic to the wonders and illusions of the screen, whom we finally confront at her apex in this classic production of *Camille*.

You will note that I say the most entrancing, not the most skillful or talented or even the most satisfying to the mass-audience taste. There have been other actresses as artful and technically proficient as she, or maybe more so—some almost as famous, some forgotten, some indifferently overlooked because they passed by in minor pictures or spent their brilliance on secondary roles; and there have been some whose popularity has been as great—if it has not, indeed, transcended hers. Mary Pickford, Gloria Swanson, Marlene Dietrich, Joan Crawford and Marilyn Monroe are a few who have been as conspicuous as personalities. In recent years, there have been such others as Sophia Loren and Brigitte Bardot. But there has not been an actress in this medium in its more than seventy years who has matched in feminine enchantment, exciting mystery and purely cinematic necromancy this elusive, expatriated Swede.

I say this with candid awareness that I am espousing a taste for a kind of extravagance in women, and a chivalry toward movie stars, that is not as prevalent today as it used to be. I do not mean extravagance as a spender (though total indifference to expense is one of the standard idiosyncrasies of woman projected by this star). I mean extravagance in image—in endowments of

Marguerite Gauthier (Greta Garbo) is a notorious Parisian courtesan who leads a wildy frivolous life through the generosity of her protector. Among her nightly playmates are Gaston (Rex O'Malley) and Prudence (Laura Hope Crews).

physical allure (as distinct from physical endowments, which countless nonentities possess), in breadth of worldly experience (which so few women actually have), in depth of capacity for loving, suffering and presumably doing things for men. It is a taste that transcends the ordinary and gropes for an iconograph of woman of a sort that rarely, if ever, exists. But it is gratified by Miss Garbo—or simply Garbo, as she will forever be known, since the evidence of her sovereign nature makes the "Miss" or merely "Greta" too banal.

Much has been written about this actress, and many have tried to analyze the compound of physical appearance and spiritual aura that she has on the screen: the languor of her tall and solid body; the beauty of her melancholy face with its large, liquid eyes, its lofty cheekbones and its wide, voluptuous mouth; the mystical calm of her manner; and the air of serene intensity she has in her every endeavor, from arranging a vase of flowers to making love.

Naturally, the essence of her nature is predominantly sexual. The key to this fabulous woman is her need and desire for men. Where other mythological females created in this medium have generated excitement through various pretexts of style and sentiment, or graphic implications of amorous aptitude, Garbo generates excitement by making you feel that she is starving for love, not obviously or obscenely, as so many female symbols do, but quietly, passionately, profoundly. She must have love or she will die. And, indeed, the evidence of her necessity is that she does die at the end of most of her films, essentially because circumstances make it impossible for her to have the fulfillment of the love she needs.

The kind of love is important. It is not simply sexual thrill, nor that plus the speechless idolatry of a handsome bore. What she craves and seeks and never reaches is a permanent conjunction with a man who is every bit as magnificent, generous and passionate as she. He must be able to meet her on that level of devotion of self that permits a complete conjunction of bodies and spirits as one. He must match her inviolate image with that of a male paragon. But since there is no such creature, and since it would be fatal, anyhow, to the illusion of her tragic isolation to put her in contact with one, it remains that this woman of Garbo must go through life (and through a fabulous film career) seeking that which her nature denies her. She is compelled to be alone.

The mythical character of Garbo began to emerge as soon as she was transplanted to the environment of Hollywood. In her first American silent pictures, *Torrent* and *The Temptress,* both 1926, she played beautiful, passionate, tragic European *femmes fatales.* It was

The beauty of Marguerite proves irresistible to Armand Duval (Robert Taylor), a young careerist of aristocratic background.

a type that was widely popular in European and American films, but Garbo brought a freshness and intensity to the hackneyed role, even though she was then but twenty-one.

In her next film, *Flesh and the Devil* (1927), she was given a go at what was to be a most popular and repeated role for her, that of a restless married woman in love with another man. Her co-star was John Gilbert, the top romantic actor of the day. His image as a lover was galvanic, so the illusion of passion in the film was helped by valid rumors of a real-life romance between the two. It is safe to say that Garbo became the foremost symbol of sex in its more elegant implications in the terminal years of silent films.

Thus there was much anxiety as to how she would do in talking films, especially since she spoke English flatly with an accent you could cut with a spoon. The inevitable day of reckoning was put off as long as it could be. Then, in 1930, Garbo "talked" for the first time, as the advertisements said. The film was *Anna Christie,* from

115

Madly in love, Marguerite and Armand are on a collision course that can only end in disaster.

the play by Eugene O'Neill. Not only did she talk with an accent, but she played a waterfront woman of low repute who falls in love with an Irish stoker. Quite a switch for the great sex symbol of the day.

The accent made no difference, however, and thereafter she played a succession of fallen women, some more elegant and plausible than others, such as the frustrated diva in *Romance* (1930), the American prostitute in *Susan Lenox: Her Fall and Rise* (1931), the Russian spy in *Mata Hari* (1931), the passé dancer in *Grand Hotel* (1932). Her appearance in *Queen Christina* (1933) brought her close to a realization of a different and devious character. This is a famous Swed-

ish monarch who likes to dress and act as a man, except (as is fully indicated) when she is making love. The hint of sexual ambivalence is clear enough in the role, but, of course, nothing could be made of it under the restrictions of the new Production Code. Garbo was brought back to her pattern in *Anna Karenina* (1935).

Now the valuable actress was at the juncture in her career where it was time for her full accreditation in the *artistic* aristocracy to which she aspired. She had never had a first-class director, really, outside of her old friend, Victor Sjostrom, who put her through a hack biography of Sarah Bernhardt, *The Divine Woman* (1928), and Jacques Feyder, the briefly transplanted

Persuaded by his ardor, Marguerite agrees to leave her Paris play set and live a country idyll with Armand.

The idyll is shattered, however, by Armand's father (Lionel Barrymore), who convinces Marguerite to give up Armand for the sake of his career.

Frenchman, who did her last woeful silent film, *The Kiss* (1929). Neither had she been acknowledged with an Academy Award, one of those Hollywood tokens of achievement which had been dispensed annually for eight years.

Considerately, Irving Thalberg, producer at Metro-Goldwyn-Mayer, the studio to which the actress was attached during her entire career in Hollywood, turned again to material that reeked of romance and tragedy, yet had in it all the implications that Garbo projected so well. It was Alexander Dumas' drama, *La Dame aux Camélias,* a classic of the nineteenth-century French theater which the great Sarah Bernhardt had acted and in which, under the title of *Camille,* Eleonora Duse made her triumphant debut in America in 1893. Dumas had based his drama on the career of a famous mid-nineteenth-century courtesan, Madeleine du Plessis, who is recorded as a girl with "a Dresden china figure and long enameled eyes." This fustian compound of romance and sentiment was turned over to Zoë Akins, Frances Marion and James Hilton to prepare for the screen, and a talented man, George Cukor, was called upon to direct.

Cukor, at this time in his thirties, had come to films from directing for the stage. He had had such striking screen successes as *A Bill of Divorcement* (1932), in which he skillfully directed a new actress, Katharine Hepburn, to her first fame; *Little Women* (1933), also with Miss Hepburn; *David Copperfield* (1934), and, at this point (1936), he was completing *Romeo and Juliet,* with Norma Shearer and Leslie Howard. Cukor had shown a sensitivity and particular aptitude for bringing out the best in women. He was what Garbo required.

Camille, as reconstructed for this offering, is in no way a transcript of the play. It is a skillful interweaving of the bare plot of the grossly sentimental old romance with studied fabrications appropriate to illusory cinema. In writing, staging and costuming, it is a thing of ruffles and frills, handsome faces, florid figures and fragile sentiments. And through it paces Garbo, luminous and serene, yet torn by all the passions that a woman in love can feel.

The heroine of this poignant story is a stately Parisian courtesan by the name of Marguerite Gauthier, who attracts and is blissfully attracted by a handsome

118

young diplomat careerist, Armand Duval. Swept off her feet by the ardor and passion he shows toward her, which is in conspicuous contrast to the effeteness of the men with whom she moves, she leaves her aristocratic patron and goes to live with Armand in an idyllic cottage in the country. But this lovely dream cannot last. Secretly, she is persuaded by Armand's father that she is bad for his career. So, thinking only of his best interest, she leaves him and returns to her wealthy baron.

Armand does not comprehend this. He thinks she is fickle, false. He does not conceive the immensity of the sacrifice she has made for him. So, when he meets her some time later in a gambling casino with her friend, he is cool and haughty. But love is still hot in him. And, after he has won a lot of money from the baron at cards, he begs Marguerite to reconsider, to go away with him. But she, knowing secretly (as we guess) that she is ill, declines, and this precipitates an ugly quarrel in which the baron challenges Armand to a duel. It is fought; Armand nicks the baron and has to go away for

a while. When he returns he has no interest in the whereabouts of Marguerite, whom we now know for certain is wasting away with lung disease. But finally he is moved to go to see her. And, yes, he arrives just in time to fill her with joy and thanksgiving that they are reunited again and to give her the longed-for opportunity of dying in his arms.

The magnificent achievement of Garbo in this romantic conceit is that she makes her extraordinary woman almost plausible—that is, within the expectations of historical reality; she makes her overwhelming within the latitudes permitted by romance. Her Marguerite is no trollop; neither is she an operatic cliché. She is a vibrant being, with heart and vitality, glowing enthusiasms and petty, even wicked, deceits, yet always impassioned generosity and basic integrity.

It is notable and meaningful that Cukor does not degrade this film with any gaudy or suggestive contrivances of amorous exercise. The kind of sensual acrobatics that Garbo does in some of her early films with

Not even his father can keep Armand from seeking out Marguerite once again, to comfort her and hold her in his arms as she dies.

Gilbert, Nils Asther and others is never intruded in *Camille,* partly because the Production Code would not allow it, but mainly because it would not be appropriate to the sort of romantic illusion wanted here. The impression communicated is that the quality of Marguerite's passion is too rich and transcendent for vulgar grappling and that of Armand too fine and dignified. And it is to the credit of Garbo and Robert Taylor, who plays the role of Armand with the zeal and concentration of an apt beginner (which he happened then to be), that they still make you sense there are warm bodies and hotly pulsing blood inside those beautifully fashioned and immaculately crisp costumes.

Significantly, the best revelations of Marguerite's emotional depths are in those scenes where she must confront painful decisions, such as that when Armand's father visits her and tactfully but forcefully reminds her that she is bad for his son's career. The fustian performance of Lionel Barrymore as the father in this exhausting scene is one of the sadder distractions of the film as it appears today. But Garbo's display of the feelings that flow and fight in Marguerite as she endures this painful confrontation—the expressions that tremble on her face, the close-up lifts and droops of her heavy eyelids that say so much more than words—is close to the best projection of emotion she does in the film.

Of course, she does have the benefit of William Daniels' indulgent camera, which catches her unusual features in the most evocative and flattering lights and shades. Daniels was the cameraman on all but six of Garbo's twenty-four Hollywood films, and he understood her face and its potentials like an engineer knows a fine machine. The glowing nimbuses he places around her profile, the shadows in the cheeks, the glints in the eyes contribute a great deal to the poetic image she conveys.

But the best scene—perhap's Garbo's greatest—is the last. Marguerite is now alone, dying abandoned by her baron and most of her friends, sadly in need of money and evidently resigned to her fate. Then Armand finally comes to her apartment. She hears that he is waiting outside and insists on getting out of her bed to greet him. She has her maid bring her loveliest negligee, then dress and arrange her to perfection and pin her invariable white camellias at her waist. She is standing as Armand enters, her eyes and face alight with hope, but with her movements remarkably suggesting a person wasted and exhausted by disease. It is wonderful how fragile and poetic she is as he sweeps her into his arms, babbles to her of his joy at seeing her again and talks of taking her to the country where she can get well and they can resume their love. She feeds on him like a famished person receiving nourishment, tangibly feasting on his ardor, pressing his passion to her heart and joyfully responding to his proposals with a flood of breathless affirmatives, "Yes! Yes! Yes!"

He lifts her from the chair in which she has been sitting; she crumbles in his arms. And while he still babbles of their future, she whispers almost inaudibly, "Perhaps it's better if I live in your heart, where you can't see me"—and she dies. Only then, in a flash of horror, does he comprehend that this is the end. And he is crying, "Marguerite, don't leave me! Come back," as the picture fades.

Thus does this classic romance conclude precisely as it should, with the ideal, illusory woman, still lovely and imperishable, in a bereft man's arms. This is not death as mortals know it. This is but the conclusion of a romantic ritual. Marguerite is really going to live forever, and not just in the heart of Armand.

La Grande Illusion (Grand Illusion)

French and British prisoners produce theatricals as a defense against the boredom of captivity.

1937

Screenplay by Jean Renoir and Charles Spaak; directed by Mr. Renoir; cameramen: Christian Matras and Claude Renoir; music by Joseph Kosma; produced by Raymond Blondy for Les Réalisations d'Art Cinematographic.

Maréchal	Jean Gabin
Captain de Boeldieu	Pierre Fresnay
Colonel von Rauffenstein	Erich von Stroheim
Rosenthal	Dalio
German Woman	Dita Parlo
Prisoner (the actor)	Carette
Prisoner (the engineer)	Gaston Modot
Prisoner (the teacher)	Edouard Daste
Prisoner (the soldier)	Georges Peclet

In 1937, just one year before Hitler began to fan his new armies across Europe and start the ominous overture to the Second World War, there was released in France a motion picture which one can confidently say is the most telling examination of the mystery of why men submit to war ever put on the screen. It is Jean Renoir's *La Grande Illusion* (*Grand Illusion*), a film which, for everything—theme, philosophy, construction, staging, performance and mood—merits the highest commendations and the monumental fame it has achieved.

Fighting as such is not its interest. The terrible, monstrous business of war, which was thoroughly excoriated in *All Quiet on the Western Front* (which see), is unmistakably realized in every implication of this film, which was written from scratch by Renoir and the distinguished Belgian scenarist, Charles Spaak. But its main concern is the slavish, automatic susceptibility of men to the complex of interlocked illusions that are used to foment and justify war—the illusions that warfare is glorious, that it is waged in a noble cause, that it induces the highest chivalry and spirit of comradeship in officers and men. And finally it is concerned with the illusion of the division of mankind into nations and political enclaves that are supposedly inviolable.

What *La Grande Illusion* boldly tells us in a drama about a group of French soldiers in German prison camps in the First World War is that war is but an extension of social conflict in which a ruling class attempts to manipulate the lower classes through illusions and deceits. Here the violence of fighting has been temporarily postponed for one group of soldiers through the military ritual of capture and imprisonment. But everything they do, all their ideas, intrigues and attitudes, and all their prickly relations with their commanders, are those of men at war. The disciplines of their involvement in the military machine derive not from any purpose of accomplishing something good for *them* but from the demand of service to some lofty and vaporous elite.

Their commanders—the German warden and the senior French officer in the camp—are aristocratic professionals committed to the interests of their class. They hobnob informally together, observe an exclusive etiquette, speak interchangeably in several languages and communicate in terms that show them to be above the pressures of nationality. They are agents of an implied economic ruling class which, for reasons of time and cohesion, the film does not attempt to clarify but which is, by reasonable assumption, responsible for the war.

On the other hand, the common soldiers—the French, British and Russians in the camp—are still explicitly conscious of their nationality. Although they get

To insure a really stiff-necked Teutonic portrayal, von Stroheim plays the prison commandant wearing a neck brace. His anti-Semitism is underscored when he sneers at one of the Jewish prisoners for translating Pindar.

along comfortably together, except for minor frictions that rise out of feelings of anti-Semitism (which stem from old nationalistic myths), and are able to project their class interests in an atmosphere of camaraderie, they are essentially chauvinistic, restless and eager to escape. They are moved by some ingrained illusion that it is their *duty* to break loose and fight again.

This aspect of *La Grande Illusion* as a metaphorical picture of class war, waged between aristocratic officers and proletarian men, rather than a simple exposure of the illusion of the officer elite, is one that was not too apparent or remarked on at the time the film was released. Then we were too much aligned with the images and conventions of the First World War. The appearance of Erich von Stroheim as the commander of the German prison camp, manifesting all his familiar char-

A scheme for escape, to be made possible by an outburst of noisy confusion, is working out by Captain Maréchal (Jean Gabin) and some of the other prisoners.

acteristics as the hateful Hun, almost dominated the picture and inevitably emphasized him, a distinctly Bismarckian Prussian, as symbolic of a national enemy.

Likewise the appearance of Pierre Fresnay as the senior French officer in the camp—elegant, suave, aristocratic and discreetly aloof from his men, yet technically considerate of them and willing to sacrifice himself to help them escape—conformed to the preconceived notion of the heroic French officer, steeped in the chivalrous traditions of the old military academy of St. Cyr. It was not convenient to see him as the exponent of a cold elite, exercising within his orbit the rigid control of a class.

Yet such is the signification of the Frenchman of Fresnay as well as the German of von Stroheim. And as we see this film today, conditioned by international conflicts and the experience of the Second World War, we can see that it states very soundly a proletarian theme, which is concluded with a characteristic surrender to cynicism and despair.

La Grande Illusion occurs in three movements, as distinct as those of a symphony. They might be described as the phases of acquiescence, rebellion and return.

The first, the phase of acquiescence, begins with two French officers—the professional captain, played by Fresnay, and a conscript captain, played by Jean Gabin —being brought into the officers' mess of a German air squadron after their plane has been downed and introduced to the squadron commander who has downed them, played by von Stroheim. Here we are given our first look at a vainglorious ritual of war. In a scene that might have been clipped from one of the many early sound films that heroized the daring fliers of the First World War, we see the German ace and his fellows solemnly pay their respects to "the gallant enemy shot down in battle." It is a romantic conceit. Then the two Frenchmen are taken, along with other French officers and men, to a dreary prisoner-of-war camp—a dull, unimpressive place of stark brick buildings and high wire fences—to be introduced to the monotony of prison life.

In various depictions, Renoir shows us the jollity of the men as they put on camp theatricals, open packages from home, or secretly dig a tunnel by which to escape. But then the tunnel-digging is discovered and the men who do not escape are moved to another camp for maximum security. Now the second, or rebellion, phase begins. And we are brought to a realization of how cruel is the enslavement of men by the rigid, relentless operation of a caste-run military machine.

Here the antagonist is presented in the person of the

To help the others escape, Captain de Boeldieu (Pierre Fresnay) has sacrificed his own life, a gesture which von Rauffenstein recognizes as the mark of breeding.

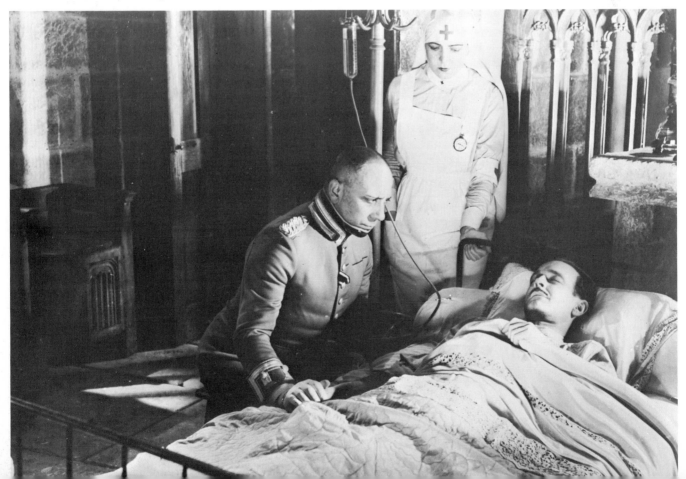

prison commander, the aristocratic flying officer from the first episode, now beached in this dismal, desolate duty because he has suffered a broken neck which is held in a brace, very stiffly, giving a rigid, steel-frame aspect to the man. Von Stroheim's tremendous inventiveness and comprehension in playing the role, for which Renoir has given full credit to the famous director of *Greed* (which see), are so sure and intense in conveying an impression of a ruthless, decadent type that the main drama of the story is almost overpowered.

He is the symbol of enslavement with whom the men now must contend—this steel-bound, taboo-ridden monster who squirts himself with perfume before he leaves his fetish-furnished chamber to confront the smelly lot of French prisoners. Quietly, efficiently, but with such sternness in his manner and voice that you know this is deadly business, he warns the men that there will be no escape from this security prison which, appropriate to the theme, is a large, old-fashioned villa with turrets and crenelated walls. And we catch his drift when he politely directs Fresnay to one side and indicates he has respect for him and confidence that he will restrain his men because he, too, is a professional soldier and an aristocrat.

Through this second phase of the picture and this significant gathering-in, there is a mood of quiet and sober tension, and a curious poetic quality, with the snow outside the old villa and a pervasive mood of antiquity.

Then this quietness is shattered with the explosion of a wild, audacious stunt which Fresnay has frankly helped a handful of rebellious prisoners arrange in order to escape—a great commotion of beating on pans and shrilling of penny flutes to disconcert the guards, with Fresnay running to the top of the highest turret, wearing white gloves and blowing a flute, to distract von Stroheim, while Gabin and a little Jew, played by Dalio, slip away. The climax of this commotion, with von Stroheim finally shooting down the elegant French officer because he truly thinks that he has gone mad, is excellent melodrama, fiercely and luridly staged, as searchlights pierce the darkness and race up and down the walls.

Now the picture goes into its third phase: the escape into open, winter country, drab and barren under a sprinkling of wet snow, and Gabin and Dalio in old clothes, walking dismally over the lonely hills, free from the restriction of prison but with no place to go. They're bickering and snarling because Dalio can't walk fast enough, and Gabin finally screams at him, "You know what you are to me? A ball and chain!" Then he cuts him most cruelly: "I always hated Jews."

This is the ultimate statement of the dehumanization caused by the enslaving disorder of the military machine. And as the erstwhile friend walks away down the road, leaving his little companion miserable and alone, we sense that this is the nadir of any hope for brotherhood. But then the rejector turns back, and a warming hope flames, which carries us on with the fugitives to the sanctuary of a remote German farm.

Here the two men are sheltered through the winter in a simple farmhouse by a peasant woman who has been widowed by the war. She treats them with respect and compassion and eventually lets Gabin make love to her, thus demonstrating the irony of nationality being aligned against nationality in mortal combat, the emptiness of artifical hate and the ridiculousness that a difference of religion should be a barrier to human regard.

Then Renoir brings us to the climax of his disturbing theme—the realization that these men, though liberated, have an urge to go back to their old ways. With the coming of spring, they are determined to move on toward their homes, to leave the generous German woman and become Frenchmen again. As they are escaping over the snow-clad Bavarian hills toward the distant sanctuary of neutral Switzerland, Gabin speaks what is probably the most trenchant line in the film: "Nature all looks alike. Frontiers are an invention of man."

When they are almost to the border, they are spotted by a German patrol, which is about to fire at them. Then the corporal shouts, "Don't shoot!" The two pathetic fugitives have passed beyond the invisible "invention of man" which separates Germany from Switzerland. They have crossed the optional line which separates the legality from the illegality of killing a man. And as the two plunge and stumble side by side in the deep snow and fade into the distance of the beautiful, peaceful alpine scene, one senses the awesome profundity of this simple revelation of man's inerasable gullibility and his continual turning back into his nationality.

Ninotchka

1939

Screenplay by Walter Reisch, Charles Brackett and Billy Wilder, from a story by Melchior Lengyel; directed by Ernst Lubitsch; cameraman, William Daniels; musical score by Werner R. Heymann; produced by Ernst Lubitsch for Metro-Goldwyn-Mayer.

Ninotchka	Greta Garbo
Count Léon d'Algout	Melvyn Douglas
Grand Duchess Swana	Ina Claire
Iranoff	Sig Rumann
Buljanoff	Felix Bressart
Kopalski	Alexander Granach
Commissar Razinin	Bela Lugosi
Count Rakonin	Gregory Gaye
Hotel Manager	Rolfe Sedan
Mercier	Edwin Maxwell
Gaston	Richard Carle

After her brilliant appearance in the tragi-romantic *Camille* (which see), for which, incidentally, fate denied her that coveted Academy Award (it went that year to Luise Rainer for her performance in *The Great Ziegfeld*), Greta Garbo appeared in one more picture in which she characteristically played a soulful, sensual woman who sacrifices all for love. This was the ironic *Conquest* (1937), in which she voluptuously portrayed the elegant Countess Walewska, mistress of Napoleon during his Russian campaign. But, alas, it was a hackneyed drama, and it did not at all utilize the manifested capacities of its luminous star. Evidently, Garbo had capped off the tragic-woman role, and her career was at another dangerous juncture, as it was when talking films arrived.

Envoys of the Soviet Union—left to right: Iranoff (Sig Rumann), Buljanoff (Felix Bressart) and Kopalski (Alexander Granach)—delay so long on a mission to Paris that a government officer, known simply as Nina (Greta Garbo), is dispatched to investigate.

A stern and disciplined comrade, Ninotchka decides to case Paris while the three envoys complete their mission of converting confiscated jewels into cash. On her tour, Ninotchka gets her bearings from a stranger, Count Léon d'Algout (Melvyn Douglas).

Then something wonderful happened. She was cast (I have never found out why) to play what would be her first all-out comedy role. It was the story of a Soviet special envoy in a satire prepared by Walter Reisch, Charles Brackett and Billy Wilder, entitled *Ninotchka*; it would be directed by Ernst Lubitsch.

This was a stroke of sheer fortune, for Lubitsch, who everyone knew was Hollywood's most perceptive craftsman at sophisticated, continental things, was available to do the picture only because he had been removed from an assignment to direct *The Women*, and this was only because George Cukor was put on that one after having been taken off *Gone with the Wind* (which see). By this fortuitous juggling of assignments at Metro-Goldwyn-Mayer, Garbo finally got as her director the man she should have had five years before.

Lubitsch was of that order of creative souls in cinema who intuitively understood the medium and were able to make a progressive transition from silent films to sound. Starting as an actor and director in postwar Germany, he had come to Hollywood in the 1920's and quickly distinguished himself with two clever, satiric entertainments, *The Marriage Circle* and *Forbidden Paradise,* both made in 1924. When sound came along, he used it in the charming *The Love Parade* (1929) to integrate commenting music with a light romantic theme. Maurice Chevalier and Jeanette MacDonald were his new, melodious stars, and he put them to further pleasant capers in *One Hour with You* (1932). But his best creations with music were *Monte Carlo* (1930), a blithe charade in which, for instance, he blended the theme song ("Beyond the Blue Horizon") with the accelerating tempo of a moving train; and *Trouble in Paradise* (1932), in which he imaged a whole sequence of bantering dialogue between two off-screen characters with a delightful montage of ticking clocks.

Lubitsch was rightly regarded as one of the most sophisticated directors in the world, obviously suitable for Garbo. Thus it was a kindly fate that brought the two together for *Ninotchka;* and it was a consummate irony that this was to be their only film together *and* the last great one of each.

The present disposition is to think of *Ninotchka* primarily as the film in which Garbo first appeared in a comedy role. But the real distinction of the picture is its velvet quality as a social-political satire that develops infectious comedy out of a topical situation that is sheer and quite apparent make-believe. Garbo's precise attunement to it is just one of its fine felicities.

Its story—a Soviet woman envoy comes to Paris to whip into line three preceding emissaries who have flubbed a mission to pawn some rare crown jewels and becomes herself diverted by the delights of the capitalist world—is a flimsy fiction which delicately balances upon the artful combination of a witty script, deft direction and a sentient star.

The major thrust of its satire is at the solemness and austerity of Marxist dogmatism and at the rigidity of a political system which compels its people to be as scornful of creature comforts and sensual pleasures as is the ascetic heroine. And its mischievous implication is that the Russians don't really want discipline.

This notion is established at the outset with the characters of the three emissaries, who arrive in front of a Paris hotel, lugging a bulging suitcase and trying to decide whether they should put up in this cheap hotel or go to the grand one—whether the latter would violate the principles of Lenin. These fellows are caricatures, clearly drawn from popular low-comedy stereotypes. There's the big, bearded, bright-eyed excited, fur-capped Germanic one, played by the talented Sig Rumann. He's ready to be corrupted right off. There's the hawk-nosed, myopic, cloth-capped one, played by Felix Bressart. He tends to be cautious and timorous. The third is a short, fat Russian, Alexander Granach. He's stupid and pliable. His reasoning is pragmatic. "So what?" is his attitude. They conclude that Lenin would want them to use the best hotel, and since the only safe there big enough to hold their suitcase is in the royal suite, they take that. Thus they are off to a luxurious and highly unproletarian start.

Now it is revealed that the suitcase contains a dazzling collection of crown jewels, former possessions of a grand duchess which were confiscated by the Soviet state and which the boys have been sent to Paris to pawn (or sell) secretly. This is quickly discovered by a hotel valet, obviously a spy, who beats it straight to the Paris apartment of the grand duchess, Ina Claire. She is with her handsome boyfriend, Count Léon, whom Melvyn Douglas plays with every indication of being a full-blooded American. He immediately gets the setup and promises to recover her jewels for her.

How he begins his campaign to make an arrangement for the purchase of the jewels is subtly described by Lubitsch in one of the classic metaphors in films. We are back at the hotel in the corridor outside the door to the royal suite. Behind the door, we hear a babble of men's voices, talking excitedly. A waiter arrives carrying a huge tray of food and goes through the door. A chorus of appreciative "ahhhs!" comes from inside the room. Then a waiter arrives carrying magnums of champagne in buckets and goes in. Louder "ahhhs!" and more enthusiastic hubbub.

Then the camera picks up a cigarette girl in tiny skirt and black silk opera hose tripping along the corridor. She enters the room, all innocence, and a terrific blast of delighted howls and hollers is immediately heard. She emerges a moment later, disheveled and flustered, and beats it down the corridor only to return with two other cigarette girls. They go in, and the din is deafening. Lubitsch holds this for a moment, then cuts to a close-up of a standing hatrack on which hang the two cloth caps and the fur hat of the fellows. In a slow dissolve, the two caps turn into derbies and the fur hat turns into

Count Léon's jokes fall flat, but when he does too, Ninotchka explodes with laughter.

The boys go to her cautiously and meekly introduce themselves. She responds to their introductions in heavy-voiced monotones. "What a charming idea for Moscow to have surprised us with a lady comrade," Rumann says. She looks at him coldly. "Don't make an issue of my womanhood," she warns. "How are things in Moscow?" another of the boys inquires. She answers flatly, "Very good. The last mass trial was a great success. There are going to be fewer but better Russians." This is a morbid reminder of the mass political trials that went on in Russia in the 1930's and resulted in the liquidation of hundreds of the enemies of Stalin.

Nina—which is her name, she tells them—is frankly here to check on the boys. Right off, she is disgusted to find them in a grand hotel. They try to explain. She scorns them. Then she asks for a cigarette, and Rumann happily pushes the bell. Here is a way to prove to her the functional efficiency of this hotel. All three cigarette girls come bounding expectantly into the room.

On a sightseeing trip in Paris, Nina meets Léon and asks directions of him. He doesn't know north from south, but he is amused by her. He brazenly tries to flirt. She gives him a cold contemptuous look. "I have heard of the arrogant male in capitalistic society," she tells him. "Your type will soon be extinct." But he invites her to his apartment, after showing her the glory of Paris from the Eiffel Tower. She calmly accepts the offer: "You might be an interesting study." Léon is voluble, romantic. "You talk too much," she admonishes him. Whereupon he kisses her, then asks, "How was that?" She ponders for a moment. "That was restful," she says. "Again!" Suddenly she finds she likes kissing. Indeed, she stoutly kisses him, but when he later remarks upon this boldness, she quietly answers, "I kissed a Polish lancer, too—before he died."

It is notable how this simple comment strikes a somber and sympathetic chord and brings us to realize Nina—or Ninotchka, as Léon nicknames her—is more than a caricature. Beneath her awkward exterior and behind those solemn eyes, implicit within the dull admissions of dedication to Communism that she makes, we sense a dreary succession of privations, sufferings and toils. We guess these are what have desexed her and deprived her of the knowledge of love. And because she is played by Garbo, who can never be totally removed from a shadow of dark and secret sorrows, we have a quick rush of feeling for her.

This solicitude for Ninotchka now becomes the compelling force that makes us both pleased and apprehensive as Léon proceeds to draw her out. We are entirely delighted when he finally gets her to laugh and when

In a fairy-tale plot the count gets the jewels from Ninotchka and gives them to their rightful owner, the Grand Duchess, who in turn gives them back to Ninotchka in exchange for the count.

a shiny silk topper. Thus does he inform us how simple the corruption of the comrades is.

Inside the room now the fellows are completely drunk, kissing Count Léon profusely and telling him he's a wonderful guy; and he, cold sober and canny, is drafting a telegram to notify the Kremlin that the jewels are to be turned over to the grand duchess and the French.

But come the dawn—and Ninotchka. Now we pick up the boys, wearing their country caps, running along the platform of a railway station, looking for the new envoy they are to meet. They are extremely nervous, wondering what's going to happen to them. Then they spot their target. It is Garbo, standing starkly alone, the image of cold austerity. She wears a limp rain hat, a shapeless raincoat, tailored suit and low-heeled shoes— a completely forbidding figure of unfemininity. Her face is a mask, without expression, except for an ominous hint of anger and sullen disapproval in her deep-set eyes.

128

With a tearful parting, Ninotchka goes back to Moscow, only to be sent off on another mission where she meets—guess who?

she shows up at his apartment uncertainly wearing a giddy Parisian hat. We are charmed when he takes her out to dinner, she dressed in an elegant evening gown, and he gives her her first glass of champagne—a temptation she accepts with as lovely a show of exploration, amazement and enchantment as ever played upon the mobile Garbo face.

But we are also nervous and uneasy when he later takes her to her room and charmingly proceeds to seduce her; not because we begrudge her the delight, for which she is obviously eager—breathlessly, radiantly so—but because we detect that the rascal is simply using her to get the jewels, playing upon her need for pleasure, the way he has played upon the boys. And we feel it is a brutal exploitation, a capitalist plot, to do

this to *her*. Thus, the delight of the picture is that Léon is the one who gets caught. It is he who succumbs to the enchantment of this fascinating, disciplined Russian girl. And though he does manage to arrange it so that she and the three comrades can defect in the end, it is he who is finally forced to a defection from the parasitic life he has led.

It is incredible that this charming picture, with its impudent mockery of Soviet chauvinism and capitalist conceit, was a box-office disappointment at the time it was released. Audiences apparently took it seriously and were confused by Garbo's unfamiliar role. But it served as a fitting capstone to her and Lubitsch's careers. It is a delightful reminder of two of the finest artists of the screen.

129

Carefree Scarlett O'Hara (Vivien Leigh) with the twins, Stuart (Fred Crane) and Brent (George Reeves) Tarleton, on the flower-wreathed porch of her Georgia home, so soon to be ravaged by the bitter winds of war.

Gone with the Wind

1939

Adapted by Sidney Howard from the novel by Margaret Mitchell; directed by Victor Fleming; production design by William Cameron Menzies; musical score by Max Steiner; photography by Ernest Haller; costumes designed by Walter Plunkett; fire scenes staged by Lee Zavitz; produced by David O. Selznick and released by Metro-Goldwyn-Mayer.

Scarlett O'Hara	Vivien Leigh
Rhett Butler	Clark Gable
Ashley Wilkes	Leslie Howard
Melanie Hamilton	Olivia de Havilland
Mammy	Hattie McDaniel
Gerald O'Hara	Thomas Mitchell
Ellen O'Hara	Barbara O'Neil
Frank Kennedy	Caroll Nye
Aunt Pittypat	Laura Hope Crews
Dr. Meade	Harry Davenport
Charles Hamilton	Rand Brooks
Belle Watling	Ona Munson
Carreen O'Hara	Ann Rutherford
Brent Tarleton	George Reeves
Stuart Tarleton	Fred Crane
Pork	Oscar Polk

Scarlett, so recently a bride, now a war widow, verbally spars with the picaresque Rhett Butler (Clark Gable), after Melanie Hamilton Wilkes (Olivia de Havilland) has introduced them at a war charity bazaar.

Prissy	Butterfly McQueen
Suellen O'Hara	Evelyn Keyes
Jonas Wilkerson	Victor Jory
Emmy Slattery	Isabel Jewell
A Yankee Looter	Paul Hurst
Bonnie Blue Butler	Cammie King

Of all the American motion pictures entitled to be designated great on the basis of *all* their qualifications, including the extent of the excitement they have caused, one towers above all the rest. That is the massive screen production of the Civil War novel, *Gone with the Wind*.

Never before or since its making has so much attention been fixed upon the urgency and the responsibility of bringing a film into being. Never has the public's interest been so attracted in the preparation stage, and never has a national volition been so generously fulfilled and satisfied. I strongly suspect a great deal of the "Civil War cult" of later years was seeded in the shaky 1930's by Margaret Mitchell's huge, nostalgic novel and the film made from it.

Miss Mitchell's novel was published in 1936 and burst upon the literary world as one of those sudden sensations that come only occasionally. Its heroine, Scarlett O'Hara, the pampered Georgia girl who emerged a tough and gaudy phoenix out of the smoldering ashes of the Civil War, swiftly became the most impressive, exciting, fascinating, discussed and certainly the most romantic female of the day. Inevitably, the production of a motion picture from such a successful book was a matter for popular speculation. And the fact that David O. Selznick had acquired the screen rights for a mere $50,000 before the novel was published was the first of many extraordinary developments in the saga of its transfer to the screen.

Selznick, a first-class showman and a gifted producer, was not slow in realizing what a remarkable property he had obtained. But even he was slow in grasping the great potential of *Gone with the Wind*. By the end of the year of publication, he had got from the distinguished playwright, Sidney Howard, a rather full treatment for a screenplay and had begun to think of casting the film. But the magnitude of the sales of the novel and the spontaneous surge of public interest in who would appear in the movie caused him to pause.

Almost from the beginning, the actor who leaped to

The railroad station at Atlanta is a charnel house of the wounded and dying waiting for medical aid and what little help Scarlett can offer.

mind as the only one to play Rhett Butler, the picaresque hero, was the tremendously popular Clark Gable. However, Gable was under contract to Metro-Goldwyn-Mayer, which was not inclined to loan him to an independent producer, except for a formidable *quid pro quo*: an arrangement whereby the big studio would finance and distribute the film. Since Selznick had a contract to release his films through United Artists until 1939, this meant that *Gone with the Wind* could not be distributed by another company until after that date. So Selznick, bent on getting Gable, was compelled to delay for two years.

The time was used to good advantage in expanding the production plans, exploring casting arrangements, working with various writers on the script and especially in contemplating the burning question of who was to play Scarlett. This was another issue that concerned the public greatly. But even as late as December 1938,

Selznick had not reached a decision as to who would play the role. And, by then, he had completed arrangements to begin shooting.

The location for the filming was to be the Pathé lot in Culver City, not far from Metro-Goldwyn-Mayer. To clear this lot of some old standing sets in order to make way for the construction of the plantation mansions of Tara and Twelve Oaks and the Atlanta buildings and streets, the art director, William Cameron Menzies, proposed that the old sets be brought down in a monstrous nighttime conflagration which could be photographed to constitute the big scene of the burning of Atlanta, a climax in the film. This heroic suggestion was enthusiastically embraced. Two stunt men were engaged to ride in an old wagon in front of the burning sets to represent in long shot the flight of Rhett and Scarlett (and Melanie Wilkes and her newborn child) out of the defeated city.

Rhett and Scarlett O'Hara flee from a burning Atlanta with the dazed remnants of the defending army.

The scene was shot on the night of December 10, 1938. And on that night, while Atlanta was burning, Myron Selznick, David's brother, came on the lot with Vivien Leigh, a beautiful green-eyed British actress, and casually presented her to the preoccupied producer as "your Scarlett." It was an arresting, dramatic gesture that Selznick could not resist. He there and then decided that Miss Leigh was to have the role.

Three weeks after shooting started in the spring of 1939, the director, George Cukor, was taken off and Victor Fleming, a close friend of Gable, was given the job. He became ill a few weeks and Sam Wood was rushed in to finish the film. Finally, on the night of December 14, 1939, the mighty *Wind* was given a triumphant world premiere in Atlanta, Miss Mitchell's home town. Its length was three hours and forty-five minutes, the longest film released in the United States up to that time.

Its reception was tremendous. But for all the public enthusiasm and critical acclaim, no one then dreamed how popular and culturally momentous it would be. It has been the most widely circulated, the most often seen, the most profitable film ever made—and that includes *The Birth of a Nation,* to which it bears an astonishing resemblance in many significant ways.

The eminence of this picture is in the richness with which it conveys a universally recognizable portrait of a many-faceted female character within a vast and tumultuous panorama of socially exciting events. But *Gone with the Wind* is more than the exposure of a vivid character, more than a superfluity of adventure, romance and spectacle. It is a superior illustration of a large chunk of American legend and myth, a grand illusion of imagined people living through a nostalgia-drenched experience.

The first title sets the stage succinctly. "There was a land of cavaliers and cottonfields in the Old South," it says; and this conception, echoing folklore and Stephen Foster songs, states the romantic environment in which the drama begins. No attempt to suggest the full reality of the antebellum South is made, or to give an intelligent comprehension of the causes of the American Civil War. This is solely an outline of the cruel "War Between the States" as it affects and alters the course of the life of a self-centered girl. It is in no sense documentary. On the contrary, it is a purely selective arrangment and coloration of historical events. But the hints of these events are so evocative, so skillfully realized, they have the effect of seeming at least to articulate history.

I will not attempt to detail or analyze the plot of this long-drawn, narrative-patterned drama. Rather I will indicate key scenes in which the character of Scarlett is

realized in the great flow of events, and the illusion of history in the making is most forcibly achieved.

There is the scene of the charity ball in Atlanta, at which money is being raised for the families of the fallen heroes in the early days of the war, and Scarlett, the belle of the plantations, in widow's weeds, flirts openly and maliciously with the debonair blockade-runner, Rhett. To her this is still but an extension of the mannered socializing of her youth.

And then there is the scene of the reading of the casualty lists after Gettysburg, with Scarlett, fearing to find the name of her adored Ashley Wilkes among them, standing detached and aloof amid a group of mothers and young wives sobbing softly, while a band made up of boys and led by an elderly home-guardsman defiantly strikes up "Dixie."

Some have professed disappointment that there are no big battle scenes, no thundering clashes of armies to convey the bloodiness of the Civil War. But the omission was judicious, for such would only distract from the concentration on Scarlett and her growing

Back at Tara, Scarlett defends her home by shooting down a Union looter (Paul Hurst).

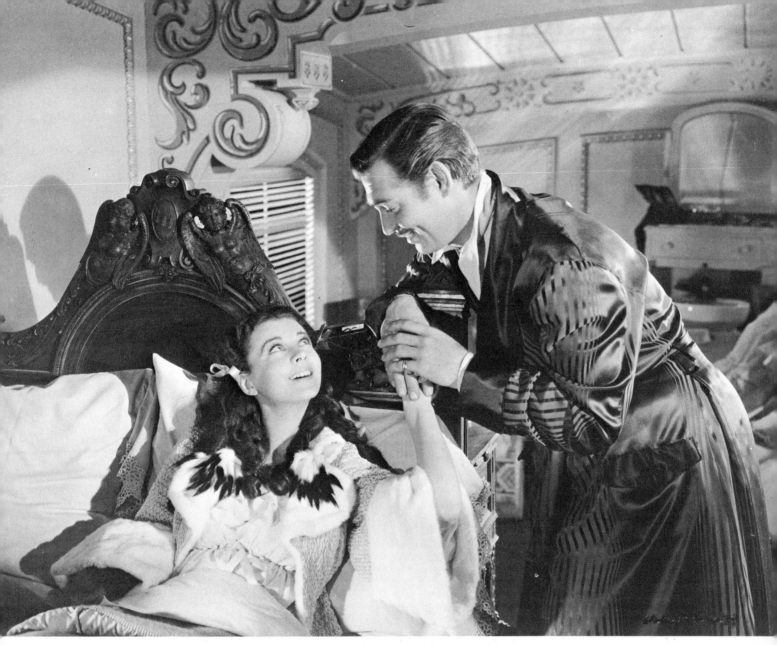

Sailing to New Orleans on a luxurious honeymoon with Rhett, Scarlett conveniently forgets all the ravages of war and reconstruction.

awareness of privation and defeat. And no battle scenes could be more eloquent of the butchery and agony of that war than the scenes in which Scarlett, working as a ladylike volunteer in a military hospital in Atlanta, observes the hideously wounded men, watches a homesick boy die and is called upon to assist in a meat-ax amputation of a gangrenous leg. Nor could anything be more eloquent of the wretchedness of the Confederacy's collapse than the scene of Scarlett, trying to find the family doctor to deliver the baby of Melanie Wilkes, moving among a horde of wounded men lying unattended and helpless on the cobblestones of a public square.

It is from this scene that the strongest and most expressive phase of the picture extends—the phase recounting the burning and fall of Atlanta and Scarlett's return to the desolation of the family plantation, Tara,

in defeat. And the depth of her disillusion is portrayed in a devastating scene where she goes out into a barren field, vomits, gets down on her knees, puts her brow against the earth and cries in anguish: "As God is my witness, I'm going to live through this, and when it's over, I'll never be hungry again!"

The succeeding phases of the film are in appropriately different, more materialistic and sardonic veins. The first, which covers the period of Reconstruction, is sturdy and often droll. It has a determined Scarlett, busying about Tara, working the fields with Melanie, scolding her and Mammy, the faithful servant, for taking care of passing Confederate homegoers, chasing the renegade ex-foreman and his "white trash" wife off the place, and then shooting the Union Army deserter, who has come to loot and rape, shooting him full in the face

135

with an old horse pistol as he threateningly ascends the stairs. "Well, I guess I've done murder," says Scarlett. "Well, I guess I won't think about that. I'll think about that tomorrow"—as she purloins the dead man's pocketbook, stuffed with greenbacks and gold pieces with which we are led to assume she gets Tara going again.

There's the return of Ashley; Scarlett's shameless attempt to get him to run away with her; her visit to the jail in Atlanta, dressed up in makeshift clothes, to try to get money from Rhett with a halfhearted offer of herself; her marriage to the well-behaved Frank Kennedy and their beginning to accumulate wealth with a sawmill worked by cheap convict labor which she persuades a reluctant Ashley to arrange. There is also the tense, dramatic episode of a Ku Klux Klan raid on Shantytown, where Scarlett has been molested; the wounding of Ashley and the killing of Frank. All this is good pictorial narration. But the apex of the story is past.

And now comes the final phase, in which Scarlett agrees to marry Rhett, whose interest in her has continued; goes on a honeymoon to New Orleans, returns to Atlanta to bear his child and settles with contented ostentation into the role of a vulgar nouveau riche, offensive to the Old Guard society, which Rhett rather wishes to embrace; and, finally, after a series of personal disasters, is deserted by Rhett.

In this phase, the hurt and disappointment the selfish woman causes the now regenerate Rhett is the only advancement of comment, and this is rather skimpy and confused because the forcefulness of Gable's performance, capped by his parting shot, "I don't give a damn!", belie the purport that Scarlett has cruelly damaged him. The chief structural weakness of the picture is the jumble of nonessentials in the last phase. We've had enough of Scarlett—and Rhett, too—long before the end. However, this needless extension of the weaker latter part of the book isn't so much of an anticlimax that it submerges that major and mighty middle part.

Naturally, there may be some objection among those who see it today that its sympathies are mainly directed to a class of people that has been historically discredited—that is, the southern slaveowners who were rightly dispossessed by the war and whose next generation generally brought forth a middle class of white supremacists. But this is no reason for resisting it as a powerful film than the same reason is for resisting The Birth of a Nation as a pioneer work of cinema art.

Scarlett is a vibrant human being, as passionately played by Miss Leigh, sharply and honestly reflective of a tangle of selfishness and sentiment. Rhett is a rich, romantic rascal in Gable's strongly muscled hands, and Leslie Howard's Ashley Wilkes and Olivia de Haviland's Melanie are true exponents of noble ideals. Colorful representations of lesser characters are given by Thomas Mitchell as Scarlett's father, Hattie McDaniel as her Negro nurse, Ona Munson as a bordello madam, Butterfly McQueen as a Negro servant, and many more. The sets, the costumes, the music by Max Steiner and the color are tributes to craft.

There have been more ambitious, more expensive and longer historical-spectacle films made in the years since this one. And there have been a few that have had more critical réclame. But there has never been one more effective than Gone with the Wind. There may never be.

The Grapes of Wrath

Pushing and shoving their ancient, overloaded truck, the Joads finally come to California and a hoped-for livelihood.

1940

Screenplay by Nunnally Johnson, based on the novel by John Steinbeck; musical score by Alfred Newman; directed by John Ford; cameraman, Gregg Toland; produced by Darryl F. Zanuck for Twentieth Century-Fox.

Tom Joad	Henry Fonda
Ma Joad	Jane Darwell
Casy	John Carradine
Grampa	Charley Grapewin
Rosasharn	Dorris Bowdon
Pa Joad	Russell Simpson
Al	O. Z. Whitehead
Muley	John Qualen
Connie	Eddie Quillan
Granma	Zeffie Tilbury
Noah	Frank Sully
Uncle John	Frank Darien
Winfield	Darryl Hickman
Ruth Joad	Shirley Mills
Thomas	Roger Imhof
Caretaker	Grant Mitchell
Wilkie	Charles D. Brown
Davis	John Arledge
Policeman	Ward Bond
Bert	Harry Tyler
Bill	William Pawley
Father	Arthur Aylesworth
Joe	Charles Tannen
Inspection Officer	Selmar Jackson
Leader	Charles Middleton
Proprietor	Eddie Waller
Floyd	Paul Guilfoyle
Frank	David Hughes
City Man	Cliff Clark
Bookkeeper	Joseph Sauers
Tim	Frank Faylen
Agent	Adrian Morris
Muley's Son	Hollis Jewell
Spencer	Robert Homans
Driver	Irving Bacon
Mae	Kitty McHugh

There has been a peculiar disposition among literary critics in recent years to downgrade John Steinbeck's historic and eloquent novel, *The Grapes of Wrath;* and some of the younger cinema critics seem to have fallen into the trap by loftily underestimating the fine motion picture made from it. They charge that is is "pseudo-documentary," a charge that can obviously be made against any film that is logically intended to recreate the raw look of actuality. They find it oversentimental. Sentiment is strong in it, that's true, but it is the sentiment of a kind of people whose natures are full of it. And they say it is grossly romantic in that it confidently assumes that a group of underprivileged proletarians, weakened by ignorance and want, would be as loyal and charitable toward one another as the people are made to appear in this film.

In my estimation, the endeavors to knock this epic film are pathetically posey. They show the urges to belittle a piece of work that is permanently reflective of a stubborn aspect of American life. They also betray some vague vexation about the failure of the characters to rise to the point of outright social rebellion some seem to think the situation compels.

That is because these critics tend to make the same mistake in estimating this picture as was made (in a different vein) by most of the critics who hailed it when it was first released: they want to see it as a film of mordant protest against social and economic inequities, a piece of anti-banker propaganda, while it really is something else.

The Grapes of Wrath is essentially a summation of the final collapse and economic disintegration of the

There is disillusionment waiting in the migrant camps where the Joads find acceptance, an existence not too much better than the one they have left behind.

nineteenth-century agrarian class—the small, hand-plow, family-unit farmers who broke the plains of the West and the Southwest and were the independent producers of grain and cotton until the tractor came along. It is a drama of the dispossessed descendants of those simple, earth-turning pioneers who settled the open lands of this country during and after the Civil War, fought for their homestead farms against the open-range cattle ranchers and nature's relentless elements, doggedly struggled for existence, until science and mechanization made the small, primitive farm obsolete and turned its owners into propertyless sharecroppers and their children into migrant employees.

This is the economic cycle that is perceived in *The Grapes of Wrath* and is transmuted into an epic drama by showing its consequence in personal terms. The sheriffs and landowners' agents who kick the sharecroppers out of their shacks at the beginning of the picture and send them on their wandering way are no more the originators of injustice than were the cowboys who cut the fences and burned the barns of the pioneering farmers, as so often represented in western films. And the big vegetable growers and orchard owners who use these people as cheap labor when they arrive in the Promised Land of California are no more willful designers of a capitalist plot than were the ancient Egyptian landowners who forced the children of Israel into peonage. They are fortuitous forces endowed with power by the circumstance of change, and are no more

responsible for the plight of the people than the people are themselves.

I feel sure it was this classic conflict in the Steinbeck novel that commended it to the attention of Darryl Zanuck, the head of production at Twentieth Century-Fox, and to Nunnally Johnson, who wrote the screenplay. It was certainly this aspect of the tale, this potential of it as a saga of earthy people carrying on in the face of mighty adversities, that rendered it apt and attractive to the directorial bent and skill of John Ford.

Even so, the producers were aware of a strong resentment of the Steinbeck work at the time they purchased the novel and put it into production shortly after its publication in 1939. Its story of the westward migration of a tatterdemalion family group of Oklahoma sharecroppers—Okies—around 1933, in the depths of the Great Depression and the calamitous Dust Bowl drought, was the digest of a tragic chapter in our nation's history, and it was a story that certain people in Oklahoma and California didn't wish to have advertised. When the company went on location to make the migration scenes in Texas, Oklahoma and California, they took no chances; they said the film they were making was to be an innocuous romance called *Highway 66*. Most of it was shot on location and at remarkably small expense. Steinbeck received $75,000 for the screen rights; the total production cost, after purchase of the story, was $800,000, more or less.

The popular awareness of the nature of the disaster

In a futile gesture, Muley (John Qualen) tries to shoot down a tractor that is knocking over the Okies' poor shacks.

To be allowed to proceed, Ma Joad (Jane Darwell) must convince the police officers that Granma is ill—when in fact the old lady has died.

that is memorialized is implicit in the fact that no time is taken to explain the reason for the Okies' movement westward, other than with a few words and the few key guides presented so graphically by Ford: the share-cropper shacks standing forlornly in the great expanses of dry and cropless land, and the bulldozers clanging and growling as they move in to knock down these shacks. The people are moving because it is their nature to seek something better for themselves. They are not helpless and hopeless "graveyard ghosts," as old Muley is—Muley, the stubborn beaten neighbor of the Joads who stays behind to die on his lost land. What is important in the drama is the persistence of these American characters: Ma and Tom Joad, a classic combine of indomitable mother and hard-grained son; the irrepressible old folks; the callow and sodden young.

From a tough and lean script prepared by Johnson, Ford assembled a sharply graphic film that has the black-and-white journalistic texture of photographed reality. Through Gregg Toland's newsreel-conscious camera, he got a picture that might almost be one of those mid-1930's documentaries of the Dust Bowl and the migration of the Okies, prepared by a government agency. (Pare Lorentz's 1936 classic, *The Plow That Broke the Plains,* is tacitly acknowledged as the model for the atmospheric and photographic style.)

The story gains momentum and reveals its characters with the start of the California exodus movement—in the childlike excitement of Pa and Uncle John, old Grampa and all the others as they load their ancient truck; in the touches of pathos and nostalgia for gone and wasted years, as Ma fingers through her family mementos in the dark of the dawn before they go; in the pouring of soothing syrup into Grampa at the last moment so they can get him drunk and into the truck, and then the pitiful death and burial of the old man by the road on their first night out.

Gusto and exhilaration, mixed with moments of

doubt and dismay, run through the exodus segment, even though the picture of America that is shown is one of depressing drabness: concrete highways, monotonous towns, standardized filling stations, junk yards full of broken cars, dog wagons, migrant campgrounds, Indian huts made of mud. How different from the scene of America that *The Covered Wagon* (which see) gives! The climax of this phase comes with the plugging of the truck up a long hill to bring the family to a glowing prospect out across the beautiful Tehachapi Valley of California at dawn—and then Ma's quiet announcement that Granma had died in her arms in the back of the truck during the night.

The next phase is that of the unfolding of discovery, disillusion and despair in the Promised Land: the first exposure of the family to the migrant camps, the human junk yards, where they see the jobless people and the hungry people, where they first sense the strange hostility of the skull-cracking vigilantes who are alien to all they've ever known, where they smell the first fumes of rebellion that smoldered during the Depression years.

The compulsion and submission of the family to be fruit pickers at wages far below a bare subsistence level are graphically dramatized, as is Tom's brief involvement with a strike movement, during which he accidentally kills a man, followed by the brightening arrival of the family at a well-run government camp. Then comes the spoiling of this haven by an abortive intrusion of goons, who nevertheless become suspicious of Tom's involvement in the killing during the strike, thus compelling him, a parolee and already a fugitive, to flee.

To me the most affecting and meaningful scene is Tom's farewell to his mother on the empty dance floor of the government camp at dawn, when he accepts his inevitable alienation and prepares to take off on his own. As overtalked and sentimental as this scene incontestably is (and Johnson has certainly filled it with unlikely loquacity, while Ford has added his measure of emotionalism by having the sad strains of "Red River Valley" played in the background by an accordion), it brings to a devastating climax the drama's major theme. For this is a brilliant symbolization of the act of

Tom Joad (Henry Fonda), marked always for trouble, must bid Ma a poignant, and final farewell.

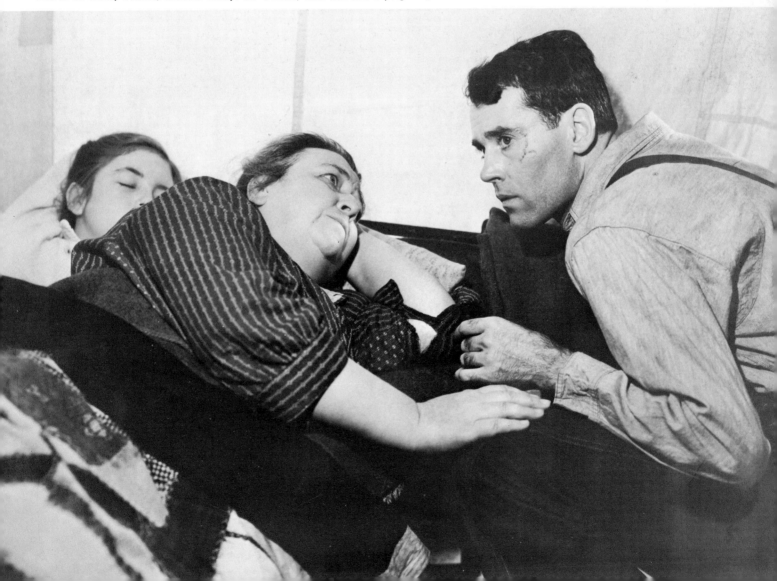

cutting the silver cord, not just the cord of Tom's attachment to his mother, as poignant as this is, but the cord of a farm boy's attachment to the nourishment of Mother Earth. Here, in this deeply personal parting, we see Tom leave the sanctuary of the soil that will no longer support him. And we know, as we see him swinging out across a distant hill, with his few belongings in a bundle, that he is gone forever from the land, that here is another bulldozed farmer who will be swallowed up in the toils of truck drivers or oil-well drillers or filling-station attendants or road-building crews or some other dreary occupation of the automotive age.

Tom, being intelligent and realistic, sees that the change which has upset their lives was inevitable. This is the revolution to which his people must adjust. And though he makes sentimental comments about being "on'y a piece of the one big soul that belongs to everybody" and about how he'll "be all aroun' in the dark . . . wherever there's a fight so hungry people can eat . . . wherever there's a cop beating up a guy," there is no real rebellion in him. He has actually abandoned the dying dream of a happy land for his poor people and is going off to seek a new world. Only Ma and Pa and the children, who are too ignorant or helpless to adjust, go on in the sad delusion that there is a bright future for them.

Clearly the foremost character, the focal interest, in the drama is Tom. He is truly a figure of classic tragedy, a strong and deserving person whom Fate (or circumstances) overwhelms. And Henry Fonda's performance presents him perfectly. It is lean, hard, laconic, tough and tender. It has muscle, humor and heart.

Complementing the qualities of this character is Ma, a monumental symbol of courage, competence and faith. She is the sort who faces forward. She fundamentally believes in her ability to take care of her situation, not in any supernatural power. She is played by Jane Darwell with great compassion and dignity.

It is interesting that there is no pushing of religiosity in this tale. These people have done their churchgoing, they have tested the power of prayer, they concede to some divine overseer, as witness the little plea for the salvation of the living that the ex-preacher Casy, makes at the burial of Grampa. But this is perfunctory, ritualistic. They have discovered they must do for themselves. In the character of Casy, the one-time country evangelist who becomes a strike organizer with the Okies in California, is conveyed a sense of the transition of spiritual fervor in the working class. John Carradine makes Casy a sardonic iconoclast.

Others are fine; Russell Simpson's Pa Joad is an American Gothic type, Charley Grapewin's Grampa is a cheerful old country-bumpkin scamp, John Qualen's reactionary Muley is a Scandinavian immigrant on the frontier. Zeffie Tilbury's Granma is a sweet, senile shell of a worked-out drudge. High marks go to everybody—Frank Darien as Uncle John, Eddie Quillan as Connie, O. Z. Whitehead as Al, Darryl Hickman as Winfield.

I have remarked on the style of Ford's direction and the realistic camerawork. Especially striking is the use of sound, the information packed in it and the emotional effect. So much of the chaos of the hegira is suggested in the rattle and clatter of the old truck, the banging of tin cans and kitchen utensils and other metallic odds and ends, all given a certain melding rhythm by the singing guitar music on the way. There is the fiddle-and-pan playing of "Red River Valley" at the Saturday-night dance in the camp, the musical theme of "Red River," the melancholy hoot of a train in the distance on the night Tom leaves, the twitter of birds, the sounds of children, the thump and hiss of the overheated motor on the old truck carrying its freight of human castoffs into oblivion.

Fantasia

1940

Story direction by Joe Grant and Dick Huemer; production supervision by Ben Sharpsteen; animation directors, Samuel Armstrong, James Algar, Bill Roberts, Paul Satterfield, Hamilton Luske, Jim Handley, Ford Beebe, T. Hee, Norm Ferguson and Wilfred Jackson; score conducted by Leopold Stokowski and recorded by the Philadelphia Symphony Orchestra; narrative introductions by Deems Taylor; produced by Walt Disney, Inc.

It simply would not stand to reason that a volume devoted to great films should be without some exemplar of the animated cartoon. This subdivision of motion photography, so complete with its own canon of esthetics and mechanical techniques, has provided not only some of the most popular entertainment of the screen but some of the most subtle evocations of feat and fantasy this medium has known.

The fact that Mickey Mouse was the delight of generations of children around the world before he was superannuated to occasional reruns on kiddie television shows, or that Felix the Cat was the darling of mere tots who are great-grandparents today, does not signify that they and their doings were any the less considerable as embodiments of cinema expression than the most serious adult work. The cartoon, or animated drawing, which is a more inclusive term—or, best of all, film animation, which is a term to embrace all techniques of single-frame, stop-motion mechanization of mobile images, whether they be drawings or puppets or inanimate objects or fanciful ideographs moved in space —is a means of designing and projecting infinite imagination with flexible ease, and it has provided countless examples of undeniable cinema art.

My difficulty here has been in choosing what animation deserves to be specified in this volume as the outstanding work in this field. So many wonderful and witty, amazing and articulate films leap to mind in a reminiscence of the whole range of animation and cartoon that I find myself bewildered and torn as to which

A zooful of terpsichoreans keeps the mood light to the tune of Ponchielli's *Dance of the Hours*.

to choose. The problem is further complicated by the fact that the majority of them—the great majority, I should say—are short films, brilliant creations in themselves and manifestations of skill, ingenuity, whimsy, poetry and thought, but short, after all, and therefore limited in concept and design.

There are, for instance, the pioneers: the first cartoon films of Emile Cohl, the Frenchman who is considered the father of the genre; or the early American innovations, such as *Gertie the Dinosaur* of Winsor McCay and *Felix the Cat* of Pat Sullivan, which were serialized and hugely popular about the time that Charlie Chaplin was making one- and two-reel comedies.

And there are the juvenilia of Walt Disney, the most famous film cartoonist of all, who began doing his own animations in 1923 and made a major breakthrough in the genre when he did *The Skeleton Dance* in 1929. This remarkable little picture, in which a skeleton does a marvelously flexuous dance in wittily synchronized rhythm to Saint-Saëns' *La Danse Macabre,* presented a whole new concoction of audio-visual elements and opened the way for the infinite perfections and variations achieved by Disney and many others.

Or there are such memorable champions as Disney's first Mickey Mouse cartoon, the first released, that is: *Steamboat Willie,* which was offered in 1928 and started this anthropomorphic rodent on a spectacular career; or *The Three Little Pigs*, that cheerful sketching of the old nursery tale, done to the tune of a catchy jingle, "Who's Afraid of the Big Bad Wolf?" which became a national resuscitant when released at the depth of the Depression in 1933; or Disney's first feature-length cartoon, *Snow White and the Seven Dwarfs* (1937).

I have been tempted to pick one of these classics as a prime example of the animator's work, and I have also contemplated Jiri Trnka's wonderous Czech puppet animation, *The Emperor's Nightingale* (1951), and U.P.A.'s witty cartoon conception of a klaxon-voiced boy, *Gerald McBoing-Boing* (1954). But I find, after much consideration, that Disney's protean *Fantasia* is the most ingenious, inclusive and impressive of all the animated films.

I know there are critics who consider this imposing assembly of eight separate animated segments, each done to the accompaniment of a familiar piece of symphonic music, performed by the Philadelphia Orchestra, to be an overly ambitious and generally pretentious work, patently "culture conscious" and often in bad taste. But it strikes me that such criticism is too quaintly prejudicial in favor of the smaller and more parochial novelties that Disney had previously done

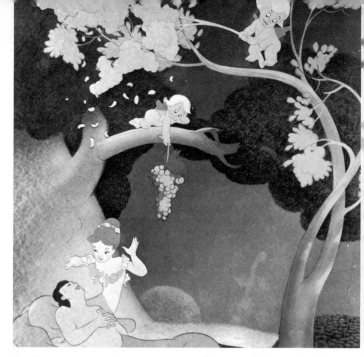

Cupids, centaurs and centaurettes are the stars of this setting for Beethoven's "Pastoral" Symphony.

and not sufficiently perceptive or elastic toward the magical ideas and dexterities in this film. To be sure, there are some flaws and missteps in it. Some parts are not good. A few are gross. But altogether *Fantasia* is the apogee—to date, anyhow—of the art of the animated film.

This picture began in Disney's mind as an idea of doing a cartoon to the music of Dukas' *The Sorcerer's Apprentice,* with Mickey Mouse as the hapless apprentice, and having the Philadelphia Orchestra perform the score under the direction of Leopold Stokowski. The conductor was keen to do a film with Disney, whom he considered one of the great artists in America.

The idea was suddenly expanded into a major project to embrace several symphonic selections, each illustrated, or accompanied, by a composition of animated images done in distinctive styles. The thought was that classical music could be given a wider audience and acceptance in this way, and that a new form of cinema entertainment would be achieved.

The project was begun with recordings of the selections to be used, then the idea men and the animators in the Disney studio went to work on their designs. The film was soon absorbing the energies of most of the studio staff. *Fantasia,* which was ready in 1940, was the biggest thing the Disney people had ever done. A special multiple-outlet sound system was designed by RCA, and the publicity people were set to beating their loudest timpani.

Because it was realized that the public might need a little explanation and aid in understanding the concept and the music, Deems Taylor, a popular music critic, was brought in to appear as a sort of master of cere-

The sorcerer orders his hapless little helper, Mickey Mouse, back to work in this scene from Dukas' *The Sorcerer's Apprentice.*

monies and to introduce the separate selections. While the format of this narration is academic and intrudes upon the cinema, and while it does tend to give the entire program the air of a concert, it binds the random segments together and may be helpful to those whose musical knowledge is scant.

The show begins before the house lights in the theater are completely doused, with vague shadows of musicians appearing on the screen and the sounds of orchestral instruments being tuned coming from the area of the pit. Then the lights go down and Taylor steps forth on the screen, on what is the orchestra platform, to introduce the show. It is, he explains, a presentation of "designs and pictures and stories" which the various musical selections have inspired. Then Stokowski—or, rather the profile of the conductor, with his mass of silver hair backlit to form a luminous nimbus—dramatically ascends to the podium and the concert begins.

The first number is Bach's *Toccata and Fugue,* and it comprises an exciting display of animated abstractions and colors flowing and merging with bold fluidity. Undefined lacy figures come through space and a magical sky-writing cipher traces patterns and creates sprays of falling stars. It is a display of pictorial pyrotechnics to get the audience into a mood of wonder and detachment suitable to surrender to the successive fantasies.

This is followed by a magical illustration of Tchaikovsky's *The Nutcracker Suite,* with tiny, shimmering fairies wielding silver wands to place sparkling dewdrops on cobwebs, a delightfully humorous dance of waddling mushrooms which take on the appearance of solemn little Chinamen, and a highly colorful flow of opening and dancing flowers.

The segment of *The Sorcerer's Apprentice,* with the agile Mickey Mouse marshaling an army of animated broomsticks to help him scrub a floor and finding him-

145

self in a familiarly hectic predicament, is a delightful composition of comedy cartooning—one of the best adventures of the irrepressible mouse.

I am not too pleased with the segment done to Stravinsky's *The Rite of Spring,* which the Disney people have made a massive animated illustration of the creation of the world, with fiery and shattering upheavals of the molten earth, roaring battles of prehistoric monsters and swirlings of glacial storms. Nor do I find especially felicitous the shrill Walpurgian revelries of a terrifying assortment of skeletons, graveyard ghouls and imps done to Mussorgsky's *Night on Bare Mountain.* This is an overdone conceit.

But delightful is a burlesque of ballet, done by elephants, ostriches, and hippopotami, to the lascivious music of Ponchielli's *Dance of the Hours*; and I also find amusing a kewpie-doll kind of confection with baby fauns and centaur maidens swishing their equine behinds for the benefit of stalwart young centaurs to the music of Beethoven's Sixth ("Pastoral") Symphony. I recall that my friend and compatriot, Olin Downes, who was the music critic of the New York *Times,* took outraged exception to this segment, saying that it "in-jected into a simple and wonderfully beautiful musical evocation of the countryside" a conglomeration of creatures that "looked like a cross between a prizefighter, a bartender and a horse's buttocks." It is inappropriate to Beethoven, he proclaimed.

A concluding illustration of Schubert's "Ave Maria" is pretty much of a cliché, except for one exquisite scene of a line of golden lanterns being carried by a file of tiny nuns through the dusk.

Fantasia was accorded a generally enthusiastic critical response, but it was not at all well supported at the box office. There were numerous explanations for this: the war in Europe, the radical change of Disney's style, the general impression that the art was too short for the longhairs and too long for the short. It was said to have cost in the neighborhood of $3,000,000 to produce, and it did not begin to earn back its cost on its first release. Nor did a new title, *Fantasia Will Amazia,* which some idiot conceived for its second-run engagements, bring even the imbeciles in. Not until it was reissued for theatrical showing in 1963 did audiences flock to see it. By then the Disney studios had virtually abandoned making big animated films.

The prehistoric past is inspired by the music of Stravinsky's *The Rite of Spring* in this epic adventure in music.

The life of publishing tycoon Charles Foster Kane is traced by many people who knew him, first by his guardian, Walter Parks Thatcher (George Coulouris), who takes him away from his mother (Agnes Moorehead) when he inherits a fortune at the age of eight. As a child he is played by Buddy Swan.

Citizen Kane

1941

Original screenplay by Orson Welles and Herman J. Mankiewicz; produced and directed by Mr. Welles; photography by Gregg Toland; music composed and conducted by Bernard Herrmann; released by R-K-O Pictures.

Charles Foster Kane	Orson Welles
Kane, aged 8	Buddy Swan
Kane III	Sonny Bupp
Kane's Father	Harry Shannon
Jedediah Leland	Joseph Cotten
Susan Alexander	Dorothy Comingore
Mr. Bernstein	Everett Sloane
James W. Getty	Ray Collins
Walter Parks Thatcher	George Coulouris
Kane's Mother	Agnes Moorehead
Raymond	Paul Stewart
Emily Norton	Ruth Warrick
Herbert Carter	Erskine Sanford
Thompson	William Alland
Miss Anderson	Georgia Backus
Mr. Rawlston	Philip Van Zandt
Headwaiter	Gus Schilling
Signor Matiste	Fortunio Bonanova

It is passionately felt by many critics that the greatest film of all time, or at least the greatest American talking picture, is Orson Welles' *Citizen Kane*. There are cogent reasons for this opinion. It is surely one of the finest specimens of sheer cinematic storytelling that has ever been thrown on a screen. It abounds in imaginative arrangements of narrative material, surprising inventions of cinema syntax and fresh techniques in the use of camera and sound. Furthermore, it tells a startling story of an American publishing tycoon that is exceptionally bold, fascinating and excitingly topical. Indeed, its penetrating scrutinization of the power urges of a man such as the great newspaper-chain owner and one-time political aspirant, William Randolph Hearst, gives intimations of more recent giants in the contemporary realm of communications and politics, so that it has immediate pertinence to the landscape of American democracy.

What is more, *Citizen Kane* has going for it the brightest legend of youthful genius bursting forth from the stuffy confines of literary fashion and studio control that the lore of films provides. The history, and all its marginal fables, of how the twenty-four-year-old Welles came thundering out to Hollywood in 1939, fresh from his innovating triumphs with the Federal Theater Project in New York and his sensational radio production of

147

H. G. Wells' *The War of the Worlds*; how he spent several months exploring the mysteries of films at the R-K-O studio and finally came forth, to the amazement of everyone, with *Citizen Kane*, has been told and retold so often I need not take time to repeat it here. All the details may be found in Peter Noble's biography, *The Fabulous Orson Welles*.

What is significant in this history and most inspiring to young people who read it today—probably more than to those who knew it at the time—is the fact that the even-then rigid and resistant Establishment of American films could be breached by the ingenuity and daring of a creative and dynamic group. I inject the word "group" at this point, because it wasn't just Welles who accomplished the astonishing construction and breakthrough of *Citizen Kane*. While he was the brilliant director-producer and extraordinarily agile star, playing the title character with full conviction in an age range between about twenty and sixty-five, he was greatly assisted and encouraged by the keenly cooperative group of producing personnel and actors of his famous Mercury Theater that he brought from New York. He was strongly indebted to Herman J. Mankiewicz, who was his collaborator on (and actually wrote)

Educated and of age, Charles Foster Kane (Orson Welles) starts building his newspaper empire.

the fluid script, and he owed a great deal to his camera-man Gregg Toland, who devised the invaluable innovations of deep-focus camera and lighting techniques. Also serving as his film editors were two bright young Hollywood men, Robert Wise and Mark Robson, who went on to become important directors themselves.

The idea for the picture—the exploration in a retrospective scan of the mystifying motivations and ambiguities in a powerful publisher's career—developed in conversations between Welles and Mankiewicz while Welles was presumably working on plans for a few other films. Welles got his close associate, John Houseman, to take Mankiewicz away to do the screenplay; then he cast it and started shooting it without letting the heads of R-K-O read it or even learn what it was about. This extraordinary caution was taken because he feared they would stop him if they sensed how much the leading character resembled the formidable and forbidding Hearst, and he wanted to have enough of the picture finished so that they could not afford to scrap it when they learned.

The subterfuges used to keep the secret were almost as ingenious as the film, and shooting was virtually completed when the secret was finally out. People in the Hearst organization—especially Louella Parsons, its Hollywood columnist—began to wax wroth about it, and a couple of powerful people (not Hearst himself) tried to prevent release. But the R-K-O president, George Schaeffer, stuck by his investment—and by Welles. *Citizen Kane* opened in New York and other cities in May 1941.

Response ranged from warm to wary. The picture's eccentric style, its rapid and helter-skelter movement, its loudness and lack of sentiment, its bruising slaps at American Philistinism and its sharply sardonic jabs at Big Money and Big Business startled and worried many critics who were not used to having their senses so assailed. There was also the valid criticism that it did not give a clear picture of the character and motivation of Kane; the viewer was left wondering what all the shooting was about. Public response was lukewarm, and the film was not an initial success.

But with time and further experience with some of the film's techniques, plus moviegoers' increasing disposition to become intrigued by elusive ideas, the audacities and intimations became more apparent and clear. At least there was more enthusiasm for the film's rich theatricality. Today it is properly regarded as one of the major pace-setters for modern films, a tremendous cinematic expression and a highly entertaining mystery.

As it opens, Charles Kane lies dying in the fabulous castle he has built in Florida, a place called Xanadu

His energy and ambition drive Kane on to run for governor of his home state.

(clearly suggestive of Hearst's San Simeon), in which he has surrounded himself with treasures and virtually secluded himself. As the camera comes up to his bedside and death closes his eyes, his heavy lips murmur one word, "Rosebud," and his slackening hand lets fall a crystal ball, containing one of those pretty snowscapes, with flecks of white swirling inside.

Sharply, this death scene is shattered: the screen becomes alive with a strident, staccato news film, similar to the famous and then-popular *March of Time*, recounting with pictures and narration the career of the dead man: how, as a boy, he came into great wealth; how he became a crusading newspaper publisher as a

149

In her palatial playpen Kane's mistress, Susan (Dorothy Comingore), is a virtual prisoner, pathetic in her need for diversion.

young man; how he aspired to political office, was defeated because of a personal scandal, devoted himself to material acquisition and finally died.

But when this news film is ended, its editor is not satisfied. He wants to know the secret of Kane's strange nature and especially the meaning of the word "Rosebud." "Was it a horse Kane once bet on; was it a woman he loved?" So a reporter is sent forth to find out, and the remainder of the picture is devoted to an elaborate and absorbing visualization of Kane's phenomenal career as recalled and described in flashback sequences by his boyhood guardian, two of his closest newspaper associates, his mistress and the major domo of Xanadu.

Their stories, picked up in succession, recall the tremendous vitality and enthusiasm of Kane—the gusto with which he started his first newspaper, the romanticism with which he married his wife, the callowness with which he took a mistress, the arrogance with which he ran for governor, and the humiliation with which he defected when his secret love life was discovered by a blackmailing, rival political boss.

They further recall the overbearance with which he tried to browbeat and buy an opera career for his mistress, the fiasco of that attempt, and the vulgarity and sterility of his later life. In some details, the recollections of these old companions overlap and contradict. Some recall incidents with humor, others with bitterness. None is altogether certain "what made Charlie tick." But all are agreed on one thing: he was a titanic egomaniac.

To the audience, it appears that he was in some way consumed by his own vast selfishness, his unrestrained ambition and his monstrous vanity. But just what it is that eats him, why and, indeed, whether Kane is really the villain he seems, or a social parasite, or the victim of his wealth and the booming age in which he lives, are not made clear by the picture. And the terminal shot, which lets us know (and only us, *not* the news-film editors) that "Rosebud" was the name of the sled with which little Charlie was playing when he was called away to his huge inheritance, sheds little more than a vague light on a weakly sentimental side of him. At the end, Kubla Kane is an enigma, just as he is at the start.

Actually, there is no more consistency, no more psychological pattern in him than there is in one of those cluttered "cover stories" of famous persons that appear in the news magazines. So fast and eclectic is the "research" done by the roving camera that the picture might be a parody of the kind of slick, superficial journalism practiced by the great mass media.

But that is what is wonderful about it. By means of the cinema device, it gives an engrossing presentation of a huge journalistic montage, a pulsing panorama of a phase of American newspaper publishing and politics between the Spanish-American War and the 1930's that smells of wealth, power and vulgarity. It holds one as much by the succession of lusty incidents and biting vignettes it peels off in profusion as it does by its gnawing mystery. One is likewise captivated by its rich, racy characters.

Kane is, of course, the most important; and, as played by the *wunderkind*, Welles, he is constantly absorbing, aggravating, amusing and bigger than life. From the bubbling bravado of young manhood, through the hungry, restless thrusts of middle age to the obscene pomposity of the old lecher lolling monstrously in his Xanadu, Welles serves us this gaudy, grotesque character with theatrical garnish and subtle taste. His Citizen Kane—and note well the sarcasm in that classic republican appellation—is one of the great characters of the screen.

Fascinating, too, as his associates (who likewise age through the film) are Joseph Cotten as a bright young reporter who becomes the conscience and gadfly of Kane, Everett Sloane as his brassy business manager and George Coulouris as his legal guardian, who symbolizes the icy austerity and the restrictive sanctions of corporate wealth. As Kane's mistress, Dorothy Comingore is properly trashy, shallow and shrill, with occasional glimmers of pathos to make us sense how tyrannically she is pushed. Ruth Warrick is prim and Procrustean as the social wife, and Ray Collins is righteously ruthless as the rival political boss. Many others from Welles' Mercury company and the Screen Actors ranks in Hollywood give shape and style to the lesser characters that pass in this roaring parade.

Kane marries socialite Emily Norton (Ruth Warrick), which assures him of status in public but boredom at home.

Much of the sense of reality and vitality in *Citizen Kane* is achieved by the amazing elasticity with which it is photographed and edited. Welles demanded pictorial textures to suit the moods of individual scenes, and tempo in action and cutting to suggest the speed and turmoil of events. For instance, the opening shots of the camera moving in on Xanadu are dark, deliberate and ominous, like mood shots in a Frankenstein film. The footage of "News on the March," which follows immediately, is bright, realistic and lively. To give a feeling of authenticity, Welles had ceilings on many interior sets, and Toland used new lenses that brought into focus everything in a room, so that action even in the deep background was as clear as one would see it naturally.

In the editing, he has what has subsequently come to be known as jump cuts—sharp transitions from one place to another (or from one time to another in the same place) without the familiar old-fashioned fades and dissolves. For instance, he has a sharp cut from the editor's instructions to the reporter in the projection room of "News on the March" to an electric sign atop a nightclub in Atlantic City advertising the appearance of Kane's mistress there. The cut is accompanied with a flash of lightning and a hissing deluge of rain, which shocks and alerts the viewer to the presence of mystery.

In one famous scene the erosion of Kane's marriage is crisply conveyed in a succession of shots of him and his wife at their breakfast table, but with each shot representing a jump of years and with their attitudes changing in each transition so that we can see the estrangement coming on. In the last cut, they are icily silent—and the wife is reading the rival newspaper!

The way in which Kane takes his mistress is short-handed beautifully in a cut from her singing weakly for Kane in her modest bedroom on the night they first meet to a shot of her screeching abominably in a richly furnished room, with a singing teacher pounding at a piano and Kane, in the background, attending stubbornly. Notable here is the meaningful carry-over of sound. Such instances of cinematic wit and cognizance are numberless.

Uplooking shots from low angles, unusual lighting of sets, and dramatic maneuvers of panning (such as a fast sweep from one small bundle of the first papers off the press when Kane takes over, to a vast field of such bundles to indicate the leap in circulation) are frequent all through the film. They add to the metaphorical language that is so fresh and fine in *Citizen Kane*.

The story is told that, some weeks after the contention over this film had slacked off, Hearst and his mistress, Marion Davies, were discovered watching it in a theater in San Francisco. Reporters gathered to ask them what they thought of it. They were reported to have said they found it entertaining, but Hearst seemed to think it was "too long."

The career of Welles after this picture is a tragicomic drama in itself. It cries for a new young Welles to film it in the style of his creative monument.

The Maltese Falcon

1941

Screenplay by John Huston, from the novel by Dashiell Hammett; directed by Mr. Huston; cameraman, Arthur Edeson; produced by Hal B. Wallis for Warner Brothers.

Sam Spade	Humphrey Bogart
Brigid O'Shaughnessy	Mary Astor
Kasper Gutman (the Fat Man)	Sydney Greenstreet
Joel Cairo	Peter Lorre
Wilmer Cook	Elisha Cook, Jr.
Effie Perine	Lee Patrick
Detective Lieutenant	Barton MacLane
Miles Archer	Jerome Cowan
Iva Archer	Gladys George
Detective Polhaus	Ward Bond
Luke	James Burke
Frank Richman	Murray Alper
Bryan	John Hamilton
Ship's Officer	Walter Huston

A doctoral thesis could be written (if it has not already been) on the changes in crime melodrama that occurred in the crowded ten years between the appearances of *The Public Enemy* (which see) in 1931 and *The Maltese Falcon* in 1941. These were years of prodigious shifting on the national economic and social scene, of significant fluctuation in public attitudes; and the contours of these modulations might be traced in the changing taste for crime in films.

The end of the Depression and the era of the lawless reign of gangs, which came with repeal of Prohibition and belated crackdowns on the barons of beer and booze, combined with the general surfeit of audience interest in repeated gangster films to render this type of entertainment temporarily *de trop*. Furthermore, an accumulation of moral outrage against violence on the screen had helped to compel the Hollywood nabobs to accept a self-restraining Production Code, which was enforced with heavy penalties, beginning in 1933. This code sternly limited the freedom with which gangsters consorted with their molls, the ferocity and noisiness of their gunfights, the grisliness of their dooms; and it compelled more forceful manifestation of the dictum that crime does not pay, even though the perceptive public was not convinced this was wholly true.

As a consequence, empathy was shifted from the gangsters to the guardians of the law. The G-man, the government agent who was bringing the gangsters to book, became the thunderous hero in the next wave of Hollywood crime films. At the same time, over in England, Alfred Hitchcock was developing a genre of fast and witty mystery thrillers pegged upon espionage and crime, in which empathy with the hunters and the hunted was elastically interchanged. His *Murder* (1930), *The Man Who Knew Too Much* (1934), *The 39 Steps* (1935) and *The Lady Vanishes* (1938) likened crime and its detection to the pursuit of an intellectual game. Then, too, there was a disposition, instigated by novels and plays, to consider the contemporary outlaws as cancers of a sick society, invading

Humphrey Bogart began building the Bogart legend with his tough, terse characterization of Spade —a bird who fits snugly between the public enemy and the international spy.

153

and corrupting a social body that was too much weakened to resist. Of such were *The Petrified Forest* (1936) and *Dead End* (1937).

Appropriately, the capstone to this cycle of reflective crime films was placed by Warner Brothers, the most prolific entrepreneur of the genre, with a picture called *High Sierra* in 1941. This was a roaring melodrama that ended with a fine Wagnerian death for "the last of the old-time gangsters," a mordant John Dillinger type, brought to bay and gunned down by a small army of state policemen on a California mountaintop. The historic thing about it is that it coincidentally joined the principal parties, John Huston and Humphrey Bogart, who were to make what turned out to be the next major prototype of American crime

melodrama. That is *The Maltese Falcon*, which followed *High Sierra* by only a few months.

Huston had been a writer at Warners' and had collaborated on several successful scripts, among them *Juarez* (1939), *Dr. Ehrlich's Magic Bullet* (1940), *High Sierra* and *Sergeant York* (1941). As a reward for his work on *High Sierra,* he was promised he might try his hand at directing, if he could come up with a good, inexpensive script. He had previously directed stage plays and had acted in the theater a bit. He was also the son of Walter Huston, a distinguished actor and motion-picture star.

One of his friends suggested he might get a good, tough script out of Dashiell Hammett's *The Maltese Falcon*, a mystery novel which appeared in 1930 and

Spade is as smooth as his opponent, the Fat Man (Sydney Greenstreet), an international crook bent on capturing a priceless *objet d'art*.

Paths cross and double-cross in this film of robbers without cops. Even the little punk, Wilmer Cook (Elisha Cook, Jr.), reaches for a piece of the action.

was the forerunner of a considerable school of hard-boiled detective fiction that had become widely popular. The screen rights belonged to Warners, which had twice made films from it, neither of which amounted to much. Huston broke down the text of the novel, roughing it out in scenes, with dialogue briefly indicated. A copy of this draft happened to reach Jack Warner, head of production at the studio. Warner was much impressed (he thought it the finished script) and immediately gave the go-ahead to Huston, who was joyfully surprised.

Hal Wallis, assigned as producer, wanted to get George Raft, one of the studio's favorite tough guys, to play the leading role. But Raft was apprehensive. He had already turned down the role of the fugitive in *High Sierra* because he thought it too much of a stereotype, and the role had gone to Bogart, who played it superlatively. Now Raft feared the fellow in this one was too

much on the wishy-washy side, so again Bogart was recruited, and motion-picture history was made.

What Huston did was trim and compress the Hammett yarn until he had but the bare bones of a crime plot to support a stunning play of characters. This was essential and accurate, for the secret of Hammett's work was the crispness of his way of writing and his tenacious knowledge of the sort of people he wrote about. He had been a private detective and understood the ways and techniques of the sleuth.

This was what Huston realized in preparing *The Maltese Falcon* as a film, and this is what he and Bogart sought in the leading character. Where Hollywood mystery crime films had pretty much emphasized the standard, surface elements of action, concealment and suspense, this would be an opportunity to generate excitement and surprise with the curiously off-beat, elusive and devastating character of the sleuth.

155

The picture begins as any average cops-and-robbers melodrama might, with a beautiful, somewhat cryptic woman calling on Sam Spade, a seedy-looking private detective, in his office in San Francisco. She wants him to help her locate a man who she says has influenced her sister to come with him out from New York. Evidently Spade is suspicious, but he agrees to take the job, he and his beady-eyed partner, when the woman puts up a $200 binder for their services.

So far, it's ordinary. But the aspect and attitude of Spade—his somewhat shoddy appearance, his cool and vaguely insolent air, his way of treating the woman with politeness but obvious watchfulness—mark him at once as different from the ordinary sleuth. This fellow is just a bit tricky, someone you've got to watch.

This becomes more apparent as dire events rapidly occur—as Spade's partner is shot while tailing the mystery man that night, then the man himself is murdered—and Spade is given a bit of a pushing around by the suspicious and inquisitive police. Is he a shady operator? Did he do his own partner in? The mystery is quickly perking, and one of the big question marks is Spade.

It perks even harder the next morning when he goes to the apartment of the dame who hired him to do the sleuthing and toughly wrings out of her an admission that she misled him, that the story of her sister wasn't true. This doesn't in the least surprise him. "We didn't exactly believe your story, Miss—what's your name?" he says. "We believed your $200." That lays it on the line. For an additional $500, he agrees to go on helping her. But what it is she wants him to do, outside of keeping her from being harmed by someone, she doesn't say.

We begin to get an inkling, however, when a peculiar, prissy little man, a possible homosexual, shows up later at Spade's office and offers him $5,000 to recover what he describes as a "certain ornament." "Five thousand dollars is a lot of money," Spade counters guardedly. The next thing he knows, the little man is covering him with a gun and saying he's going to search the office for the "ornament."

So this is it. The mystery woman is obviously mixed up in a plot of some sort involving an object of great value, and this little man, who is also in it somehow, figures that Spade is helping her, that he may even have the object or know where it is.

But now the intriguing aspect of Spade begins to emerge: he is distinctly fascinated by the temptations of this mystery. Although he is a private detective, presumably on the side of the law (he is a pal of the cops who grill him, even a drinking companion), and although there is not much question that something

Somebody's got to go, between Spade and Wilmer, outwaiting each other in a hotel lobby. And it's not going to be . . .

highly illegal is afoot, he is not going to back away from it. He's sticking with it to see what's in it for him.

Now we see Spade in action to the fullest extent of his skills—wheedling and abusing the woman, playing a cat-and-mouse game, sarcastically countering her humbug ("If you were as innocent as you pretend to be, we wouldn't get anywhere"), kissing her when she wistfully asks him, "What more is there that I can buy you with?" and then insolently giving her to realize he is not to be diverted by sex.

From here on, we follow him closely as he becomes more and more involved in what turns out to be a complicated contention over a jeweled statuette, the fabulous Maltese Falcon. We follow him as he boldly exposes himself to peril from a noxious character, Wilmer, who is clearly shadowing the dame, in order to reach the Fat Man, the focal conniver in the plot. And we stay with him through a fantastic battle of wits with this monstrous character, an elegant international criminal on the order of those in the Hitchcock films.

Some of the best scenes in the picture are the stinging confrontations between Spade and the ruthless Fat Man, in which Spade shows himself to be every bit as clever as the criminal, able to baffle and outwit his pawns, the effeminate Cairo and Wilmer, able to manipulate the dame, who is evidently in with these rascals but attempting to pull a double cross, and finally to obtain the falcon and force them to pay him $10,000 to hand it over to them.

In these tricky maneuvers, we are led to discover that

Another strong characterization of a shady character, Joel Cairo, was etched by Peter Lorre, on hand for the denouement when the Fat Man finds the falcon to be a fake.

Spade is a man of amazing audacity, cynicism and amorality. He has all the instincts of the gangster to deceive and take for himself, yet he has the wit and wisdom to guard himself by staying just within the law. He doesn't trust anybody, not his partner, his client or the police. He respects only the Fat Man and, indeed, is amused by him because he finds him to be as clever, brazen and bold as is he.

Spade stays completely uncommitted to anyone but himself, and this is magnificently realized at the climax of the film. The jeweled falcon, which Spade has obtained mysteriously from the dying captain of a just-arrived ship, he has delivered to the Fat Man and his henchmen at their hotel. They have eagerly unwrapped it, eyes gleaming with excitement and greed. Then they have shockingly discovered that it is a fake; this object they have so fiercely maneuvered to get their hands on is merely clay and glass!

They snivel and snarl in dejection, then the Fat Man and little Cairo leave, unable to compel Spade to give back the $10,000 they have advanced to him. He is left alone with the woman, who now tries to make up to him, assuming that he will take her. After all, she brought him into the case. But he icily rejects her and deliberately turns her over to the police as the one responsible for the murder of his partner and the other man.

Here is stated the essence of the personal philosophy of Spade: "If I did this (attached himself to her) and got away with it, you'd have something on me you could use whenever you wanted to. And since I've also got something on you, I couldn't be sure you wouldn't decide to shoot a hole in *me* someday." All they've got going for them, he tells her, is "maybe you love me and I love you." But what is love? A likely headache; perhaps a pair of horns! And when she indicates amazement at his ambiguous morality, he says, "Don't be too sure I'm as crooked as I'm supposed to be."

157

This fine entertainment and comment is splendidly played. Sydney Greenstreet is devilishly suave in the crucial role of the Fat Man (Huston recruited him from the New York Theater Guild), Mary Astor is deliciously and blandly deceitful as the dame, Peter Lorre is obscenely innocent as Cairo and Elisha Cook, Jr., is wicked as Wilmer. Lee Patrick as Spade's doting secretary (whose adoration is almost a joke) and Barton MacLane as the chief of detectives make it stick.

Being largely verbal in conveying the details of the plot, one might fear that *The Maltese Falcon* would be static cinema. But Huston, with the excellent assistance of Arthur Edeson as cameraman, keeps it moving, always moving. Spade is in focus throughout. The camera is virtually a detective constantly shadowing *him,* standing off to one side and peeking as he goes into a room, tailing him to the District Attorney's office, never letting him out of sight. This is camera-eye storytelling— good, straight, traditional cinema.

In the final analysis, however, it is the stringent character of Spade and Bogart's brilliant performance that make this a truly great film. It is a character that subtly communicates the attitude of an age—skeptical, disillusioned, resistant to commitment, detached. Underneath its *demimondain* surface, it states the feelings of many who were disabused of pious idealism by the outbreak of the Second World War within a decade of the Depression. And it continues, unto this day, to satisfy the youngsters who are doubtful of the society in which they live.

Shortly after release of *The Maltese Falcon,* Huston was commissioned a lieutenant in the Army Signal Corps and was called, right after Pearl Harbor, to make imformation films. His *Report from the Aleutians* and *San Pietro,* the latter a savage account of the winterlong battle of American G.I.s to capture an Italian hilltop town, were first-class war documentaries. And his *Let There Be Light*, a fact film about the treatment of psychoneurotic battle veterans, was a masterpiece of its sort. Unfortunately, the Army never allowed the last film to be publicly released.

Bogart, already past forty, made some fascinating films during the war, among them *Casablanca,* in which his character, the "saloonkeeper" Rick, is a virtual duplication of the cynical Sam Spade. Indeed, there's a little bit of Sam Spade in every role Bogart played after that, and this image he thereby fabricated is the core of the so-called "Bogart mystique."

On the bridge of the destroyer *Torrin*, Captain Kinross (Noel Coward) grimly scans the waters for German submarines during one of many convoy voyages.

In Which We Serve

1942

Original screenplay by Noel Coward; directed and produced by Mr. Coward, with David Lean as co-director; cameraman, Ronald Neame; musical score by Mr. Coward; presented by Two Cities Productions, Ltd.

Captain Kinross	Noel Coward
Alix (Mrs. Kinross)	Celia Johnson
C.P.O. Hardy	Bernard Miles
Seaman Shorty Blake	John Mills
Mrs. Hardy	Joyce Carey
Freda Leeds	Kay Walsh
Number One	Derek Elphinstone
"Guns"	Robert Sansom
"Torps"	Philip Friend
"Flags"	Michael Wilding
Pilot	Hubert Gregg
Engineer Commander	Ballard Berkeley
Doctor	James Donald
Sublieutenant	Kenneth Carton
Colonel Lumsden	Walter Fitzgerald
Captain Jasper Fry	Gerald Case
Lavinia	Ann Stephens
Bobby	Daniel Massey
Mrs. Lemmon	Dora Gregory
Mrs. Blake	Kathleen Harrison
Mr. Blake	George Carney
Young Sailor	Richard Attenborough

All hope that the motion-picture medium might continue to be used to expand and expound the antiwar theme so brilliantly advanced in *La Grande Illusion* (which see) was darkly discouraged by the onrush of Hitlerism in Germany, and it was relegated to oblivion with the outbreak of war in 1939. Now the minds and energies of film-makers in all the countries of the western world were brought to unquestioning acceptance of the absolute fact of war and to rationalization of it in terms of the posture of the country in which they worked.

The British, inclined toward pacifism until the Nazi thrust into Poland brought them face to face with the actuality of war, went to such self-defensive pictures as

159

The Lion Has Wings (1940) and the excellent documentary *Target for Tonight* (1941). And Hollywood, naturally anxious to get in on the current wave, came up fast with such military pictures as *I Wanted Wings* (1941) and *A Yank in the R.A.F.* (1941). During this early period, William Wyler's *Mrs. Miniver* (1942) was the clearest conveyance of American sentiment.

Although its visualization of the ordeal of the British during the 1940 blitz in terms of the experiences of a chintzy upper-middle-class London suburban family is heavily sentimental and is beatifically played by Greer Garson and Walter Pidgeon, it did clarify the agony of the war in terms that the American public, in its mood of outrage and compassion, could comprehend. But it was eclipsed a few months after its release by a British film that put quite clearly and appropriately the sentiment of the nation. It was Noel Coward's *In Which We Serve.*

There has been some allowable criticism of this film on the score that it is a studio-made picture. This is unmistakable to a sophisticated eye. But the exigencies of filming in 1942 entirely precluded its having a literal pictorial authenticity. It would have been out of the question to have tried to shoot this film aboard ships and in the sea. Audiences did not expect that. The illusion was satisfactory. Furthermore, belief in the characters and in their behavior under stress is what is important. This is the vital element in the film.

Actually, the difficulties of doing it at all were so great that it was truly a marvel of faith and perseverance that it was ever made. Much of the credit for this achievement went to Filippo del Guidice, one of the most interesting and original men in the history of British films.

Del Guidice was an Italian lawyer who had fled Italy in the 1930's to escape Mussolini's Blackshirts and had formed Two Cities Films in 1937. In 1940, he was briefly interned as an enemy alien. While in restraint, he conceived the notion of getting Noel Coward to make a heroic film about the British Navy, possibly on the order of his popular *Cavalcade,* which had been done as a play in the 1930's and was produced as a film in 1933.

The idea was visionary. Coward had never made or written a film, and his only experience as a film actor was in *The Scoundrel,* which he did for Ben Hecht and Charles MacArthur in 1935. But del Guidice was insistent, and he got Coward to say he would go in with him. Coward was to write, direct, play in and nominally produce the film.

While they were discussing the project, Coward's very close and greatly admired friend, Captain Lord Louis (Dicky) Mountbatten, who was in command of a

Ordinary Seaman Shorty Blake (John Mills) has a speedy wartime courtship with a fellow seaman's niece, Freda Leeds (Kay Walsh).

flotilla of destroyers, had his vessel, H.M.S. *Kelly,* shot out from under him in the battle for Crete in the Mediterranean. This inspired Coward with the idea for the film he wanted to make. He prepared the script in an amazingly short time, and then he and del Guidice began looking for a backer. This was much more difficult than they expected it to be. Most of the industry people they approached were nervous about war films. They felt this one would be too close to a documentary of the sort the government was now producing endlessly. Ultimately del Guidice was able to get a guarantee of a private loan, most of it put up by Major Alfred Sassoon.

The shooting began at Denham Studio in March 1942, with David Lean as co-director and Ronald Neame as cameraman. The opening was in October, and it was a hit from the start. The total production cost was around $1,000,000. It earned twice that in the United States alone.

Whatever basic criticism of this picture exists today derives from a lack of awareness of the condition of the British people at the time. After three years of war, in which the nation had desperately borne itself through a series of shattering experiences, the people were weary and worn. They were shaken by dread and disappointments, unsure of their destiny, thoughtful only of their stubborn resolution to save their country and themselves. There was a stout belief in their own courage, but it was not vaunted or talked of boastfully. Their nature tended to understatement. And so it is with this film.

It begins with a montage of the building of a ship and a plain, prefatory note: "This is the story of a

Called back to more antisubmarine duty, Shorty bids a plaintive goodbye to his pregnant bride, who is soon to experience the ghastly blitz of Plymouth.

ship," which it substantially is—of this particular ship, the destroyer *Torrin,* that we see and follow from the time she slides down the ways until that day she is dealt her death blow by Nazi raiders off the island of Crete and slowly, agonizingly sinks.

But the ship itself is a concept, a symbol that we are allowed to see from stem to stern and as a total mechanism only a few times in the course of the film. As a drama, this film is really a story of devotion to this ship by all the men who sail in her, and the devotion of their families to them, and thus to the vessel in which they so dutifully serve. And since the motive for their devotions is the compound of all they are—their love of country, their sense of duty, their pride and respect for their jobs—it is a comprehension of the impulse of loyalty that binds a people together and makes them strong.

In Which We Serve is not a "plot" film. It is rather a mosaic of episodes which develops in a series of flashbacks, the recollections of a handful of the *Torrin*'s men as they cling to a tiny life raft.

It is the poignant reflections of her commander on the glories of his ship: of the night that they fought her desperately against an unseen enemy in a North At-

lantic storm and brought her home badly damaged, with thirty of their shipmates dead; of his talks with the crew at commissioning ("What sort of ship do I want the *Torrin* to be? That's right—a happy ship *and* an efficient ship, a *very* happy ship and a *very* efficient ship!"); of Christmas services in the fo'c'sle, and the men singing "Good King Wenceslaus"; of the time they helped bring the Army back from Dunkirk; of his loyal wife and children and their home.

It is the memories of Chief Petty Officer Hardy (Bernard Miles) and Ordinary Seaman Shorty Blake (John Mills), typically overlapping, of their families and their Plymouth homes: of Hardy's wife and her crabby mother; of the way Shorty met Hardy's niece (Kay Walsh) on a train coming down from London and winningly married her (to the background accordion accompaniment of "If You Were the Only Girl in the World"). And it tells, in a correlated flashback, how the Nazi bombers came over Plymouth one fearful night and left poor Hardy a widower and Shorty a new father, by the grace of God.

It tells all these things and others connected with the short life of the ship in a manner more vivid and stir-

161

ring than actuality. It catches the feel of a destroyer with vibrant intensity—the sweep of her hull through the water (which was got from factual shots of a ship at sea), the rattle of orders in battle, the pounding of pom-pom guns, the coordination of the ship's crew and the officers on the bridge. And it depicts civilian life in England as it really was—the life of middle-class people doing their jobs with humor and hardihood.

When he was shooting the film, Coward was uncertain how he would structure it: whether to use the flashback technique or tell the story in a sequential narrative, which would be conventionally climaxed by the final ordeal of the ship. He wisely chose the flashback, for this allows the awareness of loss and the feeling of nostalgia for the vessel to prevail almost from the start. We know that the end of all the loving, all the build-up of eagerness and pride, all the personal sacrifice and deprivation, is to be a watery grave for the ship. It is, like the griefs and disasters the British had already experienced, a matter for patient endurance rather than theatrical suspense. But from the reflection upon this and upon the way it was endured emerges the essence of the picture, a deep involvement of admiration and pride.

There are unforgettable vignettes: the Christmas party in the captain's home at which his wife, played keenly and truly by Celia Johnson, toasts her husband's ship ("an always permanent and undisputed rival");

the lifting of Hardy's wife (Joyce Carey) from the Plymouth rubble and her dying whisper—"Tell Walter —tell him I didn't want to leave the house"; the going to Dunkirk to help evacuate the Army, and the marching of the Dunkirk survivors off the Dover dock.

So much is expressed so simply, as in the scene where the ship finally sinks, watched with mute resignation by the oil-smeared men clinging to the raft. "She's going, sir," one of them mumbles, and the captain looks, the grief in his eyes more stark and agonizing than if he were watching a loved one die. "Three cheers for the ship!" he bids them, and the men raise a weak "Hip, hip, hooray!" as the overturned hulk of the *Torrin,* in the distance, slides under the sea.

That could be the end of the picture, but Coward has a rescue sequence and a final scene which states the theme of national unity and perseverance in characteristically human terms. The survivors are taken to Alexandria, and there, in the dusty shed of a cargo pier, the captain has them gather about him, in their makeshift clothing, for a simple farewell.

"I've come to say goodbye to those few of you who are left," he calmly says, and the incident flashes a reminder of the scene of the confident commissioning of the ship. "The *Torrin's* gone. Now she lies in 1,500 fathoms and with her most of our shipmates. They lie in very good company, with the ship we love. . . ." More firmly, he continues, "We take up with a stronger

Captain Kinross and his "guest," Colonel Lumsden (Walter Fitzgerald, left), returning from Dunkirk.

The *Torrin* is hit, and fatally, sending the men into an oil-grimed sea.

The appropriate words of encouragement and commendation are difficult for the captain, whose ship shares his heart with country and family.

heart. The next time you're in battle, remember the *Torrin!* . . . Goodbye—and good luck."

And then, as the captain stands with two remaining junior officers beside him, the men file past, each to shake his hand and say a personal goodbye. When the last man has passed—the last is Hardy—and walked on into the sunlight outside the pier, the captain and his officers pause, then follow. For a moment, the pier is empty and there is no sound, except a faint, sad strain of the theme music—and a fine theme it is—creeping in. Then the voice of the narrator speaks:

"Here ends the story of a ship. . . . But there will be other ships, for we are an island race. . . . There will always be other ships, and other men to sail in them. They give to us and to all their countrymen eternal pride. . . . God bless our ships and all who sail in them!"

In Which We Serve is not jingoistic. It does not elevate the British as a super-race. The enemy is never seen in close-up. He is just an attacking plane or a distant ship. There is no indication of personal hatred of Germans or Italians. Yes, the Italians are spoken of as "bastards" a couple of times, and Hitler is called a "rat." But such things are said as expressions of resentment and repudiation, as one would speak of disease or disaster—or, more precisely, of war. This is, indeed, an antiwar film, for it clearly states and extends the agony and tragedy of warfare so that it embraces a whole society, wives as well as warriors, officers as well as men.

Captain Kinross bids good-bye and good luck to each surviving member of his crew after the *Torrin* has been sunk by a Nazi submarine.

Henry V

1944

Based on the play by William Shakespeare, edited by Laurence Olivier and Alan Dent; directed and produced by Mr. Olivier; cameramen, Robert Krasker and Jack Hildyard; scenery and costumes by Paul Sheriff and Roger Furse; music by William Walton; a Two Cities Film.

King Henry V	Laurence Olivier
Chorus	Leslie Banks
Ancient Pistol	Robert Newton
Princess Catherine	Renée Asherson
Fluellen	Esmond Knight
Constable of France	Leo Genn
Archbishop of Canterbury	Felix Aylmer
Mountjoy, French herald	Ralph Truman
King Charles VI of France	Harcourt Williams
Alice, lady-in-waiting	Ivy St. Heller
Duke of Berri	Ernest Thesiger
The Dauphin	Max Adrian
Duke of Orleans	Francis Lister
Duke of Burgundy	Valentine Dyall
Duke of Bourbon	Russell Thorndike
Captain Gower	Michael Shepley
Sir Thomas Erpingham	Morland Graham
Earl of Westmoreland	Gerald Case
Queen Isabel of France	Janet Burnell
Duke of Exeter	Nicholas Hannen
Bishop of Ely	Robert Helpmann
Mistress Quickly	Freda Jackson
Williams	Jimmy Hanley
Captain Jamie	John Laurie
Captain MacMorris	Niall MacGuinnes
Sir John Falstaff	George Robey
Lieutenant Bardolph	Roy Emerton
Earl of Salisbury	Griffith Jones
Bates	Arthur Hambling
Corporal Nym	Frederick Cooper
Duke of Gloucester	Michael Warre

In the dismal fall and winter of 1943–44, when the people of Britain were enduring the screeching perils of the "little blitz" and their tight little island was sagging under the weight of the growing invasion force, there was quietly being made at Denham, one of London's badly battered studios, a film to which even its director referred cautiously as "an experiment." This was the most that Laurence Olivier would permit himself to say for this war-born and plainly problematic production of Shakespeare's *Henry V.*

A year or so earlier, the brilliant actor had agreed to undertake the job of directing and acting in this picture under the eloquent urging of Filippo del Guidice, the same man who had persuaded Noel Coward to make *In Which We Serve* (which see). Del Guidice had heard Olivier deliver some speeches from the play on the BBC, on one of those patriotic broadcasts that were so popular in Britain during the war, and was excitedly struck with the notion of making the play into a film. What, thought he, could be more appropriate to the British mood and condition at the time than this grandly heroic and triumphant *Chronicle Historie of Henry the Fifth,* in which a stout little band of English soldiers, knights and bowmen fight their way to victory against great odds on the Continent in the fifteenth century!

At first, Olivier was resistant. He felt the film would be too great a risk, that the dramatic verse of Shakespeare was suited only for performance on the stage. Furthermore, he recalled, as did others, that the public had ever shown a discouraging indifference to motion pictures made from plays of the Bard. But del Guidice persisted. He assured Olivier that his renown as a Shakespearean actor with the Old Vic and his popularity as a star in British and American films would insure much attention for the picture, and he confidently proclaimed that the intelligence and imagination that Olivier would give it would complete the guarantee

The film opens in the Globe Theater in Shakespeare's England; the Chorus (Leslie Banks) welcomes the playgoers to a dramatized version of their history.

Against painted scenery, still charging history with poetry, Henry V (Laurence Olivier) exhorts his men on the field at Harfleur, calling them "once more unto the breach."

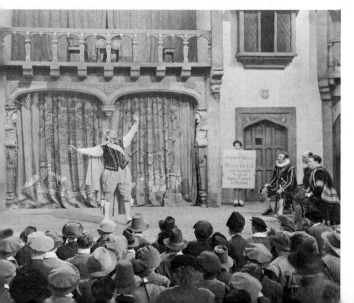

Henry climbs into a haycart and delivers the rousing St. Crispin's Day speech to his followers, just before the battle at Agincourt.

of success. The actor was finally taken with the prospect of a bold experiment.

In laying the plans for the production, he faced two major problems. First was the problem of determining the characteristic of the film. Olivier has since told me that he knew "something had to be done to give it a reality that was acceptable to the new audience without outraging the reality of Shakespeare, which can only be conveyed through the medium of the verse and a certain style of address to the matter." In short, he would have to conceive a style or manner of pictorial presentation that would be in accord with the richness of the verse and yet would develop an illusion of reality and credibility.

The second problem was that of the physical production. It was fully recognized and agreed that the film would have to be done on a large, spectacular and expensive scale. The fifteenth century was an age of knights and splendid royal households. Materials would be hard to obtain. Furthermore, shooting schedules would be subject to the uncontrollable inconveniences of war. Personnel might have to be diverted to other more pressing tasks. (Olivier himself had been temporarily borrowed from the Naval Air Arm to make the film.) And since Olivier's concept was that the Battle of Agincourt would have to be staged out in the open, on a full pseudo-realistic scale and not suggested through the eloquence of language, as it inevitably is on the stage, there was the anomalous problem of finding a location in which to perform a medieval battle in a country absorbed in a modern war.

The difficulties were tackled, and scenic designers and costumers performed miracles of ingenuity. The

166

sets and 1,000 or more costumes, including suits of armor that would ordinarily have required vast quantities of metals, brocades, leather, silks, satins and other stuffs, were fabricated from makeshifts. Suits of mail were made from heavy wrapping twine, knit and crocheted by a surprisingly eager group of Irish nuns, then sprayed with aluminum paint to simulate metal. Cheap blankets were dyed splendid colors and used for the hundreds of horse trappings in the great battle scene. Spears, swords and maces were cut from wood and coated with aluminum paint. Even King Henry's delicate crown was made from papier mâché.

The location picked for the battle was the huge estate of Lord Powerscourt at Enniskerry, near Dublin. And there, amid the green and rolling Irish hills, in the late spring and early summer of 1943, while modern armies clashed in distant places, the ancient Battle of Agincourt was staged.

The Eirean Home Guard mustered 500 sturdy young men to don the rough breeches and blouses of the fifteenth century and appear as the English foot soldiers and bowmen who are so crucial in the great battle scene. Close to 200 Irish horsemen came in with their mounts from nearby farms, the only available reservoir of men and horses, to act as the English and French knights. Though Technicolor film was at a premium, del Guidice managed to get hold of enough of this raw stock to shoot the film in color. It would have been folly to do it in black and white.

Midway through production, del Guidice ran out of money and had to sell a majority share of the film to J. Arthur Rank to complete it, but never did he suggest that Olivier should skimp on production or eliminate anything he wanted to do. The total cost was $2,000,-000 and it took eighteen months to finish the job. It

On the field at Agincourt, the battle lines are drawn between the English bowmen behind their barrier of stakes and the charging, panoplied French knights.

was the most ambitious and costly picture done in Britain up to that time.

It opened in London in December 1944, with a premiere so brilliant that it seemed to belie the fact of a nation at war. The immediate response of audience and critics was that Olivier's "experiment" had succeeded magnificently. All Britain thrilled to this extraordinary exposition of patriotism and pride, compounded from a less familiar play of Shakespeare and a masterful use of the screen.

In more recent years, some critics have quibblingly complained that the film is no more than an adroitly photographed reproduction of the play, thus consigning it to the shameful status of "noncreative cinema." But it seems to me that this contention misses the crucial point—which is that the film, while beyond question a faithful transcription of the play (considerably pruned of large and tough chunks by Olivier and the literary scholar, Alan Dent), is creative and dynamic precisely because it *does* avail the cinema device to fire the imagination, to sweep the eye over boundaries of time and space in order to give a new dimension of spiritual excitement to a traditionally limited theatrical experience. It is precisely the flow and sweep of poetic drama through a succession of ever-opening pictorial styles that renders this film cinematic, with life and vitality.

If Olivier had been so insensitive as to try to keep the action confined to one stage or even to one style of staging, as it seems about to be at the start, when the camera travels in over a model of seventeenth-century London to the hectagonal Globe Theater, there to pick up the excitement at the world premiere of *The Chronicle Historie of Henry the Fifth,* then there would be full justice in complaining that it is only a photographed play. But he doesn't try that, not by a long shot—or by many long, medium, close or other shots!

The pattern he has given the production is that of a chronicle which evolves through a casual transition out of the stagecraft and age in which it was born into modes of artistic expression and stylization characteristic of the French. Then, when the nature of the action and the intensity of the excitement become so strong that the frame of a formal stage cannot contain them, when the drama demands to be conveyed in the most striking form of illusion, the traditional devices are dismissed and an image of events is presented—something close to reality. When that is over, when the triumph of that illusion has been achieved and the spectator has been tumbled through the midst of the Battle of Agincourt, the progression is reversed. The action and emotion are again subdued as the chronicle is moved back into scenery, into the romantic aura of the Duc de Berri's France, and then back once more and finally into the cozy "wooden O" of the Globe and into the warm and ever-radiant womb of the Elizabethan age.

It is when the action progresses to the night before Agincourt, to the quiet and vigilant camp of the English and, once, to the camp of the French, that the major transition in style and mood is begun. Up to this point, the drama has been tangibly circled by the stage, by the audience's tacit awareness that it is beholding a play. But now, as the scenic structure changes into a vast vault of vague and misty night, with campfires twinkling in the distance, silent tents looming near at hand, and the voice of Chorus speaking softly,

"Now entertain conjecture of a time
When creeping murmur and the poring dark
Fills the wide vessel of the universe.
From camp to camp, through the foul womb of night
  The hum of either army stilly sounds . . ."

we are brought to the point of merging into the illusion of historical actuality.

Here, in this most exquisite passage, as Henry moves quietly through his camp, pausing to salute a fine old warrior who knows well the peril of the morrow, stopping to talk incognito with a group of untried lads who are nervous and frankly doubtful of the necessity and outcome of their cause, Olivier creates a separate philosophical, poetic realm. Now we are in a formless area of subtle intimation and anxious thought, the timeless realm of the lonely soldier who senses that he may soon die. And, as Henry draws aside to engage in his solemn soliloquy,

    "Upon the king! Let us our lives, our souls
     . . .Lay on the king! We must bear all! . . ."

an almost metaphysical communion with one man, all alone with us, is made.

This soliloquy, shot in medium close-up, with the camera focused on Olivier's face, which does not move but carries a deeply sad expression, as his voice from offscreen speaks the lovely lines, was one of his brilliant devices for acclimatizing Shakespeare to the screen. He continued to use the invention most effectively in his subsequent screen productions of *Hamlet* (1948) and *Richard III* (1955).

And so, with this moving passage, Olivier sweeps us from the stage, blurs the Shakespearean convention with a solely motion-picture device and prepares us for the spiritual breath-taking of a plunge into the real, sunlit outdoors.

Now it is the day of battle, the morning of the mo-

Henry delicately woos the young French Princess Catherine (Renée Asherson), chaperoned though she is by her lady-in-waiting, Alice (Ivy St. Heller).

The close of the film is brought back to the stage of the Globe Theater where, as it would be in Shakespeare's time, a young boy enacts the role of the Princess Catherine.

ment of truth, when the full majesterial confrontation toward which all has been directed will take place. Here, in the camp of the English, the armorers are busy at work, clanging hammers on their anvils, using derricks to hoist knights aboard their mounts as though they were helpless sea turtles. The bowmen are stretching and flexing their bows, driving stakes in the ground as vicious barriers. And, in the camp of the French, all blue and gold, the armored chevaliers are laughing, clinking glasses, drinking toasts and preparing to sweep to victory in one grand, overwhelming charge.

In the dread pause before battle, Henry, still in tunic and hose, climbs into a haycart and, with his warriors around him, gives the thundering St. Crispin's Day speech, which is, beyond any question, the grandest battle cry in literature. Notably, the camera trucks backward, not forward, during this scene. Instead of closing *in* on the speaker, as has been done in other Shakespearean films, it draws farther and farther away from him, so that when he hits those final stirring lines

> "We few, we happy few, we band of brothers . . .
> . . .That fought with us upon St. Crispin's Day!"

the whole array of the English army is envisioned, with Henry but a strong voice in its midst.

Now to the field of battle, as onward across the rolling green hills sweeps the first charge of the French knights, a vast and impressive line of brilliantly caparisoned horsemen, armor rattling, pennants snapping in the breeze, moving forward first at a slow trot then into a canter, then into a thundering charge, as the music of

William Walton increases in tempo and sweeps in a grand, martial surge, and the great battle is locked. It runs on for several minutes—a confusion of slaughter, the French knights withdrawing to reform their forces and come back across the body-spotted hills. In this one great sequence, Olivier visions the gist of medieval pageantry, the ageless, romantic, storybook notion of the Battle of Agincourt.

Olivier's direction has forcefulness and sweep, making a rich and flowing fabric of personalities and pageantry. And his own performance of Henry sets a standard of excellence. His majesty and heroic bearing, his full and vibrant use of his voice, create a kingly figure around which the others rightly whirl.

Leslie Banks' Chorus is his equal in vocal eloquence, speaking the English language with appreciation and joy. Harcourt Williams' dottering portrait of the senile King of France, Max Adrian's arrogant mincing as the wholly perfidious Dauphin, Renée Asherson's piquant Princess Catherine, Leo Genn's stalwart Constable of France, Esmond Knight's tricky Welshman, Fluellen, and Robert Newton's braggart, Pistol, are among the multitude of pleasures provided by the brilliant cast. And there are magnificent allusions and intimations in William Walton's musical score.

Within a few months after the opening of this picture in London, the war was over, but the film continued with ever-increasing popularity, a sort of phoenix of the past five bitter years. Such was the unsuspected consequence of a brilliant and brave "experiment." And the reservoir of great films was augmented by this "little touch of Harry in the night."

Les Enfants du Paradis
(Children of Paradise)

1945

Screenplay by Jacques Prévert; directed by Marcel Carné; music by Joseph Kosma, Maurice Thierte and Georges Mouque; photographed by Roger Hubert and Marc Fossard; designed by A. Barsacq, R. Cabutti and Alexandre Trauner; produced by S. N. Pathé Cinema.

Baptiste Deburau	Jean Louis Barrault
Garance	Arletty
Frederick Lemaître	Pierre Brasseur
Lacenaire	Marcel Herrand
Jericho	Pierre Renoir
Avril	Fabien Loris
Count de Montray	Louis Salou
Nathalie	Maria Cassares
Anselme Deburau	Etienne Decroux
Madame Hermine	Jeanne Marken
The Blind Man	Gaston Modot
Director	Pierre Palau
Scarpia Barigni	Albert Remy
Inspector of Police	Paul Frankeur

It was not surprising that the finest film made by the French after *La Grande Illusion* (which see) and during the Second World War should have been an expression of their fervid philosophical bent. This was Marcel Carné's *Les Enfants du Paradis* (*Children of Paradise*). Even if the nation's film-makers had not been watched by the Nazi police and if the need of making a picture of a presumably noncontroversial sort had not been imposed upon them, it is likely that Frenchmen would have chosen to make a picture very much like this to soothe and refresh the national spirit in a time of deep distress.

For *Les Enfants du Paradis* is a drama with a peculiarly Gallic theme: the predominance of chance and illusion in the lives of men. It is a romantic acceptance of the sad but seductive thought that all life is but a succession of adventures and ironies that are aptly duplicated in the make-believe comedy and tragedy on the stage. And it is an exciting exposition of the myth that the bourgeoisie, the common people of France, are still the masters, if not of their destinies, at least of the right to give expression to their feelings about how the drama of life is played.

The time of this lush and colorful picture of the theater and its personalities is the mid-nineteenth century, a period when the clamoring bourgeoisie was determined to hold its own against the forces that had been struggling to restore the *ancien régime*. Although the factor of political conflict is nowhere evident in the film, the robust spirit of the people is vocalized in the vulgar cries of the "children of paradise," the mobs that nightly fill the theaters' top galleries, howling their approval or disapproval of what they see on the stage: the simulations of life, the sly illusions and the fabrications of dreams.

It is evident that Carné envisioned—at least, unconsciously—the crowds in the peanut-galleries as the spiritual counterparts of the people of the French Revolution, the chanters of "La Marseillaise," shrilling delight and approbation for those who please their taste, howling scorn and requisition for the blood of those who offend. And the characters who play out the drama of love, lust, jealousy and hate are but symbols of the bold and elegant people who play the larger roles on life's tempestuous stage.

It is doubtful, however, whether Carné and his close collaborator, Jacques Prévert, consciously fashioned their drama to have an allegorical form when they began work on it in 1943. They had previously been collaborators on the moody, fatalistic *Quai des Brumes* (*Port of Shadows*) and *La Jour Se Leve* (*Daybreak*) in the years just before the war. Commissioned by Pathé to put together a respectable entertainment that would do credit to and earn a profit for the wartime film industry of France, they hit upon this idea of doing a spectacle that would embrace the literary fashion and the cultural ferment of the nineteenth century.

The physical problems and difficulties of getting the picture made were parallel to those encountered by the British in making *Henry V* (which see): the bottlenecks of communications and transportation; the scarcity of electricity, gasoline, hardware, materials; the constant interruptions of air-raid alarms. Also, of course, the presence of the Nazis with their manifold and ridiculous rules hampered production. And, like *Henry V* in Britain, this was the most ambitious sound film ever undertaken in France.

A further and unique problem was that the Nazis imposed a limit of ninety minutes on the length of all entertainment films. To circumvent this restriction, Carné planned to make two films, an initial one and a sequel, which could be spliced together as one as soon as the confidently expected day of liberation arrived.

This deceptive intention was kept secret from the Nazis until the end.

After six months of writing and preparation by Carné and Prévert (in association with their principal scene designer, Alexandre Trauner, and their principal musical composer, Joseph Kosma, both of whom were in constant peril of being picked up by the Nazis as Jews), a 500-foot outdoor set representing the legendary nineteenth-century Boulevard of Crime in Paris, so called because of the many theaters and music halls specializing in bloody melodramas and freak shows that lined it, was built in Nice. This was the locale of the action in the first half. The action in the second half, which has to do with the same characters several years later, moves out of this area and mostly into the interiors of two theaters constructed at the Joinville studios near Paris.

Les Enfants du Paradis presents us with more than a strong dramatic theme conveyed in an almost Balzacian exposition of crisscrossed lives and fates. It is a superior compounding of French theatrical styles, achieved through authentic designing and exquisite camera work. Since much of its character and color are evolved in reproductions of nineteenth-century theatrical performances, classical and pantomime, the quality of these reproductions is a crucial determinant. And it is in this area that the picture especially excels.

Much of the credit for this is due to Jean Louis Barrault, who plays a simulation of the famous mime, Gaspard Deburau, in a manner that brilliantly etches the artistry and poetry of mime. It is Barrault's ex-

quisite performing of the white-faced Pierrot, whose mute and poignant sufferings are significant symbols through the film and are the particular preferences of the "gallery gods," that fills the picture with a sadness, a nostalgia for *les temps perdus.* It was, indeed, Barrault who suggested to Carné a film about Deburau.

But of equal importance in imparting a luminous style and sadness to the film is the beautiful actress, Arletty, who plays a luscious courtesan around whom the rivalries and tensions of the drama circulate and unfold. It is she, introduced at the outset as the focal attraction in a notorious boulevard sideshow called *The Naked Truth,* who wins the hearts and the passions of a

Here are the "children of paradise," actually the mob that nightly fills the topmost galleries of the theaters to escape the harsh realities of life in mid-nineteenth-century France.

Jean Louis Barrault, celebrated actor and mime, suggested that a film be made based on the art of Gaspard Deburau, the great nineteenth-century pantomimist who created the forever popular character of the fanciful yet sad Pierrot.

Instant attraction brings mutual response as Baptiste Deburau and Garance (Arletty) meet on the Boulevard of Crime.

succession of men and embodies the melancholy moral that love is an illusion that is never attained. Arletty's beauty is truly electric. There is about her face, her eyes, her eloquent smile and her bare shoulders, which are ravishingly exposed in the first startling shot of her sitting naked (presumably) in a tub, a radiance of femininity such as seldom one sees on the screen. Greta Garbo and maybe one other exquisite French actress, Edwige Feuillère, have matched the mystique of woman radiated by Arletty in this film.

At the start, as we see the crowds milling along the Boulevard of Crime—stopping to ogle our beauty, known as Garance, in *The Naked Truth;* moving on to be jostled by peddlers, fortune tellers, shills for blood-and-thunder shows and to watch the come-on performance on the sidewalk platform outside the Théâtre des Funambules—we are plunged at once into the milieu and excitement of the theater, a world apart, which has the further fascination of being shady, vulgar and corrupt.

The drama begins as Garance, now walking along the boulevard with her swaggering lover, a slick and evil swindler and professional letter-writer, Lacenaire, stops to watch the performers outside the Funambules and first sees the delicate and wistful young pantomimist, Baptiste. Their eyes meet, and they exchange looks of fascinated desire. Suddenly there is a commotion and disorder in the crowd. A gentleman's pocket has been picked (by the wily and resourceful Lacenaire). Garance is menacingly suspected, until the wide-eyed Baptiste surprisingly breaks his silence. He has seen everything, he says. With that he jumps down off the platform and proceeds to act out in pantomime the entire incident of the pocket-picking, with his wonderfully eloquent hands describing all the tentative explor-

ing and comical fumbling of the thief, then alternately simulating the man who is being robbed. The crowd is amused and distracted, and Garance is hypnotized. She is entirely ready to give herself to the miraculous Baptiste.

Thus begins the strangely moody and idealistic romance of these two, which extends through the fluttering distractions of backstage feuds at the Funambules, through the atmosphere of violence and seduction in smoky cafés and music halls, all the way through the milieu of the *haute monde* which they achieve as their fortunes rise, and finally concludes with a fading away of Garance among the crowds on the Boulevard of Crime.

It is this flow of the lives of these people as they follow the leads of their careers—Baptiste to become the most famous and popular pantomimist in France, Garance to become the pampered mistress of an icy and evil aristocrat—always yearning toward each other yet never consummating their love because of their curious dispositions, that is the mainstream of the film.

It all stems out of that first night, when Garance offers herself to Baptiste in his tiny attic bedroom. "Love is so very simple," she tells him, yet he rejects it, at that moment, because he is a romantic dreamer and feels there should be more courtship, more spiritual cultivation of the divine urge. As easily as she abandons the wicked and ambitious Lacenaire, Garance goes from Baptiste's moonlit chamber into the bed of an actor, Lemaître, and then moves on from this ego-ridden lover to the lushly offered favor of a count. Baptiste is desolated and turns to an adoring dancer, Nathalie.

This is the end of the first half. In the second half,

Garance is accused of being a pickpocket, possibly because of her startling beauty, but is saved from vengeance by the diverting pantomime of Deburau.

The other men in the life of Garance as a triptych of the evils of their society. Left to right: the cruelly vain actor, Frederick Lemaître (Pierre Brasseur); the sinister cheat, Lacenaire (Marcel Herrand); and the morally corrupt Count de Montray (Louis Salou).

years later, we see Lemaître as an idolized tragedian, Baptiste as an idolized mime and Garance as the idolized mistress who still goes secretly to watch Baptiste. But all is changed. As beautiful and cool as Garance seems, she can no longer laugh as she used to. "A spring is broken in the music box," she says to the lordly Lemaître, who comes upon her one night as she is watching Baptiste. "The tune is the same but the tempo is different." Life has been kind, yet cruel, to her.

And so the fanciful pattern of this crisscross of lives is designed. The scheming Lacenaire, who has proceeded from a petty swindler to a high-class crook, is embittered because he has never achieved the success as an author that he desired, and so he vents his jealousy and frustration by first attempting to blackmail Garance's count and then by murdering him brutally in a Turkish bath. "Jealousy belongs to everybody, women to nobody," the count has aptly said. Garance revisits Baptiste, and they go together to the old attic room, which he keeps as a dreamer's sanctuary, hoping finally to realize their love. The moonlight still floods through the windows. They speak the old words they first spoke. "You were right, Garance," Baptiste tells her. "Love is so very simple." But it is not. That first long-ago breathless rapture cannot be recalled. In the morning, the prim and moral Nathalie comes to claim her husband and Garance disappears in the boulevard crowds, while the desolate Baptiste seeks after her in vain.

Thus ends this poignant fable of life as a flowing stream, never smooth and serene, as one might have it, but always vivid and interesting.

This fast résumé does not encompass the abundant flavor and excitement of the scenes of theatrical life and performance: the poetry of Barrault as the mime and the marvelously grand and sweeping postures of Pierre Brasseur as the tragedian; nor does it convey all the richness and nuances of the characters or the ambience of magic that Carné has achieved in the film.

In addition to Barrault and Arletty, there are the distinguished Brasseur, who does beautifully as the actor too pleased with his own magnificence to need a woman's love, Marcel Herrand as the basically vulgar and sinister Lacenaire, and Louis Salou as the sternly ritualistic and morally corrupt count. Each is a symbol of the vices and the failings of men who seek eternally for satisfactions that life generally withholds from them.

We are left at the final fadeout of this "gigantic philosophical ballet," as Georges Sadoul has called it, with the feeling that the past is dead, that the magic of love and enchantment cannot be recalled from the long-gone years, that the illusion of wonder and beauty does not persist beyond its momentary charm. Only the universal solvent for all the woes and despairs of this world —the ever-replenishing magic of illusion for others— remains.

That was a comforting reflection for the French at the end of the war.

In 1547, the young Ivan (Nikolai Cherkassov) is crowned Tsar of Russia, the first to bear the title, in the Uspenski Cathedral in Moscow.

(1945–46)

Screenplay and direction by Sergei Eisenstein; sets and costumes by Isaac Shpinel; musical score by Sergei Prokofiev; photographed by Edward Tisse and Andrei Moskvin; produced by the Central Cinema Studio, Alma Ata, U.S.S.R.

Ivan IV	Nikolai Cherkassov
Anastasia	Ludmila Tselikovskaya
Euphrosinia	Seraphima Birman
Vladimir	Piotr Kadochnikov
Prince Kurbsky	Nikolai Nazvanov
Prince Kolychov (Philip)	Alexander Abrikosov
Basmanov	Alexi Buchma
Fyodor	Mikhail Kuznetzov
Nikola	Vsevolod Pudovkin
Mayluta Skuratov	Mikhail Zharov
Pimen	Alexander Mgebrov

Ivan the Terrible, Parts 1 and 2

In the vast range of films from Soviet Russia, which spreads like a great mountain chain along the continental margin of European cinema, one film stands above all the rest in the jagged profile that stretches between the towering peak of Sergei Eisenstein's *Potemkin* (which see) and the much lower peaks of recent years. It is Eisenstein's last and monumental *Ivan The Terrible*, a two-part historical drama, one of the finest of film biographies.

This now inseparable pair of pictures, which contains the indubitable cream of what was at one time intended to be an Ivan trilogy, is outstanding for two reasons. It manifests a kind of cinema—an audio-visual combination—that is totally unique. In its grand and majesterial compositions of human and architectural forms, its visions of medieval circumstances and its eloquencies of music and sounds, it suffuses the mind through the eye and the ear with a tidal wave of divinations and terrors. It is also a historic memorial to the artistic independence of Eisenstein, which he innately and unconsciously erected in the last and greatest of his films.

To appreciate the phenomenon of *Ivan the Terrible,* one must know the career of the director and the circumstances which brought it about. Eisenstein, initially hallowed as "the little father of all the social realists," had been in a lot of difficulty with the Soviet bureaucrats through the early and middle 1930's as a result of his having gone abroad to work. He was employed first in Hollywood (for Paramount), where he never completed anything; then, in association with Upton Sinclair, he was to make what was intended to be an unprecedented epic of the 1910 revolution in Mexico. That turned out a fiasco of notorious complexity, which resulted in two separate and fragmentary pictures, *Que Viva Mexico!* and *Thunder Over Mexico,* neither of which was edited or sanctioned by Eisenstein.

Ivan confronts the jealous and resentful boyars (nobles) whose power he has preempted.

Returned to Russia, he was kept in the doghouse for a couple of unhappy years. Then he was assigned, expressly at the order of Premier Stalin, to undertake a patriotic epic glorifying the heroic exploits of the thirteenth-century prince, Alexander Nevsky, who defeated the invading Teutonic knights in a famous winter battle on the ice of Lake Peipus.

Eisenstein went about it with enthusiasm and intellectual serenity, first because he delighted in the opportunity to make a howling, heroic picture that would allow massive military action and triumph over the Germans (whom he despised), and second, because he was happy to be back in tentative favor again. He had the fine actor, Nikolai Cherkassov, to play the title role, and he was fortunate in obtaining Sergei Prokofiev to prepare a splendid musical score. *Alexander Nevsky* was presented in Moscow in December 1938 and was an immediate triumph. Esienstein was restored to grace.

Even so, he had to endure another period of routine and random activity on an assortment of projects for Mosfilm, the state-controlled studio. *Alexander Nevsky* had been withdrawn from circulation upon the signing of the Nazi-Soviet pact in 1939, and the endorsement of its anti-German sentiments was tactfully suppressed. However, in 1940, he was commissioned, again at the understood suggestion of Stalin, to write a scenario and begin preparation for a huge film about Ivan the Terrible.

Obviously the intention of the government bureaucrats was to have a mammoth film glorifying the sixteenth-century grand duke, Ivan IV, who became the first tsar of Russia by suppressing the independent power of the boyars (the feudal nobles) and who, though a ruthless ruler, went far toward improving the lot of the common people. It was said that Stalin was particularly eager to have this film made; it would suggest, by historical implication, the patriotism of his own policies in consolidating power in the 1930's, mainly through the notorious Moscow trials.

Eisenstein had written in 1928 that he could not see Ivan as "a personality [who] will interest the young Soviet worker." However, he did concede that, if the story were done realistically—if it told how this tsar "who enriched and strengthened Russia's economic position" went on to become "absolute monarch, head of a dominant aristocratic class"—then it might be "of more importance than a fantasy about a Mephistophelean figure, a tsar who was a wild beast."

In her biography of the director, Marie Seton says, "These were the words of a young man who was very certain what he thought about history." Now, she says, almost twenty years later, his "feelings had undergone great change." He was presumably ready to treat Ivan as a hero suitable to the Soviet mythology.

Preparations for the film were begun in Moscow, but with the rupture of the Nazi-Soviet pact and the approach of the attacking German armies upon the capital in 1941, Eisenstein was evacuated along with all of Mosfilm to a complex of studios set up at Alma Ata in central Asia. Here he continued to write and prepare for shooting his picture, which was now designed to be a massive drama in three parts, the most ambitious film ever made by the Soviets. The vast enterprise of creating a national epic in cinema in time of war was comparable to the simultaneous production of *Henry V* (which see) by Laurence Olivier in Britain and *Les Enfants du Paradis* (which see) by Marcel Carné in France. Each was an urgent summation of national pride and will.

Filming started in April 1943, and it took almost a year to shoot Part 1 and most of what was intended to be Part 2. Cherkassov was again recruited to play the title role, and Prokofiev was naturally selected to do the musical score. Sets were designed by Isaac Shpinel from drawings by Eisenstein. His favorite cameraman, Edward Tisse, did the exterior photography, while Andrei Moskvin did the interiors.

Miss Seton says in her biography that, in the five years that Eisenstein worked on this massive project, he "fought the battles of his own soul in the person of Ivan"; that he "could not immerse himself . . . without drawing a subjective parallel between Ivan and himself in a pattern of such complexity that the full meaning of it could not be fully determined by anyone except himself."

Retired to his study, Ivan plans an alliance with Queen Elizabeth of England.

This is probably accurate. There was Eisenstein, sensitive and wise, steeped in the legends and the drama of a great figure in Russian history, torn between the evidence and the fictions of this man's nature and attitudes, and seeing so much of his own turmoil in the anguishes of the tsar. Certainly the portrait of Ivan that emerges in Part 1, which was given a splendid premiere in Moscow in January 1945, is that of a hugely energetic, restless and introspective man whose nature is more that of a contemporary troubled soul, struggling with repulsive necessities, than of a great leader full of confidence and power.

The Ivan that Eisenstein first shows us in this vast, slow, majestic film, which electrically charges the senses with galvanic images and sounds, is a young man of radiant ambition, idealism and hope, as we see him crowned in the opening ceremonial of coronation in the great Uspenski Cathedral inside the Kremlin walls. But, as the drama progresses—as sinister boyar factions conspire and even close friends intrigue to shear him of his power, as his adored wife dies (of poisoning at the hands of an evil aunt, as it transpires), and he is left in

Ivan thwarts the plot against his life by dressing the imbecile Vladimir (Piotr Kadochnikov) in his own robes and sending him into the cathedral where the assassins wait.

desolate isolation at her regal funeral—we see him become more suspicious, embittered and even doubtful of himself until he finally leaves Moscow for the seclusion of a great tower at Alexander Sloboda. There, surrounded only by the Oprichniki, the loyal Lifeguards that he has set up to protect him from his unseen, unknown enemies, he awaits the call of the people to return to Moscow to be the ruthless leader he realizes now that he *must* be.

In this portrayal of the alteration of a man by the distorting burdens of a mission and the dark oppressions of surrounding treacheries, Eisenstein uses the presence and the character of scenery to convey the very massiveness of medieval Russia and the heavy, shadowy menace of Ivan's foes. The great towering vault of the cathedral in which the tall, fair youth receives his crown, surrounded by fur-capped boyars with their round, low-browed heads, reveals in pictorial dynamics the height of the youth's ideals and hopes, the expanse of the land he must encompass and the monolithic encirclement of his foes. And the increasing gloom of the chambers in which the patently aging, watchful tsar glides his gaunt form as his perils gather provides the very presence of a haunting doom.

In these significant surroundings, the quintessence of composition and decor, Eisenstein has his actors move in graphic pantomimic ways, counterpointing their attitudes and tempos to the structures and moods of the separate scenes, so that one gets from the succession of massive tableaux a stunning sense of the ponderous flow of history.

Space, light and shade and gothic faces, seen in close-up or picked out of a crowd of symbolical class groupings, become eloquent factors in his compound. Take,

Seeking refuge in a tower far from Moscow, Ivan realizes he must return and be the strong, cruel tsar his people are seeking.

175

for instance, a major sequence of Ivan's capture of the city of Kazan—a boiling, barbaric spectacle of military power played in sky-vaulted space, giving a sense of freedom when direct action is the case—followed by the grim, portentous sequence of Ivan's illness and almost death, played in a darkened palace chamber in which priests and conspirators roam like ghosts. Or watch the face of the treacherous aunt, Euphrosinia, as she plots to seize Ivan's throne for her imbecile son, Vladimir.

It is notable that the scene returns to the outdoors, to a sweeping expanse of wintery space, for the sequence in which the people come to Ivan in his tower and beseech him to resume his mission. The horizon of self-sacrifice to the greater good of Russia is frigidly but stirringly implied, and the acceptance of the challenge by Ivan is the exalting conclusion of Part 1.

This was entirely satifactory to the ideological bureaucrats, and, after the film's opening, Eisenstein was awarded the Stalin Prize. He proceeded with the final shooting and editing of Part 2. Then, in 1946, it was announced that this continuation of the epic was banned. The Central Committee, in a scathing resolution, said that, in this second part, Eisenstein "displayed his ignorance of historical facts by portraying the progressive army of the Oprichniki as a band of degenerates similar to the American Ku Klux Klan, and Ivan, a man of strong will and character, as a man of no will and little character, something like Hamlet."

Naturally, this angry condemnation bewildered and alarmed everyone who respected Eisenstein's genius and admired the massive power of Part 1. But the widespread curiosity as to what offense this sequel might contain was not completely satisfied until twelve years later, when *Ivan the Terrible, Part 2* was released. By that time, Eisenstein, devastated and forced to dis-

Euphrosinia mourns the death of her simple son Vladimir, the victim of her own deceptions.

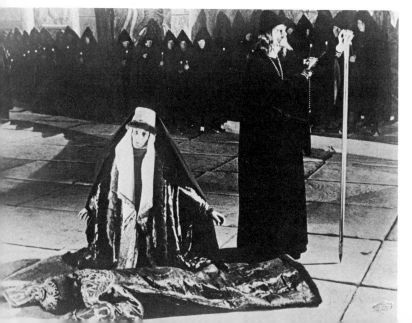

avow this second part, had died, and Stalin, whom the whole thing was intended to magnify, had gone to his reward. But now the world did have in sequence the substance of Eisenstein's epic, and the reason for its peremptory banning was abundantly clear.

Part 2 is an ever-narrowing focus upon the continuing conflicts of Ivan with his ceaseless enemies. It is ponderous and relentless melodrama that moves oppressively through a series of confrontations. And it is climaxed in a tangle of plot whereby Ivan, aware that Euphrosinia has planned to have him killed, tricks the imbecile son of Euphrosinia into putting on his robes and going into the cathedral, where the murder is to be done, and there being struck by the assassins, instead of Ivan himself.

While it does have progressive intimations of the involvements of Ivan with the Church, and while the sequence of the murder in the cathedral is a magnificently morbid spectacle, the totality of Part 2 is redundant—as history and epic, that is. But it is important—and an indivisible sequence—as the completion of the theme of Eisenstein.

For what it does is intensify awareness of the increase of bitterness and hate in the lonely Ivan. He hates the intriguers who close in on him. He even hates the mission and the obligation he has taken upon himself. While he wants to be powerful and constructive for the good of the state, he is constantly wondering and worrying whether he is right in seeking this, whether he is actually intruding upon the valid authority of the Church and committing an injustice against the boyars, whose claims may be justified. The more power he gets and the more he worries, the more he becomes ruthless and withdrawn. In the end, he is a fierce and monstrous tyrant, almost maniacal. He is, indeed, the "Mephistophelean figure, a tsar who was a wild beast," that Eisenstein anticipated in his comments in 1928.

Whether there is in this projection of a cold, vicious character some calculated aim to measure and unmask the character of Stalin is open to question. There are those who find in the film a few historical distortions, such as the poisoning of Ivan's wife, that bring the details of the drama into suspicious conformance with rumored details of Stalin's private life.

This is fruitless speculation. What is positive and permanent is that Eisenstein carries his medieval drama to a logical and artistic end. He shows in this panorama of the pitfalls of absolute power the ageless axiom that the man who must be tyrant must inevitably lose his own soul. Whether the man be Ivan the Terrible or Josef Stalin is a matter of names. Eisenstein made his last great picture nonpolitical propaganda for an awesome truth.

The Best Years of Our Lives

1946

Screenplay by Robert E. Sherwood, from the verse novel, *Glory for Me,* by MacKinlay Kantor; directed by William Wyler; cameraman, Gregg Toland; musical score by Hugo Friedhofer; produced by Samuel Goldwyn.

Fred Derry	Dana Andrews
Al Stephenson	Fredric March
Homer Parrish	Harold Russell
Milly Stephenson	Myrna Loy
Peggy Stephenson	Teresa Wright
Marie Derry	Virginia Mayo
Pat Derry	Roman Bohnen
Hortense Derry	Gladys George
Wilma Cameron	Cathy O'Donnell
Butch Engel	Hoagy Carmichael
Mr. Milton	Ray Collins
Cliff	Steve Cochran
Mrs. Parrish	Minna Gombell
Mr. Parrish	Walter Baldwin
Mrs. Cameron	Dorothy Adams
Mr. Cameron	Don Beddoe
Bullard	Erskine Sanford
Rob Stephenson	Michael Hall

It was appropriate and heartening that the first important postwar Hollywood film was a mature, engrossing drama about the return of servicemen to civilian life, a familiar cross-section estimation of the ways in which representatives of three significant types phase out of their war-conditioned thinking and back to standard peacetime frames of mind. The film was William Wyler's perceptive *The Best Years of Our Lives,* from a screenplay by Robert E. Sherwood, which Samuel Goldwyn produced. At the time it was released in November 1946, this impulsively sympathetic picture of servicemen home from the war was fully and accurately reflective of the sentiments and ethos of the times—so much so that it was warmly hailed by critics of all persuasions as the best picture of the year and was quickly inflated by the public into a big box-office hit.

It tells of three men of different ages, social backgrounds and military roles who return to the same home town together and, in their various ways, face the difficulties of readjustment that their separate circumstances impose. The eldest is a graying Army sergeant

Servicemen returning from overseas duty in the Second World War, are apprehensive about their transition to civilian life. Left to right: Navy machinist Homer Parrish (Harold Russell), Air Force Captain Fred Derry (Dana Andrews) and Sergeant Al Stephenson (Fredric March).

who had been a successful banker before the war and is returning to a wife, two full-grown children and a comfortable banking job, but whose capitalistic concepts have been jolted by his leveling experiences. Next is an Air Force captain, a much-decorated bombardier, who had been a mere drugstore soda jerk before going away to war; he is returning to a virtually unknown bride he had married just before he was shipped abroad and to the realization that he has no education for anything but jerking sodas and dropping bombs. And the youngest is a former high-school student who serves as a Navy machinist's mate and has lost both hands in an explosion; they were replaced with mechanical hands, or "hooks."

Wyler, who had been a colonel in the Air Force and had been chief of the unit that made the excellent Eighth Air Force documentary, *The Memphis Belle,* had seen an Army-made film called *Diary of a Sergeant,* which gave a stringently factual picture of how a paratroop sergeant who had lost both hands in a dynamite explosion had been outfitted with such "hooks" and trained to use them so that he could perform most of the manual functions of a normal person. Then he discovered that the amputee was a young man named Harold Russell who, though not a professional actor, was so right in appearance for the role and so eager to take it that he persuaded Sherwood and Goldwyn to let him sign Russell.

The move was providential, for a major climactic scene is one in which the troubled sailor demonstates in literal detail to his girl, the high-school sweetheart whose reaction to his injury he most profoundly dreads, how he has to get out of his harness every night when he goes to bed and thus be rendered helpless and perhaps physically repulsive to her. This scene, with its accumulated tension of uncertainty between the boy and the girl and its simply stated realization of their mutual discomfort, was one of the most affecting and compelling at the time the film was released. It gained an undoubted accretion of emotional impact and sympathy from audience awareness that Russell was a veteran and a genuine amputee. Thus did Wyler sustain, even briefly, his feeling, acquired while making *The Memphis Belle*, that some of the most convincing screen behavior could be got from people not trained to perform.

The Best Years of Our Lives is essentially a drama of the isolation and reserve of the returning veteran. It recollects and clarifies how he resists casting off his attachment to the service and the security it gave, and a bit about how the homefolk either help or resist him.

The psychological dilemma is superbly stated in the opening scene of the three men hitching a ride back to their home town in a retiring Air Force bomber. Here they are, clustered together in the Plexiglas nose of the plane, nervous and excited, still very much servicemen feeling themselves apart and alienated from the people at home. They are intensely and volubly conscious of their separateness and inwardly scared of their own individual capacities to face up to "rehabilitation." Though they talk a bit too glibly and boastfully of their desires to get out of their uniforms and again be normal, inconspicuous civilians, they fear the transition. Everything they do and say betrays their impulse to hang onto their distinctions, to the codes and *esprit* of the military caste, and signifies their skepticism toward the civilian frame of mind.

In this excellent scene in the bomber, we are quickly introduced to our men: Al, the most articulate, a sharp

At Butch Engel's bar, Homer gets "cold turkey" from the wise and sardonic proprietor (Hoagy Carmichael).

and sardonic older guy, played with appropriate ostentation and just the right shade of insecurity by Fredric March; Fred, the bombardier, whom Dana Andrews endows with a flat, formless voice and an air of reserve that barely cover his bristling watchfulness and instability; and Homer, played by Russell with an appealingly boyish clumsiness that makes all the more impressive the dexterity he displays with his "hooks."

It is remarkable how shrewdly Wyler and Sherwood have constructed the film to keep impressing by visual data the lonely isolation of these men—by showing their detachment and aloofness as they peer from the nose of the plane as it approaches their town, spotting landmarks, noting people playing golf on the local course "as though nothing had happened," sighting an unfamiliar "graveyard" for junked planes; and then by recording their amazement as they ride through town in a taxicab, catching significant changes: a used-car lot, a bunch of reckless kids riding in jalopies, a new neon sign on Butch's place, the bar run by Homer's uncle which is to be their later place of rendezvous.

Indicative of the obstructions each man has to surmount are the discomfort and embarrassment each feels within a few hours after getting home. Homer can't endure sitting sweetly and talking with his parents and his expected father-in-law, who is blunt and insensitive in referring to his handicap and his limited prospects for a job. Al is confused by his wife and daughter and miffed that his high-school son is politely but firmly uninterested in the war souvenirs he has brought home. Fred has been unable to locate his wife. Soon they have all gravitated to the masculine sanctuary of Butch's bar, seeking that place designated as a familiar haven for lonely servicemen—even though Al, in his confusion, does bring his wife and daughter along.

It is interesting and provocative that Al is the heaviest drinker of the lot, that he starts within a few minutes after he gets home and is sloppily drunk by the time

Homer is faced with the ignominy of baring his war injury to his sweetheart, Wilma Cameron (Cathy O'Donnell).

Al brings his wife (Myrna Loy) and daughter to the arranged rendezvous at Butch's bar, which starts quite gaily.

they reach Butch's bar. One begins to wonder about his relation to his wife and his environment before he left—whether possibly he went into the service because he was restless, bored; whether maybe he enjoyed his greatest sense of "belonging" in the service, and that's why he is loath to give it up.

The constant refrain is the reluctance of the serviceman to take up where he left off, to resume his previous status and function in his environment. Invariably he feels that his experience has changed his outlook and privileges. Homer has lost motivation. He isn't interested in looking for a job. He feels that his disability entitles him to live on a pension of $100 a month. Al resists the urging of the bank president to return to his old job. Scornfully, he mocks the cruel compulsion: "Last year it was 'kill Japs,' this year it's 'make money.'" And when he does settle back into harness in charge of the small-loans department at the bank, his crucial gesture of defiance is to give a small loan, without collateral, to a sturdy young former Seabee who wants to buy a farm.

Fred's resistance is tougher, more complex and justified. He doesn't want to go back to being a soda jerk in the now chain-controlled drugstore and jimcrack novelty emporium where he used to work. He feels that his experience *and* his service as a warrior qualify him for more. But he does go back, on the pretext of being an assistant manager filling in at the old job, until he finally takes a poke at a customer who talks scornfully about the worthiness of the war.

Worse for him, however, is the fact that his "warbride" wife has little respect for him and, indeed, finds him unromantic out of uniform. She cheats on him with another fellow and eventually demands a divorce.

But his hardest and most discouraging letdown is when his supposed friend Al, now returned to normal, puts him in his place by ordering him to stay away from his daughter, whom Fred has been seeing fitfully since that first night home, when she soothed him and showed him sympathy. One of the strongest scenes in the picture is one in Butch's bar, when Al, suddenly very bourgeois, brutally puts it on the line: "I want my daughter to marry a decent guy." And then, in a stunning composition, we see Fred in a telephone booth at the end of the room, calling the daughter to tell her he will not see her again, while Al stands in the foreground by the piano, watching Homer, accompanied by his uncle, play "Chopsticks" with his "hooks." All the irony of the dissolution of the service man's *esprit* is in this one shot.

Then the nadir of Fred's self-pity and desolation is conveyed in a memorable scene in which he wanders, on the verge of leaving town, through the "graveyard" of old junked bombers, standing stripped and forlorn, waiting for the junkman's sledgehammer, symbols of a glory that is gone. He climbs into the nose of a dead B-17 bomber and all the anguish of his lot comes over him. That is to say, it comes over the viewer, who is feeling with him. It is a poetic evocation of valorous and proud memories, and it sums up the evanescence of the wartime repute of the serviceman.

This is, indeed, the climax and ultimate statement of the film. Al has accomplished his transition by making that unsecured loan to an ex-Seabee and then telling his skeptical associates at a welcome-home dinner that we didn't win battles in the Pacific by first demanding collateral. That is enough propitiation for his shallow sense of rectitude. Homer has shown his sweetheart what it will mean to endure a man with "hooks," and has received her gentle reassurance. Evidently he has crossed his bridge.

But Fred is the one left hanging. He is the one revealed as having reached a peak in the service that he will never come up to again. And we know he won't, despite an effort by Sherwood and Wyler to force a happy prospect for him by giving him a small job with the junkman and making it look as though Al's daughter will "wait for him." We know he's the sort of fellow who truly had his "best years" in the war. It is too bad the ending of the picture is not that last shot of him in the junked plane.

Because he has the best role, the most forthright and meaningful, Dana Andrews is privileged to give the best performance in the film. His Fred is a poignant reflection of simple virtues and complex weaknesses, a clear and classic victim of the forces of an ironic fate. Ironically, his performance was the one that was *not* recognized by the Academy Awards. Fredric March as Al is excellent as what he was not first recognized to be—a voluble, superficial, two-faced mediocrity. His basic insincerity and fraudulence are aptly camouflaged by characteristic clowning and delivery of glib, colloquial lines.

Wyler aptly used Gregg Toland's camera to get the texture and tone of the American scene, and some very effective implications are in Hugo Friedhofer's musical score.

Later films were to look further into particular problems of ex-servicemen. Edward Dymtryk's *Crossfire* (1947) is about a veteran faced with anti-Semitic prejudice. Stanley Kramer's *Home of the Brave* (1949) is about a Negro soldier who becomes psychopathic because of the manner in which he is abused. But first and most extensive is *The Best Years of Our Lives*. It is a moving, valuable addenda to the cinema's body of contemplations of the consequences of war.

To the astonishment of his friends and associates, Al pleads for tolerance and acceptance for the less privileged at the conclusion of a dinner in his honor.

Paisan

1946

Screenplay by Sergio Amidei, Klaus Mann, Alfred Hayes, Marcello Pagliero, Federico Fellini, and Roberto Rossellini; directed and produced by Roberto Rossellini; cameraman, Otello Martelli.

Joe from Jersey	Robert von Loon
Carmela	Carmela Sazio
American M.P.	Dots M. Johnson
Boy in Naples	Alfonsino
Francesca	Maria Michi
Fred	Gar Moore
Harriet, a nurse	Harriet White
Renzo	Renzo Avanzo
Chaplain Bill Martin	Bill Tubbs
Dale, an O.S.S. man	Dale Edmonds

The irony of war is the essence of the six episodes of *Paisan*. The Sicilian girl, too, becomes a Nazi victim, but the G.I.'s buddies will blame her for betrayal.

A drunken M.P. (Dots M. Johnson) entertains a young resident of Naples on a rubbish heap.

Just as the stir of new vitality was felt after the First World War with the creation of *The Cabinet of Dr. Caligari* (which see) and other revolutionary films in Germany, so it was manifested at the end of the Second World War in a rush of outrage pictures in defeated Italy.

The reasons for this were abundant. There were locked up in warbound Italy a number of powerful film-makers who were quivering with wrath and restlessness. They were heirs of a once-proud tradition of cinema inventiveness and success that had marked the Italians as world leaders in the pristine phase of silent films. But the urges of the nation's film-makers had been stifled by the Fascist government, which imposed its wish for innocuous romances and propagandistic pictures by generous subsidies and decrees. Ornate costume dramas, banal comedies and massive, insincere pictures designed to glorify the Italian war in Ethiopia characterized the sterile nature of the nation's films in the years before the Second World War.

As the war dragged on, however, and the stark futility of it began to appear, the resentment and despair of some film-makers were subtly and guardedly expressed. Luchino Visconti's *Obsession* (1942) marked a portentous departure from the Fascist demands for sweetness and light. It was a grim, earthy exposition of lust and criminality. It signaled a gathering rebellion against compulsory make-believe. Bitter, too, was Vittorio de Sica's *The Children Are Watching Us* (1943), a tearing drama of the shock and disillusion of a boy upon discovering his mother's gross adultery, which could readily be taken as symbolistic of disillusion with the Fascist regime.

But the burst of the new Italian cinema was first recorded in 1945 with the release of Roberto Rossellini's *Open City*, a truly historic film. This devastating chronicle of the Nazi occupation of Rome—that dismal period between the collapse of the Fascist government in 1943 and liberation of the Nazi-held city in June 1944—is a violent, impassioned drama of Nazi brutality and the tough, realistic resistance of the workers' organized underground.

Disillusionment is a concomitant of war for this young G.I. (Gar Moore) and the prostitute Francesca (Maria Michi).

Rossellini had been trained to make documentaries, a genre in which the Italians were particularly adept. Following the collapse of the Fascist government and even while the Nazis were still in Rome, he started planning *Open City* and secretly filming scenes. With a few professional actors—Anna Magnani, Aldo Fabrizzi, Maria Michi, Marcello Pagliero—and people who had never appeared before the camera; with odd lengths of raw stock borrowed from Roman companies and, later, from Allied camera crews; shooting mostly on locations in the streets and workers quarters of Rome, he made this film of the Occupation entirely free of any sense of the studios.

Even though *Open City* is a plotted melodrama, in which there is an intrigue, a betrayal, the capture and torture of a working-class leader of the underground and a culminating execution of a Resistance priest, it has the appearance and the aura of a recording of raw reality. It was so real, indeed, that it wasn't popular when first shown in Italy. To the tortured and war-exhausted people, it was much too close to what they had endured. But it was hailed as a revelation when first shown in London and New York, and it was duly respected by the Italians after it was heaped with

honors abroad. This film and de Sica's subsequent *Shoe Shine* (1946), which was a harrowing and heartbreaking melodrama of the corruption of boys in the black-market environment of postwar Rome, and likewise Aldo Vergano's *Outcry* (1945), inspired the label of "neo-realism" for this kind of postwar Italian films.

The term is now used loosely, and its meaning is generally abused. The common notion is that neo-realism is synonymous with documentary. Because the Italians—Rossellini and de Sica first, then others who quickly followed them (Luigi Zampa, Alberto Lattuada, Giuseppe de Santis, etc.)—shot their films mainly in the streets, with casts of "actors" largely selected from the general populace in order to get authentic appearances and natures rather than mere professional skills, the notion is that this is the essence of the neo-realistic style.

It is not. The fundamental of neo-realism is an attitude, an esthetic philosophy that is rooted in a seeking after truth. It represents an extension of the attitude and aims of the Russian and German "realist" filmmakers in the 1920's (as exemplified by Dziga Vertov's "kino eye" productions and Walter Ruttmann's *Berlin, the Symphony of a Great City*). The idea is to abandon the rigid narrative approach and let the action seem to develop spontaneously from existing realities. The director is a passing observer who is struck by what is happening and is anxious to record it. He shuns personal involvement in the events, but his recognition of drama and of human anguish is intense.

This was an attitude most logical for the Italians. Having witnessed so much suffering, having exhausted their emotional capacities for indignation and hate, these directors were determined to get on film the forthright truth of what they were witnessing (or had witnessed) as accurately and fairly as they could.

Thus the film made by Rossellini after *Open City*—his *Paisan*—is not only the fullest indication of the neorealist style but it is the most complete communication of the disillusion and emptiness, the death of hope, the sense of letdown and utter frustration that came at the end of the war. It is, in my estimation, the greatest of the immediate postwar films. *Paisan* was made in the fall and winter of 1945–46—in the first months of postwar confusion, before Rossellini had received the international acclaim that *Open City* was to bring him, and he had not yet shaken himself free of the deep cynicism and exhaustion that the experience of the war had left.

With the same writers, Sergio Amidei and Federico Fellini, who had worked with him in preparing the script of *Open City,* plus three of four more, he cast *Paisan* in the form of a random news report of certain aspects of the last two years of the war (1943–44) while the Allies, especially the Americans, were beating their way up the peninsula of Italy. The very form of it signifies the vagrant and capricious nature of war.

It begins with actuality news shots of the Allies' invasion of Sicily, accompanied by the voice of a commentator explaining the military plan of the campaign. Then it goes into the first of its six episodes, this one a monotone account of the killing of an American G.I. and an Italian girl while they are becoming acquainted during a mop-up by an American night patrol in a Sicilian town. The next episode, after an insertion of the continuing connective newsreel device, involves an American Negro military policeman and an orphaned urchin in Naples.

The third episode is the closest to a conventional, sentimental wartime tale. It has to do with a drunken G.I. and a prostitute in Rome. He can't have relations with her because he keeps thinking about the girl he met at the time of the liberation. In his flashback remembrances of her, we see that it was the same girl, only cleaner and more wholesome than she is now. The girl, who has now recognized him, asks why he didn't return. He says he lost the address and couldn't find her. She says he should keep on looking, that there are still some decent girls in Rome. After he has gone to sleep, she sneaks out and leaves an address for him. She is waiting there the next morning, in a white dress and full of nervous hope. But he doesn't show up. Instead, we see him waiting for a troop carrier in the street, telling another soldier he is leaving because he couldn't find what he was looking for in Rome.

The next episode takes place in Florence, where an American Army nurse has come to look for a man she once knew there, an Italian artist who was evidently her lover in happier days. The city south of the Arno has been taken, but that north of the river is still being

An American Army nurse (Harriet White) returns to Florence to find an artist she once knew there. Her hopeful mission ends in tragedy.

fought for by the partisans. We learn that the fellow she is seeking is known as Lupo and is the leader of the group. Through the bare, forbidding galleries of the Pitti Palace, in the untended Boboli Gardens outside, across the river and through the streets of the famous old city, now empty and silent except for occasional Nazi patrols and the fusillades of snipers, the girl is led by an obliging partisan. They make contact with a small group of partisans who are being engaged by civilian Fascisti. One fellow is wounded and dragged into a doorway as others come around a corner, shepherding a couple of captured Fascist snipers, whom they peremptorily knock down and shoot. Then the girl goes back to the wounded fellow, who murmurs despairingly, "Everything started going wrong today when Lupo died." That's all. We have a glimpse of the girl's face when she learns her lover is dead, then a fast cut.

The fifth episode is humorous, yet expressive of the

In a Franciscan monastery three American chaplains find that even in the midst of war vows of silence are unbroken and austerity is the unchanging pattern of life.

incongruities and the truly shocking anomalies in an environment of war. Three American Army chaplains —a Catholic, a Protestant and a Jew—are paying the first formal visit to a liberated Franciscan monastery in the Apennines. They are greeted with pleasure and simple hospitality by the primitive monks. But the holy men are thrown into alarm and confusion when they learn that one of the chaplains is a Jew and another is a Protestant. This they cannot understand.

The final episode is the starkest and most overwhelming in the film. It takes place along the Po River in the north of Italy, and it simply documents the decimation of a stubborn partisan group, which includes an American O.S.S. captain and a few other Americans, by the Nazis. As the last of the captured partisans is pushed in the river to drown, a commentator says flatly, "This was in the winter of 1944. A few weeks later, spring came to Italy and the war was declared over." And on that note of desolation, of the useless wiping out of a group of remote, heroic people—Italians and Americans—the picture ends.

It is significant that, in these random sketches, there is no image of war on a large scale, no concept of armies rolling forward in a large, coordinated attack. This is essentially a picture of war in a close and concrete view, as though the camera were a reporter observing passing episodes, each an invitation to an elaborate drama, if one wished to make it so, yet each so incidental in what one realizes is the total scene that the camera merely follows it dispassionately to a significant cut-off point, and then moves on.

This method of observation might be vexatious at first to those who expect a story to be built up emotionally. Yet it actually creates such conviction as the details of the episodes unfold through the cryptic, even clumsy visualizations of Rossellini's literal style that this bluntness and studied anticlimax become the ultimate conveyance of the sense of truth.

The abrupt and unagonized snapoffs of the episodes frankly imply that the camera is turning deliberately from commitment of its own emotional reaction to the evidence so clear before its eyes. It is properly avoiding the convention of attempting to moralize on what it sees. The viewer himself is left to ponder and fill in all the ironies and griefs that are too obvious and depressing to be dwelled on, and too freighted with their own profound sadness to be commercialized.

An implicit theme in the whole is the difficulty of being understood, the bewilderments of communication among aliens, interrelated by the Italian epithet, "paisan," which is used like the American word "buddy." But, of course, the irony is that so often inability to communicate causes mistakes and griefs.

Monsieur Verdoux

1947

Screenplay by Charles Chaplin, based on an idea by Orson Welles; directed and produced by Mr. Chaplin; photographed by Curt Courant, Roland Totheroh and Wallace Chewing; music by Mr. Chaplin; a United Artists release.

Henri Verdoux	
alias Varney	
alias Bonheur	
alias Floray	Charles Chaplin
Mona, his wife	Mady Correll
Peter, his son	Allison Roddan
Maurice Bottello	Robert Lewis
Mme. Bottello	Audrey Betz

THE LADIES

Annabella Bonheur	Martha Raye
Marie Grosnay	Isobel Elsom
Lydia Floray	Margaret Hoffman
Annette	Ada-May
Yvonne	Helene Heigh
Maid	Marjorie Bennett
The Girl	Marilyn Nash

THE COUVAIS FAMILY

Pierre	Irving Bacon
Jean	Edwin Mills
Carlotta	Virginia Brissac
Lena	Almira Sessions
Phoebe	Eula Morgan

THE LAW

Prefect of Police	Bernard J. Nedell
Detective Morrow	Charles Evans

Switching to subtle comedy, Chaplin continues his artistry as a suave stockbroker, a naval officer, an engineer who marries and murders rich widows for the money to support a son and an invalid wife.

Gently but firmly, Monsieur Verdoux gets assurance that the game is worth the candle.

It is a far cry from the baggy, comic character that Charlie Chaplin performs in such classics as *The Gold Rush* (which see) and *Modern Times* (1936) to the elegant, energetic murderer he plays in *Monsieur Verdoux*, the last of his outstanding pictures, which the great comedian released in 1947. It is a distance that must be measured in something more than the passage of time and the technical changes in concept and comedy style, which are immense. It must be measured in the manifold personal troubles and emotional crises that Chaplin went through in the years that were most profoundly burdened by the anguish of the Second World War. These were the things that conditioned him for this most extraordinary of all his films.

The first were the worries and confusions that crowded in on him with the production of *The Great Dictator*, which he started preparing early in 1939. Struck (as everyone was) by the resemblance that

Monsieur Verdoux, clutching a single rose—reminiscent of the Little Tramp's delicacy—senses a prospective victim in the rich widow (Isobel Elsom) who comes to consider renting his house.

Most difficult to murder is Annabella Bonheur (Martha Raye), who survives drowning and poison to the disgust of the much-marrying Monsieur Verdoux (Charles Chaplin).

Adolf Hitler bore to his altogether dissimilar and universally beloved Little Tramp, Chaplin felt it would be fitting for him to satirize the fiendishness and folly of the Nazi leader in terms of the ludicrous behavior of a remarkably familiar-looking clown.

Already he had decided, despite the success of *Modern Times,* that the Little Tramp was finished as a viable character. He was a fanciful concept of a passing age and taste, and Chaplin was ready to ditch him when the idea for *The Great Dictator* occurred. However, he would retain the character in this new film to the extent of having a little German Jewish barber of customary personality to represent the antithesis to the fanatical dictator and to take over from him at the end. While the dictator, Hynkel, would exhibit many of the familiar mannerisms of the Little Tramp, he would be a heinous parody of him, an egregious paradox. Chaplin, of course, would play both roles.

The picture was in production when the war began. Chaplin was in a quandary. Should he abandon it or go on? Had the monstrousness of Hitler become too sinister for jokes, or would ridicule still be effective in exposing the monstrosity of the man? Chaplin decided to continue. But when the film was released in October 1940, the war had taken an ominous turn and critics were of the opinion that the time for laughing at Hitler was past. Although Chaplin superlatively mimics the mincing mannerisms and shouting oratory of the demagogue, and Jack Oakie parodies Mussolini in a comparably devastating way, the film struck too many

people as insensitive and distasteful at the time. Chaplin was criticized for it, which evidently hurt him very much.

Then he got into trouble in 1942 by making speeches advocating that the Allies open a "second front" to divert the pressure of the German assault on Soviet Russia. He was challenged for getting himself involved in political and military matters. Newspaper columnists lambasted him, charging him with being a Communist sympathizer, which they had done ever since he made *Modern Times.* This was followed by the drab experience of being dragged through a sordid paternity suit brought against him by a disappointed woman shortly after he had married his fourth wife in 1943. All these things aroused the ire of Chaplin and subtly embittered him. He was ready for a radical departure when he made his next film.

This was to be a "comedy of murders," suggested to him by Orson Welles and based on the grisly story of a notorious French wife-killer, Henri-Désiré Landru. Chaplin, now parted completely from the spirit and mood of the Little Tramp, decided that his emancipation would be displayed in a complete paradox.

His *Monsieur Verdoux,* which is the outcome of this decisive move, is an extraordinarily daring example of what we later came to call "black comedy," a fascinating presentment of the oncoming "theater of the absurd." The deeply humanistic attitude, naturally expected of Chaplin, which is still in *The Great Dictator* in the little barber's role, is blandly diluted and diverted

186

into a mischievous attitude of intellectual justification of obvious inhumanity. The nimble and comical Bluebeard, whom Chaplin enacts with great *élan*, is a startling exposure of the incongruity of the values and behavior of modern man.

At the start of the film, this Monsieur Verdoux is a dapper and exquisitely mannered little Frenchman in his well-cut vests, his batwing collars and with his pencil-mark moustache and silver hair. Indeed, he has all the appearances of a gentle and potentially tedious fop, amusingly fancy and fastidious but otherwise shallow and dull. And his ardent pursuits of middle-aged women, conducted in beautifully exaggerated comic styles, might be but dandified extensions of the romantic manners and innocent pursuits of the Little Tramp.

But soon it becomes apparent by innuendoes of the daintiest sort, such as smoke rising from an incinerator at the back of a garden in which Verdoux is cutting flowers, that he is a secret, shameless murderer—that he fraudulently marrries well-to-do women, as he explains, and then quickly polishes them off as soon as he has their affairs in order so that he can come by their wealth. This he does because he has discovered that, as a bank clerk, he could not earn enough to support a crippled wife and their small son, whom he loves and who do not for a moment suspect that his long periods away from home are for the purposes revealed.

Obviously such a character is a monster by all our sane and ethical lights, and his ultimate unmasking and destruction are only right and just. But, as Chaplin plays this rascal, he is both a satan and a faun, a devil in gentleman's clothing and a charming innocent with the perfidy of a rogue. For each of his well-selected victims, he plays a different role. For one he is a dandy naval officer, for another a pompous engineer, for a third a successful stockbroker. And for all he is a man of the kindest mien.

In this way, Chaplin is able to show great comic variety and avoid the possible tedium in his fellow's monotonous career. The funniest of his murderous endeavors are directed against Martha Raye as a lady of uncouth and raucous manner whom he finds impossible to destroy. One crafty attempt to get her by putting poison in her drink and having it backfire on him when he thinks he has switched the drinks and poisoned himself, and another by trying to dump her out of a rowboat while fishing on a lake and falling overboard himself in the process and having to be rescued by her, are as comically inventive as any Chaplin ever played.

When Verdoux is finally captured—after a typical Chaplin episode in which he, an older man now, and widowed, is being gallant to a beautiful young woman

A tramp no longer, but still a satirist of contemporary manners.

—he frankly acknowledges his identity as the notorious Bluebeard of the past and explains himself, at his trial, as a diligent small businessman. He says he was simply in the business of "liquidating persons of the opposite sex," which, unfortunately, is considered illegal when pursued on a small, personal scale but is tolerated and even applauded when practiced on a large scale as in war.

"Mass killing," he says; "does not the world encourage it? I am an amateur by comparison."

This paradoxical argument is the crux of the film, and Chaplin extends and expands it in his final scenes. In prison, awaiting execution, he has Verdoux casually expound a philosophy of ruthless pragmatism to a group of reporters interviewing him. Crime doesn't pay —not in a *small* way, Verdoux knowingly states. Good and evil, he says, are arbitrary forces; "too much of either would destroy us all."

When a priest comes to confess him and asks if he has no remorse for his sins, Verdoux answers, "Who knows what sin is, born as it is from heaven, from God's fallen angel? Who knows what ultimate destiny is served? After all, what would *you* be doing without sin?" And when the priest concludes his mission with a

187

prayer that God have mercy on the condemned man's soul, Verdoux responds politely, "Why not? After all, it belongs to Him."

The picture closes with Verdoux being led to the guillotine—an image more stark and disturbing than ever was that of the Little Tramp going his lonely way.

Monsieur Verdoux was found quite shocking at the time it was released, and there were sharp criticisms of its structure, which were fully justified. It is slow in many stretches; it is sadly sentimental in the scenes of Verdoux with his wife and youngster (brightened only by the father chiding his son at one point for pulling the cat's tail: "There's a cruel streak in you; I wonder where you got it.") The bursts of comic invention do fall a bit uncomfortably into the grimly gothic pattern of murders (none of which, thankfully, is ever shown), and the philosophical argument does not begin to emerge until near the end.

Except for Chaplin's brilliant performance and the wonderfully comic one of Miss Raye, there is little distinction in the acting. A repeated shot of train wheels humming along the tracks to give the notion of transitions in place and time is annoyingly trite and monotonous. And the whole thing is too long—almost two hours.

But the very audacity of it—the fact that Chaplin dared to depart from his customary brand of humor to project this harsh and glibly ghoulish homily on the difficulties of survival in a mass-organized world—and the continuing impressiveness of it as pristine "black comedy" from the world's most famous comedian render *Monsieur Verdoux* a deathless film.

Understandably, it was confusing and upsetting to audiences who could not have sympathy or pity for the ambiguous murderer. It was not successful at the box office, and Chaplin ordered it withdrawn from distribution after two fruitless years. Except for one theatrical revival in New York in 1964, it has not been available for viewing in this country—and that is a loss! It stands at the end of the gallery of great works of a great man of the screen.

Chaplin's next film was *Limelight,* a sweetly sentimental tale of an aging music-hall comedian and his generous befriending of a lonely girl, which is an obvious reflection of his feelings of self-pity in 1952. Alas, it was the last picture he made in Hollywood. A shameful move to harass him by the Attorney General of the United States while he was on a trip to Europe with his family in the fall of 1952 caused him to take up residence in Switzerland and refuse to return to the land in which he had such a splendid and anomalous career.

Comfortable at last and a gallant companion of the girl (Marilyn Nash) whom he had befriended earlier, Monsieur Verdoux is spotted by the sister and son of a former dupe, the start of his undoing.

1948

The Treasure of the Sierra Madre

Screenplay by John Huston, from a novel by B. Traven; directed by Mr. Huston; cameraman, Ted McCord; music by Max Steiner; produced by Henry Blanke for Warner Brothers.

Fred Dobbs	Humphrey Bogart
Howard	Walter Huston
Curtin	Tim Holt
Cody	Bruce Bennett
Gold Hat	Alfonso Bedoya
McCormick	Barton MacLane
Presidente	A. Soto Rangel
El Jefe	Manuel Donde
Pablo	José Torvay
Pancho	Margarito Luna
Flashy Girl	Jacqueline Dalay
Mexican Boy	Bobby Blake
Man in White Suit	John Huston

Wealth and the acquisition of it have been exalted so often on the screen (I would reckon that, next to matrimony, getting rich is the most popular happy ending in American films) that it is rare to have a picture that cruelly and candidly states that too-avid pursuit of this temptation may lead to disaster and death. Especially is it exceptional to have one that illustrates this theme with an artistry sufficient to elevate it to the class of a universal moral fable, on the order of Erich von Stroheim's *Greed* (which see). Such a film is John Huston's *The Treasure of the Sierra Madre,* which was the first turned out by the director of *The Maltese Falcon* (which see) upon his return from World War II.

I find it significant that this most prominent of the young Americans who were involved in making documentaries for the services during the war should have chosen for his first effort on his return to Hollywood this stark and realistic contemplation of the brutal consequences of sheer, raw greed upon a trio of gold prospectors on a lonely and perilous expedition into the mountains of Mexico. It is evidence that Huston, whose Army documentaries were *Report from the Aleutians, The Battle of San Pietro* and the extraordinary (and never released) study of "battle fatigue" veterans, *Let There Be Light,* had truly acquired a broadening of his philosophical view of life as a result of his war experience. He was probably the sole American film-maker who was markedly imbued with the spirit of cynicism evident in the early works of the Italian neo-realists.

In fact, there is such ironic scorn for the convention of gold in *The Treasure of the Sierra Madre,* such somber display of distaste for the way in which the gross idolatry of this monetary metal can destroy the simplicity and enjoyment of life, that the film is an interesting parallel to Vittorio de Sica's *Shoe Shine* and his *The Bicycle Thief* (which see). While it does not have their topicality and social immediacy (since its time is the 1920's or the early 1930's at most), it has the same tone of frustration about the frailties and

In a grubby bar in steamy Tampico, Fred Dobbs (Humphrey Bogart) convinces a new-found friend, Curtin (Tim Holt), that a rich grubstake can be found in the nearby mountains.

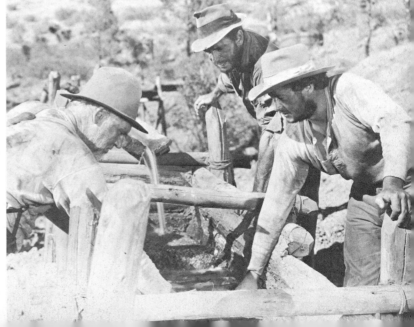

Enormously authentic was the location chosen for the film—an area where John Huston as a very young man had served in the Mexican Army.

vulnerability of human beings when confronted by the juggernauts of the social systems in which they live.

In telling a tension-stretching story of how the cancer of greed expands in one wormy prospector until it drives him mad and causes the dissolution and failure of a successful cooperative enterprise, *The Treasure of the Sierra Madre* juxtaposes this evidence of disease in civilized man against tacitly humiliating evidence of the generosity of man in the primitive state.

In the mountains from which the three prospectors laboriously dig a treasure of gold, there lives a community of Indians who have no awareness of or interest in the metal locked in their hills. Their only interest is living serenely, without discomfort and strife. When one of the three prospectors leaves his enterprise to respond to their plea for medical assistance to one of their sick children, their concept of compensation is to compel him to accept the luxury of lying in a hammock all day while they load him with food and drink. This is much more enjoyable, they believe, than the useless substance of gold.

At the same time, there are in the mountains other strata of human beings ranging between the primitive Indians and the prospectors. The most aggressive are the native bandits who are moved by a cruel cupidity quite as evil and dangerous to their welfare as that of the prospector who succumbs to the greed for gold. But the irony is that their cupidity (which traps them, too, at the end) is for guns and donkeys and bits of clothing. They, too, are unaware of the substance of gold. Thus the final implication of this aggressively moralistic

With a third prospector, Howard (Walter Huston, father of the director), a grizzled veteran of the hills, the group set out on their search for gold.

film is that man may be ruined by obsession for the symbols of "property" that prevail in his social state.

How Huston made this picture is a clue to the conditioning of his mind and the bent of his thinking about film-making when he returned to Hollywood. He had found the story in a novel by B. Traven, which had been published in 1935 and which he had read with possessive interest before he went off to war. Its essential observation of the corruptive effect of avarice was much the same as that in *The Maltese Falcon,* and it ends with a similar irony. Only here the calamity of too much wanting is completed upon the protagonist.

The novel was owned by Warner Brothers, and all the while Huston was away he thought about it and kept beseeching the studio to hold it for him to do on his return. He did not return immediately, however. He spent most of 1946 in New York preparing and directing a stage production of the play, *No Exit,* by Jean-Paul Sartre. This stark, existentialist reflection of dead souls doomed to the fate that their individual sins had ordained for them was not a box-office success, but it helped to condition Huston for *The Treasure of the Sierra Madre.*

All along, he had thought of Humphrey Bogart to play the focal role of an American vagrant, stranded in Tampico, who gets enough money to grubstake himself and two companions on a search for gold and then becomes monomaniacal when the stuff starts rolling in. It made a challenging role for Bogart, an initially sympathetic character who combined the perfidy and ferocity of some of his gangsters with the cool detachment and self-serving of Sam Spade. His Fred C. Dobbs in *Treasure* could be Spade after several turns of hard luck and financial setback had driven him into exile in Mexico and left him mentally unsettled and obsessed with a desire to recoup.

As ardent in Huston's calculations was his wish to have his father, Walter, play a sassy old sourdough named Howard whom Dodd accidentally comes upon in a Tampico flophouse and with whom he and a younger newly found friend named Curtin arrange to form a prospecting partnership. This character, picturesque but slippery, is at first the doubtful element in the group, but it is he who turns out to be hero and humanitarian of the tale.

Essential to the project, however, was Huston's determination to make the outdoor scenes of his mostly outdoor picture on location in Mexico. His experience in documentary filming had impressed him with the worth of authentic atmospheric settings, especially for a picture of this sort. His faithful producer, Henry Blanke, finally cajoled Jack Warner in to approving this departure (which was a big one at the time, you may be

The expedition goes beyond its goal of finding treasure and becomes a struggle between individuals.

sure), and the company went on location, first in steamy Tampico, and later in the mountain country near the village of San José Purua, about 80 miles west of Mexico City.

Before they left for Mexico, a bizarre encounter occurred that was in keeping with the exotic and sardonic flavor of the film. B. Traven, the author of the novel, was a man of mystery. All that was known about him was that he lived in Mexico and could be reached only through his agent, who transmitted messages to him. Huston was anxious to have Traven read the screenplay he prepared, so he had a copy sent to him and received such a lengthy and interesting reply from the author that he thought it would be helpful if they met. Through the agent, he arranged a meeting in a Mexico City hotel, but when he got there on the day appointed, Traven did not show up. Then he received a message that Traven was ill and couldn't come.

In the middle of the night before Huston was planning to fly back to Hollywood, he awoke to find a small man standing at the foot of the bed in his hotel room. The man presented a card which identified him as "Hal Croves, Interpreter—San Antonio and Acapulco," and he said, "Traven asked me to come to see you." He then showed Huston a letter signed by Traven which said, "This man knows more about me than I know about myself."

Huston was fascinated. He immediately suspected the man *was* Traven, and he tried by various methods in subsequent conversations to draw him out. Later, when they went on location, the little man showed up again and was signed on as technical adviser. He knew a great deal about Mexico, especially the jungle, but he

continued to insist he was Croves. He stayed through the location shooting, which lasted for two months, and when the company was about to leave Mexico, he quietly disappeared. Huston, involved in his story of greed and rapacity, could not imagine why a prominent author—if he really was—would be so anxious to deny himself the pleasure of the respect of the company. So Croves remained a mystery—until recently, when it was publicly revealed that he actually was Traven, and that both names were pseudonyms for Traven Torsven, a Chicago-born novelist who now lives in Mexico City.

Huston himself was sufficiently familiar with Mexico, having served in the Mexican cavalry when he was in his early twenties, sowing his wild oats. He understood the wildness of the mountains, the raw boom-town quality of Tampico, the viciousness of some Mexicans and the innocence and gentleness of others. These are all very vivid in his film.

But the crux of *The Treasure of the Sierra Madre* is in the conflict of characters, played against the rugged background of adventure, toil and peril. Dobbs, when we first meet him in Tampico, is a forthright, likable bum, bland about panhandling a fellow American (a small role played by Huston himself), nonchalant about losing in the lottery, ready to take a hard job for small pay. He appears droll and fatalistic, and when he gets together some money from a job (which he and his casual sidekick, Curtin, have to beat out of their sly employer), he is thoroughly ready to risk it on the exciting hope that old Howard has enough knowledge of the mountains to take them to where there may be gold.

Howard is equally intriguing—a toothless, garrulous old scamp who, when we find him in the flophouse, sitting there in a dirty union suit and regaling anyone who will listen with his opinions of the fatal lure of gold, seems a cracky old windbag, amusing but undependable. He scarcely appears the person to lead a dangerous expedition into the wilds. Both comical and cagey, he is obviously a bird you have to watch.

In visualizing him, John Huston recalled a man he once met at a bar in Durango, an old prospector who talked rapidly with his arms tightly folded and seldom looked anyone in the face. He described this character to his father, and added the clarifying note, "This man has never listened to himself talk. He has never heard himself."

"Dad took it from there," said Huston, in telling of the making of the film. "That was the only piece of direction I ever gave him, outside of where to stand and such." However, when Huston first telephoned his father to tell him he wanted him to do the role, he informed him he would have to learn some Spanish (which he did) and also to discard his false teeth. Walter balked at this requirement. He had recently bought a new set of dentures, for which he paid a lot of money and of which he was very proud. He still resisted the instruction to remove them when they started to film, but he reluctantly tried it and discovered the effect of chattering. "It just flowed from there on," Huston said.

The viewer is involved intensely as the trio goes into the wilds, shoots at attacking bandits from a rattling train, buys burros and camp equipment at a village and climbs into the Sierra Madre. Everyone yens for El Dorado, and there is a strong thrill of questing it here. The suspense takes a sharp turn, however, when the men, having found a vein of gold and gone through the weeks-long labor of digging a mine and building a sluice, find themselves suddenly confronted with the ominous divisiveness of Dobbs, who demands that they start splitting up their gold dust and letting each man take care of his own "goods."

It is at this point that the bold adventure flows into a study of characters and the drama becomes a perilous conflict of the individual men. While the menace of outside interference is variously and startlingly maintained with an American lone-wolf prospector coming to the camp and demanding to be cut in, a vicious

There's more than gold to be reckoned with in the mountains.

visitation from bandits and an eerie call in the night by Indians, the major suspense and anxiety lie in the viperous uncertainty of Dobbs. With him becoming more and more fanatical over the acquisition and guarding of his gold, and with old Howard becoming more alert to the danger that he presents, the tension grows taut over the issue of whether they will ever get out alive, not alone because of the bandits and the Indians but because of the possible treachery of Dobbs.

And, sure enough, it is Dobbs' treachery that very soon does for him and for the successful conclusion of the enterprise. Old Howard has gone off with the Indians to be rewarded for curing their sick child; Dobbs and Curtin are left to make their way out of the mountains with the gold. In the night, Dobbs attempts to murder Curtin, fails and tries to go it alone. En route, he is waylaid by the bandits, and they finish him.

This crucial scene of the bandits overtaking the famished and desiccated Dobbs, a figure of utter foulness, as he and his burros go for water in a shallow arroyo, is the most horrifying in the picture and perhaps the most memorable. For, in the very way that the bandits come upon this evil man, giggle and gloat over his defenselessness and even start stripping him of his tattered clothes before killing him, then fight for the burros and, in doing so, scatter the precious gold, is visioned a ghastly parody of the Furies destroying a marked man. It is a blood-curdling verification of the likely wages of greed.

Anticlimactic but poetic is the final sequence in which old Howard and Curtin arrive at the village, discover that Dobbs has been killed, the bandits apprehended and their gold scattered to the wind. "It's a great joke, Curt," the old man cackles, as he laughs hysterically. "The gold has gone back to where we found it!" An empty bag on the windswept ground is the last we see.

Except for Max Steiner's music, which is too obvious and insistent in some scenes, the techniques in this film are splendid. Huston's direction—his grasp of atmosphere, got with Ted McCord's camera, and his overlaying of character and suspense—is a model of excellent structuring. The performances are superb—Bogart's and Walter Huston's perhaps the best either man ever did, while Tim Holt's stolid Curtin, Alfonso Bedoya's bandit chief and Bruce Bennett's intruding prospector are totally in tune.

Huston and Bogart did other films together—*Key Largo* (1948), *The African Queen* (1949) and *Beat the Devil* (1954)—and each did some good ones separately. But neither, in my estimation, has topped *The Treasure of the Sierra Madre*.

The Bicycle Thief

Antonio (Lamberto Maggiorani) is at his new job, plastering the walls of Rome with posters advertising a Rita Hayworth film, when a thief makes off with his much-needed transportation.

1948

Story and screenplay by Cesare Zavattini, based on the novel of the same name by Luigi Bartolini; directed by Vittorio de Sica; cameraman, Carlo Montuori; music, Alessandro Cicognini; produced in Rome by de Sica Production Company and released in 1949 in the United States by Mayer-Burstyn.

Antonio, the husband	Lamberto Maggiorani
Maria, the wife	Lianella Carell
Bruno, the son	Enzo Staiola
The Medium	Elena Altieri
The Thief	Vittorio Antonucci
Baiocco	Gino Saltamerenda

Early in Vittorio de Sica's *The Bicycle Thief,* which emerges with time as the most poignant and one of the two most significant of the true Italian neo-realistic films, the focal character, a poor bill-poster in Rome, has occasion to make an urgent and desperate appeal to the police. His bicycle has been stolen right before his eyes, while he was up on a ladder, his very first day on a new job. Without this small means of conveyance, the last valuable thing he owns, he will lose his job and be deprived of his only way to support his wife and child. Naturally, acting on instinct, he rushes first to the police to seek the assistance of their power to apprehend a thief.

But the desk officer is impassive. Rome is full of bicycles, he says. It would take every man on the police force to search for a missing one. This sort of thing is a nuisance; it happens dozens of times every day.

The poor man is dumbfounded. Can't the authorities do *something* to help? "Did anyone witness the incident?" the officer wearily inquires. The bill-poster answers him grimly, "People saw it, sure—but nobody cared. . . ."

That one line contains the bitter essence of the rueful and devastating theme of this beautifully pure and tender picture: People see, but nobody cares. And it also identifies the transit of the Italian neo-realist group, and especially of de Sica, away from their first black films. Whereas the techniques and the terseness of the free-shooting realistic style are continued—even carried further—in *The Bicycle Thief,* and whereas the implication of injustice and social apathy are still as strong, the film itself sees to arranging that a lot of people care—that is, the lot of people who see this agitating film.

You will recall how totally uncommitted Roberto Rossellini keeps us in *Paisan* (which see), how purposely he sees to it that we are permitted to observe and partake of the painful details of tragic wartime experiences, yet never assists or even allows us to surrender our hearts to the people we see. They are random and quickly passing figures in the turgid stream of all those countless others who have been washed along by the war. Our sympathies and imaginations may be momentarily tangled with them, but we are cut away and carried on to others at the very junctures where we might become emotionally involved.

To a certain extent, de Sica does something of the same in *Shoe Shine,* his tragic picture of Rome's homeless delinquents, made in 1945. He lets us observe the drab confusion and black corruption of newly liberated Rome, and he brings us in contact with two youngsters who are sucked up and destroyed in this morass. But he doesn't induce us to linger too long or sympathetically

193

Antonio, accompanied by his son Bruno (Enzo Staiola), begins a fruitless search for the thief through the seamy working-class area of postwar Rome and the spare-parts market where stolen bikes are sold bit by bit.

with these boys. They are part of the already ruined and discarded wreckage of war.

The attitude changes, however, in *The Bicycle Thief,* the next film de Sica directed, in 1948. Here he involves us totally with the bill-poster and his small son as they search through a long and cheerless Sunday for the stolen bicycle in Rome. Here he maneuvers and compels us to identify ourselves with this average working-class father and his wonderfully loyal little boy as they desperately quest for that object which symbolizes survival and a fruitful life in this great city where they find themselves hopelessly disregarded and alone. Everything in the picture is designed to make us sympathize with these two absolutely prototypical samples of average humanity. Everything draws us completely into

compassionate sharing of their plight. And when we have to bid goodbye to them at the end of the film, it is as though we are being wrenched unmercifully from loved ones, from ourselves.

Thus, in this Spartan picture, which takes place mainly in one day and concentrates only on two people, the intent is to *make* us care, to view with concern and compassion an isolated instance of misfortune in a troubled world, and to leave us so attached to these small victims that our eyes and hearts should be forever more alert.

In making plans for this picture, de Sica and his inveterate scriptwriter, the eminent Cesare Zavattini, recognized immediately that it could only be done with pictorial authority, in authentic settings and preferably with a real-life cast. Their story was from a novel by Luigi Bartolini that was in the contemporary idiom of social reportage, and that's what they aimed to make their picture—a reportage of the streets.

But finance was not easy to come by, and for a brief time de Sica was lured by an offer from David O. Selznick to put up the money for the film. Selznick had been impressed by *Shoe Shine* and was anxious to have de Sica direct for him. (Five years later, he did get him to do *Terminal Station,* an unfortunate effort with Jennifer Jones and Montgomery Clift.) But Selznick's choice for the Roman bill-poster was Cary Grant, and de Sica, for all his eagerness to get some money, could not see Grant in the role. He told Selznick he would take Henry Fonda, but Selznick vetoed that. He said Fonda was "not box office." Negotiations were fortunately dropped.

De Sica eventually raised his money, approximately $100,000, from friends and other Italian financial sources, and he found a Roman electrician, Lamberto Maggiorani, to play the role. A wonderful, chubby-faced youngster, Enzo Staiola, was discovered to play the boy. The rest of the cast were all people found here and there in Rome. The only professional actor is Vittorio Antonucci, who is tentatively identified toward the end as the thief.

The opening of the picture sets the atmosphere of working-class want in the city that is still recovering from the disaster of war. After seeking fruitlessly for employment, the father is promised a job as a bill-poster if he has a bicycle, whereupon he pawns the family bedsheets, the last of his wife's dowry, so that he can get his own bike out of hock. And the scene of him going to the pawnshop, where bundles of family possessions are piled high on the storage racks, gives mute testimony to the massiveness of poverty and insecurity in Rome.

But the father is happy about his new job. The night before he is to start, there is a charming business of the wife fixing his new workman's hat to fit him and the son polishing the bicycle. And the next day, he is cheerful as he starts work, slapping Rita Hayworth posters on walls—until three men come along and divert him while one snatches his bicycle and rides away. In the confusion of a chase through the jammed streets, the bill-poster loses the thief in the crowds, and finds himself suddenly confronted with the terrible realization that the bicycle is gone.

Now begins the long procedure of a needle-in-the-haystack search, wherein the father and son, compelled to their own devices by the indifference of the police, start off the next day looking for the bicycle through the whole morning and afternoon of a Sunday in Rome. It

Ironically, a suspect eludes them by taking refuge in a church during mass.

Bruno, resigned, patient, but uncomprehending, waits in the street while his father searches a brothel for the culprit.

is in this phase of the picture that all its strong and subtle values emerge: the discovery of the loving attachment between the father and son, the exposure of myriad aspects of human nature in the people of Rome, suggestions of harshness and hypocrisy in the charitable pretensions of the Church, a realization of the plight of all poor people in a vast society of competitive enterprise. In it are finely modulated the rhythms of hope and despair, humor and heart-tearing pathos, comedy and, yes, tragedy.

The day starts with a serio-comic expedition to hunt the stolen bicycle's parts in a secondhand bicycle market, crowded with sullen people and tough police; rolls on with a ride aboard a trash truck through a sudden shower of rain, and a funny scene of the father and the youngster being crowded out of a shelter by a flock of babbling German seminarians. There is a quick burst of hopeful excitement when the father sees a suspicious-looking fellow making a deal with an old man; they follow this old fellow into a mission and then a church, with a succession of funny and grim encounters that lead to naught.

Then there is a beautiful interlude in which the father, having squabbled with the son and having been

Antonio catches the thief, but is beaten off by bystanders protecting the stolid epileptic.

separated from him, thinks an accident has happened to the lad, and is wonderfully relieved when he sees him standing sturdily at the top of a flight of stairs.

Eventually, they spot the thief, and the father chases him into a bordello, with a comical touch of making the youngster stay outside; but when the father drags the thief forth, he finds him to be a poor epileptic. And there is nothing he can prove, anyhow.

Frustrated now, and thoroughly without hope, the father and son sit forlornly on the curb, watching a swarm of bicycle racers go past, or look at racks full of bicycles outside a stadium.

Then the father spots an unguarded bicycle leaning against a wall in a side street. Without mentioning it to the youngster, he gives him streetcar fare to ride home, then goes back to the bicycle and tries to ride off on it. But as he swings out into the main thoroughfare, he is chased, just as he himself chased the thief of his own bicycle. And, sure enough, with his horrified son watching, he is caught and thrown down by a mob of people swarming out of the stadium. The shocked boy runs to him, and together they persuade the owner of the bicycle to let the father go. Both are speechless with shame and exhaustion as the son takes his father's hand, and they walk away together, weeping softly, in the faceless, dusty crowd.

Thus does de Sica end his picture with an image that pierces the heart. This is his conclusion—or inconclusion—for the "comedy" of life: Man carries on, toiling bravely to do the best he can for himself and his loved ones, cheered only by their contact and love, amidst the general indifference of other men. It is an ending reminiscent of that to King Vidor's *The Crowd* (which see) or several of Charlie Chaplin's wistful and fatalistic films.

No effort is made to define character or character development in *The Bicycle Thief*. Its two people are simply personalities viewed under painful stress. That is why untrained performers could be used in the roles: they had only to do the physical actions the director told them to do. But so acute was de Sica's direction and so responsive were Maggiorani and young Staiola as father and son that we learn all we need know about them—the father's stubbornness, tenderness and pride; the boy's valor, humor, devotion and his encouraging precocity. If there is one inducement to optimism at the end of the film, it is the feeling that this bright youngster will do all right in the world.

De Sica and his cameraman, Carlo Montuori, have found pictorial poetry in the streets of Rome—not in the usual tourist areas, but in the working-class quarters, in Trastevere, and in those sections where mundane commerce is done. And the music of Alessandro Cicognini is beautifully written and used to raise the emotional potential. Note the plaintive theme that accompanies the father and son, the music of rolling bicycles and the "morning music," full of freshness and bells.

The Bicycle Thief won tremendous critical approval in Italy and abroad, and it clearly established de Sica as one of the great film directors in the world. A man of strong emotion and vitality, he has brilliantly manifested both in his later output of pictures, which have been an adornment to the cinema culture of Italy.

Sunset Boulevard

On the neglected grounds of her creepy Hollywood palace, Norma Desmond (Gloria Swanson) and her devoted former director, Max von Mayerling (Erich von Stroheim), conduct the eerie funeral for Norma's pet chimpanzee.

1950

Screenplay by Charles Brackett, Billy Wilder and D. M. Marshman, Jr.; directed by Mr. Wilder and produced by Mr. Brackett for Paramount Pictures; cameraman, John F. Seitz; music by Franz Waxman.

Joe Gillis	William Holden
Norma Desmond	Gloria Swanson
Max von Mayerling	Erich von Stroheim
Betty Schaefer	Nancy Olson
Sheldrake	Fred Clark
Morino	Lloyd Gough
Artie Green	Jack Webb
Undertaker	Franklyn Barnum
First Finance Man	Larry Blake
Second Finance Man	Charles Dayton
Themselves	Cecil B. De Mille
	Hedda Hopper
	Buster Keaton
	Anna Q. Nilsson
	H. B. Warner
	Ray Evans
	Jay Livingston

It is surprising how loath film-makers have been to make films about themselves, or about the magic medium of illusion they transmit to the world. As egotistical and narcissistic as most film artists are—including the writers and directors, who are the crucial creators, of course—they have seldom dared turn their cameras on their own involuted lives or explore the cultural importance and impermanence of most of the work they do. For that reason, *Sunset Boulevard,* a picture about a passé silent star who still maunders in the memories of her glories and of movies in an era that is gone, was not only rare as an invasion of a ticklish subject when it came along, but it was—and still is—the most arresting and subtly philosophical film about Hollywood that there has been.

I say this with grateful recollection of such interesting previous ones as George Cukor's serio-comic *What Price Hollywood?* (1932), Victor Fleming's sardonic *Bombshell* (1933), William Wellman's sharp but sentimental and surface-skimming *A Star Is Born* (1937) and Preston Sturges' trenchant *Sullivan's Travels* (1941); or such subsequent cynical observations as Vincente Minelli's *The Bad and the Beautiful* (1952) and John Cromwell's *The Goddess* (1958).

These are all various contemplations of workaday Hollywood—of film people's problems of adjustment to the turns of their fortunes, up or down, and the humorous or bitter consequences of their involvements in the business of making films. But *Sunset Boulevard* takes a long look at the past of this mesmeric medium and makes the sardonic discovery that most of its yield is vaporous and vain, that the seeming triumphant creations accomplished in one age will be, with but few exceptions, crumbling celluloid in the next. It offers the sobering implication that the major output of movies is myth, momentary excitements and exaltations that are as evanescent as dreams.

This may sound a strange interpretation to put upon a picture that seems to be simply about the grotesque eccentricities of a daft old actress in contemporary (1950) Hollywood. But the point is that Norma Desmond, one of the great, glamourous stars of silent films who now dwells in a musty mansion set back from Sunset Boulevard, where she has been in archaeological seclusion for a couple of decades when the story begins, represents more than the delusions of grandeur of one old star. She represents the ostentation and arrogance of a whole generation of film-makers which has passed —a generation that produced a glittering output of gaudy trumperies and vast vulgarities, yet whose craftsmen assumed the postures and played the roles of great creators of Art.

She is further a haunting reminder of the massive mythology of silent-screen gods and goddesses whose well-advertised images drew millions of devoted worshipers into darkened temples all over the world. She is altogether a living relic of a tempo and taste that are dead. And the rising of her live ghost in the present, domineering and absurd, when she goes, toward the end of the picture, to the studio of Cecil B. De Mille and is illumined for one last appearance in the blinding radi-

Surrounded by the gaudy souvenirs of a once-glamorous career, Norma enacts a fantasy of a New Year's Eve celebration with Joe as the sole guest.

Cecil B. De Mille plays himself, patient and kind but unyielding when Norma visits his studio hoping for a return to glory—and a contract.

ance of a light they aptly call a "brute," is an eerie and chilling implication of the transience of all things in films.

This is not the morbid demonstration that Charles Brackett and Billy Wilder wished to make when they started this devastating picture. Their modest intention was to present an entertaining revelation of the folkways of Hollywood, a sharp, realistic comprehension in their customary super-graphic style of the kinds of peculiar people who have inhabited the place, along with a blistering exposition of the vaingloriousness of one old star.

The integrity of their intention is conveyed in the early scenes, which begin with an awesome discovery of a murdered body floating in a swimming pool and the exploding of one of those headline scandals so peculiar to Hollywood. Then, in the format of the flashback, the victim is identified and the misfortunes of his career as a screenwriter are prefatorially explained. In the crafty and cynical endeavors of this young fellow, Joe Gillis, to sell a script to a wary and cynical producer and in his frustrating conversations with a slippery talent agent, the authors crisply convey the cautiousness and pettifoggery typical of contemporary Hollywood.

But the balance of their intention is given an upsetting tilt the moment Joe swings his car into the driveway of a secluded estate in Beverly Hills in order to elude credit agents and finds himself looking at a mansion as strange as a haunted castle in a fairytale. For the aura of this old mansion, which we soon learn encloses and enshrines the person and the myth of Norma Desmond, who "used to be big in silent films,"

Left now by Joe, a distraught and hysterical Norma attempts suicide by cutting her wrists.

swiftly pervades the picture. The feeling it exudes of the rococo habitations and the fabulous ways of living of the old stars engrosses the mind with an excluding sense of involvement in a barbaric past, but a past that is now deteriorated and buried in weeds and dust. The strong personality of Norma, who emerges as the place's chatelaine, immediately dominates the action and becomes the major fascination of the film. Norma, trailing her delusions, takes over the bearing of the theme and guides it straight to the conclusion that there, in time, goes all Hollywood.

The inevitability of this predominance may have been in the script, which is probably the best and most expressive of their own sardonic natures that Brackett and Wilder ever did. (Others of their characteristic pictures were *A Foreign Affair* [1948] and *The Lost Weekend* [1945].) But I feel sure it is due, in large measure, to the brilliance of Gloria Swanson in the role of the old silent star, which she so fully and intimately understood, and to the subtle authority of Erich von Stroheim as the present butler and first director and husband of the ex-star.

These two conspicuous celebrities from the era of silent films, both draped with laurels and legends of their own eclipses when "talkies" came in, take such command of the features and the fabrics of these grim symbols of the past that they overwhelm the picture with a thunderous volume of authenticity. It is remarkable how weirdly genuine they make such bizarre and baroque scenes as that of a candlelit burial of the shrouded corpse of a pet chimpanzee, or of the screening of faded silent movies in the cluttered drawing room of the vast old house or of a lonely New Year's Eve party attended only by Norma and Joe, served wine by the stony-faced butler, while a solemn string quartet plays "Charmaine."

The grotesqueries of the set-up, the mausoleum atmosphere of the place and the chill breath of dead and dying devotions that still rustles through the cheerless rooms are amplified in the bold performances that Miss Swanson and von Stroheim give. The latter was also helpful with suggested touches and ideas. As the legendary director of the classic *Greed* (which see) and the actor of the role of the German officer in *La Grande Illusion* (which see), he was immensely respected by Brackett and Wilder, and he was allowed to do what he wished to invest the patient, loyal butler with much of his own caustic personality. The total disillusion of this fellow and his fierce determination to protect Norma from the bruises of her follies and the shattering of her hopeless fantasies are among the few touching manifestations in *Sunset Boulevard*.

For it is notable that it is not a touching picture. As loaded as it is with what might be easy inducements to tearful nostalgia, it is brutal and unrelenting in its exposure of the haughty vanity and selfishness of Norma, who is wholly without true sentiment. There is only one moment when one is likely to let one's heart go out to this woman in her self-imposed solitude. That moment comes after she has got her clutches on the accidentally interloping Joe in the hopes that he might help her complete a screenplay she's trying to write about Salome, after she has craftily turned him into her gigolo and tried to complete his sequestration with that ludicrous party on New Year's Eve. He has broken away from that engulfment to seek the company of some of his own contemporaries, and while he is away, the desperate Norma slits her wrists with a razor blade.

Joe is called back by the butler (who evidently has a mystical knowledge of where he is), and there is one passage of genuine pathos when he returns to her in her room.

At first she doesn't want to see him. Why not, he wants to know. "Great stars have great pride," she tells him, with her face hidden by her bandaged wrists. He goes to her bed and leans over her. The little orchestra is still playing "Charmaine" downstairs. "You're the only person in this stinking town who's been good to me," he says softly, close to her face. Suddenly we sense two desperate people, a lonely has-been and a never-has-been, reaching across the yawning gulf between them, and we are tenderly moved as they embrace.

But the pathos is quickly dissipated in the successive scenes, in which Joe complacently squires Norma as her dutiful gigolo, goes with her to the studio to call upon the great De Mille, who Norma is now vainly hopeful will direct her in a comeback production of Salome, sits around in anguished boredom while she does imitations for him (one of which—of Charlie Chaplin—is terrific), and finally sneaks off to another girl.

For Joe, too, is patently selfish, without compassion or sentiment. As played perfectly by William Holden, he is basically as cold and self-centered as Norma is. He moves in with her for no reason but to try to advance himself, and he stays with her simply for the comfort and the luxuries she provides. When he tentatively makes a secret attachment with a nice young woman at one of the studios and tries to settle down to writing with her, he is even self-serving about that. He is as cruel to this girl as he is to Norma. So it really is not a surprise when he counters Norma's jealous intervention by dragging the girl to her house and brutally exposing his debasement, thus hurting everyone. The appropriate solution for this impasse is that Norma, now thoroughly deranged, shoots Joe and sends him staggering to plunge, dead, into that Elysian swimming pool.

There are those who think there is some pathos in the final scene, in which Norma, about to be taken away from her home forever by the police, can be persuaded to go quietly only by being made to think she is to shoot a scene for De Mille. A camera is set up at the foot of her stairway and the butler, good old loyal Max, is there to "direct" the demented actress in her final "scene." As she gropes to the head of the stairs and says, "Where am I?" Max calls out confidently, "This is the stairway of the palace! Camera! Action!" And as Norma ostentatiously descends, for an audience of gawking policemen and reporters, the camera whirrs and the lights blur conclusively.

Yes, there is something sad about it. But I find this calculated scene more a pointedly ironic comment upon the phoniness of much that is in films. Like everything else in the picture, it is a shrewd reflection of the basically evanescent creation of Hollywood.

But note well that Brackett and Wilder do not ridicule the *making* of films. They are entirely respectful of craftsmanship—even the massive engineering of the latter-day De Mille. They catch the pitch and the tempo of the everyday working stiffs, such as the girl, played by Nancy Olson, and an assistant director, played by Jack Webb. They show the vitality of these people in the hustle around the studios. The melodrama of the community is highlighted in the police cars screaming at dawn along Sunset Boulevard. But what we have to realize is that all of them are passing in a parade, like the card-playing friends of Norma—Buster Keaton, Anna Q. Nilsson and H. B. Warner—who have already passed and are now "waxworks" to Joe.

For all the excellencies of this picture, it was not a big box-office hit. (Paramount, the producing studio, was wary of it from the start, and let it sit on the shelf for almost a year before releasing it.) The public, like Norma Desmond, preferred to preserve its myths. It wasn't eager to be reminded that its cherished dreams fade and disappear.

Clearly insane, Norma descends her marble staircase in queenly regalia, "performing" only for the police waiting below.

Rasho-Mon
(In the Forest)

1950

Screenplay by Akira Kurosawa and Shinobu Hashimoto, based on the two-part novel by Ryunosuke Akutagawa; directed by Akira Kurosawa; photographed by Kazuo Miyagawa; music by Fumio Hayasaka; produced by Daiei.

The Bandit	Toshiro Mifune
The Woman	Machiko Kyo
The Merchant	Masayuki Mori
The Woodchopper	Takashi Shimura
The Priest	Minoru Chiaki
The Beggar	Kichijiro Ueda
The Medium	Fumiko Homma
The Policeman	Daisuke Kato

The delicate beauty of Machiko Kyo, combined with her ability to excite rousing lust and passion, is an important part of the film's intricate story pattern.

A bandit (Toshiro Mifune) meets a merchant (Masayuki Mori) and his wife in the forest, in the first of three versions of the dramatic encounter.

On a pleasant evening in September 1951, the audience at the Venice Film Festival gathered in the handsome festival hall to view a token Japanese entry entitled *Rasho-Mon*. Neither the audience nor the jury knew much about it, except its title, which the program said should be translated as "In the Forest," and that it was credited to Akira Kurosawa (which the program incorrectly spelled). A few may have heard incidentally that it was showing at Venice because the enterprising festival director had requested an entry from Japan, which had not been represented at a major European festival since the Second World War. However, since it was known that Japanese production was recovering from the disruptions of the war, the director thought that the cinema artists of the East should be accorded some polite recognition in this international forum of films.

How right he was became apparent as the lonely picture was unreeled; the audience was practically bowled over by its strong and mature qualities. Overnight it was the festival sensation, and no one was greatly surprised when the jury gave it the best film award, over such worthy competitors as Elia Kazan's *A Streetcar Named Desire,* Robert Bresson's sensitive French film, *The Diary of a Country Priest,* Jean Renoir's exquisite *The River* (which technically represented India) and Charles Crichton's memorable British comedy, *The Lavender Hill Mob.*

Clearly, it isn't a picture of a conventional and easy sort. It hasn't the usual narrative structure of beginning, middle and end. It is simply a series of observations of a violent criminal act involving the rape of a woman, as seen from the points of view of the three individuals involved in it, plus that of a secret on-looker whose presence at the occurrence is only later revealed.

As the picture pursues its peculiar and sometimes perplexing way through the various accounts of the violence, the viewer is led to assume that the quest is a subtle probing by the dramatist for the solution of the crime. It appears that it is a surprisingly clever, off-beat mystery, and the viewer is held in keen suspense watching the details of the action and looking eagerly for

Although the bandit and the merchant battle fiercely, the result is total frustration: the merchant is dead and the woman has escaped, according to the bandit's recital at court.

clues. But, at the end, there is no solution. No detection of "who done it" is achieved. The ephemeral significance and importance of the crime itself evaporate. We are not even told what happens to the characters involved. What emerges from these vivid observations is a bitter realization that man is a vain and callous creature who thinks only of himself, who sees things only as it suits him, as it favors his repute and vanity.

It begins with three Japanese wanderers—a beggar, a woodcutter and a poor young priest—sheltering themselves from a rainstorm within the porch of a ruined gatehouse, long ago. It is evident that the times are parlous, the country desolate and the people depressed, as the three men ruefully reflect on an act of violence that has recently occurred nearby. It seems that a notorious bandit has waylaid a merchant and his wife as they were going alone through the forest . . . and now the scene dissolves from the gatehouse to the local police court, which is no more than a bare, open space, dazzlingly bright in the sunshine. Here the bandit sits trussed up on the ground, facing squarely at the audience. He's a burly, ferocious brute who grunts and howls with contempt and arrogance as he gives his account of the crime. . . .

We are in a peaceful forest of tall trees, the sunlight splattering through, and the boastful bandit is lying drowsing against a tree. Through his sleepy eyes, he sees a merchant coming along a forest way, leading a horse on which sits the merchant's wife. She is dressed all in white and is wearing a large, broad-brimmed hat

from which hangs an encircling veil of diaphanous material, behind which the bandit perceives a fragile, serene, exquisite creature so delicately shielded from the vulgar gaze.

At first the bandit is indifferent, but as he watches the wary travelers pass and senses the beauty of the woman, he is moved by a surge of lust, which Kurosawa subtly indicates by the bandit's indolent posture on the ground, his ruttish grunts and then the phallus-like lifting of the scabbard of his sword. He gets up and follows the travelers, then accosts the merchant and tells him of a treasure of swords he has hidden in the forest and is willing to part with, cheap. The merchant, tempted, goes with him, leaving the woman in a hidden glade beside a stream. In the forest, the bandit jumps the merchant, overpowers him, ties him with thongs and leaves him sitting on the ground while he returns to fetch the woman.

He finds her serenely trailing her beautiful pale hands in the stream. She is terrified when he rudely grabs her and drags her to where her husband is, struggling and wrenching violently as they move through the peaceful woods. When the woman beholds her tied-up husband, she makes a frantic attempt to flee, but the bandit catches her, wrestles with her, and then, as his passion is fired by her strangely erotic squirming and her provocative panic-stricken cries, he twists her pretty head into position and lustfully kisses her. As he does so, the tree tops wobble, the woman becomes flushed, her hands go slack and she drops the tiny dagger she

203

has pitifully tried to use. Then her arms go tight around the bandit and she yields to his lusty embrace.

Afterward, with the woman lying spent upon the ground, the bandit goes to the husband, who has helplessly watched the brute offense, cuts him loose and offers to fight him fairly for possession of his wife. But the husband, blanched with rage, attacks the bandit. They fight with swords and the husband is killed. Then the bandit goes to retrieve the woman and finds that she has fled.

That is the bandit's story, which is concluded as the scene returns to the court and the prisoner boastfully confides to the audience, " 'Twas her temper that fascinated me."

. . . Back now to the gatehouse and the three vagrants sheltered from the driving rain. "Man can't speak the truth—the mortals!" blurts the woodcutter, obviously disturbed by this story, which has been recounted by the beggar, who evidently heard it at the court. "Mortals are cowards, that's why they have to lie," replies the beggar.

The young priest disagrees. "Instead of a hot temper, I found in her face a pitiful sadness," he says—and with that the scene returns to the inquest, with the beautiful, fragile, nervous wife now telling *her* story to the audience. Here we dissolve again to the forest—a forbidding place now—and we see the woman lying on the ground, obviously ravished and disheveled. The cowardly bandit has fled, leaving her alone with her husband, who looks upon her with icy scorn as she finally rises and comes toward him, whimpering pitifully. She cuts him loose and offers him her dagger to kill her, but he refuses. Knowing she is now debased in his eyes, she implores and beseeches him, ever more

agonized and frantic. As the music rises to a wild bolero beat, the woman flails about her husband and tugs at his clothing in hysterical despair. "Then I fainted," she says, "and when I came to"—here a burst of sobs and wailing—"my dagger was in my husband's breast!" She intended thereafter to kill herself, but she was found, she says. . . .

"All women deceive us with their tears—and themselves, too!" the beggar snorts. "Men want to forget things they don't like—that's easier," growls the woodchopper.

Now comes the story of the husband, as reported to the inquest by a weird-looking, chalk-faced medium whose incantation comes hoarsely from her throat. After the assault, says the medium (as the scene dissolves to the forest again), the wife looks radiant. She begs the bandit to kill her husband and take her away with him. Then, abashed and panic-stricken, she and the bandit flee. For a long spell, the husband sits alone in the forest. There is soft music and the tinkle of little bells. Dismay suffuses his countenance, as sadly he gives way to tears. Then he sees his wife's dagger lying on the ground near him. He bends toward it and . . . Back at the inquest, the medium throws herself on the ground in a state of violent convulsion, obviously communicating that the husband has committed suicide.

At this report, the woodchopper, at the gatehouse, blurts out that this is not so. "No dagger was in his breast," he hollers. "He was killed by a sword!" Whereupon his two companions suspect that he knows more than he has told. They persuade him to tell them, at least, whatever he knows.

Yes, he was in the forest when the violence occurred, he admits. He did (he does) see the assault, then the

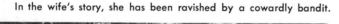

In the wife's story, she has been ravished by a cowardly bandit.

The dead husband's story is told by a medium, whose message from the departed relates a wife's perfidy.

woman break loose and go to her husband, whom she cuts free from his bonds and implores to avenge her honor. But the husband will not. "I regret more the loss of my horse," he tells her scornfully. Whereupon she berates her husband and the bandit for their cowardice and selfishness, and, in an accumulation of frenzy, the two men finally fight. It is a long, violent, groaning, sweating sword duel. There is no music now, just the natural sounds of the forest, the labored panting and snarling of the men and the ringing of their swords. The length of the fight betokens how inflamed the mind of the woodchopper is by the haunting memory of the battle.

Finally the bandit plunges his sword into the husband's chest and tries to clasp the woman, who has watched the violence, transfixed. But now she disgustedly repulses him and runs away. He, lacking the strength to follow, lies panting on the ground, as a bird trills a distant, cheerful song. The contrast is awesome and ironic. Then the bandit rises, sardonically scans the scattered scene, goes to the gaping dead man and contemptuously steals his sword.

This is the end of the episode. And this is the point at which the story of Ryunosuke Akutagawa, on which the film is based, concludes. But Kurosawa, unwilling to finish this cynical account on that note, arranged a postscripted ending to provide a lift of hope.

As the three vagrants finish their recollections and stand dejectedly in the rain, the feeble wail of a baby is heard in the gatehouse nearby. The vagrants look and find the infant, deserted. The beggar wants to steal its clothes, justifying his shameful intention by remarking, "We can't live unless we act selfishly these days." But the woodcutter prevents him. He snatches up the infant and says that, even though he has other children, he will take it and care for it. With that, the storm ends and the three men go their separate ways, now looking a little less drab under brightening skies. "It's only natural, these days, we doubt people," says one; and the priest observes, "I have regained my faith in men."

It is evident that Kurosawa intended this film to express a philosophical recognition and sympathy for the frailty of man and for the notion that reality is only what each individual makes it for himself. It is possible, though he has never said so, that he was moved to articulate this theme by the depressed and disillusioned condition of the Japanese at the end of the Second World War. Lied to and betrayed by their leaders, they had fabricated their illusions of reality according to what each desired. When their illusions were shattered, they were left with a sense of sadness and ruin.

Most appreciable in the picture is its poetic quality, the eloquence that emerges as by witchcraft from its pictorial style and pace. These vary with the levels on which the story unfolds. Fascinating, too, is the entirely stylistic and (to us) unfamiliar manner in which it is played. Toshiro Mifune acts the bandit with great, bold, exaggerated sweeps of physical movement. His facial expressions are contorted and fierce. His vocal sounds are mainly grotesque grumbles and animalistic grunts. As the woman, Machiko Kyo conveys many concepts and moods. In the scene where we first meet her, she is serene and infinitely remote, an idealization of feminine beauty and aristocratic dignity. But as she proceeds through the various phases, she changes to correspond to the individual notions of her. To the bandit, she has winsomeness and grace. She is a rare and fragile vessel out of which comes a strong, voluptuous surge. To her husband, she is coarse and callous, with the painted eyes of a prostitute. To the woodchopper, she is hypnotic. To herself, she is wan and pitiful. Miss Kyo's fluid performance and her exquisite exotic quality account for much of the poetry and magic in the film.

When *Rasho-Mon* opened in Japan, it got a confused, even antagonistic, response. One respected critic called it "a dark and dirty film with poor sound and coarse dialogue." But after its triumph at Venice, it became a sensational success. The notice it received inspired the Japanese film industry to give more opportunity and leeway to a group of thoughtful and talented film-makers, most of whom were carry-overs from prewar days, and this has resulted in a succession of excellent, world-ranging Japanese films.

Kurosawa frames his film with three ragged commentators, waiting out a rainstorm under the village gate, underscoring the narrative with skepticism: a woodchopper (Takashi Shumira) who claims to have been a witness; a priest (Nimoru Chiaki); and a beggar (Kichijiro Ueda).

Jeux Interdits
(Forbidden Games)

1952

Adapted by Jean Aurenche, Pierre Bost and René Clement from an original story by François Boyer; dialogue by M. Aurenche and M. Bost; directed by René Clement; music by Narciso Yepes; produced by Robert Dorfman.

Paulette	Brigitte Fossey
Michel	Georges Poujouly
Father Dolle	Lucien Hubert
Mother Dolle	Suzanne Courtal
Georges Dolle	Jacques Marin
Berthe Dolle	Laurence Badie
Father Gouard	André Wasley
Francis Gouard	Amedée
The Priest	Louis Saintève

The drift of French motion pictures after the Second World War betrayed a state of exhaustion and pessimism among artists and producers of France, which was summed up by Claude Autant-Lara's *Le Diable au Corps* (*Devil in the Flesh*, 1947). This sad and despairing drama of the frustrating love affair of a youth and an older woman whose husband is away at war, played with supreme sensitivity by Micheline Presle and Gerard Philippe, denotes the bent of French film-makers to turn back to the patterns of prewar films, to themes of individual frustration and sheer fatalistic mischance.

Then, like a light out of darkness, there came, in 1952, René Clement's tremendously pertinent and vital *Jeux Interdits* (*Forbidden Games*). This sharp and unmistakable indictment of a stupid, insensitive society, conveyed in a strange, macabre story of two children betrayed in time of war, suddenly crashed through the clutter of indulgent and delusive films and slapped the self-piteous French people directly in the face. At last, in a film that should have happened shortly after the war, a quality of biting self-inspection and self-criticism to compare with that which Jean Renoir achieved in his classic *La Grande Illusion* (which see) and in his subsequent *La Regle du Jeu* (*The Rules of the Game*, 1939) was returned with exciting vitality to the moribund body of French films.

Significantly, it was disturbing and quickly became a *cause célèbre*. Passed over by the committee that picked the French entries for the Cannes Festival that year (those picked were *Fanfan la Tulipe, Nous Sommes Tous des Assassins* and *Trois Femmes*), it was shown out of competition by its indignant producer to the critics assembled at Cannes and provoked them to wrath at the selection committee. "Scandal!" they openly cried.

Then, almost barred from the Venice Festival on the grounds that it had been shown at Cannes, *Jeux Interdits* went on to win the Venice grand award and

The war orphan Paulette (Brigitte Fossey) is comforted by the farm boy Michel (Georges Poujouly) when he makes a cross to mark the grave of her bullet-riddled puppy.

accumulate assorted honors around the world. Even so, it was openly resented by certain French critics, notably those of the Communist press, who charged that it gave an unfair picture of the peasantry of France.

Ironically, its haunting story of the bond of sympathy that grows between a bright farm boy and a little girl war orphan through a secret game with animal corpses provided an opportunity, which Clement embraced magnificently, to combine and communicate two components that have been traditional adornments of French films. These are a feeling for children, their genuine natures and proclivities, and a feeling for peasants and provincials, for rural life and bucolic scenes.

No national group of film-makers has surpassed, or even matched, the French in conveying the subtleties of children. Masterpieces leap to mind: Jean Vigo's *Zero de Conduit* (1933), Julien Duvivier's delightfully humorous *Poil de Carotte* (1935), Jean Benoit-Levy's lovely *La Maternelle* (1932) and his poignant *La Mort du Cygne* (*Ballerina*, 1938). Likewise, a genius for distilling the character and flavor of rural life has been manifest in such films as the classics of Marcel Pagnol —his *Regain* (*Harvest*, 1937), *La Femme de Boulanger* (*The Baker's Wife*, 1939), *La Fille de Puisatier* (*The Well-Digger's Daughter*, 1940)—and in the monumental performances of that supremely accomplished portrayer of Gallic characters, Raimu.

Jeux Interdits is in both traditions. Its children—an eleven-year-old boy, son of callow peasants on a farm in the south of France, and the five-year-old girl that he finds wandering in the woods after her parents have been killed while fleeing in a refugee column and whom he takes into his home—are intensely real and candid youngsters, he a pliant sprig of the ambient soil and she a wide-eyed little creature with all the naïveté and trust

The rude farmer, Georges Dolle (Jacques Marin), is an object of great interest to Michel as he writhes in pain after being kicked by a horse.

of the well-bred city child. And the crude and ignorant adult peasants who give this child a place in their home and try to treat as kindly as they are able are compellingly authentic types.

That's just it. They may be too authentic. Their helpless illiteracy, their proneness to superstitions, their dull obedience to the rituals of the church, coupled with their earthy, ribald humor and their placid stupidity, may be glaringly recognizable as familiar peasant traits, but the consequence of them in this drama make them painful to tolerate.

For the import of this picture is that the good, solid peasantry, which is supposed to be the backbone of the nation's strength, is not strong. It is not intuitive in comprehending human foibles and the eternal verities. It does *not* possess the innate wisdom so charmingly and comfortingly compacted in Raimu. It is pitifully and painfully unable to cope with the challenges of the disordered world, or even with the shock and confusion of a war-shattered child. It is so lacking in comprehension that it hews to certain shibboleths of death, and yet it chastises children who imitate these common shibboleths. It is not willfully wicked or knowingly, complacently weak. It is purely and simply ignorant. That is the painful tragedy. What is essentially transmitted in this oblique reflection upon war and upon the scourging of children in it is that society is still playing games—games of war and death and betrayal—that are morally forbidden. But it goes on playing them.

Clement began his career as a cameraman, and became a director of short films for the resistance movement during the war. After the liberation of Paris in 1944, he began what was intended to be a documentary of the wartime resistance activities of the French rail-

In death Georges is irresistible to Paulette and Michel, as they are obsessed by their secret game of playing undertakers.

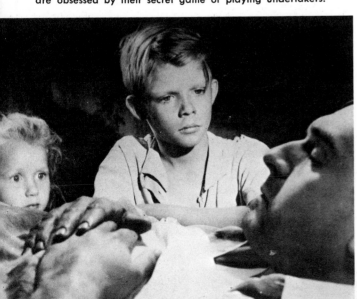

way workers. It was called *Le Bataille du Rail* (*The Battle of the Rails*), and it was markedly successful when released in France in 1945. It is really a dramatic reenactment of actual episodes put together in a plot that is climaxed with the blowing up of a Nazi munitions train, and it vibrates with powerful heroic overtones. It is the only French film of this period that compares at all with the Italian resistance films.

After it, Clement was permitted to do another war film, *Les Maudits* (1946), about a rabble of leftover Nazis and French collaborators who try to escape from Europe in a German submarine. But it was not a success, and thereafter the director was compelled to accede to the tacit embargo by French producers on pictures having to do with war.

Then he got his hands on a novel, *Jeux Interdits,* by

There is black humor in the graveside battle of two bumpkins who blame each other for the disappearance of the cemetery crosses.

François Boyer, who had first written this story as a screenplay in 1946 but because of the resistance to war stories could not get it produced. With Robert Dorfman now agreeing to produce it (after the novel was something of a success), and with a new script prepared by the distinguished screenwriters, Jean Aurenche and Pierre Bost, Clement proceeded to make the picture in a grittily realistic style, shooting most of it (all the exteriors) on a poor farm in the Maritime Alps and using a cast of generally unfamiliar actors who made

excellent peasant types. His two children were inexperienced youngsters, Georges Poujouly and Brigitte Fossey, whom he found after careful searching and from whom he got superb performances.

The remarkable feat of the picture is that it makes a powerful statement about war with a minimum of graphic description of war activity and a great deal more diverting humor than is ordinarily found in war films. The only showing of war's hideous violence is in the opening scenes of a column of refugees fleeing along a country road, trying to find some haven in the south of France. Suddenly there is the familiar terror of a German plane swooping down out of the sky, machine-gunning the column, causing the people to run into the fields. Then, as suddenly as it has descended, the instrument of death is gone, leaving the column riddled, the parents of a little girl dead in a ditch, and this terrified little creature, unscratched, beside them, clutching the body of a dead puppy in her arms.

From this aspect of death and terror, the scene is as quickly moved into the peaceful country, as the little girl, still terrified, runs along the bank of a river, following the body of her puppy, which has been tossed into the stream by some heedless person who has taken it from her arms. So the context of war's morbidity is projected into the peaceful countryside.

Having retrieved the body and wandered off with it into the woods, the little girl is found by the astonished farm boy, who proudly takes her to his home, shows her off to his family, arranges for her to stay and happily appoints himself her protector. She is his trophy of the vague and distant war. In the night, when she wakes from a bad dream and calls his name—"Michel!"—he goes to her in the loft above the rude home, tries to soothe her and assure her that her parents have been put in a hole so they will keep dry. His childish explanation comforts and quiets her.

The next day, he comes upon her in the woods, trying to bury her puppy, which she left there the day before. Sensing her yearning for contact with her parents through this tiny corpse, he conceives an appropriate diversion that will turn her bewilderment over death into a game. He arranges for them to bury the puppy in a secret place in an old abandoned mill. Michel constructs a rude cross, puts it over the tiny mound, and the little girl wonderingly contributes her rosary beads to be draped around this cross. Then, in order that the puppy will not be lonesome, Michel takes the carcass of a mole from the nest of an owl in the mill loft and buries that beside the puppy's grave.

The imitation of the ritual of burial diverts and delights the little girl. To keep her absorbed and contented, Michel collects the bodies of other animals,

208

buries them in the secret cemetery and rounds up crosses to put over the graves. Some of the crosses he steals from the churchyard cemetery, and he even tries to filch a crucifix from the altar of the country church, but he is caught by the astonished country priest before he can manage this profanation. The whole enterprise becomes for the children a private and exhilarating game.

Meantime, the grown-up members of the family are fretting over an older son who has been kicked in the stomach by a "war horse," a frightened runaway from the same shambles in which the parents of the little girl were killed. The measures these poor, stupid peasants take to ease and entertain this injured bumpkin, as he lies propped up in the old square bed, are funny and pathetic. And when he dies, likewise funny and pathetic are the gathering of the family and relatives in the tiny church to go through the requiem mass that clearly has little comfort or meaning for them. It is patent that Michel and Paulette, the little girl, derive much more from their "game" than these dourly mundane and pragmatic grown-ups derive from theirs.

The vacuity of their ritualism is suddenly turned into

Paulette, taken away from Michel by the perfidy of his family and brought to a refugee center, thinks she hears Michel's voice in the film's heart-wrenching finale.

grotesque comedy when, going to the churchyard the next Sunday to decorate the son's grave, they find the cross from his grave lying in the road and other crosses missing from the family plot. Jumping angrily to the conclusion that this desecration has been done by one of their neighbors with whom they have been feuding, the father of Michel grabs this neighbor by the ears when he comes along with his son a few minutes later to decorate the grave of his wife. And in a flash, these two middle-aged peasants are tumbling around the graveyard in a fight, grabbing and wrenching at one another, until they fall into a freshly dug grave.

Peace is restored, however, when the funny little priest jumps in, separates the fighters and tells them he knows what has happened to the crosses. Michel has taken them! Now they all go after Michel who runs away and hides. But in the night he sneaks back to see Paulette, to reassure her that all is well.

Then gendarmes come to the farmhouse. Michel sees them and thinks they have come to get him. But when he hears they are seeking Paulette, whom they have learned disappeared in this area, he comes out after they have gone and offers to make a deal. He will tell where the crosses are, if his parents will promise not to give up Paulette. They promise. But the next day, when the gendarmes come, they betray their promise and ruefully surrender the bewildered child.

This scene of the children's parting, the little girl rigid with dread and the boy, restrained by his father, kicking and screaming with anger and chagrin, is one of the most heartbreaking I have ever seen. And the boy's exploding rebellion is poignantly put in the following scene, when he goes alone to the old mill, breaks up the crosses, scatters the mounds of the graves and, as a last heart-tearing gesture, takes the little girl's rosary beads and places them in the owl's nest, saying bitterly to the old bird, "Keep it a hundred years!"

But the tragedy is imaged completely in the final scene. It is a crowded refugee center with distraught people all over the place. There, all alone in a chair against a wall, sits little Paulette, her eyes literally blank with confusion, her body motionless. No one is paying attention to her. Then she hears someone call the name Michel in the hubbub of voices at the far end of the room. Her eyes come alight, she stirs expectantly, jumps down from the chair and starts running wildly in the direction from which she heard the voice, crying frantically, hopefully, receding in the distance, "Michel! Michel!" The beautiful, plaintive guitar music of Narciso Yepes, which has been the only music in the film—a soft, four-note theme of gentle sadness—comes up strongly to drown the echoes as the picture ends.

Shane

1953

Screenplay by A. B. Guthrie, Jr., based on the novel by Jack Schaefer, with additional dialogue by Jack Sher; directed and produced by George Stevens for Paramount Pictures; cameraman, Lloyd Griggs; music by Victor Young.

Shane	Alan Ladd
Mrs. Starrett	Jean Arthur
Mr. Starrett	Van Heflin
Joey Starrett	Brandon de Wilde
Wilson	Jack Palance
Chris	Ben Johnson
Lewis	Edgar Buchanan
Ryker	Emile Meyer
Torrey	Elisha Cook, Jr.
Mr. Shipstead	Douglas Spencer
Morgan	John Dierkes
Mrs. Torrey	Ellen Corby
Grafton	Paul McVey
Atkey	John Miller
Mrs. Shipstead	Edith Evanson
Wright	Leonard Strong
Johnson	Ray Spiker
Susan Lewis	Janice Carroll
Howells	Martin Mason
Mrs. Lewis	Helen Brown
Mrs. Howells	Nancy Kulp

An errant gunfighter, Shane (Alan Ladd), turns up at the Starrett farm and is offered the meager hospitality of the farm by Starrett, his wife (Jean Arthur) and the hero-worshiping Joey (Brandon de Wilde).

The cattle baron escalates the homesteaders' woes by sending in a professional killer, Wilson (Jack Palance), whose first act is mowing down an impulsive farmer, Torrey (Elisha Cook, Jr.).

Perhaps the most regnant phenomenon of the international culture of films is the persistence of the western as a genre. It began, as we have noted in the chapter on *The Covered Wagon* (which see), before the fledgling "flickers" were even out of the stage of

Torrey's funeral, conducted by Starrett (Van Heflin) on Cemetery Hill, is attended by a pathetically small group of neighbors backed by the majesty and glory of the Grand Tetons.

novelty, and it has continued as a clear and thriving species to the present day. But despite this longevity, the fundamental theme of the western film has changed very little since the species was born. Basic in the western postulations is the brave and "decent" man with a gun. Be he a law-keeping marshal in a frontier community, a cavalry soldier, a virtuous "bad man," a noble Indian opposing evil whites, a trail rider, a wagon-train master or any variation thereof, this man with the weapon and the impulse to use it *rightly* is the crux of the genre. Set against some form of evil, he is the central figure in the vast mythology built up and perpetuated in almost all western films.

And it *is* a mythology, as powerful and indigenous as that which the Greeks clarified in dramatic poetry 2,500 years ago. It embraces the bold, romantic legends of the development of the American West, and it sets up a sturdy hero image as essential as that of

Provoked beyond endurance, Shane takes on the troublemakers in a vicious one-sided battle.

Hercules. Appropriately and precisely, the homesteader boy in *Shane,* this picture that I here proffer as the most exemplary western in sound, awesomely says of the heroic gunman who has come to help his father, "He's like God!" There *is* a hint of divinity about the hero figure in the western film.

Of course, there are other implications and excitements generated in the genre, other reasons for popular acceptance than the symbol of individual courage and power. There are the enduring implications of national enterprise and growth, as manifested in the broader epics such as *The Covered Wagon* and *The Iron Horse,* or in the latter-day sagas of western folkways, such as this picture, *Shane.* There are the magnificent excitements of beautiful scenery and visions of open space, giving a thrilling inducement to the urge for spiritual escape. There are pictorially electrifying actions, such as cavalry charges and cattle stampedes, and the surges of energy and rhythm that the well-directed camera can achieve.

For instance, it is in such excitements, more than in a strong heroic theme, that the vitality and fascination of John Ford's *Stagecoach* lies. The beauty and thrill of this picture made in 1939, are in the artistry with which Ford has laid out and galvanized a story of eight assorted people rolling west across the wide-open plains of Arizona in an old Concord coach, which looms large

and important in the scenes of storytelling, then appears disturbingly small as the camera is drawn back in the distance to view it weaving infinitesimally among the majestic mesas of Monument Valley, almost lost in the landscape and the sky. They are in the skill and dexterity with which Ford has used his camera to suggest the lurking menace of Geronimo and his Apaches out there among the mesas someplace, waiting to waylay the travelers, and in the tempo with which he has shown a chase of the stagecoach by the Indians across a salt flat, before a troop of cavalry arrives just in time to save its people and provide the epiphany.

I was strongly tempted to pick *Stagecoach* for prime citation in this book, as I was also tempted to pick Fred Zinnemann's equally famous *High Noon.* This latter, produced by Stanley Kramer in 1952, is a major example of the extension of the genre after the Second World War. Here, in this bone-bare drama of a brave sheriff in a western town who, on the day of his marriage and retirement, stubbornly opts to stay around and confront a returning badman who has threatened to get him and presumably take over the town, is another superior achievement of stating in pictorial terms a dramatic societal confrontation within the generic frame. And Gary Cooper's performance as the sheriff is perhaps the best of many ever done by this incalculably fine actor in a long career.

211

But *High Noon,* like *Stagecoach,* is a western by marriage, as it were, the marriage of an unlocated story and a familiar western locale. So *Shane,* which was made by George Stevens in 1953, just one year after *High Noon,* is the film I have come to select as the truest and most affecting western produced with the benefit of sound.

Immediately and clearly in its favor is the fact that its story of the brave and lonely resistance of a little group of homesteaders in the Wyoming Territory to an open-range cattle baron who wants to drive them off their farms is uniquely western. It presents a confrontation of a sort that did occur, historically and often, during the agricultural settlement of the West. The range rancher versus the fenced-land farmer was an intrinsic rivalry; and although it has been made platitudinous by frequent repetitions in films, it is presented authentically by A. B. Guthrie, Jr., who did the script of *Shane.*

Further, the intrusion into this conflict of a strong, silent man with a gun, a specimen of the traditional gunfighter, who was a folk-hero type on the frontier, aligned with the harassed homesteaders to use his bravery and skill on their behalf, is an exciting injection of this popular element of myth. The fact that the gun

of this stranger, who arrives out of nowhere to partake of the ordeal of these farmers, becomes their salvation in the end is in line with the ritual and reason of frontier rectitude.

After all, it is fully manifested that this erstwhile gunfighter, Shane, does not wish to get mixed up in trouble any more than the homesteaders do. When he comes to the farm of Joe Starrett and accepts an invitation to stay awhile with this good-hearted man, his wife and youngster—to help Joe with the chores—it is clear that he is grateful for this chance to rest quietly in a home.

Like Joe and the other homesteaders, Shane tries to avoid brawls with the cattle baron, Ryker, and his bullies. When they come around, Shane stands beside Joe in support of his wish to escape gunfighting. But a showdown cannot be avoided, not with Ryker determined to drive the "sod-busters" off their land. So it comes, after Shane and Joe have beaten Ryker's bullies in a smashing fistfight in the saloon; after Ryker has brought in a hired gunman who casually kills a farmer in cold blood; after this pitiful victim has been buried and another farmer's home has been set afire. Only now is it desperately accepted that the farmers must fight guns with guns. Even so, Shane, who asks for the as-

Shane leaves as he came, without explanation or purpose, with the touching wail of Joey reaching him, "Shane . . . come back, Shane. . . ."

signment—"This is my kind of game"—has to beat Joe into insensibility before he can assume the job, ride fearlessly to Ryker's hangout and kill the hired gunman and a couple of others in a blazing duel.

This is all according to the ritual, the code of justice and honor, in the western film. And it is put on the screen by Stevens with artistry and style. The scenic magnificence of the country is got in location settings within the area of the Grand Teton Mountains, which rise snowcapped across the countryside as glorious symbols of the poetic beauty of the West. Throughout there are stunning visions of the grandeur of the mountains and plains, sometimes radiant in the glow of western sunshine, sometimes shrouded in torrential, black-browed rains that sweep across the country in majestic insolence. Stevens has shot this film in color and it has been adjusted to the large screen, so that it has the pictorial authority of the grander epic efforts in this genre.

Likewise, his staging of details is strongly evocative of American frontier folkways, barring a small anachronism here and there (a familiar imperfection in even the best of western films).

There is the vivid incident of the killing of the farmer who allows himself to be goaded into drawing on the gunman by a deliberate slur on the Confederacy (which is another convenient device of sentiment in western films). And then, in the burial of this fellow on Cemetery Hill, Stevens pulls all the stops with skillful staging —the placing of the pitiful little group of farmers on the hilltop, lonely against the sky; the solemn and fumbling delivery of a fighting eulogy by Joe; the sad and squeaky playing of "Abide with Me" on a harmonica; the farmer's dog scratching and whining at the coffin as it is lowered into the ground; and then the camera panning slowly across the windy hill to focus on a lone covered wagon, with the Grand Tetons looming behind and the harmonica faintly finishing the playing of "Taps."

But what I find best about this picture—and what, indeed, lifts it far above the level of the conventional western—is the establishment within its narrative flow of the little homesteader boy, Joey, as the key observer of all that goes on. For it is in this eight-year-old youngster, performed by Brandon de Wilde, that is crystalized and communicated the popular point of view toward western films—the penchant for hero worship (which Joey develops for Shane out of the same enthusiasm for legend that later generations have had), the wide-eyed excitement and wonder at the occurrence

of the cliché, the wistful reluctance to accede to the termination of the ritual.

When he watches the fistfight in the barroom from behind a pickle barrel, nibbling with nervous excitement in a peppermint stick, we have an incisive reflection of audience feelings toward these standard battles in saloons. Happily, this one is better than most. When he asks his mother if she loves Shane, he articulates what fancy infers. And when he wanders away from the burial to watch a colt nursing at a mare, he conveys the inevitable unawareness and indifference of a child toward the finality of death.

But the strongest commentary on the ritual is Joey chasing after Shane when he rides off to his desperate rendezvous. The youngster running across the country, wading the river, crossing Cemetery Hill and arriving in time to watch the showdown from beneath the swinging doors of the saloon—all utterly implausible—is the candid visualization of the myth. This is the concrete symbolization of the hero worshiper pursuing the idol to the end.

Likewise, the sentimental parting of Joey and Shane, after the latter has finished off the gunman and most of the Rykers with a blazing fusillade in the saloon, is like a poetic *envoi* to the concluded ritual. Shane has completed his function; now he must go on. And all that's left is the desolated youngster, alone on the bare porch of the store, calling after the departing hero, the passing legend, "Come back, Shane!"

Thus, by one simple narrative arrangement, Stevens and Guthrie have devised a broader intellectual and emotional proportion for the western formula.

The acting is excellent, for the most part, especially that of Van Heflin as the stalwart, stubborn Joe, and Jean Arthur as the wife with just a faint trace of feminine adoration toward Shane. Unfortunately, Alan Ladd is not precisely what one would prefer as Shane. He is too young and good-looking, for one thing. He should be older, weatherworn and gray. And he inclines to *act* the cryptic hero rather than *be* him, as Gary Cooper is in all his western portrayals.

But young de Wilde is perfect, unforgettable as the boy—rugged, square, authentic in his collarless blue shirt, his knee-length pants supported by country galluses, with his shiny pink cheeks, his blue eyes, his towhead and squared-off haircut that attests to a mother's tidy hand. He's all boy, a nostalgic stand-in for every participant in the fantasies of the frontier. With him, millions of bearded and balding "boys" have teared a bit at the departure of Shane.

On the Waterfront

1954

Original story and screenplay by Budd Schulberg, suggested by a series of newspaper articles by Malcolm Johnson; directed by Elia Kazan; photography by Boris Kaufman; musical score by Leonard Bernstein; a Horizon picture, produced by Sam Spiegel and released by Columbia.

Terry Malloy	Marlon Brando
Edie Doyle	Eva Marie Saint
Father Barry	Karl Malden
Johnny Friendly	Lee J. Cobb
Charley Malloy	Rod Steiger
"Pop" Doyle	John Hamilton
"Kayo" Dugan	Pat Henning
Big Mac	James Westerfield
Glover	Leif Erickson
Gillette	Martin Balsam
Truck	Tony Galento
Tillio	Tami Mauriello
Barney	Abe Simon
Mott	John Heldabrand
Moose	Rudy Bond
Tommy	Thomas Handley
Mrs. Collins	Anne Hegira
Bartender	Pat Hingle

The immensity and complexity of American industry, with its power of billions of horses and its drama of millions of men, have strangely escaped the attention and inspection of the makers of films. Very few have been excited by the vastness and color of the industrial scene, or concerned about the problems of the working man. D. W. Griffith touched upon them in his *Intolerance* (which see). Charlie Chaplin satirized them in his *Modern Times* (1936). A couple of pictures were made in the 1930's about working conditions in the mines. King Vidor tried to tell the massive story of the growth of the steel industry in his *American Romance* (1944). But, for the most part, the controversial subject of industrial affairs has been taboo, blacked out by a tacit prescript as firm as the stevedores' "d and d" (deaf and dumb) in the film we now review.

This is just one of the reasons why Elia Kazan's *On the Waterfront* is an exceptional motion picture. As vivid and exciting as it is, it merits particular attention because it fearlessly breaks the rule of silence (or inattention) that prevailed in Hollywood. It is totally and vitally concerned with the attitude of the working man.

To be sure, the area of its inspection is marginal to the vast and throbbing scene of familiar mass production. It is not concerned with manufacturing. It is focused upon the business of cargo handling in a great American port. And the issue it shapes is not the large one of man versus the machine, but that of man versus the elements that would bind him to the industrial complex in peonage.

Its hero is an unschooled longshoreman, a thick-headed young stevedore who belongs to a wildcat waterfront union controlled by labor racketeers. And the gist of it is simply what happens when this dense but dogged chap is made to see how cruelly he is being exploited, not only by the racketeers but by his own patronizing brother, who is the sharp-witted lawyer for the goons. It is a limited and simplified inspection of the evil of union control, and it leaves several questions unanswered, including who it is that lets the union prevail.

But it does very much confront the issue of the individual working man caught up in the bewildering network of service to giant industry. It states the uneasy relation of the worker and his fellow working men, whereby each is in lonely isolation within the pseudo-brotherhood of the group. It does this against the awesome background of imperious machines, the machinery in this case being the great and voracious cargo ships that the stevedores fill and empty with the perseverance of ants. And it beautifully catches the rhythms and the raw, powerful poetry of workers enclosed in an environment that feels and sounds and smells of industry.

It was virtually predestined that Kazan should have made this film. It is the achievement upon which his whole career converged. Starting as an actor with the dynamic Group Theater in the early 1930's, he went on to gangster roles in Hollywood, and got his first assignment as a film director for *A Tree Grows in Brooklyn* (1945). This is a rebellious but radiant reminiscence of a slum childhood, steeped in the kind of feeling for the working class that later appears so strongly in the fabric of *On the Waterfront*.

Doubling as a stage director and a power at the Actor's Studio, which was the center of the Stanislavsky "method" in the American theater, he directed the stage production of Tennessee Williams' *A Streetcar Named Desire,* in which a young actor, Marlon Brando, first came to prominence. When he brought this play to the screen in 1951, with Brando repeating his stage role of an angry Polish truckdriver and Vivien Leigh cast as the tragic, neurotic heroine, he clearly displayed his ability to get actors to deliver tours de force. Brando was a splendid exponent of Kazan's freely realistic style —a natural flowing together of personality, sensitivity, mood and intellectual improvisation to create and make

214

profoundly real all the difficult aspects of a raw, agonized character.

In the late 1940's, Kazan directed two Arthur Miller plays, *All My Sons* and *Death of a Salesman*. He and Miller became close friends, and they often spoke of doing a film together about longshoremen on the New York waterfront. Miller had written a story, "The Hook", which he and Kazan had brought to the stage of discussion with people at Columbia Studios. Then, in 1951, Kazan submitted to interrogation by the Un-American Activities Committee of the House of Representatives, and gave testimony as to what he knew about Communists in the theater and in Hollywood. As a consequence, his friendship with Miller chilled, and their project was dropped.

However, Kazan did not abandon his wish to do something on this waterfront theme. Now, more than ever, he was eager to make a socially expressive film. He soon teamed up with Budd Schulberg, a liberal writer, to pursue the subject, and they spent a lot of time scouting around the New York and Hoboken waterfronts, observing the brutal conditions under which the dockers worked. They also enlisted Malcolm Johnson, a reporter for the New York *Sun*, whose series of articles on waterfront labor conditions won a Pulitzer Prize in 1949.

Eventually they got Sam Spiegel, then a producer of minor repute, excited about their story, and he soon worked Columbia into a deal. He also made a verbal agreement with Frank Sinatra to play the lead. Sinatra was fresh from his surprising dramatic performance in *From Here to Eternity* (1953), which was a Columbia picture, and was considered a hot property. Then Kazan found he could get Brando, his proud creation, to play the role, and Sinatra was eased out of the picture. He was very angry with Spiegel and Kazan.

Kazan was determined to shoot the picture in its authentic locales, a way of semi-documentary shooting to which he was introduced when he directed *Boomerang* for Louis de Rochemont in 1947, and arrangements were made for filming in Hoboken, New Jersey, on the piers and in adjacent streets and parks, with Boris Kaufman, a New York cinematographer, handling the camera. Spiegel kept after Schulberg to fine down a lean, hard script, and an excellent cast was assembled, mostly from the Broadway theater. There was Lee J. Cobb from *Death of a Salesman* to play Johnny Friendly, the union boss; Rod Steiger to play the stevedore's brother, Charley; Karl Malden to play Father Barry, a waterfront priest; and Eva Marie Saint to play a young woman, Edie, whose stevedore brother is murdered and who has a passion for justice and revenge. Kazan also recruited three former prizefighters

Labor boss Johnny Friendly (Lee J. Cobb) encourages Terry Malloy (Marlon Brando) to keep his mouth shut along the waterfront; Terry's brother Charley (Rod Steiger) approves.

In a bar, Edie Doyle (Eva Marie Saint) pleads with Terry to help find out the circumstances of her brother's death.

In a bitter exchange Charley warns his kid brother of the danger of "singing."

Attempting to avenge his brother's murder, Terry brutally battles with the union boss.

to play henchmen and body-guards of the union boss.

While shooting in Hoboken, Kazan was constantly watched by the real waterfront mobsters. Just to be on the safe side, he had his own guards around the company. As the shooting went on, he got to know some of the mobsters, and occasionally he would ask them how they liked a scene, whether they found it authentic. They would approve or merely shrug. Happily, Kazan noted that most of them showed up in the audience on opening night.

What they saw might not be precisely the aspect of the waterfront they experienced and comprehended, for Kazan made this film more than the studied documentary many viewers initially thought it to be. In its narrative essence, it is simply a recount of how this punchy young dock-walloper, who initially is willing to go along with the tyranny of the racketeers, is brought to a realization that something is wrong by the girl, whose brother has been bumped off for squealing, and by the militant Catholic priest (the latter role, incidentally, based on a real-life character). Confronted with this awareness, which is hideously confirmed when his own brother is bumped off by the boss' killers for failing to muzzle him, Terry breaks the waterfront code of silence —the voodooistic rule of "d and d"—and squeals to the crime commission investigating conditions on the waterfront. For this, he is ostracized by his fellow workers, to whom he is a "canary," the worst thing one can be. However, he has his ultimate triumph when he beats up the union boss, revealing him to the union members as a bully, and thereby compels his right to go into the shape-up (fill a job) without the favor and consent of the racketeers.

But essentially—and what the actual mobsters might not have understood—this is a presentation of the universal theme of the impersonalization and alienation of the inarticulate, regimented working man. It is, indeed, a powerful statement in motion-picture terms of the pathos and distant, muted protest of the inarticulate.

Expressive of this, for instance, is an eloquent scene in the hold of a cargo ship. "Kayo" Dugan, one of the few increasingly rebellious stevedores, has been killed when a sling of Irish whisky cases has been "accidentally" allowed to fall on him, and Father Barry has come to administer the last rites. Over the broken body, the priest stands up angry and tall to deliver a spontaneous sermon to the circle of silent stevedores. "Boys, this is my church," he thunders, with passion in his voice. "And if you don't think Christ is down here on the waterfront—in the shape-up—you don't know nothing!" Then the tarpaulin-covered body is raised from the hold on a platform sling, with Father Barry standing beside it, and Edie's father kneeling mournfully alongside the companion of his own sacrificed son. It is a scene full of Christian allegory and proletarian significance.

There is a major question that the screenplay fails to discuss: why does such a ruthless wildcat union exist and carry on? Actually, the prevalence of vicious labor conditions on the waterfront was due to a deep conspiracy among high-level labor racketeers, political fixers and acquiescent shipowners, as Malcolm Johnson's newspaper stories showed. But the film bridges all this with but one shot (from behind) of an unidentified man, sitting in an elegant apartment watching a television news broadcast of the union boss' eventual appearance before the crime commission, and then peremptorily switching off the set when the boss becomes hysterical. Who this gentleman is—the governor, the kingpin of the shipowners—the film does not indicate.

Kazan has explained this shortcoming: "We were striving for a dramatic unity in the flow of the story, so we didn't want to bring it to a halt at any point and go off into a subplot. We felt the one hint of an unspecified Mr. Big was enough to make the viewer understand there was something mysterious and sinister behind all this, and let him figure it out for himself."

Likewise, the picturing of the crime commission's hearings is so general and vague, and so neglectful of evidence that should be sufficient to get the boss indicted, at least, that this is an irritation. The best way to take it is as a tacit, sardonic acknowledgment of the deliberate ineffectualness of the many official investigations of crime on the waterfront.

The concluding episode, too, in which Terry, after testifying and being ostracized, walks boldly into the union office and engages the boss in a splashing, smashing fight which he wins, is a theatrical presumption. It isn't likely that such a thing would have occurred. It is a romantic climax that Schulberg and Kazan contrived.

But then Schulberg and Kazan were not able to invent a formula for correcting conditions on the waterfront—or, indeed, in any other area of injustice in American industry. All they could state was the eternal idealistic and romantic hope that the working man could be more knowing, cohesive and articulate in protecting himself and his fellows against those who would take advantage of him.

For all its conspicuous weak points, *On the Waterfront* is such a fine film, such a fierce and poetic articulation, that it needs no apologies. There are many stunning things in it—for instance, the scene in which Terry finally owns up to Edie that he is guilty, though unintentionally, of having led her brother to his murder, telling her this horrible truth against a background of ships and the river, but with his awful words drowned out by the deafening roar of a ship's whistle, communicating utter shock and pain.

Or the scene of Terry and his brother in the back seat of the taxicab, with Terry struggling to explain in his poor, fumbling words and helpless pauses, indicating the confusion of his thoughts and the terrible hurt his brother has caused him by betraying his early boxing career. And in this quiet exchange we suddenly sense the bitter boyhood of these orphaned brothers, the cruel expediences that have driven them apart, and the economic and moral imbalance of their so close and yet so distant careers.

This is near to Brando's best performance, this portrayal of Terry Malloy, conveying so much articulation of the inarticulate in so few words. Rod Steiger, too, is superior as the brother who has chosen to use his better intellectual equipment for his own brutally selfish gain. Lee. J. Cobb's union boss is a bruiser who glibly makes, with barroom charm and weasel words, a loud, brazen representation of a hideous hypocrite. And Eva Marie Saint plays Edie with tremendous intensity, yet fragile grace.

There has been some niggling criticism of Leonard Bernstein's musical score. It is too bold, too brassy, too pretentious, some disaffected critics say. I find it apt and expressive of tortured feelings in a dynamic film that has, in the very rhythm of its rattling and clanging sounds—the coughing of donkey engines, the whir of cargo slings, the jangle of all the natural music of a busy waterfront—the throbbing intoxication of a great modern symphony.

Actual use of the waterfront streets and docks of New York and Hoboken balanced the strength of Brando's performance as Terry, here staggering back to join the shape-up, the alloting of the day's jobs.

The Seventh Seal
(Det Sjunde Inseglet)

1956

Written and directed by Ingmar Bergman; photographed by Gunnar Fischer; music by Erik Nordgren; produced by Svensk Filmindustri.

The Knight	Max von Sydow
The Squire	Gunnar Bjornstrand
Jof	Nils Poppe
Death	Bengt Ekerot
Mia	Bibi Andersson
Lisa	Inga Gill
The Witch	Maud Hansson
The Knight's Wife	Inga Landgre
The Girl	Gunnel Lindblom
Raval	Bertil Anderberg
The Monk	Anders Ek
The Blacksmith	Ake Fridell
Skat	Erik Strandmark
The Church Painter	Gunnar Olsson
The Merchant	Benkt-Ake Benktsson

Returning from the Crusades, a knight (Max von Sydow) meets the figure of Death (Bengt Ekerot) on a lone stretch of beach, and a Gothic tale begins.

While the ferment of cinema creation was bubbling in many countries after the Second World War, there was in Sweden a young man whose destiny was to restore the fame of Swedish motion pictures to the eminence they had enjoyed during the "golden age" of Mauritz Stiller and Victor Sjostrom, between 1918 and 1925.

This young man was Ingmar Bergman, a name that sounded so much like that of the famous Swedish actress, Ingrid Bergman, that for several years, even after his own fame was established, he was often referred to flippantly as "Sweden's other Bergman." That isn't done any more.

Bergman, whose childhood and boyhood were spent under the stern eye of a Lutheran-minister father, broke into motion pictures in 1944 as a scriptwriter. His first script, for a picture called *Hets* (*Torment*), told a suspiciously intimate tale of a schoolboy tormented by a sadistic teacher to the point where his life was almost ruined. The next year, he began directing and went through a period of several years in which he wrote and directed a variety of pictures in a variety of styles.

The titles—*Crisis, Prison, Illicit Interlude, The Naked Night*—signpost a spate of heavy dramas, solemn and tormented things in which the maturing Berg-

man worked out his agonies and hates. Then suddenly he did an about face and followed with three comedies. The third one, a sparkling charmer, sophisticated and erotic, called *Smiles of a Summer Night,* won a special commendation at the Cannes Film Festival in 1956. Bergman, up till then a nobody—outside his own country, at least—was now recognized as a writer-director who gave promise of following in the old Ernst Lubitsch vein.

But his very next picture confounded all expectation of such a thing and served notice that here was a cinema creator of extraordinary range and magnitude. For that next picture was his philosophical and poetic allegory, *The Seventh Seal,* which was immediately hailed as a triumph and is now established as a screen masterpiece.

The strong intellectual passion of it took viewers by surprise, mainly because such powerful brooding as it contains was so unusual in latter-day films. In a sense, it is in the great tradition of Strindberg and Selma Lagerlöf, deep probers of man's inner nature, and it follows in the philosophical line of the films that were made by Stiller and Sjostrom in the early days. Indeed, it is evident that Bergman has been very strongly moved by the strange contemplative nature of the great Swedish silent films. He has acknowledged himself in the tradition, and has said that *The Seventh Seal* was inspired by the film that Sjostrom made from Lagerlöf's *The Phantom Chariot* in 1920. That, too, was a fantasy-

A foolish juggler, his pretty wife and baby are the first symbols of simplicity and beauty that the knight finds.

The awesome intensity of fourteenth-century Scandinavia was a preoccupation of Ingmar Bergman, a minister's son whose questing for the meaning of life dominates in several of his fine films.

allegory in which man was confronted by Death and placed the strength of his virtue in conflict with the forces of doom.

The Seventh Seal is essentially the story of a lonely man's search for God—or, perhaps it might better be said, the story of a man's search for meaning in life. Its hero is seeking the Answer. "I want knowledge, not belief," he cries, "not faith, not suppositions, but knowledge!" This ageless cry of anguish is the theme of only a few great films. And the extraordinary thing about this one is the forcefulness with which it conveys the magnitude of its abstract ideas with visual images, the manner in which it makes you fathom the loneliness of man, the mystery of God, the fearful shadow that lies between life and death, the hideousness of superstition and the piteousness of blind faith.

The specified time of its action is the fourteenth century and the locale is Sweden or Denmark, a primitive, rude and forested land that is suffering a terrible epidemic of bubonic plague. It begins with a knight, returning from the Crusades, met on the rocky, wind-lashed coast by a black-robed, chalk-faced figure who announces himself to be Death. Death is waiting to take him, as he is taking so many in the land, but the knight bids for time to do a good deed and make one final attempt to fathom life. He challenges Death to a chess game on condition that he may live as long as he avoids a checkmate. If he wins, he will be released.

And so, while the game is in progress (which it is, as shown in cut-back scenes throughout the film), the knight and his squire, a wholesome skeptic, go riding through the land observing the behavior of the people under the lurking menace of doom. Some are giving themselves to cruel self-torture under the brutal goading of their priests, assisted by brutish soldiers who whip the people into line. Others, a group of seeming wardens, are preparing to burn a girl as a "witch," on the clearly preposterous charge that she has trafficked with the Devil.

Still others, scornful of religion, are wallowing in pleasure like pigs, feasting and fornicating, or ribaldly amusing themselves by watching an entertainment put on by a tiny strolling troupe. But in this band of players, the knight and his faithful squire, both of them weary and cynical of meaningless mouthings about God, find three innocent persons—a juggler, his wife and their infant child—who are as simple, fresh and wholesome as the morning dew. Except that the juggler sees visions, bright illusions, from time to time (to his pretty wife's tolerant amusement), the happy couple are as normal as their child. They are the concentration of simplicity, love and purity.

And so it is this little family that the knight, still unsatisfied in his quest for understanding, arranges to have elude the destruction of Death at the climax, when he and a piteous band of wanderers he has picked up must surrender themselves to Death at the end of the game.

Of course, one may see this picture as nothing more than a Gothic fantasy, a fearful descriptive visualization of morbid and medieval horrors. And there is enough horror and ugliness in it to make the blood run cold. Bergman is a passionate zealot for frank, realistic imagery, and his pictorial presentations of a people whose bodies and minds are diseased by corruption and ignorance are more eloquent than any words.

For instance, his scene of a procession of religious masochists—a gaggle of hollow, howling creatures, some dismally hooded and cowled, some staggering under the weight of mammoth crosses, some lashing themselves with thongs; crippled, diseased and maniacal—that comes straggling over a hill, marshaled by priests and soldiers, pacing to a grim, liturgical chant, is a scene right out of the Dark Ages. Indeed, Bergman took his cue for its design from old paintings on Swedish church walls.

A young girl (Maud Hansson) who has been accused of witchcraft is to be burned at the stake by a group of soldiers.

At last the knight comes home to join the family he could not accept earlier.

Or his scene of the preparation to burn the girl at the stake is a blood-chilling documentation of human savagery. There's the child, paralyzed with terror, the fright of hell in her staring eyes, resigned long since to her ordeal, while callow men go about the task of piling wood on a platform and lighting the unrelenting fire. The scene can only be compared to the fine one of a witch-burning in Carl Th. Dreyer's impressive Danish film, *Day of Wrath* (1948).

Yes, there is plenty of horror in this picture—and intentionally, be it said, because Bergman believes in involving the emotions of his viewers with shocks. He has stated without hesitation that he cannot abide that his films be exposed to "the merely indifferent presence of a popcorn-chewing audience."

But it should be obvious that there is much more in it than sheer Gothic fantasy. It should be obvious that the knight is intended as a symbol of modern man, a modern intellectual, such as Bergman himself. He is weary of war, disillusioned about serving an unknown God that permits the injustices, cruelties and sufferings that occur in the world, and shocked by man's fear and trembling in the face of prophesied doom—in this case the plague, which plainly symbolizes the nuclear bomb.

Likewise, it should be obvious that the characters met by the knight and his squire in their patient travel-

Death leads a weird dance at the end.

ing toward the knight's long-unvisited home are symbols of various types of humans. There's the crude actor in the strolling troupe who shirks his responsibility to go leching after the blacksmith's wife. There's the latter, a lusty, selfish woman, full of deceit and fickleness; and there's her husband, a harmless dullard who contributes nothing but muscle to the world.

More significant, there is a perfidious ex-seminarian who robs, cheats and bullies the pure and helpless. And there is a fiery-eyed minister who shouts about doom and damnation and fills his listeners with fear of God, not love. These rascals symbolize the treachery of religious teachers, just as the awesome parade of masochists is symbolic of enslavement to ritualized beliefs. At one point, the knight complains darkly, "We make an idol of our fear and call it God."

To be sure, there are other symbols, other aspects, that are not too clear, and this has been one of the reasons for some criticism of the film. What precisely is the idea behind the character of Death? Is it but the end of existence of each individual? If it is—if that's all one can fathom from this complicated film—then it is, indeed, shallow and romantic and Bergman might be called immature.

But I see Death as much more than a warder who simply rings down the curtain on life. He, or it, is a sort of cosmic conscience that every man must confront. Death is the constant observer who challenges every one of us, watching our every action, demanding our measuring up, and ready to lead us to oblivion when we have played our games and lost. Thus Death takes each of the characters who symbolizes some weakness or error, some one of the human deficiencies that are dispensable in the world. But Death does not get the juggler, his wife and their infant child because these people possess the virtues of purity and generosity that must not die.

Actually, Death as an assassin is not the antagonist. The antagonist is the moral and spiritual condition of man. It is this, the state of evil that man has allowed to occur, that confronts the knight throughout his wanderings and causes him to question God. Death is the visual presentation of the device by which man is erased—that is to say, the conscience—that takes all but the pure in the end.

Many techniques and tendencies of Bergman are richly revealed in this film—his use of natural beauty, for instance. His camera is quick to catch the esthetic essence of nature, whether it be in the cold and rocky coast, swept by strong winds from off the ocean and pounded by the sea, or in the immediately juxtaposed radiance of an early morn. His sensitive use of nature distills a strongly characteristic poetry. And especially so because he puts it in sharp contrast to other elements that communicate the aberrations and artificialities of man in the social state. For instance, there is a simple, exquisite moment in *The Seventh Seal*: Death has sawed down the tree into which the deceitful actor, Skat, has tried to flee, showing in one awesome image the fate of this wickedness. Then, onto the tree stump, in close-up, leaps a tiny squirrel with bright, beady eyes, all charm and innocence. This is nature compensating for ruin.

Now a word for the acting. Bergman has regularly drawn from a small group of excellent Swedish actors for the casts of his films. Their frequent collaborations with him and his knowledge of their individual skills have made for an ideal condition of creative give and take.

Here he has Max von Sydow as the knight, a tall, thin man, exuding the strength, the stoicism and the inner spiritual fervor of the Swedes; and Gunnar Bjornstrand, who has been a performer in more Bergman films than anyone else, has the prize role of the incisive, sardonic, implacable squire. Nils Poppe is charming as the bright-eyed and bouncy little juggler who goes free, and Bibi Andersson is delicious as his wholesome, adoring wife.

After this classic picture, Bergman went on to make a succession of brilliant screen dramas—the nostalgic *Wild Strawberries*, for which he had aged Victor Sjostrom play the leading role; *Brink of Life; The Magician*; the highly moralistic *The Virgin Spring*. And then he embarked upon a morbid and deeply contemplative trilogy, in which he returned to the theme of the anguish of the individual who feels lost or neglected in a search for God. Bergman persists in being a believer, although publicly tortured by doubt, and he maintains that every drama should in some way attempt to clarify the relation of man to God. "I will never give up the discussion," he has solemnly proclaimed.

Yet I doubt that he will ever make a picture that will surpass *The Seventh Seal* as a cosmic contemplation of the eternal man-God theme. And I am sure that he will never catch an image that will move me, at least, any more than the scene at the end, wherein Death leads a saraband of the departed souls of the drama across a hilltop against a clouded sky.

Simple-minded Gelsomina (Guilietta Masina), bought out of poverty by the brutish Zampano (Anthony Quinn), tries her best to add cheer to the strong man's show.

La Strada

1956

Story and screenplay by Federico Fellini and Tullio Pinelli; directed by Signor Fellini; dialogue by Signor Pinelli; cameraman, Otello Martelli; music by Nino Rota; produced by Dino de Laurentiis and Carlo Ponti.

Zampano	Anthony Quinn
Gelsomina	Giulietta Masina
Matto (the Fool)	Richard Basehart
Colombaini	Aldo Silvani

and
Marcella Rovere and Livia Venturini

Federico Fellini's *La Strada* is such a genuinely poetic film and it so intimately involves the audience with the personalities and feelings of individuals that it represents a far extension of the neo-realist sweep in Italy. While it does play its tragic story of a carnival strongman and the simple-minded girl he keeps as his clown and slavey, in streets and empty lots and country roads that are as real and reflective of postwar poverty as the streets in Vittorio de Sica's *The Bicycle Thief* (which see), it is so completely concerned with subjective variations of mood that it stands at the opposite pole from Roberto Rossellini's grimly objective *Paisan* (which see).

At the same time, it cannot be regarded as a form of fanciful romance, except insofar as its conception of a pure and innocent spirit in the girl does have a certain romantic buoyancy. Most of it is a harsh exposure of the capacity of cruelty in the man to batter and eventually destroy the unselfish and loving spirit of the girl. And it comes to a hopeless conclusion that is the antithesis of romance.

I dwell on this point that *La Strada* is neither a prime neo-realist film nor a modified carry-over of the old prewar sentimental street romance because I feel we should recognize clearly how much this haunting picture represents a transition in regard for the spirit and the suffering of individuals that occurred in Italian films. It is the ultimate projection of what de Sica began with *The Bicycle Thief* and continued more expressly in his *Miracle in Milan* (1951) and *Umberto D* (1952). And it is also the simplest and fullest manifestation by Fellini of his lyrical power to express the deep pathos in people.

Perhaps the main reason we continue to class it as a neo-realist film is because we recall that Fellini was a mover in the early postwar surge. After a youth and young manhood of traveling with circuses and vaudeville shows, doing cartoons for newspapers and gag writing for humor magazines, he became associated with Rossellini in 1944 and helped write the scripts of *Open City* and the prototypical *Paisan*. The first film he fully directed gave a hint of things to come. It was a natural and wistful contemplation of the peril of romantic daydreaming, entitled *The White Sheik* (1951). He followed this with *I Vitelloni* (1953), a ruthless and often poignant study of aimless and restless postwar youth. Then he produced *La Strada*, and his reputation was made.

The story is that he wrote this picture expressly for his wife, Giulietta Masina, who was a moderately well-known screen actress and comedienne. But he couldn't find a producer to finance it. They all wanted him to do another *I Vitelloni*, which had won the grand prize at the Venice Festival and had been a big commercial success. Certainly they did not want him to do a raggle-taggle tale of low-class street performers without an insuring star. Dino de Laurentiis and Carlo Ponti did offer to back the film, if he would use Silvano Mangano and Burt Lancaster and rewrite the story a little bit for them. He refused. He would do it with Miss Masina or he would not do it at all.

Then one night he called for Miss Masina at the Cinecitta studio where she was working in one of those big costume dramas that were so gruesomely characteristic of commercial production in Italy during the 1950's. This was *Attila the Hun*, and it had the American actor, Anthony Quinn, in the title role. Fellini met

223

Quinn, and immediately he wanted him to play the brute—the gypsy strong-man, Zampano—in his projected film. At first Quinn was totally uninterested, but then he saw a screening of *I Vitelloni*, which excited him immensely, and he agreed. With Quinn willing to work in *La Strada* during the mornings, before he reported to *Attila the Hun*, Fellini was able to get financing from Ponti-de Laurentiis, and shooting was started.

There is no question that much of the power and veracity of *La Strada* is due to Quinn's extraordinary appearance and performance as the overbearing brute who buys the simpleton girl, Gelsomina, from her poor peasant mother for 10,000 lire and takes her to travel with him in his grotesque motorcycle trailer. His sullen, insensate domineering as the vagrant entertainer whose act is doing feats of strength, the most impressive of

which is breaking chains by the expansion of his chest, is the menace of evil that carries through the film and pervades it with a thickening ooze of poisonous and impermeable stupidity. At the same time, his cloudy indications of anguish and loneliness give a dimension of pathos to the character. Quinn's raffish get-up in cheap clothing and an American G.I. knit cap, with his heavy, creased face and guttural voice (which is well dubbed in Italian) magnifies all the clumsiness and grossness of the man.

But it is Miss Masina's Gelsomina who gives the picture its rich authority and lifts it, through her sweet and gentle nature, to a lyrical level that she remarkably sustains. This surprising little creature, with her round, bright-eyed, serio-comic face that is a lot like that of Harry Langdon, the old silent comedian, is the essence

At last Zampano displays a glimmer of emotion when he misinterprets the kindness and simplicity of Matto, the Fool (Richard Basehart), an acrobat in the traveling show which Zampano elects to join.

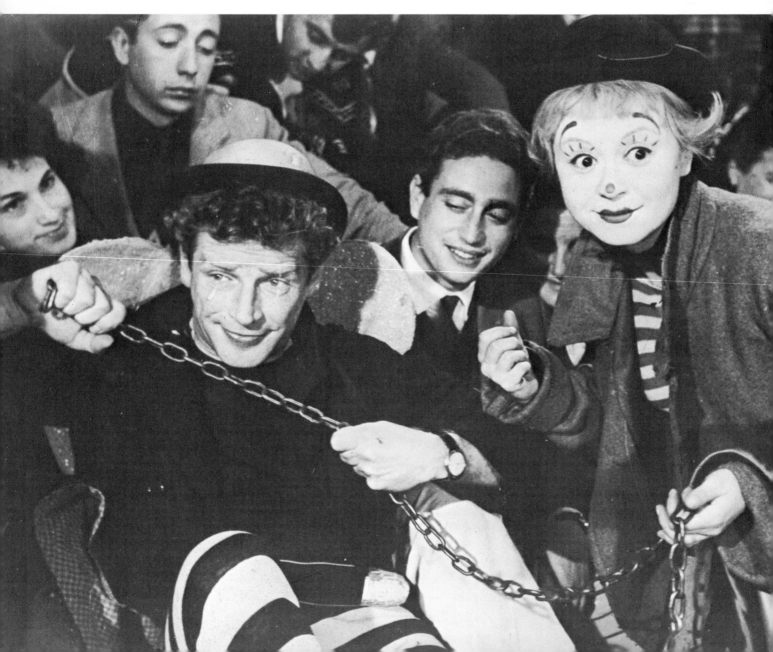

Zampano abandons the grief-stricken Gelsomina, sneaking off while she sleeps.

him, with Gelsomina as a horrified witness, and hides the body in a culvert under a road. This vengeful killing so shocks Gelsomina that she is deadened and demented with grief, and becomes so cheerless and torpid that Zampano finally abandons her, going away while she is sleeping, unable to do it otherwise.

Thus little Gelsomina passes, and this all might mean nothing to us save a dismal demonstration of the poignant waste of a pure soul. But Fellini has put a classic postscript, an epilogue, onto his film that provides an emotional catharsis for this heartbreaking parable. . . .

Zampano murders the Fool in a fit of insane anger, an act which plunges Gelsomina into inconsolable grief.

of cheerfulness and sadness constantly intermixed, of humor and pain compacted in one sturdy, stubborn little frame.

Her delight when she is allowed to work with Zampano, wearing a clown costume and tootling a trumpet and beating a drum to announce his appearance, is counterbalanced by her distress and dismay when she finds she cannot make contact with him through the friendliness and affection she has for everyone. And although she is beamingly happy as they go around the countryside, doing their act at village fairs and weddings, she is vaguely oppressed by the saddening thought that she is of no use to Zampano, except to drudge for him and occasionally give him sex.

The moment of her greatest joy is when she is made to understand by an acrobat whom she has met in a small traveling circus which she and Zampano have joined that "everyone serves some purpose" and that her purpose clearly is just to serve Zampano, no matter what his feelings for her. This so delights the little creature that, when Zampano gets out of jail (where he has been at the time of this conversation for attacking the acrobat with a knife), she devotes herself to him with contentment. Her assurance to him is that she "no longer dreams of going home."

But her joy is shattered, some time later, when they again meet the genial acrobat, who cannot refrain from taunting the stupid strong-man, and Zampano murders

Gelsomina is dead and Zampano, a lonely drunk, is left with the realization of his brutality.

Months later, the sullen Zampano is in a seaside town when he hears the distant strains of the music that Gelsomina has played, a little song that runs as an exquisite melodic counterpoint through the film. He follows the sound to find the music being sung by a girl who is hanging up clothes, and from her he learns the blunt fact that Gelsomina is dead. That night Zampano is unable to go through with his monotonous strongman act. He goes to a bar and gets drunk, wrangles with other men, goes off alone and walks out upon the beach, where he finally sinks down in a broken heap at the edge of the water, moaning his loneliness and grief. Thus are we sadly afforded the shattering spectacle of man dimly comprehending the cost and cruelty of his selfishness—too late.

Fellini has crowded this picture with such a wealth of significant detail—of humorous, picturesque, pathetic, lyrical incidents—that it carries more implications than are in its most obvious parable. There is a charming incident in which Gelsomina comes upon a retarded child stuck away in a bedroom of an old farmhouse where she and Zampano are entertaining at a wedding feast, and at once, without any sense of incongruity, she starts to do little things to amuse the child. It is a beautiful glimpse of her spirit of generosity, and it is capped with an interesting irony when she is chased away by a couple of nervous nuns.

There is also the perfectly magical sequence in which the wandering Gelsomina, having run away from Zampano, comes into a town at night and finds it aglow with the lights of a religious festival. There, for the first time, she sees the acrobat doing a high-wire balancing act over the main square, and she is utterly enraptured by the mystery and the brilliance of it all.

But I find the whole phase of the friendship of Gelsomina and the caustic acrobat, who is played by the American actor, Richard Basehart, in an eerie, mischievous way, to contain such beautiful moments of communication between spirits that are akin—except that one is more prescient than the other—that it holds the loveliest lyricism in the film. The parting of the two in the dawn light, after the acrobat has imparted his little homily about serving to the girl and has given her a cheap trinket as a souvenir, is Fellini at his poetic best.

Obviously, the fact that Zampano cannot abide the acrobat—the Fool, as he is known around the circus—is symbolic of the eternal clash between the free and soaring spirits and the brute oppressors in this world.

The music of Nino Rota is one of the fine, effective elements in the film.

Patience, forebearance, the monotony of life form the substance of existence in the Bengali village where Satyajit Ray starts his *Apu Trilogy*. The old woman is Chunibala Devi.

The Apu Trilogy

1956–1959

Pather Panchali, screenplay by Satyajit Ray, based on a novel by Bibhuti Bannerji; directed by Mr. Ray; cameraman, Subrata Mitra; music by Ravi Shankar.

The Father	Kanu Banerji
The Mother	Karuna Banerji
Apu	Subir Banerji
The Daughter	Uma Das Gupta
Old Woman	Chunibala Devi

Aparajito, screenplay by Satyajit Ray, based on a novel by B. Bannerji; directed by Mr. Ray; same cameraman and music.

The Father	Kanu Banerji
The Mother	Karuna Banerji
Apu, as a boy	Pinaki Sen Gupta
Apu, as an adolescent	Smaran Ghosal
The Uncle	Ramani Sen Gupta
Headmaster	Subodh Ganguly

The World of Apu, original screenplay by Satyajit Ray; directed by Mr. Ray; same cameraman and music.

Apu	Soumitra Chatterjee
His Wife	Sharmila Tagore
Kajol	Alok Chakravarty
The Grandfather	Dhiresh Mazumaer

People communicating with people through motion pictures extending around the world, which has been such an evident and felicitous phenomenon since the Second World War, is in no instance manifested more affectingly and successfully than in the conveyance of the people of India through these films of Satyajit Ray. This beautiful triptych of features, known as *The Apu Trilogy* from the name of the lad whose development from childhood through maturity is traced, is a lovely illumination of a way of living and looking at life in a land where mysticism and misery have sadly gone hand in hand. And it has probably done more to give a picture of the great middle class of India, caught in a tangle of cultures, than any other communication we have had.

The secret of its ingratiation is the sensitivity and candor with which its extraordinary writer-director has brought together on film the strangely lethargic mood and tempo of life in the rural areas, the crush of congestion in the cities, the softness of sentiments that pass between gentle, stoical persons and the sadness of the shattered hopes of youth, all composed in a visual flow to music that achieves the most touching harmony.

It is remarkable how this group of pictures came to be made at all, and how it has drawn the world's attention to the ambiguities of film production in India. Ray was a young commercial artist, capriciously interested in films, when he was commissioned to do a series of illustrations for a new edition of a popular novel of Bibhuti Bannerji. While he was doing the drawings, he wrote a screenplay from the book in the hope that someday he might be able to put it into a film.

On an extended trip to London in 1949, he saw a great many movies and became excited by the work of Vittorio de Sica, especially *The Bicycle Thief* (which see). When he returned to India in 1950, he tried to obtain financial backing to do a production in neo-realist style of the Bannerji story, the rights to which he had obtained. But no one in the heavily populated, strictly commercial Indian film industry would think of extending him money to do a picture, especially one of the sort he had in mind. So Ray was thrown upon his own devices, which were to obtain the help and backing of friends.

With very little money, but with the assistance of Bansi Chandragupta, a friend who had worked as art director for Jean Renoir when he was doing *The River*

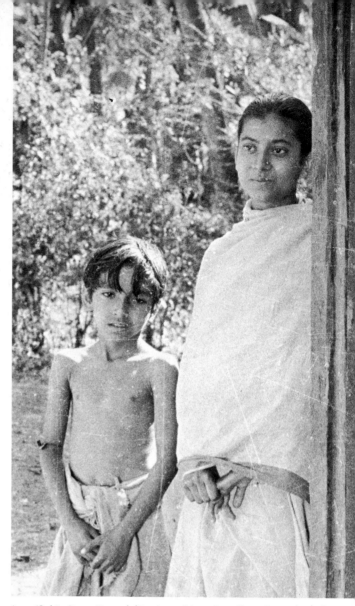

Apu (Subir Banerji) and his sister (Uma Das Gupta) await their father's return from a religious mission.

After the death of the daughter, the father (Kanu Banerji) moves his wife (Karuna Banerji) and the young Apu (Pinaki Sen Gupta) to bleak quarters in the bustling city of Benares.

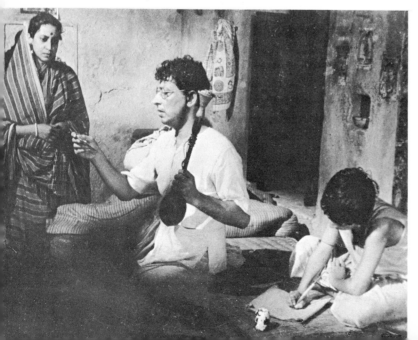

(1951) in India, and with Subrata Mitra, a still photographer, recruited to be his cameraman, Ray assembled a cast made up largely of nonprofessionals and went to work shooting the film in a village many miles from Calcutta. They worked largely on weekends and holidays.

In addition to getting money to keep going, one of his foremost anxieties was the survival until she completed her role in the picture of an aged woman he got to play an old aunt. This woman had been a popular stage actress, but her career had been ended by ill health, and she had survived for years on opium tablets. Ray virtually kept her alive for this film. And well he did, for her fragile performance is one of the picture's most poignant elements.

A few sequences of the incompleted project were

With his mother and father dead, the adolescent Apu (Smaran Ghosal) leaves his uncle's farm to study at the university in Calcutta.

shown to John Huston while he was visiting in India. He was so impressed by them that he suggested the finished film might be shown in connection with a forthcoming exhibition of the arts of India at the Museum of Modern Art in New York. This was a thrilling idea, but how were they to finish the film? At this point, Ray went to the highest level of the government of the state of West Bengal and asked for funds. Evidently the prospect of a showing in America did the trick, for the government put up sufficient money. The invitation from the museum came, and, in a burst of feverish activity, during which Ravi Shankar composed an exquisite musical score, the film was finished and shipped to New York.

Though it made a very good impression when it was shown at the Museum of Modern Art in 1954, many months passed before the picture, called *Pather Panchali (Father Panchali)*, was opened commercially in Calcutta. And it did not attain wide attention until it was shown at the Cannes Festival in 1956, where it was one of those occasional "sensations" and was given a special award as the "best human document."

On the strength of this exceptional recognition and growing commercial success in West Bengal, Ray was given backing to do a sequel by a regular commercial company. This sequel, also based upon the novel of Bannerji, was called *Aparajito (The Unvanquished)*, and it won the award as best film at the Venice Festival in 1957. So excited was Ray on this occasion that he recklessly announced there would be yet a third film in the series. To keep this promise, he wrote on his own *Apur Sansar (The World of Apu)*, which carries forward into melancholy manhood the hero of the two previous films. This, perhaps the strongest in the series, was released in 1959. It rounds off what is no doubt the greatest of only a few memorable film trilogies.

This series should now be seen in continuity and all at one time, if possible, because the experience of it is strongest when it can be absorbed as a full turn of the cycle of life. However, one must be prepared to accept it at the slow and pensive pace at which it moves, relaxed before its unhurried transit and its timeless serenity. This is especially necessary when one confronts the first of the three, *Pather Panchali*, which in this country

Apu (Soumitra Chatterjee) agrees to marry a country girl (Sharmila Tagore) after she has been jilted by an epileptic.

Apu and his wife are happy together, bearing their poverty as an accepted course of life, until the young wife's death in childbirth.

Indulging his grief in lonely wandering until chided by a friend, Apu returns to his son, Kajol (Alok Charkravarty), whom he has left for so long with the grandfather (Dhiresh Mazumaer).

was subtitled *Song of the Road*. For here, in beginning his story of a poor middle-class family living in a Bengali village—a husband and wife, a small daughter and smaller son and an aged "aunt" whose connection is so tenuous she is treated as an object of charity—Ray patterns a formless mosaic of rambling and crude domestic scenes that appears to be purely "documentary" before anything of consequence occurs.

There are shots of the frail old woman, the harassed mother, her lively little girl and her cheerful husband, a priest by profession who is so poor he has to eke out a living collecting rents. There are scenes of familiar burdens: of the mother trying to get the child to eat, washing clothes, quarreling with her husband or pushing the little boy toward school. And only slowly there emerge suggestions of tender and sad relationships—between the little girl and the frail old woman, the father and daughter, the mother and son.

Even amid such poverty and scrimping, there is evidence of faded quality. The husband has some education; the mother has some taste. For all their humiliating poorness, they have honor and dignity. And the children are lively and happy, the little girl as graceful as a bird. They dream of distant places, the mystery and magic of trains.

Then misfortunes come upon them. The old woman dies in the woods, and the children find her body. They are horrified. The father goes away on a priestly mission, and it looks as though he's gone for good. The little girl catches pneumonia from standing thankfully in a drought-breaking rain. She dies after an agonizing illness, and the mother is left alone with her little son. Then the father returns, bringing a present for his little girl, and the anguish of the mother finally bursts in a flood of tears.

That is all. The father, discouraged, decides to move with his wife and son, go elsewhere. Before leaving, the little boy takes a trinket of his sister's and tosses it sadly into a pool. That is his farewell to her. The three ride away in an old cart, and the gentle strains of Shankar's Indian music phrase the end of childhood and village life.

The second film, *Aparajito*, begins with the family arriving in Benares, where the father, after what has evidently been some fruitless wandering, hopes to find something to do. Here, again, Ray constructs a mosaic of teeming city life: of priests and pilgrims wandering along the Ganges, of the mother and son strolling through a festival, of ritualistic ostentation and grinding poverty.

Then the father dies, and mother and son go to live with a great-uncle in a small town where the boy is educated, as his mother wishes him to be. The two are separated when Apu, now a tall and wistful youth, wins a scholarship to Calcutta University and goes to live in the city again. And the sadness of their separation, the back and forth tracking of their lonely lives, is climaxed with the death of the mother and Apu's going forth into the world.

The third film, *The World of Apu*, tells of the young man's facing up to life—of his unsuccessful attempts to make something of his learning as a teacher in Calcutta, then as a worker in a factory; of his virtually accidental marriage to a beautiful, fragile country girl; of his trying to write a novel; of the distant death of his wife in childbirth while staying with her mother; of his lonely wandering across India for several years and his final return to the home of his in-laws to see and embrace his little son. Thus *The World of Apu* concludes symbolically as *Pather Panchali* begins, with a small boy, eyes wide with wonder, and with sadness, on the threshold of life.

There is, in this series of pictures, some subtle criticism of the play of religious superstition and old traditions affecting the people's lives. For instance, there is an implication that the father takes ill and dies as the consequence of bathing in the Ganges with the swarms of pilgrims that visit the Benares shrines. And the sanction of an ancient superstition that induces Apu to wed the country girl who has been abandoned by her intended husband is implicitly and gently ridiculed. But the virtue of the series as instruction in the characteristic of life in India, prior to the so-called Liberation from British rule, is in the awareness of the sweetness and the sorrow of a people they convey, and in the great sweep of compassion for the helpless and the doomed they provide.

I cannot begin to name the countless beautiful and poetic ways in which Ray imparts the message of tenderness and sorrow. But there are a few things I must mention, such as the experience of the little girl and boy as they break away from the village and run across a flax field, bursting in delicate bloom, to a distant rise from which they can watch a steam train rolling across the countryside, and then the experience of the boy when he puts his ear against the frame of an electric transmitter tower and hears the magical hum of all the world; or the delicate glimmer of fireflies in the twilight on the evening the mother dies; or the flinging by Apu of the pages of his novel from the top of a hill in the luminous dawn.

The Apu Trilogy says and implies so much more than is ordinarily said in motion pictures that it is no wonder it towers above all the thousands of films that have been made in India, and marks the peak of the rich career of Ray.

La Dolce Vita

1960

Story by Federico Fellini, Tullio Pinelli and Ennio Flaiano; screenplay by Signor Fellini, Signor Pinelli, Signor Flaiano and Brunello Rondi; directed by Signor Fellini; director of photography, Otello Martelli; music by Nino Rota; produced by Giuseppe Amato and Angelo Rizzoli.

Marcello Rubini	Marcello Mastroianni
Paparazzo, the photographer	Walter Santesso
Maddalena	Anouk Aimée
The Prostitute	Adriana Moneta
Emma, Marcello's mistress	Yvonne Furneaux
Sylvia, a Hollywood star	Anita Ekberg
Robert, Sylvia's fiancé	Lex Barker
Frankie Stout	Alan Dijon
Steiner	Alain Cuny
Paola	Valeria Ciangottini
Marcello's Father	Annibale Ninchi
Fanny, a chorus girl	Magali Noel
Nadia	Nadia Gray
Matinee Idol	Jacques Sernas

With the success of his *La Strada* (which see), Federico Fellini might have been thought to have achieved the eminence that would have assured him financing for any film he wanted to make. But he hadn't. His next film, *Il Bidone* (1955), made with the American actor, Broderick Crawford, was a failure, and once again he was in the position of having to scramble for funds. It took him more than a year to raise the money to make *The Nights of Cabiria* (1957), in which he again had his wife, Giulietta Masina, this time playing a poignant prostitute. Although it was vastly successful, artistically and commercially, it set up another roadblock to his ambitious designs.

For again the producers were after him to make the same sort of film, and again he resisted their persuasions. He now had turning in his head an idea for a film that would be bolder and bigger than anything he had done to date. What he wanted to do was a picture about the Rome he had come to know in the years of his growing importance as a world-famous film-maker.

"Rome had become a big place in the 1950's," Fellini recalled to me several years ago. "It was full of all kinds of new people, activities, an international crowd, and I was being shoved along in it, not knowing exactly what was happening. I had been to a lot of film festivals, rushed through airports, stayed in strange hotels. Life had become like a carnival—disordered and unreal. There was an unsettled climate. This is what I wanted to get in a film—this climate of activity, excite-

ment, nervousness and uncertainty. I had come to the point where I wanted to stop and inquire, 'What's going on?'"

The picture Fellini envisioned would be made up of several episodes, each episode representing a slice of life in Rome, reflective of things the director had seen or heard about. One of the first he wished to do was that of an American actress coming to Rome to play in a salacious picture and cutting up scandalously. This would have the weird disorder and carnival atmosphere he wanted to convey.

To hold his episodes together, Fellini wanted an observer of the passing scene, a logically present onlooker who would, in effect, be himself. He thought of several possibilities—a film-maker, a tourist guide—then he hit upon a reporter, a popular journalist. And because he sensed a fascinating motif in the swarms of free-lance photographers that had become an uncontrollable annoyance in the journalistic life of Rome, he decided to make his observer a reporter for a popular picture magazine.

But when Fellini tried to sell his idea, producers shied away. They wanted another *Nights of Cabiria*, not this loose-jointed, uncertain thing. A year passed. Then Angelo Rizzoli, a wealthy financier and publisher

A helicopter carrying a statue of Christ over the ancient Roman aqueduct for delivery to St. Peter's Square is the shocker to start Fellini's mosaic of the sweet life in the Eternal City.

Marcello Rubini (Marcello Mastroianni), a third-rate journalist, starts his night-life scandal hunting when he picks up the insatiable Maddalena (Anouk Aimée) on the Via Veneto, where the night-blooming *paparazzi* (news cameramen) hold sway.

in Milan, put up the money and Fellini was able to start shooting in the summer of 1959. He decided to call his film *La Dolce Vita* (*The Sweet Life*)—an ironic phrase for the life of abundance and leisure into which many Romans of various shadings had come.

Even before it was finished, word was going around that Fellini had a picture that would set the country on its ear. Rumors of its sensational nature were briskly circulated in Rome, and an explosive reception was prophesied. The anticipation was accurate. When *La Dolce Vita* was released in early 1960 in sixty-four cities throughout Italy, it was greeted with unprecedented brickbats and bouquets. Some critics called it the greatest Italian film ever made; others slammed it as hideous, offensive, outrageous, a shocking disgrace. The Roman Catholic newspaper, *Il Quotidiano,* gave it a rave review. The Vatican's *L'Osservatore Romano* called it sacrilegious and obscene. There was talk that the government might ban it or demand that it be cut. Fortunately, it did neither. The popular response was immense. Consistent with expectations, it won the grand prize at Cannes that spring and went on to harvest countless laurels and be a smash hit around the world.

What is the basic fascination of this tremendously agitating film that has now caused millions of viewers to be delighted, bewildered and disturbed? Is it simply the unabashed candor with which Fellini exposes and dissects the gaudiness and corruption of certain phases of life? Is it merely the fact that he affords us the position of a privileged *voyeur* on several kinds of sexual indulgence, as performed or clearly specified by the wide range of sensualists and deviates that appear in almost all the episodes? Not entirely, I would say, although there is no doubt that the scent of eroticism that pervades the whole film is a considerable and exciting

Sylvia (Anita Ekberg), a moronic Hollywood star, floats through an evening in Rome with Marcello, ending up with a quixotic bath at dawn in the Trevi Fountain.

blandishment. The fact that modern life in a great city is acknowledged to be plagued with the compulsion to achieve and display sexual prowess is certainly one of the powerful themes.

But I think the reason *La Dolce Vita* engrosses and agitates the viewer and leaves one staggered and empty, as though having watched a fatal accident, is because it so vividly envisions a kind of calamity that might occur to anyone—at least, anyone exposed to the modern culture of luxury and joy, easy success and self-indulgence, that is promoted in this super-salesman's age.

Marcello, the roving hero, is a fellow whose connections with life are pretty much those of any average middle-class urban bachelor. Although he pursues an occupation that takes him into all sorts of areas and permits him bizarre and weird adventures that most men would have to fantasize, he is shown, as the drama develops, to be personally and emotionally involved and beset by the same kinds of urges and anxieties that beset the average young man.

While he moves from one experience to another—from a night in a prostitute's bed with an elegant, unpredictable nymphomaniac to a curiously comical encounter with a voluptuous Hollywood star; from a sobering involvement with mob hysteria at a television-covered "miracle" to a cynical saturnalia with a gaggle of bored aristocrats—he is constantly being hung on to

233

by a frantic woman with whom he lives and who tries to scare, shame or nag him into marrying her. And, in one of the more revealing and affecting episodes, he is shown to be deeply sentimental about his provincial father and nostalgic about his prewar youth.

In short, this fellow Marcello, whom Marcello Mastroianni plays with a disarmingly genial, casual manner that betrays the hero's immaturity and lack of strength, is just a footloose person seeking guidelines in a world in which old values and old systems have been unsettled and all that is sought after is sensation for sensation's sake.

The characteristic of the environment and the iconoclasm in the approach is brilliantly brought to the audience in the first episode. The opening shot is a broad scene on the edge of Rome, with the great towering arches of the ruins of the San Felice aqueduct rising eloquently against the sky. Two thousand years ago, this structure was one of the lifelines of imperial Rome; now it is a stark and crumbling relic, a gaunt reminder of a greatness that is gone.

As the camera scans this prospect, noting a soccer field in the shadow of the ruins, we hear the distant whir of a helicopter. Then the camera picks it up, and we see two low-flying choppers approaching, with an indeterminate object dangling by a cable beneath one. As it comes closer, we discover the object is a massive statue of Jesus Christ, soaring rakishly over the landscape with beneficent arms outstretched.

The chopper flies on efficiently, above piles of ugly new apartment houses, above a flock of hooting youngsters who chase the swiftly moving shadow of the statue in the street, above a group of shapely young women in bikinis, sunbathing on a penthouse roof, who shout gleefully, "Look, it's Jesus!" And, along with it, in the other chopper, flies Marcello, with his photographer, taking shots of this incongruous transportation and shouting gags at the girls on the roof. Thus, in this ribald exposition of the image of Christ as a passing performer in an aerial circus, as it were, a pithy statement is made of the ambiguities of contemporary Rome—the scrambling of values and the reduction of dignity to mechanical expediency.

This same note is picked up later in the garish episode in which Marcello, along with his mistress, Emma, and his photographer, are on hand to observe a disgusting display of hyperinduced religious hysteria mixed with cheap commercial showmanship in a staged enactment with two working-class children of a fake "miracle," for the benefit of television cameras.

The bizarre nature of this incongruous happening is matched in lighter vein by the experience of Marcello in following the Hollywood star all over the city—on a press-agent visit to St. Peter's, on a jazz-inflamed jamboree at a nightclub in the Baths of Caracalla, on a bathing jaunt in the Trevi Fountain at dawn—all the while trying to seduce her, never quite being able to grasp the vitality and childish pretense of this empty-

A pitiful fake "miracle" is used to arouse false hopes in the sick and crippled when two misguided children claim to see a vision of the Madonna.

Marcello's father (Annibale Ninchi) makes a business visit to Rome and almost succumbs to a heart attack when he goes home with a nightclub chorus girl.

headed and emptyhearted American. Anita Ekberg's performance as this voluptuous, frigid star is one of the amazing surprises and indelible memories of the film.

From this—and from the earlier episode with Maddalena, the whimsical nymphomaniac—one might think that Marcello is nothing but a rounder, a semiprofessional gigolo. But his more serious side is indicated in his encounter with his friend, Steiner, in a church and, on an evening, when he and the bovine Emma attend a soirée in Steiner's home. To be sure, he is shown to be superficial, an intellectual poseur, perhaps. But he is obviously trying to find a pattern, even trying to write a book. However, the book goes out the window—and all else goes with it—when Steiner inexplicably murders his two small children and then commits suicide. This is the climax of the erratic but rising action of Marcello's career.

The film has been criticized often because the reason for Steiner's act is not explained. Yet this lack of explanation, this enigma, is the very point of Fellini's exposé. People are so complicated, so confused and irrational in this age, that there are no simple explanations. The "sweet life" is totally absurd. Fellini told me he took his incident from an actual case of which he had heard, a similar murder-suicide by a successful and apparently happy engineer in Milan. Presumably life had become too barren and the future too bleak for this man. He had become demented.

The most poignant moment in the picture is when Marcello, leaving the room in which Steiner has exploded disaster, looks back at the body of his friend slumped in a chair. This is the cold, silent moment in which the glass of Marcello's life is shattered, too. This goodbye to Steiner is clearly goodbye to everything for him. And the conclusion of this episode, with the camera zooming in to catch a brash photographer trying to snap the horrified face of Steiner's homecoming widow, is the peak of the journalist motif.

The last episode, the so-called "orgy", is a Walpurgian epilogue in which Marcello abandons himself to the excesses of a group of homosexuals and hedonists, mocking all the hallowed symbols of sentiment and respectability at a costume party (celebrating a divorce) in a luxurious house near the beach. And, at dawn, all the revelers file grimly to a spot on the sodden sand where a monster fish with one great glazed eye has been hauled from the sea. This fish is the symbol of the veracity and futility of life, and its eye is the eye of death peering at those who gawk at it.

Then, from the other side of a sea-cut inlet, comes

A huge Cyclopean fish, dragged from the sea, casts an uncomprehending eye on the Jet Set as they wind up at Ostia in the dawn's light.

the faint voice of a young girl calling to Marcello. It is a girl whom he had met some time before at a beachfront restaurant, while he was working on his book. He turns and goes toward her, trying to hear her, but her voice is drowned out by the sound of the surf. He shrugs and turns back toward the fish. The last shot is a close-up of the girl's sweet, young, wistfully smiling face.

In sum, this is an awesome picture, licentious in content but deeply moral and vastly sophisticated in its excoriation of the "sweet life" and its degeneracies. And an excellent cast performs it. In addition to Mastroianni and Miss Ekberg, there are Yvonne Furneaux as Marcello's mistress, Anouk Aimée as the nymphomaniac, Annibale Ninchi as Marcello's visiting father, Magali Noel as a nightclub chorus girl, Alain Cluny as Steiner, Walter Santesso as Marcello's agile photographer, and many more whose faces are vivid in the minds of many who have seen this film.

An excellent musical score by Nino Rota is full of sweet melodies and mockeries. It is a score almost as varied and eloquent as the script, and it does a great deal to give character and emotional momentum to the film.

In a very real sense, *La Dolce Vita* is a cultural and social document, as well as an exciting entertainment. Its whole graphic scan of Rome—its rain-washed and dawn-grayed environs, its crowded Via Veneto with its prostitutes and perverts etches the character and mood of one large area of the great city at a point in time. It is a point in time between eras of incalculable difference, perhaps. Fellini has done this great service with a poet's heart and film-maker's eye.

His next great film after this one was his autobiographical *8½* (1963), in which he psychoanalyzes a distinguished film director who has just completed an extraordinary picture and is worried about being able to make another one. It is a superlative achievement in a brilliant, revolutionary cinema style. And it thoroughly manifests that Fellini's do-it-yourself psychoanalysis was a success!

A collection of decadent citizens celebrate Nadia's (Nadia Gray) divorce with an orgy that starts with a striptease in her husband's invaded villa.

The magnificent portrayal of Hugh Griffith as the lusty, earthy Squire Western, here triumphant at the hunt's conclusion, is one of the film's many gems.

Tom Jones

1963

Screenplay by John Osborne from the novel by Henry Fielding; produced and directed by Tony Richardson; music composed and conducted by John Addison; production designer, Ralph Brinton; director of photography, Walter Lassally; film editor, Anthony Gibbs; produced for United Artists.

SQUIRE ALLWORTHY'S HOUSE

Squire Allworthy	George Devine
Bridget Allworthy	Rachel Kempson
Mrs. Wilkins	Angela Baddeley
Jenny Jones (Mrs. Waters)	Joyce Redman
Partridge	Jack MacGowran
Tom Jones	Albert Finney
Blifil	David Warner
Molly Seagrim	Diane Cilento
Black George	Wilfrid Lawson
Square	John Moffatt
Thwackum	Peter Bull
Mrs. Seagrim	Freda Jackson
Lawyer Dowling	Redmond Phillips

SQUIRE WESTERN'S HOUSE

Squire Western	Hugh Griffith
Sophie Western	Susannah York
Parson Supple	James Cairncross
Miss Western	Edith Evans
Honor	Patsy Rowlands

ON THE ROAD TO LONDON

Lieutenant	Mark Dignam
Northerton	Julian Glover
Landlady, George Inn	Avis Bunnage
Mrs. Fitzpatrick	Rosalind Knight
Susan, Upton Inn	Lynn Redgrave
Mr. Fitzpatrick	George A. Cooper
MacLachlan	Jack Stewart

LONDON

Lady Bellaston	Joan Greenwood
Mrs. Miller	Rosalind Atkinson
Lord Fellamar	David Tomlinson

Narration spoken by Michael MacLiammoir

Henry Fielding's *Tom Jones,* that massive novel of the amorous adventures of an indefatigable young man in eighteenth-century England, may be the literary source of the beautiful color film of the same name that Tony Richardson made, with the help of a multitude of artists, in England in 1963. But the spiritual source of this movie, which richly and suitably conveys the essence of the narrative content, the flowery rhetoric and the ribald wit of the Fielding novel, is the whole range of boisterous cinema, from the slapstick conceits of Mack Sennett to the frisky montages of the French New Wave.

That is what is so commendable about this picture. It

Master Blifil (David Warner), nephew of Squire Allworthy, flanked by his and Tom's tutors, Thwackum (Peter Bull) and Square (John Moffatt), are the malevolent fingers reaching out to seal Tom's fate, especially when they "catch him wenching."

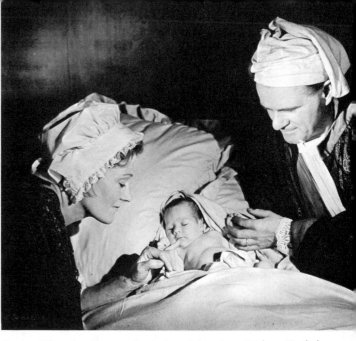

Squire Allworthy (George Devine) and his sister Bridget (Rachel Kempson) are charmed by the innocent foundling whom the Squire names Tom Jones.

On the road to London, Tom (Albert Finney) rescues Mrs. Waters (Joyce Redman) from the cruel hands of a brawling soldier and is nearly skewered as a result. Outcome: the rescue is a comforting one.

recreates upon the screen a classical entertainment that develops its own energy as much from its cinematic gusto as from the racy material it presents. It departs almost completely from the standard and static ways of transferring costume novels to the screen with a reverential air, and it goes at the task by employing the liveliest and, indeed, most impudent and trenchant of movie comedy concepts and syntactic techniques.

Mr. Richardson and his scriptwriter, John Osborne, shrewdly and rightly perceived that the essence of Fielding's novel is the humorous, almost mocking, attitude with which it describes the manners and morals of the eighteenth century. Life in the beautiful west country, among the landed squires, and in the elegant drawing rooms of London, where the grand and lecherous ladies hold sway, offers a sweeping panorama of social shams and moral hypocrisies; and this both amused and sickened Fielding, who satirized it with pungent wit.

So do Richardson and Osborne in the tone they set in the film, which is cheerfully derisive of pomposity and deceit. They pattern and play the gusty story of wenching and bastardy, of honorable intentions and dishonorable legalistic tricks, so that it all comes out in

At an inn en route to London, Mrs. Waters and Tom are startled by a jealous husband, Fitzpatrick (George A. Cooper), who is first jealous, then contrite when he discovers the lady is not his wife, then content when he takes over from Tom.

a great rush of noisy and ribald incidents that are made both laughable and shocking by a style of cinematic ridicule.

For instance, at the very beginning, before the main title comes on, they serve astonishing notice that this is to be a lark in movie terms. Home comes the righteous Squire Allworthy to his comfortable Somerset farm to find a newborn male baby lying in his bachelor bed and the smell of an amatory scandal seeping up from belowstairs. But don't think this conventional prologue is done in conventional style. Not at all. It is done in mock depictment of an old melodramatic silent film, with the action fast and the cutting rigid, printed titles instead of dialogue and a wild din of pseudo-spinet music setting a nervous tone. And then, as a frightened barber is brought up from below to confess to being the father, and a buxom Jenny Jones is brought up to admit to being the mother, Squire Allworthy piously proclaims (in a printed subtitle) that he will adopt the infant and give him the name Tom Jones—"of whom (the next title tells us) the opinion of all was that he was born to be hanged!"

Such is the brisk and delightful way the picture begins, packing the whole sordid legend of the hero's bastard birth into a few hundred feet of film. And then, after the title and the credits, the story gets off at full speed, now some twenty years later, with Tom a lusty young man (played with a wonderfully open, guileless and raffish attitude by the fine actor, Albert Finney), and with a lively, exhilarating pace marked by the always apt measures of a musical score by John Addison.

I mention the score so directly because it is such a vital element in this constantly mobile and chromatic visualization of a racy, romantic conceit. Addison's score is bursting with mischief and sauciness, melodic and instrumental, commenting in delicious ways on the sparkling and spicy action, the pell-mell frolicings in the woods and in the hay, the totally bold and bravura displays of character. It becomes as much a factor in the fashioning of feeling and pace as Richardson's staging and his eclectic use of techniques.

And what old and new tricks he uses—some that go back to the style of the Keystone chases and some as fresh as those Richardson himself perfected in some of his more serious British films. For instance, he loves to cut an action with a fast across-the-frame wipe or a rapid clock-hand rotation to clear the screen for the next scene. He will stop the action at a crucial moment for a split-second freeze and hold the characters in embarrassed suspension before letting them continue or jumping on to the next scene. He will spot a character's face in an iris. He even has his characters address the audience directly, as Groucho Marx sometimes does in his farcical films. Take the scene in which Tom Jones, the lusty scapegrace, having been turned out of Squire Allworthy's home and, making his way to London, during a stop at Upton Inn, finds he's been robbed, and accuses the landlady of picking the pockets of his pants. In the wrangle with her, he turns to the audience and demands hotly, "Did *you* see her take that five hundred pounds?" Or again, when he has picked up Mrs. Waters, a lady of easy virtue, on the road and is going toward Upton with her, his passion is conveyed by having him look at her, back at the audience, and then reach forward and place his hat over the camera lens.

By such prankish and flippant devices, Richardson gives his film the spontaneity and bounce of a spicy contemporary satire dressed in knee breeches and tent-sized skirts. He states, by such cinematic comments, a current sophisticated attitude toward the absurdities and incongruities that Fielding had to define in words. His is a twentieth-century method of making sport of eighteenth-century manners and morals.

Such manners and morals does he show us, such characters and episodes! There's the big, brawling fight in the churchyard over Molly, the incorrigible slut (a word often used with rich expression), whom Tom has presumably got with child. There is Squire Western's roaring deer hunt, with the horses and dogs racing crazily across the beautiful green fields of the Somerset countryside, the hand-held cameras pitching wildly in the midst of the huntsmen and the hounds or flying over the scene (in a helicopter), surveying the madness below. (That madness, incidentally, is descriptive of

239

Molly Seagrim (Diane Cilento), daughter of the squire's gamekeeper, is an early conquest of handsome Tom (Albert Finney).

the fierce, sadistic streak that courses in the hot blood of some of these country gentlefolk, and it is brought to sharp definition by flashing glimpses of spurs raking horses' sides or barnyard fowl killed by passing riders or the triumphant huntsmen clubbing to death the run-down deer.) There is likewise that madhouse explosion of righteous and unrighteous characters through the corridors and bedchambers—mostly bedchambers—of Upton Inn after an irate husband breaks in upon Tom with a woman the fellow thinks is his wife.

What is certainly the most extraordinary sequence in the film is the scene in which Tom and Mrs. Waters eat a meal together at Upton Inn, each trying to outdo the other in the juicy voluptuousness with which they suck lobster claws, gnaw chicken drumsticks, lap up raw oysters with tongues and lips and chomp into pears and apples as though caressing pliant flesh with their teeth. It is a scene so lewd, yet so clever and unassailable, that it marks what is certainly the high point of the lusty licentiousness of *Tom Jones*.

The acting is manifestly expert. I have mentioned Albert Finney as Tom. He is the perfect exemplar of the romantic young gentleman and scamp. But Hugh Griffith is his match as Squire Western, the snorting, cursing, barnyard-mannered goat who is the traditional prototype in literature of the eighteenth-century boor. Griffith is everything that Fielding could have wanted him to be—fire-eater, hypocrite, lecher—and with a maniacal gleam in his eye that is all his own.

Susannah York as his daughter, the lovely Sophie, whom Tom hopes to wed, is a warm little package of passions; Diane Cilento is all teeth and claws as the insatiable Molly; Joyce Redman is brazen and bold as the naughty Mrs. Waters, originally Jenny Jones, who for a brief and sardonic moment has the disquieting impression that she has gone to bed with her own bastard son; and Dame Edith Evans as the prudent and meddling sister of Squire Western.

There is George Devine as the gracious Squire All-worthy, and John Moffat and Peter Bull as the evil, scheming tutors of Tom Jones, and David Warner, who is now more widely famed for his splendid performance in *Morgan!* (1966), as Blifil, the unctuous rival of Tom.

In the London phase of the story, which so richly states in a few scenes the Hogarthian squalor of that fine city in the eighteenth century along with a sparkling impression of its Georgian elegancies, there is Joan Greenwood to give sly humor to the urbane Lady Bel-laston, and David Tomlinson to make a mockery of the stylish suitor, Lord Fellamar.

Sets and costumes are of an order to compare more than favorably with the best that have been presented in British period films, primarily because they are honest and look lived in—especially the costumes, which are usually rumpled and often a little dirty, the wigs frequently askew.

Appropriate also to the spirit are the prim remarks an off-screen narrator throws in, from time to time, as commentary—of the author, as it were, on the scene. For instance, there is his wry conclusion after the clearly seductive eating bout of Tom and Mrs. Waters: "Heroes, whatever high ideas we may have of them, are mortal, not divine. We are all as God made us—and many of us much worse." Or his lip-smacking observation upon Tom's lustiness when in his cups: "It is widely held that too much wine will dull a man's desires. Indeed it will—in a dull man."

And I cherish in my mind one grand shot of a group of raffish English soldiers whom Tom has met while on his way to London, filing drunkenly across a hill, bawling "Rule, Britannia," to the accompaniment of the baaing of a nanny goat.

Some have considered this picture a deliberate and illiterate caricature of a vital period in English history. Well, caricature it may be; but no more so than the graphic engravings of Hogarth or the words of Fielding's own *Tom Jones*. The period was one that cried for lampoon in its own bold and bawdy terms, properly displaying its pious pretense and its sprawling vulgarity. Richardson's picture does it, in familiar and arcane movie terms, appropriate to our modern comprehensions. What is more, it entertains superbly.

Seeking fortune in London, Tom is waylaid by a lady of fashion, Lady Bellaston (Joan Greenwood), who strives to make a "gentleman" out of him.

Blow-Up

1966

Screenplay by Michelangelo Antonioni and Tonino Guerra; inspired by a short story by Julio Corazar; directed by Signor Antonioni; cameraman, Carlo Di Palma; music by Herbert Hancock; produced by Carlo Ponti for Metro-Goldwyn-Mayer.

Thomas	David Hemmings
Jane	Vanessa Redgrave
Patricia	Sarah Miles
Model	Verushka
Blonde Teenager	Jane Birkin
Brunette Teenager	Gillian Hills
Bill	John Castle
Ron	Peter Bold
Man in Park	Ronan O'Casey
Shop Owner	Susan Broderick
Shop Employee	David Hutchinson
Patricia's Husband	Piers Haggard
Models	Jill Kennington
	Rosaleen Murray
	Peggy Moffitt
	Ann Norman
	Melanie Hampshire

Thomas (David Hemmings), a leading London photographer, excites his model (Verushka) with erotic music to get the filmic expressions for which he is noted.

The emergence of Michelangelo Antonioni as one of the stronger cinema stylists of our day and thereby one of the major communicators of mid-twentieth-century malaise has been a painful one, almost as painful and uncertain as the course of one of his agonized characters through the opaque areas and stretches of one of his films. It has been as though Antonioni himself has been seeking to cut through the confusions, hesitations and illusions that can cloud a contemporary mind, groping to find a comprehension of what it is he really has to say and a pictorial grammar and rhythm by which to make it clear. Well, if not *exactly* clear, to make it perceptible.

Waiting for him to deliver a knockout film has been a suspense. But achieve it he did with *Blow-Up,* and we may rest content. For, in this elaborate color picture about a London photographer who is so deceived by the very artifice of his profession and the dazzle of his milieu that he cannot distinguish reality from surreality, we are given a superior exposition of an enervating sickness of our age and a thoroughgoing demonstration of Antonioni's way. What is more, we are given some humor in an Antonioni film.

Beginning with *L'Avventura* (1960), which was the first of his works to achieve a vagrant theme in his groping and a thin coagulation of style, he has been concerned with exposing the roiled and obfuscated states of mind of persons who are baffled and frustrated by the circumstances of their lives. He has been making an effort to say in pictures how their worlds *look* and *feel* and especially how they seem to give back something to persons—all of them women, until now—who are rootless, frightened and lonely because of not being able to become involved. His effort has been to show us, from the outside looking in, how life appears to these persons, from the inside looking out.

A high-fashion photo session is speedily handled by Thomas in his white-walled studio.

His character in *L'Avventura* is a moody young woman who adopts the restless lover of her closest friend when the latter mysteriously disappears. Her world is a cheerless wasteland of ugly volcanic rocks (which is the topographical nature of the island on which her friend disappears) and then of barren Sicilian homes and churches and a lifeless modern concrete town in which she tries to make contact with the lover, who is just as lost as she. In the landscape and other graphic features, we see the landscape of this young woman's mind; and in the torpor of the film's tempo we feel the dankness and chill of her fears. *L'Avventura* rambles and maunders in a sometimes exasperating way, but it conveys Antonioni's method of communicating sentience without clear narrative.

In his succeeding *La Notte* (1961) and *Eclipse* (1962), he goes on to further expositions of the troubled states of mind of more young women, the one in *La Notte* being a wife who is disillusioned and bored with her shallow husband, and the one in *Eclipse* a letdown mistress who tries to find some contact with a vigorous young stockbroker and discovers he has nothing for her.

Until then, all his pictures were photographed in somber black-and-white, but for his next, *Red Desert* (1964), Antonioni went to color and made a marked advance. Here he has color, hot and molten or cool and ephemeral, suggesting more elusive tonal levels in the state of his subject's mind. This is not only more sophisticated but more appealing to the eye. But again his subject is a woman—a psychoneurotic woman, this time —and her ultimate arrangement is no better than that of the women in *La Notte* and *Eclipse*. Antonioni's

subjects were becoming monotonous. Then he crashed through with *Blow-Up,* and the pain of his emergence was justified.

Even though this erratic picture is ambiguous in much of its strange communication and may require more than one viewing to assure a satisfactory understanding, it clearly implies the dilemma of its focal character. He is deluded and bewildered by the massive mirages of our age. He is fooled by the very mechanism that is an indivisible part of him—the camera, which catches but a shadow of reality and truth and may be manipulated to create sheer fantasy. He is hooked by the stimulants of high style, feverish music, slick décor, automobiles, mechanical gadgets, cigarettes, wine and noise. His affairs form a steady melodrama, engineered by his nervous whims, which spring from his overstimulation. And, amid it all, he is poignantly alone.

This much is easily apparent in the frenetic flow of the film, which packs a wealth of involved activity into a chronological span of twenty-four hours. From a sweaty night in a flophouse, where he has been making photographs of derelict men to be published in a volume depicting the London scene, the young man plunges without letup into a hectic day of photographing weirdly dressed mod models for a high-style magazine, casing a curio shop for possible purchase and snapping candid photos in a park. He is spontaneous, volatile and tireless, commanding and self-assured; and a pleasantly insolent expression never changes on his handsome, sensuous face.

But, during that interlude of making photos in the park, something extraordinary happens. He has been furtively snapping a girl and a man engaged in what appears to be quite innocent kissing on a wide, empty lawn, when the girl suddenly perceives him and chases

Discovered filming a love scene in the park, Thomas is pursued by Jane (Vanessa Redgrave), who pleads for the negatives.

after him to demand that he give her the film. She is fiercely insistent, but he refuses to surrender the roll. Without his knowing how she has located him, she later appears at his studio. There she makes another stubborn endeavor to get the roll of film.

Now his curiosity is tingled. What does this young woman have to hide? Why is she so eager to kill those photos that she will go to bed with him to get the roll of film? He has no idea who she is. Nor do we know. Antonioni doesn't tell. He regularly puts characters in his pictures without troubling to explain who they are. The mystery of the girl becomes part of the interest.

After the chap has had a wry time teasing the girl, mischievously got her to like him and has evidently gone to bed with her, he gives her a roll of blank film and sends her on her way. Then he puts the real roll through his developer and casually studies the snaps. There's nothing unusual about them. Just a girl and a man kissing; a pleasant, romantic idyll of a couple in a park. But let's have a better look at them, make a few blow-up prints. Wait! What's that shape among the bushes at the edge of the lawn? And why is the girl looking in that direction, with a possible expression of concern on her face?

Alone in his darkroom, our photographer intently studies the snaps, makes further blow-ups from them, isolating details, until slowly he is convinced that he can see a hand holding a gun and an indistinct face in the bushes. And in a blow-up of the last snap he made, as the girl was going away from him and presumably seeking the man who had disappeared, he is sure he sees a body lying under a clump of trees!

So *that's* why the girl was apprehensive! The man was evidently shot, and the girl either knew it was going to happen or ran away when she discovered it had been done. Without any question, the photographer concludes that this is what occurred, and the significant thing is that the audience is inclined to go along with him. We, too, have become so accustomed to accepting what we see in photographs—or *think* we see, or in movies are *told* we see—that we proceed on that evidence.

In this case, the evidence is supported when Thomas, now curious and disturbed and evidently involved emotionally in the output of his camera for the first time, goes back to the park at night; sure enough, there beneath the trees he sees the rigid body of a gray-haired man. This is sufficient evidence for him, enough to startle and arouse him to want to do something about it, to let somebody know, to relieve himself of this grim knowledge that his camera has given him. So off he goes again, seeking the counsel of the man who is to

Tracking down Thomas, Jane offers herself in exchange for the films.

publish his book of candid photographs. And finally he discovers him, groggy and apathetic, at a marijuana party in a fine old London mansion!

Most people, seeing the picture for the first time, are sure at this point that a murder *has* been committed and that our photographer is correct in his surmise. But the fact is that Antonioni is making us see as he wants us to. He is making us see with the eyes of the photographer and feel as the photographer feels. He is making us sense this whole experience as it is sensed by this strange, detached young man, who is in a world of mirages and is something of a mirage himself.

He does this by subtle devices. When the man goes into the park that second time and sees the body lying under the trees, wind blowing in the branches is the only sound—just as this was the only sound apparent when the young man took the photographs—except that when he bends over to scrutinize the body closely, there is the distinct sound of a click. It is the sound of a camera shutter snapping—in the photographer's mind.

Or when the troubled fellow is driving to find his publisher, he is diverted by what he thinks is a glimpse of the girl of the photographs going into a rock-'n'-roll dance hall. Immediately he leaps to follow her, but inside he cannot find her. However, he becomes briefly embroiled in a struggle with other fellows for a piece of broken guitar thrown away by one of the mod musicians, races outside with it, and then, when he sees he has escaped the others, casually throws it away. This may seem an irrational sequence, a surrealistic episode, but it is in such insertions of elliptical imagery that Antonioni compels us to feel the way his characters feel. This is a visualization of the young fellow's conflict in himself: his struggling to get something and, when he has it, throwing it away.

Again, in his wanderings, Thomas' car is blocked by a puny parade of ban-the-bomb agitators. He is unmoved when one of the paraders dumps her cardboard banner in his car, equally unmoved when an errant breeze blows it into the street. Another symbol of his utter lack of commitment.

The denouement of the mystery comes at dawn (it usually does in Antonioni pictures), when the young fellow goes again, this time with his camera, to make a photograph of the body and finds it isn't there. The melodrama he has fancied has vanished into thin air. And then, as he leaves the park, he encounters a gaggle of chalk-faced mimes—the same ones that open the picture, clattering around the London streets at dawn. They are coming to have a game of tennis on the dew-spangled park tennis court.

Only it isn't a game of tennis. It is a pretense done in pantomime, but with as much energy and excitement as

Thomas finds what looks like a concealed figure in a blow-up of one of the pictures.

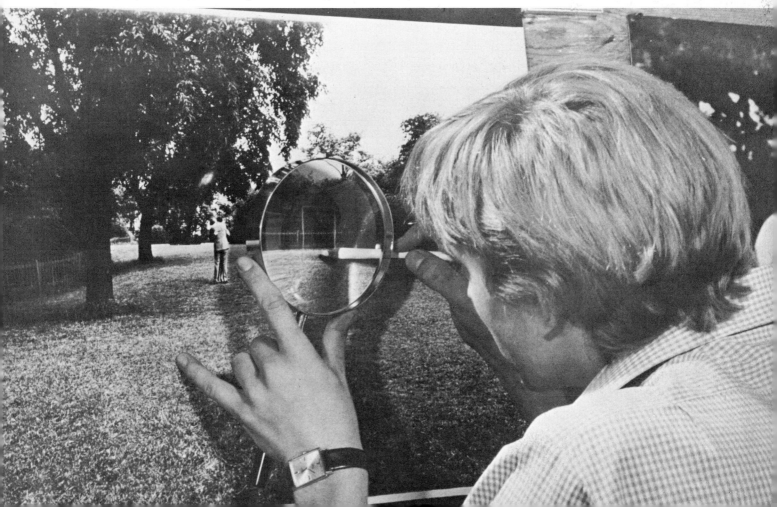

if it were genuine. Thomas stands off and watches, wistful and faintly amused. Is this real or is it imagined? It doesn't matter. It is the image of the young man's state of mind. And when he compliantly trots off to pick up an imaginary ball that has been knocked over the fence and makes a pretense of heaving it back to the players on the court, the whole paradox of the young man— and of many of us, too—is visualized. Antonioni leaves him standing alone and quite pathetic in a park field, surrounded by the ambience of London, yet not surrounded by anything.

One may ask what is stated by *Blow-Up*. Is it simply that illusion and reality are so intermingled in our conditions that it is difficult to distinguish them, and that one can find oneself in trouble by making a mistake? This is certainly the major implication. But there is also a great deal said about the hopeless diffusion and frustration of sex competence. There is an extraordinary scene of the photographer making shots of a model pretending sexual excitement, straddling and stimulating her as he snap, snap, snaps with his camera, until he has her aroused to the state he wants. Then he walks away, unimpassioned, leaving her squirming on the floor.

There is also the controversial sequence of the photographer dropping his work to have an erotic frolic with a couple of teenage girls who have come to him seeking work as models. It is a frenzied and reckless episode, vulgar and funny—and, because it reveals the man as immature, pathetic.

Indeed, one feasible reason for the photographer's creating the complex illusion of a murder is that he may have failed sexually with the girl when she came to his studio, and his mind was concocting a revenge. It is interesting that Antonioni does not allow the audience to have a vicarious sex experience with him, except for the sexual skirmish with the girls.

Otherwise the state of mind of this young man is captured visually in elaborate optical suggestions—the heightened colors of buildings, the various planes of transparencies set up for staging fashion shots in his studio, the relation between the graininess of his blow-ups and the stippling of a modern painting done by a friend.

And David Hemmings' appearance as the photographer is sensuous and poetic; his movements suggest a performance of ballet. His is the major characterization. Vanessa Redgrave is elusive as the girl in the two sequences she has in the picture. Others, seen briefly, are the model, Verushka, and Sarah Miles.

Consistently, the picture leaves us wondering where Antonioni himself goes from here.

A mad rumble in his studio with a pair of teenagers (Jane Birkin and Gillian Hills) is considered one of the film's controversial scenes.

Ulysses

1967

Screenplay by Joseph Strick and Fred Haines from the novel of James Joyce; directed by Joseph Strick; cameraman, Wolfgang Suschitzky; music composed and conducted by Stanley Myers; produced by Walter Reade, Jr.

Molly Bloom	Barbara Jefford
Leopold Bloom	Milo O'Shea
Stephen Dedalus	Maurice Roeves
Buck Mulligan	T. P. McKenna
Haines	Graham Lines
Gerty MacDowell	Fionnuala Flanagan
Bella Cohen	Anna Manahan
Zoe Higgins	Maureen Toal
Josie Breen	Maureen Potter
Blazes Boylan	Joe Lynch
Nurse Callan	Rosaleen Linehan
Alexander J. Dowie	O. Z. Whitehead
The Citizen	Geoffrey Golden
Lieutenant Gardner	Tony Doyle
Garrett Deasy	Dave Kelly
Lynch	Leon Collins
Bantam Lyons	Des Perry
Florry	Claire Mullen
Kitty	Pamela Mant

The choice of the fiftieth film in this volume is one that I purposely postponed until the deadline was upon me, thinking there might just arrive a last-minute, unexpected entry that would qualify to be pegged as one of the greats. The prospect was not propitious, it seldom is in this medium. But a surprise by the unanticipated is always a glittering outside hope.

And, sure enough, one came—as usual, from a source I hadn't looked to at all, and in the shape of a film I would have reckoned the least likely to leap forth as great. I would have said this because the very greatness, and the very uniqueness, of the book from which it was made would have seemed to preclude the probability of its being cramped into the formats of the screen. Furthermore, the novel's notorious candor in carnal revelation by words would have seemed an essential feature that could not be expressed or exchanged. By all the rules, I would have forecast this film had little chance. Yet here it is—Joseph Strick's splendid production of James Joyce's *Ulysses*.

There are several compelling reasons for my amazed admiration for this film and my confidence that it will stand forth as a classic of the screen. It is a welcome simplification and clarification of a massive literary work that has been a puzzle and a struggle for English scholars for the past forty years. While it could not presume to be a compound of all the substance and vast complexity of Joyce's herculean novel, which is generally acknowledged to be the most famous, controversial and influential of the twentieth century—and, indeed, no one could possibly have expected it to be all that—it does a remarkable job of pulling the fantastic account of events in the lives of three persons in Dublin during the course of one day into a sequential pattern that makes it reasonably comprehensible. It firmly compresses the stories of Leopold and Molly Bloom and the ambitious poet, Stephen Dedalus, into a kind of cinematic narrative that knits their mundane activities and their abundant fantasies into a relevant form.

Here, in a properly open and wanton performance by Milo O'Shea, is Bloom, the insurance agent whose awareness of being a Jew is aggressively superseded by his pride in being an Irishman, and whose small life is troubled and brightened by wistful wishes and wondrous fantasies. Here, in Barbara Jefford, is Molly, his lumpish wife, whose sexual affairs and dull frustrations are jumbled in lurid memories. And here, in a perfectly measured and darkling portrayal by Maurice Roeves, is Stephen Dedalus, the renegade Catholic, who is a simulacrum of Joyce himself. Here, too, are several strong impressions of typical Dublin characters from the large and rich assemblage in the book.

Further, these warmly living people and the whole ambience of Dublin, with its old gray buildings and groaning graveyards and challenging vistas out to the Irish Sea, are defined by conception and camera in a visual and verbal poetry that is sensitively reflective of the novel and consistent with the best work on the screen.

But the paramount distinction of this picture and the reason it constitutes a shattering and inevitably potent breakthrough in the culture of films is the fullness and absolute naturalness with which it uses and articulates the sensuality of the novel and the language in which it is conveyed. Nothing of Joyce's startling candor in describing the carnal thoughts and the vagrant erotic impulses of his very human and true characters is stinted or weakly obfuscated. Strick and his fellow scenarist, Fred Haines, have these people state explicitly what is in their minds—the longings for self-satisfaction, the expiations of their insecurities, the oppressions of their animal instincts, the verbalizations of their sex experiences. They dare to express in motion picture the deep libidinous realities and the consequent human revelations that are basic in Joyce's book.

It was mainly because of these exposures, which society had chosen to describe and conceal with the prohibitive word "indecent," that most critics generally

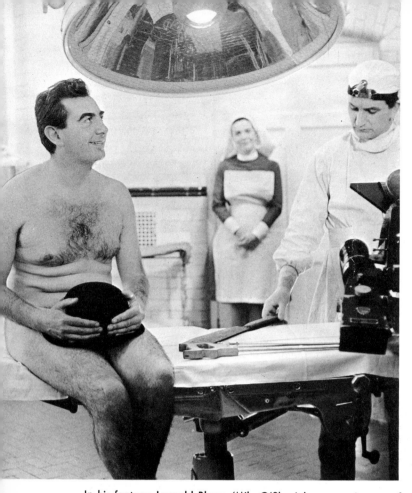

In his fantasy, Leopold Bloom (Milo O'Shea) has many images of himself; one as being pregnant and in the delivery room of Trinity Hospital in Dublin.

assumed no one would ever venture to bring *Ulysses* honestly to the screen. The fact that Joyce had spoken to Sergei Eisenstein in the early 1930's about his doing a film from the book, and that Eisenstein had abandoned the task after preparing a tentative script, seemed a fair indication that the job could not be done. The language, much more than the complexities and obscurities in the structure of the book, made it seem highly unlikely it would ever be made into a film—at least, not one that could be taken as anything but a cheap parody. Just as the novel was pilloried and obstructed for eleven years following its publication in Paris in 1922 before it was admitted, on a memorable ruling by Federal Judge John M. Woolsey, to be published in the United States, so it was reckoned that any picture that dared treat the novel faithfully would be pilloried, or totally discouraged, by the elements that pressure films.

Thus the report was taken lightly when it was announced in 1961 that Jerry Wald, a Hollywood producer, had acquired the screen rights to *Ulysses* and intended to make a picture, with John Huston as director. Especially was it discounted when rumors got around that the British comedian, Peter Sellers, would play the role of Bloom. Subsequent indications that the project would be directed by Jack Cardiff, a British craftsman who had previously directed D. H. Lawrence's *Sons and Lovers* (1960) for Wald, did little to lift expectations. *Sons and Lovers* had clearly revealed the customary film-maker techniques of softening realities and obscuring basic revelations in bringing strong literary material to the screen. Then Wald died, and his option on *Ulysses* was allowed to lapse.

In the meantime, Strick, an independent American producer and director, who had been involved in several varied and interesting minor works—the most impressive of which was a drama of alienation, *The Savage Eye* (1960)—had been hopefully eyeing *Ulysses* and laying out in his mind how it could be digested and articulated on the screen. He had attempted to get screen rights in 1960, before Wald stepped in. Now, when he heard the rights had reverted to the Joyce estate, he tried again. This time he gave the executors a frank and encouraging account of how he intended to do the picture, and they optioned the rights to him.

Obtaining financial backing was much more difficult. No major American company would touch the project. Interest among British producers was glacial. Then Walter Reade, Jr., a New York theater owner, independent producer and distributor, got excited about it and agreed to put up the money, in association with the combine of British film-makers known as British Lion. That group was dubious, however, and stipulated that its investment would be contingent upon the granting of a British censor's certificate to the finished film. Reade was compelled to guarantee that he would assume the total cost, which was calculated at $700,000, if a certificate was not obtained.

With this support and understanding, Strick went to work on the film. He arranged to shoot it in Dublin, which was essential to get authentic atmosphere, and also allowed a saving of money through use of an Irish staff and crew. His cast was studiously selected from promising people without star names. Miss Jefford had been spotted by him when he saw her play Shakespeare with the Old Vic company in Los Angeles. O'Shea had been discovered in a Dublin musical revue, and Roeves, a young Scottish actor, was found on the recommendation of Laurence Olivier. Top salary for these players was £100 a week. The rest of the cast was picked in Ireland and England, and there was one American.

Shooting was started in Dublin in the early summer of 1966, with a house in the Sandymount section used for interiors of the Bloom house on Eccles Street—Molly's bedroom and the kitchen—and also the parlor of the brothel of Bella Cohen. The enterprise was remarkably similar to Erich von Stroheim's shooting

Greed (which see) in San Francisco more than forty years before. Sixteen weeks were spent filming; then the editing and scoring were done in London. The picture was ready in early 1967.

Reade's distributing organization was aware that the film would be a faithful reproduction of the candor of Joyce's *Ulysses,* and the possibility that it would run into trouble with censors was fully realized. A pattern of exhibition whereby it would be shown simultaneously for three-day premiere engagements in a number of theaters all over the United States at a $5.50 top scale of prices was calculated and arranged. It was hoped that by booking it this way, in 130 theaters, enough money would be made in one go-round to pay off the cost of the negative, at least.

However, in writing contracts with the theaters that agreed to show the film, the distributors were compelled to make the provision that any theater operator could cancel out, if he was displeased or worried after seeing a preview of the film. As it turned out, the Reade organization could not obtain a finished print in time to provide the scheduled previews, so several sections of the sound track were obtained—those sections containing the most candid language—and these were audited in New York, Chicago and Los Angeles. Following these auditions, 100 theaters canceled their contracts. The distributor had arranged only 5 more bookings; he was left with the dismal prospect of a total of 35 dates. (When the film opened in March, the number was up to 65.)

There was a further grave anxiety—getting the film through customs into the United States. The federal government still has authority to deny admission to any material considered of a "lewd or obscene" nature, just as it had at the time the novel was originally banned. Whether the customs inspectors would appropriately abide by the ruling of Judge Woolsey that *Ulysses* was not "obscene," or whether they would find the film guilty of that of which the judge had absolved the novel —namely, "the leer of the sensualist"—was altogether uncertain. It was a desperate two and a half hours for the distributor while the inspectors were viewing the film. But within a few minutes after they had seen it, they voted to pass it intact. The decision was a prognostication of critical reaction to the film.

For the general and often amazed discovery of critics and customers has been that *Ulysses,* while startlingly outspoken, is wholly without lasciviousness. It is so shamelessly open and natural in expressing "unrefined" thoughts and in using notoriously vulgar but familiar and robust words that it is frequently characterized by critics as being in surprisingly "good taste." The phrase defines precisely the paradox exposed by this film. It is the completely uninhibited nature and performance of the mind in its private ruminations and reflections, so often pervaded by sex, in contrast to its public inhibitions: this becomes the dominant theme. It is the indifference of the psyche to any of the socially imposed restraints of "good taste" or of canonical circumscription when communicating solely with itself. And it is the true aspect of *being* that this film so recognizably reveals.

The film begins, as does the novel, with Buck Mulligan atop the Martello Tower, speaking his impious praise to the early morning and calling up Stephen Dedalus to consider with him the ironies and absurdities of life. It briefly establishes these young scholars and their pedantic English visitor, Haines, then cuts without cluttering introductions to the home of Bloom and Molly, his wife. In crisp and droll domestic glimpses, it tacitly indicates Bloom's generous indulgence of the sullen Molly, his knowledge of her infideli-

Maurice Roeves is seen as the young scholar-poet, Stephen Dedalus, walking along the beach in the early morn.

Impotent since the death of their son, Bloom comes back to bed with Molly (Barbara Jefford) who, in her revery, somehow senses a change in Bloom.

ties and yet his wistful attachment to her through the bond of their baby boy that died.

Hence it proceeds to weave a chronicle of episodes in the day's activities of Bloom and Stephen—Bloom's accidental tipping of a horse to an inveterate gambler, his attending Paddy Dignam's funeral, his visit to the newspaper office to negotiate an ad, and his serio-comic encounter with an anti-Semitic citizen in a flavorsome saloon; and Stephen's poignant confrontation with one of his pupils at Mr. Deasy's school, his unpleasant conversation with Mr. Deasy and his lonely ramble on Sandymount Beach.

The two are eventually brought together in the interns' room at Trinity Hospital, where Mulligan, Stephen and others are indulging in a spree of irreverent banter while in their cups; then Bloom and Stephen go off together to the red-light district of Nighttown, and there Bloom surrenders his mind and spirit to a series of elaborate and revealing fantasies while visiting the brothel of Bella Cohen. What the film conveys through this exuberant and witty flow of figments of imagination is the cheerfulness, sentimentality and sexual insecurity of Bloom and the restlessness and self-doubt of Stephen, who has a fantasy of causing his mother's death. Each, in his way, is compensating for his inner despairs and loneliness—Bloom because he has no son to succeed him, Stephen because he isn't a great poet.

The brief intermingling of their spirits is recognized in a sequence where they go to Bloom's home together for cocoa after their Nighttown escapade, and their moods are sardonically translated in a disembodied, quizzical dialogue. Then Stephen leaves, Bloom goes to bed with Molly, and there follows her great silent soliloquy reflecting, at last, her own feelings. Thus the film ends as the novel does.

It is in this amazing soliloquy, this "internal monologue" with its stream-of-consciousness cerebration complemented by pictorial images, that the whole vulgar life of Molly, her pathetic union with Bloom, her shattered hopes of being a concert singer, her contempt and her need for men, her tawdry affair with Blazes Boylan, her voracity in sex, all run together (but with Miss Jefford providing punctuation with the measure of her speech) to coagulate the sadness of this woman. It runs for twenty-three minutes, and is the staggering climax to the whole.

Inevitably, many of the characters and much of the novel is left out of the film. No effort is made to emphasize the classical parallels—Bloom as a modern-day counterpart of the ever-questing Ulysses, Molly as the restive Penelope and Stephen as the son, Telemachus—nor any of the numerous literary parodies that are so much the delight of Joyce. Mulligan, Boylan, Stephen's

father, the crippled girl, Gerty MacDowell, and many others of major consequence in the novel are briefly sketched, in the film.

But the essence of this symbolic story of man's eternal longing and loneliness is grandly distilled in the poetry of Joyce's language and Strick's images and in the excellent performances that every member of the cast gives. And after one has the experience of Molly's soliloquy, with its passages of carnal realism and its beautifully supporting visuals, one has a sudden awareness of how tongue-tied the screen has been in trying to articulate feelings that Joyce expressed half a century ago.

It is, I feel, highly appropriate and also poetically just that this film comes last in this volume, for it stands as such an interesting summation of past and probable future trends. By at last giving Joyce's great novel the cinematic visualization it cried to have—and which, indeed, was anticipated in numerous intervening stream-of-consciousness films, such as Ingmar Bergman's *Wild Strawberries* (1957) and Federico Fellini's *8½* (1963), all of which owed their conceptual nature to the inspiration of Joyce's work—it sets up a suitable monument in this medium to an artist from whom much has been derived.

But, more than this, it establishes a model of mature approach and artistry in articulating experience of a sort that is being examined more and more in films. The delicate areas of the human libido, the depths of the subconscious mind, the alienations of the procreative impulse and the sterilities of sexual appetite are matters of increasing interest. Copulation has been explicated on the screen in such fine films as the Swedish *Dear John* (1965) and the Japanese *Woman in the Dunes* (1963). Homosexuality has been detailed in Bergman's *The Silence* (1963) and Andy Warhol's artless indulgence of sheer voyeurism, *The Chelsea Girls* (1966). Clearly this medium, which can so graphically comprehend and communicate the mysteries of psychological movement, will be called upon to do so more and more.

It is well, then, that there should be a compound of image and verbal poetry to mark the channel in this direction. And it is most felicitous that it should be the film of Joyce's *Ulysses*.

So long ago Bloom and Molly were happy together, he vigorous and full of manhood, and she satisfied with his love.

250

Supplemental List of 100 Distinguished Films

This is a further selection of films I have admired and enjoyed for their artistic distinction and their exceptional entertainment qualities. They are listed in alphabetical order, with year of production and director specified, and the nationality indicated thus: (A) American, (B) British, (D) Danish, (F) French, (G) German, (I) Italian, (J) Japanese, (R) Russian, (S) Swedish.

Alexander Nevsky (R), 1938, Sergei Eisenstein
All the King's Men (A), 1949, Robert Rossen
Around the World in 80 Days (A), 1956, Michael Anderson

The Bank Dick (A), 1940, Edward Cline
Ben Hur (A), 1926, Fred Niblo
Berlin, the Symphony of a Great City (G), 1927, Walter Ruttmann
The Big Parade (A), 1925, King Vidor
Bridge on the River Kwai (A), 1957, David Lean
Brief Encounter (B), 1946, David Lean

Cabiria (I), 1913, Giovanni Pastrone
Casablanca (A), 1943, Michael Curtiz
Chang (A), 1927, Ernest B. Schoedsack and Merian C. Cooper
Chapayev (R), 1934, Sergei and Georgi Vasiliev
City Lights (A), 1931, Charles Chaplin

Darling (B), 1965, John Schlesinger
David Copperfield (A), 1935, George Cukor
Day of Wrath (D), 1948, Carl Th. Dreyer
Divorce, Italian Style (I), 1962, Pietro Germi

Earth (R), 1930, Alexander Dovzchenko
8½ (I), 1963, Federico Fellini

The Fallen Idol (B), 1949, Carol Reed
Farrebique (F), 1948, Georges Rouquier
La Femme de Boulanger (F), 1940, Marcel Pagnol
The 400 Blows (F), 1959, François Truffaut
From Here to Eternity (A), 1953, Fred Zinnemann

Gate of Hell (J), 1953, Teinosuke Kinugasa
General Della Rovere (I), 1960, Roberto Rossellini
The Goddess (A) 1958, John Cromwell

The Great Adventure (S), 1950, Arne Sucksdorff
The Great Dictator (A), 1941, Charles Chaplin
Great Expectations (B), 1947, David Lean
The Great McGinty (A), 1940, Preston Sturges

Hail the Conquering Hero (A), 1944, Preston Sturges
A Hard Day's Night (B), 1964, Richard Lester
He Who Must Die (F), 1957, Jules Dassin
High Noon (A), 1952, Fred Zinnemann
Hiroshima Mon Amour (F), 1959, Alain Resnais
How Green Was My Valley (A), 1941, John Ford
Hud (A), 1963, Martin Ritt
The Hustler (A), 1961, Robert Rossen

Intruder in the Dust (A), 1949, Clarence Brown
The Iron Horse (A), 1924, John Ford

Kameradschaft (G), 1931, Georg W. Pabst

La Kermesse Héroïque (F), 1936, Jacques Feyder
The Lavender Hill Mob (B), 1951, Charles Crichton
The Life of Emile Zola (A), 1937, William Dieterle
Little Caesar (A), 1930, Mervyn LeRoy
The Long Voyage Home (A), 1940, John Ford
Lost Horizon (A), 1937, Frank Capra
Lust for Life (A), 1956, Vincente Minnelli

M (G), 1932, Fritz Lang
The Magnificent Ambersons (A), 1942, Orson Welles
Marty (A), 1955, Delbert Mann
Meet Me in St. Louis (A), 1944, Vincente Minnelli
Million Dollar Legs (A), 1934, Edward Cline
The Miracle of Morgan's Creek (A), 1944, Preston Sturges
Modern Times (A), 1936, Charles Chaplin
Murderers Are Among Us (G), 1946, Wolfgang Staudte
Mutiny on the Bounty (A), 1935, Frank Lloyd

The Navigator (A), 1924, Buster Keaton

Open City (I), 1945, Roberto Rossellini
The Ox-Bow Incident (A), 1943, William Wellman

Pinocchio (A), 1940, Ben Sharpenstein and Hamilton Lusk
Pygmalion (B), 1938, Anthony Asquith and Leslie Howard

The Quiet One (A), 1948, Sidney Meyers

The Red Badge of Courage (A), 1951, John Huston
The Red Shoes (B), 1947, Michael Powell and
  Emeric Pressburger
Rififi (F), 1956, Jules Dassin
The River (A), 1937, Pare Lorentz
Room at the Top (B), 1958, Jack Clayton

Safety Last (A), 1923, Harold Lloyd
The Search (A), 1948, Fred Zinnemann
She Done Him Wrong (A), 1933, Lowell Sherman
Shoe Shine (I), 1946, Vittorio de Sica
Shors (R), 1939, Alexander Dovzhenko
The Sign of the Cross (A), 1932, Cecil B. de Mille
Singin' in the Rain (A), 1952, Stanley Donen
  and Gene Kelly
Sous les Toits de Paris (F), 1930, René Clair
Stagecoach (A), 1939, John Ford
Stalag 17 (A), 1953, Billy Wilder
The Stars Look Down (B), 1939, Carol Reed
A Streetcar Named Desire (A), 1951, Elia Kazan
Sunrise (A), 1927, Friedrich Murnau

The Ten Days That Shook the World (also *October*) (R),
  1927, Sergei Eisenstein
Thérèse Raquin (F), 1928, Jacques Feyder
The Third Man (B), 1950, Carol Reed
The 39 Steps (B), 1935, Alfred Hitchcock
They Won't Forget (A), 1937, Mervyn LeRoy
To Live in Peace (I), 1946, Luigi Zampa
Top Hat (A), 1935, Mark Sandrich

Umberto D (I), 1952, Vittorio de Sica

Variety (G), 1925, E. A. Dupont
The Virgin Spring (S), 1960, Ingmar Bergman

Westfront 1918 (G), 1930, Georg W. Pabst
West Side Story (A), 1961, Robert Wise and
  Jerome Robbins
Who's Afraid of Virginia Woolf? (A), 1966, Mike Nichols
Wild Strawberries (S), 1957, Ingmar Bergman
The Wizard of Oz (A), 1939, Victor Fleming
Woman in the Dunes (J), 1964, Hiroshio Teshigahara

Zero de Conduit (F), 1933, Jean Vigo

Bibliography

HISTORY AND CRITICISM

The Rise of the American Film, by Lewis Jacobs. Harcourt, Brace, 1939, 585 pp.

The Film Till Now, by Paul Rotha and Richard Griffith. Funk & Wagnalls, 1949, 755 pp.

The Liveliest Art, by Arthur Knight. Macmillan, 1957, 383 pp.

The Movies, by Richard Griffith and Arthur Mayer. Simon & Schuster, 1957, 442 pp.

Agee on Films, by James Agee. McDowell, Obolensky, 1958, 432 pp.

Grierson on Documentary, by John Grierson. Harcourt, Brace, 1947, 324 pp.

The History of Motion Pictures, by Maurice Bardeche and Robert Brasillach. Norton, 1938, 412 pp.

Classics of the Foreign Film, by Parker Tyler. Citadel, 1962, 254 pp.

The Western: From Silents to Cinerama, by George N. Fenin and William K. Everson. Orion, 1962, 362 pp.

50 Years of Italian Cinema, by E. Ferdinando Palmieri, Ettore M. Margadonna, and Mario Grommo. Bestetti, 1964, 76 pp.

The Italian Cinema, by Vernon Jarratt. Macmillan, 1951, 115 pp.

Italian Cinema Today, by Gian Luigi Rondi. Bestetti, 1966, 280 pp.

French Film, by Georges Sadoul. Falcon, 1947, 131 pp.

50 Years of German Films, by H. H. Wollenberg. Falcon, 1948, 48 pp.

From Caligari to Hitler, by Siegfried Kracauer. Princeton, 1947, 361 pp.

Kino, a History of the Russian and Soviet Film, by Jay Leyda. Macmillan, 1960, 494 pp.

Soviet Cinema, by Thorold Dickinson and Catherine de la Roche. Falcon, 1948, 136 pp.

Scandinavian Film, by Forsyth Hardy. Falcon, 1952, 62 pp.

The Japanese Films, by Joseph I. Anderson and Donald Richie. Tuttle, 1959, 466 pp.

Indian Film, by Erik Barnouw and S. Krishnawamy. Columbia, 1963, 301 pp.

Novel into Film, by George Bluestone. California (paper), 1961, 237 pp.

Film Notes, the Silent Film. Museum of Modern Art, 1949, 68 pp.

Rotha on the Film, by Paul Rotha. Essential, 1958, 338 pp.

The Immediate Experience, by Robert Warshow. Anchor (paper), 1964, 212 pp.

The School and the Art of Motion Pictures, by David Mallery. National Association of Independent Schools (paper), 1966, 147 pp.

All Talking, All Singing, All Dancing, by John Springer. Citadel, 1967, 256 pp.

TECHNIQUE

The Art of the Motion Picture, by Jean Benoit-Levy. Coward-McCann, 1946, 263 pp.

Film as Art, by Rudolf Arnheim. California (paper), 1957, 238 pp.

Theory of Film, by Siegfried Kracauer. Oxford, 1960, 364 pp.

Film, an Anthology, edited by Dan Talbot. Simon & Schuster, 1959, 649 pp.

Film, a Montage of Theories, edited by Richard Dyer MacCann. Dutton (paper), 1966, 384 pp.

The Film Sense, by Sergei M. Eisenstein. Harcourt, Brace, 1942, 288 pp.

Film Form, by Sergei M. Eisenstein. Harcourt, Brace, 1949, 279 pp.

The Filmviewer's Handbook, by Emile G. McAnany, S.J., and Robert Williams, S.J. Paulist Press, 1965, 208 pp.

The Art of Walt Disney, by Robert D. Field. Macmillan, 1942, 290 pp.

BIOGRAPHY

D. W. Griffith, American Film Master, by Iris Barry. Museum of Modern Art, revised edition, 1966, 40 pp.

Douglas Fairbanks, the Making of a Screen Character, by Alistair Cooke. Museum of Modern Art, 1940, 36 pp.

A Tree Is a Tree, by King Vidor. Harcourt, Brace, 1953, 315 pp.

Charlie Chaplin, by Theodore Huff. Schuman, 1951, 354 pp.

The World of Robert Flaherty, by Richard Griffith. Duell, Sloan, 1953, 165 pp.

Sergei M. Eisenstein, by Marie Seton. Wyn, 1952, 533 pp.

The Fabulous Orson Welles, by Peter Noble, Hutchinson (London), 1956, 276 pp.

Garbo, by John Bainbridge. Doubleday, 1955, 256 pp.

John Huston, King Rebel, by William F. Nolan. Sherbourne, 1965, 242 pp.

The Stars, by Richard Shickel. Dial, 1962, 287 pp.

The Films of Josef von Sternberg, by Andrew Sarris. Museum of Modern Art, 1966, 56 pp.

Index of Films

Index